INTERVIEWING

Michael Z. Sincoff
The Mead Corporation

Robert S. Goyer
Arizona State University

Macmillan Publishing Company
New York
Collier Macmillan Publishers
London

Copyright © 1984, Michael Z. Sincoff and Robert S. Goyer.

Printed in the United States of America

All rights reserved. No part of this book may be reproduced or transmitted in any form or by any means, electronic or mechanical, including photocopying, recording, or any information storage and retrieval system, without permission in writing from the Publisher.

Macmillan Publishing Company
866 Third Avenue, New York, New York 10022

Collier Macmillan Canada, Inc.

Library of Congress Cataloging in Publication Data

Sincoff, Michael Z.
  Interviewing.

  Includes bibliographical references and index.
  1. Employment interviewing. 2. Interviewing.
I. Goyer, Robert Stanton, . II. Title.
HF5549.5.I6S56 1984   658.3'1124   83-11969
ISBN 0-02-410840-5

Printing: 1 2 3 4 5 6 7 8 Year: 4 5 6 7 8 9 0 1 2

ISBN 0-02-410840-5

Preface

During the past twenty-five years we have discussed the topic of interviewing with practitioners ranging in experience from undergraduate college students to chief executive officers of both private and public organizations. In classes, seminars, and workshops they asked us for a text that applied the substantive theoretical background on human communicative behavior to the interview. They made suggestions concerning their practical needs, including an introduction to relevant theory, examples, and exercises that would demonstrate the nuances of the most commonly used forms of the interview, and practice in using specific interviewing techniques.

Interviewing is such a text. It is designed for the beginning student as well as the working manager of people and is based on our extensive experience both outside and inside the classroom. It begins with a systematic description of the process that is intended to result in communication, including the generation, transmission, and perception of messages and the evocation of desired meaning. The interview is placed within the spectrum of human communicative behavior and is defined from the perspectives of both event and process.

Different interviewing situations are described, based on two general purposes for engaging in an interview: (1) giving and/or getting information (Chapter 2) and (2) influencing the behavior of others through persuasion (Chapter 4). The most prevalent types of interviews using principles of both informational and persuasive interviewing receive special attention: survey interviewing (Chapter 3), employment interviewing (Chapters 5, 6, 7), appraisal interviewing (Chapter 8), exit interviewing (Chapter 9), and counseling interviewing (Chapter 10). Each treatment is characterized by simply written theory, tested prescriptive techniques, illustrations and examples, practical exercises, and case studies when applicable. For those who desire additional information or points of view on any particular topic, a brief bibliography is provided at the end of each chapter.

A significant feature of *Interviewing* is the discussion of Equal Employment Opportunity (EEO) as it relates to employment interviewing. Three chapters are devoted to the legal environment of, preparation for, and conduct of the employment interview. In addition, we provide in the appendixes the complete texts of the federal enabling legislation concerning EEO and employment guidelines. Specific techniques that we recommend and solutions to problems raised by the employment situation are presented consistent with the current legal interpretation. When the law is clear, we so indicate, and when the law is unclear, examples are provided illustrating the current border line between what is probably lawful and what is probably unlawful.

Also unique to this text is a detailed section on the career-planning process in the chapter on appraisal interviewing, including a sixty-six-item career-planning questionnaire designed for the person who wants to come to grips with personal motivational factors, strengths, and weaknesses.

When preparing this text, we envisioned a book soundly grounded in theory, thorough in the areas it covered, readable and useful both to the student just learning interviewing techniques and the practitioner who wanted a refresher text. Our intent was to capture the essence of the subject without presuming to exhaust it. We chose to draw heavily from the common body of knowledge on interviewing, augmented substantially by our own experiences, research, understanding, and perspectives. When appropriate, we have cited some of the classic research or theory on a given topic, while maintaining a commonsense, application-oriented approach. We believe that *Interviewing* has achieved these goals, and we invite you to learn with it.

Michael Z. Sincoff
Kettering, Ohio

Robert S. Goyer
Tempe, Arizona

Acknowledgments

We wish to acknowledge the following persons and organizations for allowing us to reprint in our text the following materials:

Stanley E. Degler, Executive Editor, *Fair Employment Practices Manual,* The Bureau of National Affairs, Inc., Washington, D.C., "Title VII of the Civil Rights Act of 1964" and "Uniform Guidelines on Employee Selection Procedures (1978)."

Capt. James F. Donovan, Acting Deputy CNET, U.S. Naval Education and Training Command, NAS Pensacola, Pensacola, Florida, "The ABMS Hatton Story."

Carl W. Hendrickson, Vice President, Market Opinion Research, Detroit, Michigan, "Telephone Interview Questionnaire."

Bruce A. Hubler, Corporate Director, Executive Staffing, The Celanese Corporation, New York, New York, "The Chronological Résumé," "The Functional or Results-Oriented Résumé," "The Directed Résumé," and "The Letter Résumé."

Dudley P. Kircher, Vice President, Corporate Communications, The Mead Corporation, Dayton, Ohio, "Communication Audit Survey Instrument: General Interview Questionnaire."

Keith G. Rasmussen, Senior Vice-President, Lynchburg Foundry Company, Lynchburg, Virginia, "Telephone Interview Questionnaire."

Stephen J. Wall, Director, Corporate Management Development, Union Carbide Corporation, Danbury, Connecticut, "External Management Training Survey Questionnaire."

A *Fortune* 500 company that wished to remain unnamed, "Employment Application Form" and "Internal Job Application Form."

In addition, for their critiques and suggestions for improvement of the chapters covering the employment interview—its legal environment, preparation, and conduct—we thank Eugene G. Ayton, Corporate EEO Manager and David H. Germann, Manager, College Recruiting and Relations, both of The Mead Corporation, Dayton, Ohio.

For assistance with manuscript preparation, we thank Cynthia A. Romano and Lillian G. Smith, both of the Corporate Staff Human Resources Department, The

Mead Corporation, Dayton, Ohio, and Marion H. Yakerson, Department of Communication, Arizona State University, Tempe, Arizona.

For their overall assistance, for being a sounding board for many of our ideas, and for their encouragement, we thank Kathleen D. Sincoff, Kettering, Ohio, and Patricia A. Goyer, Chandler, Arizona.

Finally, we thank Karen, Susan, Linda, Amy, Jim, and all those students and colleagues past and present whose support and friendship were so instrumental in bringing this work to completion.

Thank you all.

M.Z.S.
R.S.G.

Contents

1 Basic Principles of Interviewing   1

Introduction 1
Human Communicative Behavior 2
Language and Symbol Systems 3
Definitions 3
Interview Situations, Purposes, and Variables 4
  Participant Behaviors 5
  Message Components 8
  Climate of the Communicative Act 8
Anatomy of the Interview 10
Summary 12
Exercises 13
Notes 13
Additional Readings 14

2 Informational Interviewing   15

Introduction 15
Information Forfeiture 16
Barriers to Sharing Information in the Interview 17
Asking Questions and Providing Responses 18
Summary 22
Exercises 22
Notes 23
Additional Readings 23

3 Survey Interviewing — 24

Introduction   24
Interviews and Questionnaires   25
   Constructing the Interview Guide   27
   Conducting the Interview   27
   Training Interviewers   28
   Additional Considerations   29
Sample Questionnaires   29
Summary   49
Exercises   49
Notes   49
Additional Readings   50

4 Persuasive Interviewing — 51

Introduction   51
Persuasion Defined   52
Ethical Dimensions of Persuasion   53
Problem and Participant Analysis   54
   Problem Analysis   54
   Participant Analysis   56
Structuring the Interview   57
Summary   60
Exercises   60
Notes   60
Additional Readings   67

5 The Legal Environment of the Employment Process — 68

Introduction   68
Equal Employment Opportunity   69
Lawful and Unlawful Questions   73
Responding to Questions That You Believe Are Unlawful   80
Summary   81

Exercises 81
Notes 81
Additional Readings 82

6 Preparing for the Employment Interview 83

Introduction 83
Search Firms and Employment Agencies 89
The Job Application Form 90
Job-Posting Systems 93
The Résumé 95
Cover Letters 102
Representative Excerpts from Cover Letters 102
Recommendations, References, and Background Checks 107
Summary 108
Exercises 109
Notes 109
Additional Readings 109

7 Conducting the Employment Interview 110

Introduction 110
The Employment Interview 110
The Employer's Behavior in the Employment Interview 112
The Applicant's Behavior in the Employment Interview 114
Physical Behaviors and Cues 115
Employer's Questions in the Employment Interview 116
Applicant's Questions in the Employment Interview 119
A Word About Salary Questions 120
Panel Interviewing 121
The Employment Offer 122

Summary 123
Exercises 124
Notes 125
Additional Readings 125

8 Appraisal Interviewing 126

Introduction 126
Appraisal System Objectives 128
Appraisal Interview Objectives 128
Common Performance Appraisal
  Situations 129
Preparing for the Appraisal
  Interview 133
Conducting the Appraisal
  Interview 139
Job Variables Discussed in the
  Appraisal Interview 140
Environmental Variables Discussed in
  the Appraisal Interview 141
Representative Questions in the
  Appraisal Interview 141
Career Planning 142
  Assessment 143
  Analysis and Insight 144
  Decision Making 145
  Change 146
  Reassessment 146
Summary 146
Exercises 146
Note 147
Additional Readings 147

9 The Exit Interview 155

Introduction 155
Company Benefits 157
Terminating Employee Benefits 157
Conducting the Exit Interview 160
  The Opening 160
  The Body 163
  The Close 163

Pitfalls   164
Outplacement   164
Summary   165
Exercises   165
Notes   165
Additional Readings   166

10 Counseling   167

Introduction   167
Directive Versus Nondirective
  Counseling   168
The Supportive Counseling
  Climate   169
Listening and Counseling   171
Conducting the Counseling
  Interview   172
   Preparation   172
   The Opening   172
   The Body   173
   The Close   175
Summary   175
Exercises   175
Notes   176
Additional Readings   176

Appendixes   177

Appendix A: Title VII of the Civil
  Rights Act of 1964   177
Appendix B: Uniform Guidelines on
  Employee Selection Procedures
  (1978)   195
Appendix C: Standard Form 171,
  Personal Qualifications
  Statement   244
Appendix D: The Joe Hatton Situation:
  An Action Maze   252

Index   267

List of Figures

FIGURE 3.1: Telephone Interview Questionnaire   30
FIGURE 3.2: External Management Training Survey Questionnaire   38
FIGURE 3.3: Communication Audit Survey: General Interview Questionnaire   41

FIGURE 4.1: Persuasion Case: Problem and Participant Analysis   61

FIGURE 6.1: Position Specifications   85
FIGURE 6.2: Employment Application Form   91
FIGURE 6.3: Internal Job Application Form   94
FIGURE 6.4: The Chronological Résumé   97
FIGURE 6.5: The Functional or Results-Oriented Résumé   99
FIGURE 6.6: The Directed Résumé   100
FIGURE 6.7: The Letter Résumé   101
FIGURE 6.8: Recent College Graduate Résumé   103
FIGURE 6.9: Soon-to-Be College Graduate Résumé   104

FIGURE 8.1: Career Planning Questionnaire   148

FIGURE 9.1: Employee Termination Notice   158
FIGURE 9.2: Supervisor Checklist for Terminating Employees   159
FIGURE 9.3: Personnel Department Checklist for Terminating Employee   159
FIGURE 9.4: Exit Interview Form   161

1

Basic Principles of Interviewing

CHAPTER OBJECTIVES

1. Explain "intent."
2. Define and explain the process of communication.
3. Explain the concept of "purposeful sharing."
4. Differentiate between "trying to communicate" and "communicating."
5. Define "meaning."
6. Explain why we use language codes.
7. Define and explain components of the interview.
8. Identify and explain categories of variables that influence interview effectiveness.
9. Identify and differentiate among participant behaviors, message components, and climate factors.
10. Explain motivational conditions found in the interview.
11. Explain goal-orientation in the interview.
12. Explain "reciprocity."
13. Describe how your attitudes and expectations affect your ability to listen.
14. Describe purposes of the opening, body, and close of the interview.
15. Identify specific techniques used in the opening, body, and close of the interview.

Introduction

Next to social conversation, the interview is undoubtedly the most common form of interaction between people, regardless of the situation or context. Whereas social conversation is casual and incidental, an interview requires intent; it is planned and prepared for before it occurs. Whether you are an employer or employee, buyer or seller, parent or child, teacher or student, physician or patient, counselor or client, or newsmaker or newsgatherer, you undoubtedly at some time will be a participant in an interview. Whenever you make a conscious, planned effort to inform or influence another person in an interactive setting, or whenever you are on the receiving end of such an effort, you are participating in an interview.

Because effective interviewing is both an art and a science, it is possible to learn how to do it well. Gaining experience in interviewing is necessary if one is to theorize and comment about it. Keep in mind, however, that practice tends only to make permanent, not perfect. What is needed to achieve effectiveness in interviewing is a combination of background knowledge and theory based on practice and research, plus guided application.

Human Communicative Behavior

People's efforts to adapt to and to influence their environment depend substantially on their abilities to communicate with other people concerning their problems and those of the groups to which they belong. Our ability to communicate and our methods of doing so are unique among the world of living organisms in that we can share experiences (we can communicate) indirectly and vicariously by means of sophisticated sets of signs and symbols.

Communication is probably the basic ingredient in most human interactions. Although there are many definitions of communication, we view it here as the purposeful sharing of experience between people. Evidence that communication has occurred is found in the behaviors resulting as a consequence of the sharing acts.

Implicit in the notion of purposeful sharing are two assumptions: (1) the individual who has something to share must want to share it; and (2) the individual who initiates the sharing retains the very thing that is shared (that is, we give of ourselves; yet we keep what is given). An individual's conscious (purposeful) or unconscious (inadvertent) interpretation of those behaviors displayed by another person should not be confused with communication between the two parties, as interpretation, by definition, is private and unique, and communication is shared.

Although we cannot communicate without some amount of interpretation occurring, we are almost constantly involved in interpreting events and behaviors whether or not communication occurs. Thus, genuinely to communicate (to share, to make common) is a remarkably satisfying experience when it occurs to a high degree of perfection, and an overwhelmingly frustrating experience when it occurs hardly at all. Very often the trying ("I communicated") is mistaken for the fulfillment. On other occasions, the message is mistaken for the event itself; but simply receiving a message certainly does *not* guarantee that communication has occurred between two persons.

We suggest that experiences are considered "shared" (that communication has taken place) when a positive correlation of responses occurs between the people involved in the communicative event. The behavioral evidence of this occurrence (sharing) is defined operationally by the responses of the participants to the shared message stimulus. These responses also provide an operational definition of meaning. If the response made by the perceiver of a stimulus message corresponds to the response intended by the message generator, then communication has occurred. If there is no such correspondence of responses, then there has been no communication, even though the sign/symbol stimulus may indeed evoke independent meaningful responses for both the generator and the perceiver. The main point is that sharing the message stimulus does not mean that communication has taken place; the responses must also be shared.

When human beings interact, the failure or success of the interaction from the participants' standpoint is typically a function of their respective communicative behaviors. To improve the probabilities of success, the variables in the process should be examined carefully and attitudes and skills improved accordingly. This is why we have written this book.

Language and Symbol Systems

As we just noted, our capacity to communicate is greater than the capacity of other organisms, because of our ability to use a wide variety of symbols. As a result, we can refer to ideas and events past, present, and future, as well as to physical objects that are either present or not present. We also can store these references for lengthy periods of time. We do all of these things by means of language codes, which are symbol systems (verbal and nonverbal) consisting of systematic combinations of stimuli perceived through one or more of the sense organs. Once we have learned the arbitrary but conventional rules (grammar) for combining and organizing a given set of symbols, as well as the referents for them, we then can generate messages and share referents (experiences) with others who also have learned the same language code. Although individuals learn a variety of language codes (music, dance, speech, gestures, facial expressions, and the like), most of our conscious efforts are devoted to verbal language codes, either oral or written.

Researchers consistently report that for about seven out of every ten minutes that we are conscious and awake, we communicate through oral and aural modes. An average percentage breakdown of time spent in verbal communicative behaviors would look something like this: 9 percent writing, 16 percent reading, 30 percent speaking, and 45 percent listening.[1] For our purposes, the interview is a human interaction involving primarily the behaviors of speaking and listening (although it typically incorporates nonverbal visual and tactile behaviors as well).

Definitions

Communication, then, is the sharing of experience.[2] For the involved parties, the sharing may be either direct (real) in terms of the time and space dimensions of the event, or it may be indirect (vicarious), removed in some way from the original experience and thus a substitute for it. Direct sharing occurs at a very elementary biochemical and physiological level and is not unique to humans. Vicarious experience (or perhaps more accurately, vicariously shared experience), however, occurs only symbolically and insofar as is known, only humans are capable of communicating at this level with a high degree of sophistication and skill.

The process of communication refers to that combination of sequential ingredients that produces a communicative event, including (1) a generator of a (2) stimulus message that is (3) purposefully projected to (4) a perceiver who (5) responds discriminatively (assigns meaning). Note that although on occasion the message generator may desire some knowledge or indication of the perceiver's response (sometimes labeled *feedback* or *feedforward*) and will indicate in the stimulus message that such knowledge is expected (such as when asking a question), the provision of such knowledge by the perceiver is not a necessary condition for the occurrence of communication. Indeed, an examination of your own experience will reveal many occasions when messages have been generated and transmitted to another person without your knowing whether the message was received and the desired response made (e.g., oral requests or videotaped presentations made but not responded to, or acted upon without the generator's knowledge; letters and phone calls that are not answered). This does not mean that communication (i.e., the response, meaning, or behavior you desired from your stimulus message) did not occur; it simply means that you do not know whether it occurred.

The interview is a goal-oriented, dyadic human interaction involving primarily oral and aural communicative behaviors.[3] The term *goal-oriented* in this definition implies that at least one (and perhaps both) of the participants in the interview has a preconceived purpose for engaging in the interview and influencing the behavior of the interview partner in a desired way. "Dyadic human interaction" means that there are only two parties involved, typically meeting face-to-face, with each party usually (but not always) a single individual. (In some panel interviews, one party may consist of several persons, such as in an employment interview when two or more employer representatives simultaneously interview a single applicant or when two or more law enforcement officers interrogate a single suspect.) The phrase "involving primarily oral and aural communicative behaviors" indicates that both parties participate in the interview by alternately speaking and listening, although these primary behaviors are by no means the only ones used (except perhaps in the telephone interview). Nonverbal behaviors also can occur (observation of dress, movement, gesturing, judging the firmness of a handshake, noting the scent of perfume, and so forth), reflecting nearly the full range of human sensory perceptions.

Interview Situations, Purposes, and Variables

Based on this definition of interviewing, it is obvious that interviewing occurs in many situations and for a variety of purposes, although the interviewing label is not always used. Regardless of the purpose or type of interview, there are three categories of relatively discrete variables that, individually and in combination, strongly influence the effectiveness of the interview: (1) participant behaviors, (2) message components, and (3) climate of the communicative act.

Participant Behaviors

In the interview it is to the advantage of both participants to be as thoroughly prepared as possible in regard to each of these three variables (including arranging the physical setting) before the actual interview meeting. Neither the interviewer (R) nor the interviewee (E) should enter an interview "cold" (without preparation) if it is possible to avoid doing so. To the extent that the R takes the initiative in seeking the interview to accomplish a given purpose, it is particularly important that at least the R be thoroughly prepared.

When an interview is initiated, it is useful to identify the responsibilities of R and E. For example, the R typically requests the interview and has the "burden of proof" in regard to changing the status quo in some way that requires a decision by the E. Conversely, the E is assumed to have a kind of "power of decision" concerning whatever has prompted the R to seek the interview—to provide information, buy a product, or offer a job. Note that in many interview situations the roles of R and E often alternate from moment to moment. Consequently, the participant's communicative behaviors will vary as each one's role shifts in accordance with that person's objectives and the development of the interview.

In the preceding section on definitions, the participants were represented by the generator and perceiver. In the interview, the participants are typically referred to as the "interviewer" and "interviewee" (the "persuader" and "persuadee," the "employer" and the "applicant," the "appraiser" and "appraisee," the "counselor" and the "counselee"). For each participant, factors to be noted include: physical characteristics (appearance, observable skills, physical habits and mannerism, vocal quality, and the like) and their cognitive/affective characteristics (attitudes, intelligence, mental quickness, motives, feelings, and so forth).

As mentioned earlier in this chapter, the participants represent one of the key variables in the interview situation. The fact that only two parties are involved usually causes each to focus on the other and makes the participants' behaviors especially important. What are some of these behaviors?

Physical Characteristics. Although you occasionally hear or read that a person cannot *not* communicate, such an assertion is quite inconsistent with the definition of communication discussed earlier. As individuals, we constantly provide a multitude of behavioral stimuli; similarly, we are almost constantly (when conscious) interpreting and evaluating the behavioral stimuli of others. Accordingly, as long as the special condition of purposeful sharing (as contrasted with the more pervasive condition of constantly interpreting) is the necessary requirement for communication to occur, the physical behaviors of one person may frequently influence the behaviors of others in a unidirectional, noninteractive, and noncommunicational way.

It is useful therefore to keep in mind that any behavioral act, whether intentional or unintentional or verbal or nonverbal, may influence an observer, particularly in the intimate, face-to-face interview situation in which many stimuli are present. This is especially important when the behaviors can be interpreted as contradictory (e.g., the ideas presented orally by Participant A are perceived by Participant B as inconsistent with the latter's interpretation of A's facial expressions, posture, or dress). As an illustrative exercise showing such inconsistency, look at yourself in a mirror, frown, slouch, and say out loud, "This is the happiest day of my life." Physical appearance and bearing (including gestures, mannerisms, and use of voice) will be interpreted (accurately or inaccurately) by your interview partner and compared with what your words ostensibly intend to communicate.[4]

Many physical characteristics (e.g., age and sex)[5] are not under individual control (despite efforts to disguise them); conversely, however, many such characteristics and behaviors are subject to the individual's control (e.g., clothing, posture, gestures, neatness, and vocal characteristics such as volume and rate, vocabulary). You should be sensitive to this fact and assess the likely impact of your behavior before the interview, as part of your preparation.

Cognitive/Affective Characteristics. Although physical behaviors and cognitive/affective behaviors often overlap, in our discussion the latter term will refer to attitudes, motives, feelings, intellectual abilities, and mental quickness.

The attitudes, motives, and feelings you bring to an interview will have an immediate and direct bearing on the probabilities of achieving your interview goals. If you approach the interview from the standpoint that it is inherently an adversarial contest in which the object is to overcome an opponent, the point of effective interviewing as a means of communication will have been missed. A consistent theme in the literature on effective interviewing is that both parties have something to gain from the interaction between the participants and that both can and will contribute something to the final outcome. In order to be successful in interviewing, even when the participants strongly disagree, they must be open and cooperative with each other.

Attitudes reflect our feelings toward an object or event and hence suggest motives and goals that prompt us to participate in interviews. Accordingly, we should identify these attitudes and goals before the interview. In some interviews (e.g., job employment) this will be relatively simple, whereas in others (e.g., clinical counseling) it may be extremely difficult.

A useful description of participant motivation can be found in the journalistic reportorial interview (a type of informational interview):

	Motivational Condition			
	I	II	III	IV
Reporter	Willing	Willing	Unwilling	Unwilling
Respondent	Willing	Unwilling	Willing	Unwilling

In Motivational Condition I, both the reporter and respondent are motivated to participate. This is the optimum condition, as each party wants to contribute to the outcome. Motivational Condition II suggests that the reporter wants to be involved (in order to obtain a story) but that the respondent is reluctant to participate (perhaps because of distrust of the reporter). Motivational Condition III may occur when the reporter thinks that the respondent is trying to use the reporter in some way (perhaps to obtain favorable publicity or to plant a story). Note that in this situation the respondent may have initiated the interview. Finally, in Motivational Condition IV neither the reporter nor the respondent has any intrinsic desire to participate in the interview. Yet, for extrinsic reasons (e.g., the editor and/or the respondent's employer insists on the interview) the interview occurs.

For any interview, each participant's preparation should include identifying and assessing both R's and E's objectives (immediate and delayed). Although the interview as a means of communication can be relatively unstructured, by definition it is goal-oriented. Therefore, the extent to which R and E can identify common goals will largely determine the range and pertinence of the subject matter and logic that can be usefully employed. If no common ground can be identified, the preparation of one or both parties will have been inadequate, and the interview will be of little use.

The participants' intellectual abilities and mental quickness refer to the cognitive and conceptual skills that are revealed by means of oral language usage and listening behaviors during the interview. The ability to organize ideas quickly and to process, store, and retrieve pertinent information as a basis for discussion and decision making is very important to the interaction that occurs in interviewing. Despite individual differences in cognitive abilities, these abilities nevertheless can be identified and improved. In the interview these skills are reflected largely in the questions that participants ask and the answers they give. Language usage and listening skills are essential.

As the term suggests, *language usage* is how one uses a particular symbol system. Although both nonverbal and verbal language codes may be used, the emphasis here is on the latter as the primary language used in the typical interview. Chief among the characteristics of language usage that reveal a participant's ability to "think straight" are the vocabulary employed (including grammar), the type and insight of questions asked, and the organization and thoroughness of the responses to questions.

Because the mode of participation in interviewing is reciprocal (both parties speak and listen, with each party reacting to the other), often involving only fragmentary sentences and phrases, it is important to choose carefully one's vocabulary and style. To talk down to or to talk over the head of your partner is counterproductive, whether done unconsciously or otherwise. Similarly, if you cannot organize your thoughts in such a way that the question or the response can be understood by your partner, the problem of achieving communication will be compounded. Chapter 2 will discuss questioning techniques and the problems of using emotionally "loaded" language.

Listening refers to a presumed skill about which there is much conjecture but relatively little rigorous research.[6] Most professionals in the field would agree that listening involves a combination of physical hearing acuity (the ability to receive sound) and focused cognitive attention/perception. If the task requires listening to oral language materials (in contrast with music, for example), general intelligence also is important when listening success is measured by comprehension, recall, or retention of the material presented. Whatever listening does entail, it can be learned and improved, just as skill in reading can. The ability of your interview partner to respond intelligently to a question frequently is taken as evidence of listening ability. If the response to your question or comment is not clear or relevant, you may be inclined to blame your partner's listening ability rather than your own ability to state (organize) the question. Because it is likely that your willingness (attitude) to listen affects your ability to do so, you should prepare for the interview expecting your partner to make valid points and offer pertinent information. Both participants should recognize that failure to listen to the other's contributions probably will result in failure to accomplish interview goals.

Message Components

There are a number of message-related variables that affect the probabilities of having a productive interview. The problems of language usage are also relevant to message components. Languages consist of arbitrary sets of signals and symbols that we perceive through our senses (particularly sight, sound, touch, and smell). Over a period of time, the meanings that these signals and symbols suggest are agreed upon by the users of that language. The objects, ideas, and events that the symbols represent thus constitute the content of a message, as influenced by the context in which the symbols are used and the purposes of the participants. In an interview, content is a function of the knowledge and purpose of both parties in the interview situation. Other components of messages include language characteristics (vocabulary, organizational structure and logical complexity, timeliness and pertinence, and so on) and sensory channels (aural, visual, tactile, olfactory, and so on).

Language Characteristics. Although you automatically may assume that your interview partner will share your language, be alert to differences in the degree of sharing. Although everyone in a given community may speak the same language, differences in regional dialects and specialized jargons or simply maturity and experience may have the same effect as if a substantially different language were being used, particularly when it is spoken. This is especially important in informational interviewing (see Chapter 2). The way in which the interview participants organize their thoughts for presentation, the degree of abstractness and logical complexity involved, the relevance of the information and point of view being expressed all will influence the effectiveness of the interview.

Sensory Channels. In interviewing, you should realize that you are generating behavioral stimuli for your partner in a variety of ways, and vice versa. Although the perfume or after-shave lotion you wear may not be intended to influence your partner, it nevertheless may have a subtle effect—or even be overpowering! The point is that you should be sensitive to how you may affect the other party, from whatever sensory source. An alert person will observe and interpret things about an interview partner that, accurate or not, may hinder or prevent understanding and acceptance rather than encourage it.

Climate of the Communicative Act

The environment in which the interview takes place can influence its effectiveness, particularly in regard to the following variables:

1. Physical setting (such as temperature, light, noise, odors, humidity, and physical placement of participants).
2. Social setting (cultural customs and taboos, nature of the occasion).
3. Time dimensions (time of day/week/month/year, length of interview).
4. Psychological climate (stress variables, relationship of participants to each other and to the message).

Physical Setting. Fortunately, the actual physical setting of the interview can be controlled, within limits. If the temperature or humidity level is too high or too low, an adjustment probably can be made. The same is true of light, noise, and distracting odors, even if it means moving the participants rather than removing the causes of the discomfort. You should remember to plan and arrange the location of the interview and adjust the physical characteristics of the meeting place.

Even the choice and placement of the furniture are matters for consideration affecting the comfort and the participation of the interview partners. The distance and barriers (desks, etc.) you put between yourself and your partner may help or hinder the interview interaction (e.g., putting several feet of table top between you and your partner may encourage or emphasize the psychological distance between you, rather than reduce it). In this context, you should be particularly sensitive to the fact that personal space is culturally related. Research in proxemics (the study of relationships in the use of personal space) reveals, for example, that North Americans generally prefer greater distances between themselves and others than do Latin Americans or Arabs.[7] When these distance expectations are violated, problems often result. Hence, the physical setting of the interview is an obvious, although easily overlooked, variable influencing the interview's effectiveness.

Social Setting. In addition to the intercultural variables that affect the physical interview setting, the participants' social or cultural customs may create problems in interpersonal relations, if they are unknown or ignored. In general, the guest in the situation should adhere to the customs and manners of the host, regardless of which party is the R and which the E. Both parties should be sensitive to the other's sociocultural background, as it is often easy to offend the other unconsciously. Even though one participant usually has no control over the cultural norms of the other participant, nothing can destroy a positive interview climate more quickly than a lack of sensitivity in this area.

Time Dimensions. The length of the interview and its time of occurrence may also influence its outcome. If you know that a prospective employer regularly schedules staff meetings from 1:00 to 2:00 P.M. on Wednesday and reserves 9:00 to 10:00 A.M. daily for checking the day's mail, you would be unwise to call for an interview during either of those times. Interrupting an established procedure is upsetting and should be avoided when possible. Similarly, be alert to the timeliness of the interview in terms of the goal or action to be sought. An action requiring three to five weeks of planning by your partner should not be brought to your partner's attention ten days before the implementation deadline (or ten months before it, either).

If you seek from your interview partner thirty minutes of that person's time and proceed to stay sixty minutes (without your partner's encouragement), you should not be surprised at a negative response. Similarly, if you are the host, you should be willing to terminate an interview gracefully but firmly when the requested amount of time has expired.

Psychological Climate. An interview's psychological climate is something that you may not be able to investigate in advance or control if known. The personal causes of stress that participants bring with them to an interview may remain hidden or appear unexpectedly during the interview. When the latter occurs, it often sidetracks the participants and the interview goals and requires both patience and sensitivity on the part of the other party, even if it means terminating the interview. What you can do, however, is avoid making the situation worse. Tact, patience, sensitivity, and language skill can help alleviate such tensions.

Anatomy of the Interview

It is not practical to partition the typical interview arbitrarily into discrete parts, because an interview requires highly fluid interaction between the parties. A psychological differentiation, however, suggests three identifiable parts: the opening, the body, and the close. Just as there are psychological problems facing the two parties in the opening (attention getting, rapport building, orienting, conciliating), there are similar tasks to be accomplished in the body and in the close. The purpose and substance of the interview dictate what happens in the body and, to a lesser extent, in the close. Therefore, when beginning the interview, you may want to follow one or more of the now common techniques first suggested by Goyer, Redding, and Rickey in 1964:[8]

1. Brief statement or summary of the problem (need) facing E and/or R.
   (Appropriate when E is vaguely aware of the problem but not well informed on the details.)

   Example (Assistant plant manager meeting with the foreman of the third shift): "As you may have heard, our latest quarter report reveals that manufacturing defects of the widgets produced in our plant here in Los Angeles increased by 5 percent over the previous quarter, and it's over 8 percent higher than for the equivalent quarter a year ago. The plant manager has asked me to meet with each of the foremen to see if we can't figure out what is causing the problem."

2. Brief explanation of how you (R) happened to learn that a problem exists—coupled with suggestion that E will want to discuss it.
   (Avoids appearance of lecturing or talking down to E; encourages spirit of cooperative, objective discussion of a mutual problem.)

   Example (Assistant plant manager to plant manager): "Bill, in reviewing the corporation manufacturing report that arrived yesterday, I noticed that the manufacturing defects in the widgets we produce in our plant increased by 5 percent over the previous quarter figure and 8 percent over the equivalent figure a year ago. I've been reviewing our inspection procedures and have an idea that might help us get a handle on the problem."

3. Statement of an incentive (goal or outcome) desired by E that may reasonably be expected if the proposal is accepted.
   (Potentially the most powerful opening of all but easily abused—frequently corny, too obvious, or exaggerated. Avoid making it sound like a high-pressure sales pitch. Emphasize honesty and sincerity.)

Example (First-shift foreman to assistant plant manager): "Mr. Jones, I received your note about the increased rate of manufacturing defects last quarter, and I think I know how to save the company $100,000 a year by reducing the number of unusable widgets we manufacture."

4. Request for advice or assistance on a problem from E.
(Good when it is sincere! Don't use it as a gimmick.)

Example (Assistant plant manager to budget director): "Ms. Smith, I've got a real problem in manufacturing, and I need your help. Could you compile figures for me on the comparative salary and associated costs for widget inspectors at our Los Angeles, Phoenix, Indianapolis, and Atlanta plants during the last five years? I also would appreciate your analysis of the relative cost effectiveness of the widget inspectors in those plants over that period of time."

5. Statement of a striking, dramatic fact.
(Again, potentially very powerful but can be corny. Must be sincere, logically justified, and related to E's motivations; usually can be tied in with the incentives in the third technique. Particularly appropriate when there is real emergency and E is apathetic.)

Example (Treasurer to plant manager): "Bill, I just noticed in the corporate manufacturing report that our widget manufacturing defects percentage increased 5 percent over the previous quarter figure. Do you realize that that translates into almost a quarter of a million dollars on the negative side of the ledger?"

6. Reference to E's position on a given problem.
(This is a "common-ground" approach. Excellent to use when E has taken a public position or has already asked R to bring in proposals.)

Example (Plant manager to assistant plant manager): "Bob, I know that you have been working on this manufacturing defects problem and that you think our inspection program leaves something to be desired. Would you please review for me the dimensions of the problem as you see them, the necessary criteria that must be satisfied before the problem can be resolved, and some possible solutions?"

7. Reference to the background (causes, origin, etc.) of a problem (but not a statement of the problem itself) when E is fairly familiar with this background.
(Another application of common ground. May be useful when E is expected to react in a hostile manner after discovering what the proposal really is.)

Example (Assistant plant manager to plant manager): "As you will recall, corporate headquarters notified us last month that our current manufacturing defects figure did not look good and that we might want to think about its impact on our profit and loss figures for the quarter."

8. Statement of person who sent you to see E.
(Appropriate when E is a stranger and an entrée is necessary; can be used, of course, only when *true*—and when the third party is respected by E.)

Example (Private consultant to plant manager): "Mr. Jones, I'm Sam Namloz. Your corporate vice-president for manufacturing, Mr. Pavidic, suggested that I talk with you about a problem you seem to be having with manufacturing defects, to see if I might be of some assistance."

9. Statement of the company, organization, or group you represent.
   (Appropriate when added prestige is needed or when necessary to explain why you are there.)

   Example (Sales representative of a large industrial machinery manufacturing company to the vice-president for manufacturing): "Mr. Jones, I'm John Reyog of the Turnsteel Company. We have developed a new machine for the manufacture of widgets that I think you might find of interest."

10. Request for a specified, brief period of time.
    (Caution: don't be apologetic in asking, and don't exceed the time requested. Use only when necessary, in dealing with impatient, irritable, or very busy E.)

    Example (Shift foreman to assistant plant manager): "Mr. Adnil, I know you have a full schedule this morning, but I need ten minutes of your time to describe a problem on the widget line that is affecting quality control."

11. Question (various types: direct interrogation, yes-response, etc.).
    (Advantage: encourages E to respond in some manner. Pitfalls: can be tactless, abrupt, or too obvious. Question should be related to E's motives, mood, background, etc.)

    Example 1 (Shift foreman to assistant plant manager): "What's this I hear about unusually high manufacturing defects on the widgets?"
    Example 2 (Shift foreman to assistant plant manager): "The crew on this shift has heard about the widget problem, and we're eager to do whatever we can to improve the situation. Is there any way we can help?"

Remember that the opening of the interview should be planned in advance and based on the interviewer's analysis of the partner's knowledge, motives, and attitudes.

The body of the interview clearly is content oriented and is also the result of the direction and flow of interactions between the parties. The sequence of ideas presented is subject to some degree of patterning and control by both parties. The amount of preparation of each party in regard to knowledge of the topic and the interview partner will be most evident in this portion of the interview.

The close of the interview should be designed to give both unity and coherence to the entire interview. Both parties should be willing to take the initiative to summarize areas of agreement and disagreement and to decide what they should do next.

SUMMARY

The success or failure of people to relate to one another and their environment is basically a function of their ability to communicate, that is, to share their experiences. Although all living organisms are capable of communication on at least a biochemical level, humans have a unique ability to use symbol systems that permit the vicarious sharing of experiences occurring in the past, present, or future and in dealing with objects or events that are either physically present or absent. Verbal language codes used in oral and aural modalities are the chief examples of such symbol systems.

The interview is a goal-oriented, dyadic human interaction involving primarily (but not exclusively) oral and aural behaviors. In preparing for the interview, both parties should be familiar with the roles and goals of both the interviewer and the interviewee, as well as with each one's physical and cognitive characteristics. For an effective interview, the participants should have positive attitudes and competent skills. In preparing for the interview, remember that your analysis of the interview situation should include:

1. *Participant behaviors* of both R and E (self and partner), including both physical characteristics and cognitive/affective characteristics.
2. *Message components,* including characteristics of language (vocabulary, organizational structure) and sensory channels.
3. *Climate of the communicative act,* including the physical and social characteristics of the interview setting, time constraints, and the likely psychological climate of the interview.

EXERCISES

1. Interviewing has been defined as "a goal-oriented, dyadic human interaction involving primarily oral and aural communicative behaviors." Describe two recent interview situations in which you have been involved, one a positive experience and the other negative. What participant behaviors, message components, and climate caused the situation to be positive or negative?
2. Your instructor will assign you to interview a classmate. Prepare an analysis of the interview situation based on the variables identified in this chapter. The interview will take place after you have read Chapter 2.

NOTES

1. Andrew D. Wolvin and Carolyn G. Coakley, *Listening* (Dubuque, Ia.: Wm. C. Brown, 1982), pp. 4–5.
2. Robert S. Goyer, "Communication, Communicative Process, Meaning: Toward a Unified Theory," *Journal of Communication* 20 (1970):4–16.
3. For other definitions of interviewing, see R. S. Goyer, W. C. Redding, and J. T. Rickey, *Interviewing Principles and Techniques,* (Dubuque, Ia.: Kendall/Hunt, 1968), p. 5; R. F. Kahn and C. F. Cannell, *The Dynamics of Interviewing* (New York: John Wiley, 1964), p. 16; M. E. Stano and N. L. Reinsch, Jr., *Communication in Interviews* (Englewood Cliffs, N.J.: Prentice-Hall, 1982), p. 5; and C. J. Stewart and W. B. Cash, Jr., *Interviewing Principles and Practices,* 3rd ed. (Dubuque, Ia.: Wm. C. Brown, 1982), p. 7.
4. For a thorough discussion of the roles of nonverbal behavior and nonverbal communication, see R. P. Harrison, *Beyond Words: An Introduction to Nonverbal Communication* (Englewood Cliffs, N.J.: Prentice-Hall, 1974); M. L. Knapp, *Essentials of Nonverbal Communication* (New York: Holt, Rinehart & Winston, 1980); J. Ruesch and W. Kees, *Nonverbal Communication* (Berkeley and Los Angeles: University of California Press, 1964); and M. Wiener, S. DeVoe, S. Rubinow, and J. Geller, "Nonverbal Behavior and Nonverbal Communication," *Psychology Review* 79 (1979):185–214.

5. M. Benney, D. Riesman, and S. Star, "Age and Sex in the Interview," *American Journal of Sociology* 62 (1956):143–152.
6. For a thorough discussion of the role of listening in human communication, see R. O. Hirsch, *Listening: A Way to Process Information Aurally* (Dubuque, Ia.: Gorsuch Scarisbrick, 1979); C. H. Weaver, *Human Listening: Processes and Behavior* (Indianapolis: Bobbs-Merrill, 1972); and A. D. Wolvin and C. G. Coakley, *Listening* (Dubuque, Ia.: Wm. C. Brown, 1982).
7. C. H. Dodd, *Dynamics of Intercultural Communication* (Dubuque, Ia.: Wm. C. Brown, 1982), pp. 230–236.
8. R. S. Goyer, W. C. Redding, and J. T. Rickey, *Interviewing Principles and Techniques* (Dubuque, Ia.: Wm. C. Brown, 1964), pp. 10–11.

ADDITIONAL READINGS

Downs, C. W., G. Paul Smeyak, and Ernest Martin. *Professional Interviewing.* New York: Harper & Row, Pub., 1980.

Siegman, A. W., and S. Feldstein, eds. *Nonverbal Behavior and Communication.* Hillsdale, N.J.: Lawrence Erlbaum Associates, 1978.

Sommer, Robert. *Personal Space: The Behavioral Basis of Design.* Englewood Cliffs, N.J.: Prentice-Hall, 1969.

Informational Interviewing

CHAPTER OBJECTIVES

1. Explain the role of "information" in the interview.
2. Define "information forfeiture."
3. Describe six practices that will reduce the likelihood of information forfeiture.
4. Describe three barriers to sharing information.
5. Explain the influence of language choice, types of questions, and pattern of questions on success in the interview.
6. Explain the need to adapt your language to your interview partner.
7. Differentiate between open and closed questions.
8. Explain the pros and cons of using open and closed questions.
9. Identify types of follow-up questions, including when and where to use them.
10. Give examples of "yes-response" questions.
11. Conduct an information-gathering interview.

Introduction

As noted in Chapter 1, a common purpose in interviewing is to obtain information (i.e., to induce other people to share their experiences with you) or to give information (i.e., to share your experiences with other people). As will be pointed out in later chapters, even when the purpose of the interview is to persuade one's partner to agree to a particular point of view or course of action, the sharing of information will be involved to some degree. In this context, information refers to any portion of an individual's experience (knowledge, point of view, attitude, feeling, etc.) that has not been perceived previously by the interview partner.

Information Forfeiture

An individual's efforts to provide or to obtain information frequently are thwarted because of a lack of sensitivity to the interpersonal relationships between the interview partners, a lack of communicational skills, or both. As a result, information is lost, as evidenced by changes (omissions, additions, or transpositions) in the message provided. The following six practices will help prevent, or at least reduce, information forfeiture:

1. *Preview the information.* By briefly previewing the purpose and general content of the information to be offered, the information giver can alert the respondent to what is to follow, thereby providing for the respondent a mental set and a frame of reference for processing the information. Particularly in the opening of the interview, once you have established rapport with your partner, you should preview what will be discussed as a transition into the body of the interview (e.g., "As you may recall, the purpose of my visit is to review with you your office computer needs, suggest some alternative solutions, and discuss cost and installation problems.").

In addition to an initial general preview statement, the information giver should use summary-preview transitional statements as the interview progresses (e.g., "We've agreed that joining this organization will benefit you in two respects: meeting people your own age and giving you an opportunity to be of service to community development. Now let's review the time and energy costs that are involved.") Effective transitions help hold together the information and help introduce new topics into the interview.

2. *Be systematic (organized) in giving details.* The way that the information giver organizes the message can either inhibit or facilitate both the sharing process itself and the ability of the interview partner to recall the information later. Evidence from a number of researchers supports the view that one's ability to organize ideas is a function of the individual's skill in presenting and identifying (1) component relationships (part to part and part to whole), (2) material-to-purpose relationships (the relevance of one idea to others), (3) sequential relationships (the logic in a sequence of ideas), and (4) connective relationships (conjunctive or transitional links between ideas).[1] All of these skills can be learned, and skillful information givers will organize their ideas clearly in order to help the interview partners receive and retain information. Guidelines for ordering specific topics in the interview will be discussed later in this chapter.

3. *Use emphasis and attention factors.* The research literature confirms that we remember best that to which we have paid the most attention. Therefore, the careful use (but not overuse) of selected emphasis techniques can help prevent information forfeiture. Although such techniques as repetition, vocal pause, varying the rate of speech, changing volume, and using gestures can result in an emphasis pattern, the most consistently successful technique is simply to indicate to one's partner that what is to follow is of particular importance (e.g., "This next point is critical . . ." "Now note this . . ."). This technique is often referred to as "proactive emphasis" and is very effective if not overused.[2]

4. *Encourage oral reaction from the respondent.* Often the simplest way of checking to make sure that information has not been lost is to ask the respondent to repeat or restate the information presented. If this technique can be used with-

out talking down to the respondent, the provider of the information can be satisfied that at least the words in the message were received as intended. If the respondent paraphrases or repeats exactly the message received, the information giver may have even better evidence that the point of the message was perceived as intended. Responses can be encouraged through such requests as "Tell me in your own words what I have just said" or "What do you think I've been trying to say?"

Note that the respondent's ability to repeat or paraphrase your message correctly is not necessarily evidence that the respondent understands, agrees with, or is persuaded by your message. To determine the latter, ask the appropriate question (e.g., "Do you agree?") and listen for cues (e.g., "I agree with you on this point, but . . .").

5. *Use more than one medium of presentation.* It probably is not true that "a picture is worth ten thousand words" (pictures can be meaningless too), but often one will find that a combination of sight and sound (and perhaps even touch and smell as well) can be of tremendous help in clarifying the information to be shared. In the interview, this means being prepared not only to talk about a set of statistical figures but also to display them in the form of charts, diagrams, and the like. It means being willing to gesture, move, or touch if necessary. Such aids can help both participants, in that the additional medium provides another means of organizing the material and reinforcing its effects on the interview partner. When using visual aids, however, be careful not to lose control of them. If you give a sheet of statistics to your partner to read, your partner may be reading them when you are ready to move to another topic. Avoid letting an audiovisual aid become an audiovisual distraction!

6. *Summarize frequently.* Particularly when you are the information giver in an interview, you should frequently summarize the information shared, in order to monitor your own exposition and to ensure that the receiver has accurately followed and interpreted the message. If the information giver does not volunteer summaries, the information getter either should request them or make them. Among other benefits, such summaries will reveal the consistency (or lack of it) of the giver's remarks and point up possible forfeitures as the summaries progress. Depending on the clarity of or the uncertainty about what has been said, summaries should be offered whenever either participant feels the need.

Barriers to Sharing Information in the Interview

We have just seen how information can be forfeited as a result of the participants' oral behaviors. In addition to the participants' behaviors, other kinds of barriers can prevent information from being shared between the partners. Particularly in a face-to-face interview, the physical distances between the participants (proxemic relationships) can affect the interaction between them, and furthermore, the optimum distance may vary considerably from culture to culture. These proxemic relationships clearly are subject to some degree of control and should be considered as part of the preparation for the interview. For example, in the United States a distance of three to eight feet between interview participants is usual, although the intrusion of furniture such as a desk or table may emphasize the distance and create a kind of barrier in itself.[3]

The arrangement of furniture in the interview can encourage or discourage face-to-face participation. The larger the desk between an interviewer and an interviewee, the more formidable the psychological distance between the two parties will be. Similarly, the more cluttered the desk and the larger and more luxurious the interviewer's chair compared with that of the interviewee, the greater the perceived difference will be between the two parties in terms of role and stature. If the interviewer deliberately uses such a furniture arrangement in order to intimidate the interviewee, and the interviewee perceives it, that behavior in itself will communicate a message that bodes ill for the occurrence of productive interaction in the interview. Potentially confounding the situation even further are intercultural assumptions (or the lack of them) when the participants are of different nationalities or backgrounds and are accustomed to different conventions regarding expectations of "personal space" requirements.[4]

Individual physical limitations or inabilities (e.g., hearing impairment or speech dysfunctions) also may prevent the sharing of information. In preparing for the interview, be aware of both your own and your partner's possible restrictions and prepare accordingly. Usually this simply involves being sensitive to the other's needs and adapting to them graciously.

Role differences between the participants can also prevent the effective sharing of information, as will be discussed in later chapters. Perceived differences in social standing, economic class, ethnic or religious background, job level, and the like, whether accurate or not, can be one of the greatest of all barriers to effective communicative behavior of any kind, including the interview. Fortunately, it is possible to clarify and alleviate, if not totally neutralize, possible role differences in the interview if the participants are sensitive to each other's needs, skillful in using interviewing techniques (preventing information forfeiture), and genuinely interested in achieving commonly defined goals. The assumptions, habits of thinking, and attitudes regarding the other person's characteristics, viewpoint, and experience can either create barriers or remove them, depending on the sensitivity of the involved parties. Sensitivity and politeness toward the interview partner do not mean automatic acceptance of the other's point of view. But they do mean that genuine differences of opinion can be discussed and mutual respect maintained, even when progress toward a common goal is extremely limited.

Asking Questions and Providing Responses

When you seek information from another person, it would seem obvious that all you need to do is ask that person a question. Actual experience in interviewing, however, quickly reveals that the ability to ask the "right" question (or sequence of questions) often is not an easy task. Keep in mind that the interview occurs in a context reflecting a variety of different attitudes, abilities, and experiences for both participants. Thus, it is not surprising that questions (and the responses to them) are subject to different interpretations by each of the participants. In preparing interview questions, be alert to the possible influences of these three factors:

1. *Language choice.* As was noted in Chapter 1, the possibility of communication occurring (as contrasted with simply transmitting and receiving messages)

is largely a function of the participants' sharing the same language codes. Because of the richness and variety of experience associated with verbal language codes, the specific words chosen to ask a question are of critical importance. The broader and more precise the participants' experiences are with regard to the subject of the interview, the greater the probability will be that the choice of words (given the same language code) will not be a critical factor in asking questions and providing responses. On the other hand, the greater the discrepancy is in the participants' range and detail of experience, the greater the probability will be that language usage and choice will be a problem. The more technical or sophisticated the topic is, the greater both participants' responsibility will be to be sensitive to possible language problems. A general rule of thumb to follow is to avoid the use of acronyms, jargon, colloquialisms, and regional slang in favor of simpler, more generally accepted language. This does not mean that you should sacrifice precision and detail for simplicity and conciseness but that your language level should be geared to your interview partner's understanding level, if you are to avoid confusion, ambiguity, and information forfeiture.

For example, if the interviewer asks, "Have you seen a boilermaker?" a yes response may be unintentionally inaccurate or quite misleading. Depending on the correspondence of experiencing between the participants, a "boilermaker" may refer to at least one of the following: (1) a metal worker who makes boilers, (2) a U.S. Navy seaman who carries a boilermaker rating, (3) a student who attends Purdue University, or (4) an alcoholic drink. This kind of semantic ambiguity pertains to much of our everyday language usage and requires that the information giver and receiver recognize this in order to be clear and precise. Consider the numbers of possible meanings that might be associated with such words as "bear," "coat," "act," "air," "bow," "box," "charge," "dog," "good," "play," "review," "set," "race," and so on. When such words are used, we typically examine the context in which they appear in order to find clues to their intended meaning, if we are aware of more than one possibility. Even then, we often make false assumptions or lack the necessary experience to interpret words or phrases as the speaker intended.

Finally, when dealing with an interviewer partner who is emotionally involved with the subject of the interview, be cautious in using "loaded" language in your questions or responses. Although such language may prompt immediate active participation, it may so prejudice the interview partners against each other or sidetrack the direction of the interview that it becomes nearly impossible to identify, much less to satisfy, the goals of the interview in a rational way. If you know, for example, that your partner feels strongly about a given political party or system (e.g., Republican, Democrat, Communist, Socialist), religious or racial group (Catholic, Protestant, Jew, Arab, Indian), or emotionally charged issues in the public consciousness (e.g., euthanasia, capital punishment, abortion, gun control), you should avoid references to your partner's position if they are not relevant to the interview topic or purpose.

2. *Types of questions.* Because the purpose of an interview question is to elicit pertinent information from your partner in the most efficient and least offensive way, the types (forms, styles) of the questions that you ask can greatly influence the response you receive. Although a question may contain all the "right" words, the way the question is phrased and vocally presented will greatly affect the response made. Question types are typically classified as either open or closed

in regard to the content of the desired response and as either direct or indirect in regard to the questioner's approach to the respondent.

Open questions, by definition, offer the respondent a variety of response possibilities within the framework of the topic identified in the question. In addition to their possible use in building rapport, open questions are designed to (1) involve the respondent, (2) indicate to the interviewer the depth and breadth of the respondent's knowledge of a topic, and (3) suggest the respondent's attitudinal and emotional involvement with the topic.

The degree of the question's openness may vary, depending on the question's purpose. For example, when a prospective employer asks a job applicant, 'What do you know about our organization?" the respondent has an extremely wide range of response options, from "nothing" to a detailed review of its products or services offered, its organizational structure, its financial status and future prospects, and so forth.

Open questions are not without their problems, however. Though allowing the respondent to control the nature and detail of the response, open questions often can be inefficient in terms of the amount of useful information gained per unit of time, because of disorganized, rambling, or irrelevant responses. Separating the wheat from the chaff often is a difficult task for even highly skilled interviewers, because of the quantity of information to be gleaned from open-ended questions. "What do you think about the president's new tax proposal?" and "What do you think are its strong and weak points?" are examples of questions that are relatively open and designed to get the respondent involved. These types of questions are not meaningfully answered by a simple yes or no but still provide substantial leeway for responding.

Closed questions are intended to restrict the range of responses available to the interview partner in an effort to ensure relevance to the topic of the interview. By using them, the information gatherer controls the nature, type, and detail level of the response. "Which political party do you think has done the best job of administering state government during the last decade?" "What childhood illnesses have you had?" These examples of closed questions demand a more restrictive response than do those in the preceding section and are intended to help focus the respondent's experiences in terms of sharing information. Usually they can be answered with yes or no or with specific information. Although the closed question can be controlled somewhat better by the questioner, resulting in more specific information in less time, it also can mean finding out less valuable and less pertinent information than otherwise might have been volunteered. The outcome may be a reduced or distorted understanding of the response by the questioner. Concentrating on individual trees sometimes makes one oblivious to the outlines of the forest.

Whether open or closed questions are appropriate in a given situation should be determined by the questioner (whether R or E) on the basis of the objectives of the interview and the breadth and depth of knowledge of the participants. Thus the concern for the content of the responses to questions is reflected in the decision to ask an open or closed question. Of equal concern is whether to approach the interview partner directly or indirectly in regard to the partner's possible emotional involvement with the topic. If the topic of the interview is one that is apt to produce psychological discomfort or defiance on the part of the respondent, particular care should be taken to avoid asking questions that will make the interview partner defensive or antagonistic. Any interview that may include unpleasant decisions and consequences for the interview partners requires careful questioning techniques, because the respondent consciously or otherwise may seek opportunities to rationalize or prejudge responses or not to respond at all. In any event, the objectives of the interview may be put completely out of reach.

Interviews involving counseling, complaints, correcting, reprimanding, performance appraisal, and termination are particularly susceptible to such problems, but no interview situation is completely devoid of such a possibility if either party is insensitive to the interview partner or clumsy in using interviewing techniques. If an academic adviser is seeking information from a student about the content and teaching methods in Professor X's course and knows that the student did not do well in the course, then directly asking the student ("What did you think of Professor X's course?" or "Is Professor X a good teacher?") may be a less useful way of eliciting the desired information than is asking one or more indirectly related questions ("What kind or progress are you making toward your degree requirements?" "What was the value of the courses you took this last term?" "Which course did you have difficulty with, and why?"). Note that direct or indirect approaches may be used with either open or closed questions.

Probing and follow-up questions are used to obtain clarification of or more detailed information on a topic already under discussion, and they carry many descriptive labels (e.g., "secondary" questions, "mirror" questions). They may be either open or closed and are used when the questioner seeks to confirm what has already been said or to enlarge the explanation of a topic by focusing on some aspect of it. Some examples are:

"Can you give me an example of that last point?" (clarification)
"You say that you haven't been feeling well and that your head hurts?" (more detail)
"I think I understand your procedure, but just how would you handle a problem like this? (explanation and application)

Leading questions often are used in persuasive interviewing when the questioner wants to establish a sequence of responses (the "yes-response" technique).[5] In informational interviewing, however, neutral rather than leading questions should be used, as the latter tend to provoke unreliable responses. The leading question often tells you what the respondent thinks you want to hear, topically or emotionally, regardless of whether or not the respondent honestly knows or believes it. For example, when the office manager says to the secretarial assistant, "You certainly like the present open-space office arrangement, don't you!" the likelihood of a positive response is great, particularly given the role differences between the participants. Similarly, the parent who says to the child, "You want to be like me when you grow up, don't you?" expects the answer yes—and probably gets it. Note that the answer to a yes-response question does not have to be yes. For example, the questioner who asks, "You don't want to make that mistake again, do you?" expects a no answer.

If gathering information is the interviewer's goal, both the wording of the question and the vocal and physical manner of the questioner must be designed to facilitate a clear, thorough, and sincere response. Intentional or unintentional verbal browbeating, aided and abetted by physical mannerisms, discourage the revelation of useful information and should be avoided at all costs in informational interviewing.

Encouraging a general willingness to respond should not be confused with encouraging a *given* response: probing and follow-up questions refer to the former, and leading questions refer to the latter.

3. *Pattern of questions.* In planning the interview, make it a point to organize the sequence of the most important questions in regard to the objectives of the interview and the topics to be covered. In effect, such a plan provides an outline of the proposed interview and permits assessment of mutual progress as the interview proceeds. Be flexible about implementing the prepared outline, and adjust it as the interview progresses, in accordance with unexpected information or points of view and the necessity of asking follow-up questions based on the responses of your partner. Perhaps most importantly, be sensitive to the likelihood of questions from your partner and the importance of integrating these into the total interview. Too rigid programming of questions may stifle the interaction, whereas too flexible programming (or no programming at all) may result in haphazard information and ultimate confusion.

SUMMARY

The object of informational interviewing is to give and to receive information. When information is forfeited, the chances of achieving the goals of the interview suffer accordingly. There are many skills that can be used to enhance efforts to share information, just as there are many physical and attitudinal barriers that can prevent such sharing. Skill in asking questions and providing responses can be learned and centers on language usage, the types of questions asked, and the pattern of questioning employed.

EXERCISES

1. Complete Exercise 2 from Chapter 1 in preparation for conducting an in-class interview with another class member with whom you are not familiar (the instructor may choose to make this assignment for you). Gather as much information from and about each other as you can, so as to provide a strong information base for formally introducing your partner to (1) the rest of the class, (2) a potential employer, and (3) a group of professionals in your partner's intended career area.
2. Conduct an in-class interview with another class member, with the object of providing detailed information to your partner concerning a process, event, decision, or whatever, about which you are probably more knowledgeable than any student in class and which your partner must relay to another person who is unfamiliar with the information.
3. Arrange an out-of-class interview with a professional in your career field. Select a person who does a considerable amount of interviewing as part of

his or her job, and seek information about such items as (1) interview training received (e.g., formal course instruction, self-instruction, on-the-job experience), (2) interviewing practices (e.g., types and kinds of interviewing situations encountered, favorite techniques and methods employed), and (3) suggestions (general and/or specific) for improving your own ability to conduct an interview. Submit a written report describing the interview from the time of its inception to its termination, including the questions you asked and a detailed summary of the information you received.
4. Locate an interview in a newspaper or magazines (e.g., *Wall Street Journal, Business Week, Time*) and critique it in regard to the variables discussed in this chapter.

NOTES

1. Robert S. Goyer, "A Test to Measure the Ability to Organize Ideas," *Journal of Educational Measurement* 4 (1965):63–64.
2. Ray Ehrensberger, "An Experimental Study of the Relative Effectiveness of Certain Forms of Emphasis in Public Speaking," *Speech Monographs* 12 (1945):94–111.
3. Alan Hartter, "The Relationship Between Physical Separation and Comfortableness In An Interview," (Master's thesis, School of Interpersonal Communication, Ohio University, 1975).
4. Robin Widgery, and Cecil Stackpole, "Desk Position, Interviewee Anxiety, and Interviewer Credibility: An Example of Cognitive Balance in a Dyad," *Journal of Counseling Psychology* 19 (1972):173–177. See also C. H. Dodd, *Dynamics of Intercultural Communication* (Dubuque, Ia.: Wm. C. Brown, 1982).
5. Robert S. Goyer and Michael Z. Sincoff, *Interviewing Methods* (Dubuque, Ia.: Kendall/Hunt, 1977).

ADDITIONAL READINGS

Payne, S. L. *The Art of Asking Questions*. Princeton, N.J.: Princeton University Press, 1951.

Stewart, Charles J., and William B. Cash, Jr. *Interviewing Principles and Practices*. 3rd ed. Dubuque, Ia.: Wm. C. Brown, 1982.

Richetto, Gary M., and Joseph P. Zima. "Fundamentals of Interviewing." *Modcom* (Science Research Associates), (1976):1–36.

3

Survey Interviewing

CHAPTER OBJECTIVES

1. Explain how an interview can help gather information systematically.
2. Explain when you would engage in a face-to-face interview instead of sending the respondent a written questionnaire.
3. Give examples of two ways to record data obtained in a survey interview.
4. Identify and describe the steps to be taken in constructing an interview guide.
5. Describe steps you can take to help ensure objectivity when conducting a survey interview.
6. Identify key issues in sample selection and coding of response data.
7. Understand principal differences between highly structured and highly unstructured questionnaires.
8. Write a survey questionnaire and conduct a survey interview.

Introduction

The use of the interview as a means of systematically gathering information occurs in a variety of settings (e.g., business, government, education, politics, journalism) and for a variety of purposes (e.g., market analysis, conducting organizational climate surveys, and collecting data for scholarly research, censuses, assessment of voting behaviors, readership surveys). Whatever the setting and purpose, the object is to gather from a respondent information that can be compared, collated, and used with information gathered from other respondents replying to the same questions.

Survey interviews are a type of self-report device and therefore are subject to the problems of the respondents' giving (intentionally or otherwise) distorted information and the interviewers' making distorted interpretations of those responses (again, intentionally or otherwise). Although there are inherent disadvantages in self-reporting techniques, the interview (and its handmaiden, the questionnaire) are widely used to collect immense quantities of data from millions of people. In the discussion that follows, we shall consider some of the variables that influence the effectiveness of survey interviewing.

Interviews and Questionnaires

When researchers decide to collect data by means of a self-report technique, one of their first decisions is whether to approach respondents in a direct face-to-face manner, in a relatively direct but not face-to-face manner (telephone), in an indirect, mediated manner (written questionnaire that the respondent reads), or in some combination of these. Each has its own advantages and disadvantages.

1. *Need to target specific respondents.* If the interviewer must get responses from specific individuals, the chances of doing so clearly are much better in the face-to-face situation than in either the telephone interview or the mailed questionnaire. Conversely, if the researcher seeks a response simply from "a member of the household," a telephone call or mailed questionnaire probably will suffice.

2. *Time frame for gathering data.* The time dimension in gathering self-report data is important in two respects. First, the interviewer's time in meeting and talking with the respondent in the face-to-face situation (including getting to and from the interview site) will be more time-consuming (and financially costly) than will calling a respondent on the telephone, and both of these techniques will take the interviewer more time than will mailing a questionnaire to a respondent who may or may not answer the questions. Second, almost all survey research has identifiable time constraints (e.g., political polls on a candidate's popularity are conducted at specified intervals before the election; communication audit data in an organization must be gathered only during certain times of the workday). These time constraints may dictate a particular self-report technique.

3. *Eliciting respondent cooperation.* When the questions to be asked are relatively short, simple, direct, and closed (see Chapter 2), and the questioner makes this clear in the opening of the interview or on the instructions on the questionnaire, the respondent can be expected to cooperate willingly. On the other hand, if the questions to be asked are open, multifaceted, intentionally ambiguous, or sensitive, resistance should be expected. When the latter is the case, the face-to-face or telephone interview (particularly the former) gives the interviewer a much better chance of eliciting cooperation from the respondent. If the respondent does not wish to cooperate, it is a very simple matter to throw a mailed questionnaire in the wastebasket or just to hang up the telephone receiver.

4. *Amount and quality of information sought.* A long list of questions or questions that require long and carefully constructed answers requiring considerable time and effort to record are less apt to be answered on a mailed questionnaire than in an interview, particularly a face-to-face interview. In the latter, a skilled interviewer can take time to clarify questions and responses immediately, which is not possible with the mailed questionnaire.

5. *Ease of recording responses.* From the standpoint of the researcher, it is much easier to have the respondent take the time and effort to complete a mailed questionnaire form, thus permitting the researcher to concentrate on tabulating data or other tasks. If the questionnaire itself is carefully constructed and permits the

respondent only to mark choices and not to write out responses, so much the better. But if the respondent gives overly long answers to the questions, which in turn must be interpreted by the questioner, more valid and reliable results may be obtained in the interview, permitting the questioner to code responses quickly and consistently according to an established format. In general, the self-administered questionnaire should avoid open-ended questions and rely on closed response questions for ease of recording responses. If the questionnaire is being administered by a skilled interviewer, a greater variety of follow-up questions and detailed responses is possible.

The following two examples demonstrate variations in the ease with which responses can be recorded:

> "To what extent in your job as a survey interviewer do you use the skills and procedures in which you were formally trained?"

In the self-administered questionnaire, the answers to this could be difficult to record, because of the tremendous range of responses possible. If administered by an interviewer who has some classification scheme in mind (e.g., not at all—somewhat—mostly—all of them), a somewhat more precise response can be sought and categorized. If these same response categories were offered in a self-administered form of the questionnaire, the respondent might decide that none of them fits and might ignore the question or write in an option not provided (e.g., "sometimes 'not at all', and sometimes 'mostly', depending on the specific task.").

> "In your job as a survey interviewer, what percentage of your workday do you typically spend in the following activities?"
>
> 1. Writing interview questions.   _____
> 2. Selecting respondent samples.   _____
> 3. Mailing questionnaires.   _____
> 4. Participating in telephone interviews. _____
> 5. Participating in face-to-face interviews. _____
> 6. Tabulating data.   _____
> 7. Writing reports.   _____
> 8. Other (list).   _____
>   _____
>
> Total: 100%

Notice that this question lends itself very easily to the self-administered questionnaire format, as specific typical behaviors are listed, with the "Other" category a possibility.

6. *Financial cost.* Gathering self-report data can be expensive in both time and money. If mailed questionnaires are used and the sample size is large, mailing costs (both original and follow-up) can mount quickly. If telephone interviews are used, there will be both telephone and interviewer costs. If interviewers are hired for face-to-face interviews, the cost per interview will probably far exceed either the mailing or the telephone costs.

You should weigh each of these six considerations before deciding which technique for gathering the self-report data will be most appropriate for your purpose. You should not assume that just because you are planning to use an interview technique, you will have no need for a questionnaire. The fact is that almost always you will be using some form of questionnaire (also called an interview "protocol," "schedule" or "guide") in all of your survey interviews.

Constructing the Interview Guide

The objective of the questionnaire used in survey interviewing is systematically to secure valid and reliable responses to a set of questions asked individually of a group of people. Inherent in the process is the assumption that the respondents will give truthful answers and that the interviewer will ask questions and record all answers accurately and consistently across all respondents. The former assumption is not under the interviewer's control (although the consistency of answers provided by the respondent to selected questions may in part be controlled), and the latter assumption is a function of skills that can be learned and developed.

In constructing the interview guide, you must be sensitive to the survey's objectives (what information you are seeking and the uses to which the information will be put) and the characteristics of the respondent population (particularly language behaviors and willingness to participate). The format of the guide thus should include (1) a set of standardized opening remarks to introduce the topic and purpose of the interview and to establish rapport with the respondent; (2) a clear transition into the questionnaire itself; (3) the specific questions to be used (including clarifying explanations you may be asked for); and (4) a closing statement, including thanking the respondent for participating. In general, the questions should be as simply worded as possible, using language that is not controversial to the respondent, and they should be organized in a nonthreatening and logical sequence from the viewpoint of the respondent. When quick recording and tabulation of results are required, direct, closed questions should be asked.

After the guide has been formulated, it should be pretested on a sample of the population for which it is to be used, until each of these four format characteristics has been thoroughly refined.

Conducting the Interview

You will recall from Chapter 1 that there are many variables that affect the likelihood of communication occurring in any interactive situation. In survey interviewing, the interviewer must be particularly sensitive to the opportunities for biasing responses that are inherent in the interviewer's behaviors (particularly verbal behaviors) and avoid them. In survey interviewing, the interviewer's object is to draw from respondents information, reactions, or opinions politely, neutrally, and impartially, without the slightest suggestion, verbally or otherwise, of influencing or evaluating the response, before or after it is given. In those interviews using direct, closed questions, the task is usually much easier than in those interviews using open-ended questions and considerable probing, because in the latter the interviewer clearly has many more opportunities, in word and manner, to bias the responses. Interaction is unavoidable in any kind of interview situation, but it is the interviewer's responsibility in survey interviewing to encourage some response behaviors and to discourage others. Accordingly:

1. Ask the questions exactly as worded on the interview guide, using the same vocal inflections, pronunciations, and so on for each respondent. If you are asked

to repeat the question, repeat it exactly as you first asked it. Do not offer opinions or suggest answers, and do not let your physical actions (posture, gestures, facial expressions) indicate approval or disapproval of responses. For questions that your pretest or field use of the questionnaire suggests will occasionally require explanation or clarification, plan and practice the clarifying remarks so that they too will become standard in both wording and expression.

2. Be friendly, gracious, but businesslike to all respondents. Each respondent and situation may require a somewhat different approach in establishing rapport and inspiring cooperation, requiring the interviewer to be adaptable and sensitive.

3. Focus your words and actions on the information being sought, and anticipate and practice verbal and nonverbal behaviors that will keep the respondent on target without giving offense. For example, do not let either your voice or posture show impatience; instead, be alert to verbal cues that will let you return to the interview's purpose and questions.

4. Ask every question on the interview guide, in the order that each appears. Even when the respondent unknowingly gives what you consider an answer to Question 10 while answering Question 3, ask Question 10 when it appears in context, exactly as it appears and without apology. (Often this procedure will give the interviewer clues to the reliability of the respondent's answers.)

5. Interview respondents individually and privately. The more distractions there are in the environment (e.g., other people, noise, interruptions), the more likely that unreliable and invalid responses will result.

6. Assure the respondent that his or her answers will be confidential, and then behave accordingly. If you reveal the details of specific interview responses to others, you will have breached the ethics of the interview and damaged your own credibility and that of the organization you represent, as well as perhaps invited legal action.

7. Conclude the interview on a positive note so that the respondent will think well of you, your organization, and the entire experience.

Training Interviewers

Selecting and training of interviewers to carry out survey interviewing deserves a special comment. An employer of trained survey interviewers looks for persons who are likely to be accepted by the public, whose appearance and psychological makeup reflect attitudes and sensitivities that will instill confidence and cooperation in others, and who have the necessary skills and training to perform well (or who can be taught those skills). The prospective survey interviewer typically will be screened and/or receive instruction in the following areas:

1. *Basic speaking and listening skills.* If you are unable to speak the standard language of the area being surveyed, clearly articulated and resonated, a career as a professional interviewer, survey or otherwise, will be extremely difficult to pursue. Similarly, if you do not have the patience to focus on and listen carefully to what the respondent is saying (or if you have a physical hearing dysfunction that is uncorrected), your effectiveness as a survey interviewer will be limited.

2. *Understanding and appreciating the role and significance of interviewing in the research process.* Without understanding the importance of interviews, it will be difficult for the interviewer to be conscientious in asking questions and recording responses faithfully and reliably and to take pride in the task performed.

3. *Basic interviewing skills.* Learning the manner and style of opening an interview, asking questions and recording responses, handling language ambiguities and misunderstandings, and closing an interview gracefully are skills that can be refined with practice, by means of role playing and actual interviews in the laboratory and the field. Practice without professional supervision in this area only makes permanent; critical supervised practice will help make perfect.

Additional Considerations

There are other considerations involved in planning and conducting survey interview projects that are outside the purpose and scope of this discussion, but that you should know about, including

1. *Sample selection.* Extremely important to survey research is the selection of the sample of persons to be interviewed. In order to generalize confidently the results of the survey to a much larger group of people, the sample of people interviewed must be an accurate representation of the larger group to which they belong. Consequently, even though other significant sources of error variance (interviewer behaviors, questionnaire guide characteristics, situational variables in the actual interivew) may be controlled or neutralized, a nonrepresentative sample of prospective respondents will produce survey research that lacks validity. It is sufficient here to point out only that a "good" sample selection procedure is one that clearly (1) identifies the population that is to be studied, (2) defines the number of respondents required to generalize reliably to the larger population, and (3) provides a systematic selection procedure for discovering respondents representative of the larger population according to the variables and population characteristics pertinent to the study.

2. *Coding and processing results.* Another potentially serious source of errors in survey research occurs after the interviewing has been completed. No matter how valid and reliable the interview questionnaire is, the interpretation of those responses for purposes of coding and processing (summarizing and collating) data require interpretation by the person doing the coding (even though the responses may subsequently be processed by a computer). This is particularly true for questions that involve probes of the respondents' answers and the recording of free responses. Accordingly, it is important to translate the questionnaire information into categories that accurately represent the data, yet permit classification of the data into categories amenable to mathematical data tabulation and reduction techniques.

For a more thorough and detailed discussion of procedures and techniques for selecting samples and coding and processing results, you are urged to examine one or more of the books listed at the end of this chapter and to study the sample questionnaires that follow.

Sample Questionnaires

Figures 3.1, 3.2, and 3.3 illustrate three different types of survey questionnaires. Figure 3.1 shows the first twenty-one items of a fifty-one-item telephone interview questionnaire designed to elicit information about the respondent's interest in and willingness to support a new heavy industrial manufacturing facility in

FIGURE 3.1. Telephone Interview Questionnaire[1]

Hello, I'm _____, from _____, a national survey research company with headquarters in _____.
We're conducting a survey about employment opportunities in this area.

1. How many persons 18 years or older in this household are currently (CIRCLE ONE RESPONSE PER ROW)

	None	One	Two	Three	Four	Over 5	DK	Ref/NA	
a. Employed full or part time?	[0]	1	2	3	4	5	8	9	37
b. Homemaker?	0	1	2	3	4	5	8	9	38
c. Unemployed?	0	1	2	3	4	5	8	9	39
d. Retired?	0	1	2	3	4	5	8	9	40

a. Is there someone 18 years or older in this household that is actively seeking employment?
- Yes 1
- No   (TERMINATE) 2
- Don't know (TERMINATE) 8   41
- Refused/NA (TERMINATE) 9

(ASK TO SPEAK TO THE PERSON WHO IS 18 YEARS OR OLDER AND SEEKING EMPLOYMENT)

b. What was your job title in the last working position you held? (RECORD JOB TITLE)

(GO TO Q.11)   42-43

2. Are you presently employed in a full or part time job?
- Yes 1
- No (ASK TO SPEAK TO SOMEONE WHO IS EMPLOYED FULL OR PART TIME AND RE-READ INTRODUCTION) 2
- Don't know (TERMINATE) 8   44
- Refused/NA (TERMINATE) 9

3. Would you describe *your* job as being white collar or blue collar? (IF NECESSARY, EXPLAIN THAT WHITE COLLAR USUALLY MEANS OFFICE WORKERS OR PROFESSIONALS LIKE TEACHERS, WHILE BLUE COLLAR USUALLY MEANS MILL, FACTORY OR PLANT EMPLOYMENT)
- White collar 1
- Blue collar 2
- Other _____ 3
                 (SPECIFY)
- Don't know 8   45
- Refused/NA 9
- (IF MILITARY, GO TO BLUE SECTION)
- (IF FARMER, GO TO GREEN SECTION)

FIGURE 3.1. Telephone Interview Questionnaire (continued)

a. Are there any persons in this household that are employed in a blue collar job?	Yes (ASK TO SPEAK TO THAT PERSON AND RE-READ INTRODUCTION) 1 No (GO TO PINK SECTION) 2 Don't know 8 Refused/NA 9	46

4. Let's discuss some things about your current job. First, what is your job title? (PROBE FOR TITLE OR DESCRIPTION OF WORK)	_____ 01 (RECORD TITLE) Don't know 98 Refused/NA 99 (IF MILITARY, GO TO BLUE SECTION) (IF FARMER, GO TO GREEN SECTION)	47–48

5. Approximately how many miles is it, *one way,* from your residence to your work location? (IF "DON'T KNOW," PROBE FOR BEST ESTIMATE)	Distance varies 01 Less than 5 miles 02 6–10 miles 03 11–15 miles 04 16–20 miles 05 21–25 miles 06 26–30 miles 07 31–35 miles 08 36–40 miles 09 Over 40 miles 10 Don't know 98 Refused/NA 99	49–50

6. About how many minutes does it take you to drive to work? (PROBE FOR BEST ESTIMATE)	Less than 15 minutes 01 16–20 minutes 02 21–25 minutes 03 26–30 minutes 04 31–35 minutes 05 36–40 minutes 06 41–45 minutes 07 Over 45 minutes 08 Don't know 98 Refused/NA 99	51–52

7. Do you usually drive to work alone, or does someone else drive with you?	Drive alone 1 Drive with someone else 2 Don't drive to work 3 Don't know 8 Refused/NA 9	53

FIGURE 3.1. Telephone Interview Questionnaire (continued)

8. Does your job involve the supervision of other employees? (READ RESPONSES)	Often Sometimes Rarely Never Don't know Refused/NA	1 2 3 4 8 9	54
9. Approximately what hourly wage rate are you now paid?	Under $3.00 an hour $3.00–$3.99 an hour $4.00–$4.99 an hour $5.00–$5.49 an hour $5.50–$5.99 an hour $6.00–$6.49 an hour $6.50–$6.99 an hour $7.00–$7.49 an hour $7.50–$7.99 an hour $8.00–$8.99 an hour $9.00–$9.99 an hour $10.00 or more an hour Don't know Refused/NA	01 02 03 04 05 06 07 08 09 10 11 12 98 99	55–56
10. Would you say that you have the *opportunity* to work overtime? (READ RESPONSES AND ROTATE)	Often Sometimes Rarely Never (GO TO Q.11) Don't know (GO TO Q.11) Refused/NA (GO TO Q.11)	1 2 3 4 8 9	57
a. Do you actually *work* overtime as often as possible, sometimes, or do you never work overtime?	Often as possible Most of the time Never Don't know Refused/NA	1 2 3 8 9	58
11. Would you be willing to work on a rotating shift, that is, working first shift one week, second shift the following week, and third shift the week after that? (READ SLOWLY)	Yes No Don't know Refused/NA	1 2 8 9	59
12. Is there a shift you would *not* be willing to work?	Yes No Don't know Refused/NA	1 2 8 9	60

SURVEY INTERVIEWING   33

FIGURE 3.1. Telephone Interview Questionnaire (continued)

a. Which shift(s) would you *not* be willing to work? (READ RESPONSES IF NECESSARY)	Days Afternoons Nights Don't know Refused/NA	1 2 3 8 61 9
13. How about rotating off days? Would you be willing to work on different days of the week rather than always having weekends off?	Yes No Don't know Refused/NA	1 2 8 9 62
14. What shift do you currently work on? (IF NOT EMPLOYED, ASK WHAT SHIFT THEY LAST WORKED ON)	Days Afternoons Nights Don't know Refused/NA	1 2 3 8 9 63

A new, semi-automated *industrial plant* may be constructed in this geographical area. The jobs would be generally heavy work requiring some physical effort and exposure to *heat* producing materials and equipment.

15. How willing would you be to work at this new plant if it were built within the next two years? Would you say you would be (READ RESPONSES AND ROTATE)	Very willing Somewhat willing Only slightly willing Not at all willing (GO TO Q.18) Don't know Refused/NA	4 3 2 1 64 8 9

16. I would like to mention several jobs that may be available at this new plant. As I mention each one, I would like you to tell me whether you have *training* or *experience* in each job.

	Have Training or Experience	Do Not Have Training or Experience	Don't know (VOLUNTEERED)	Ref/NA	
a. Skilled maintenance	1	2	8	9	65
b. Large machine operator	1	2	8	9	66
c. Small hand tool operator	1	2	8	9	67
d. Quality control	1	2	8	9	68
e. Crane operator	1	2	8	9	69
f. Fork truck operator	1	2	8	9	70
g. Cleaner or painter of small parts	1	2	8	9	71

34 INTERVIEWING

FIGURE 3.1. Telephone Interview Questionnaire (continued)

| 17. | If this new plant is built, how willing would you be to receive training in one of the jobs I just mentioned? Would you be (READ RESPONSES AND ROTATE) | Very willing
Somewhat willing
Only slightly willing
Not at all willing
Don't know
Refused/NA | 4
3
2
1
8
9 | 5 |

| 18. | Are there any other persons in this household that are employed in blue collar jobs? | Yes
No   (GO TO Q.19)
Don't know (GO TO Q.19)
Refused/NA (GO TO Q.19) | 1
2
8
9 | 6 |

| a. | Could I ask you some questions about each additional blue collar worker in your household? | Yes   (GO TO NEXT PAGE)
No   (GO TO Q.19)
Don't know (GO TO Q.19)
Refused/NA (GO TO Q.19) | 1
2
8
9 |

| A1. | What is their job title? (PROBE FOR TITLE OR DESCRIPTION OF WORK) | _____ (RECORD TITLE)
Don't know
Refused/NA | 01
98
99 | 7–8 |

(IF FARMER, ASK TO TALK ABOUT SOMEONE WHO IS EMPLOYED IN A JOB OTHER THAN FARMING)
(IF NO OTHER BLUE COLLAR WORKERS, GO TO Q.19)

| A2. | Approximately what hourly wage rate are they now paid? | Under $3.00 an hour
$3.00–$3.99 an hour
$4.00–$4.99 an hour
$5.00–$5.49 an hour
$5.50–$5.99 an hour
$6.00–$6.49 an hour
$6.50–$6.99 an hour
$7.00–$7.49 an hour
$7.50–$7.99 an hour
$8.00–$8.99 an hour
$9.00–$9.99 an hour
$10.00 or more an hour
Don't know
Refused/NA | 01
02
03
04
05
06
07
08
09
10
11
12
98
99 | 9–10 |

| A3. | What shift do they currently work on? | Days
Afternoons
Nights
Don't know
Refused/NA | 1
2
3
8
9 | 11 |

FIGURE 3.1. Telephone Interview Questionnaire (continued)

A4. Is there another blue collar worker in your household?	Yes (GO TO NEXT PAGE) No (GO TO Q.19) Don't know (GO TO Q.19) Refused/NA (GO TO Q.19)	1 2 8 9	12

B1. What is their job title? (PROBE FOR TITLE OR DESCRIPTION OF WORK)	_____ (RECORD TITLE) Don't know Refused/NA	01 98 99	13–14

(IF FARMER, ASK TO TALK ABOUT SOMEONE WHO IS EMPLOYED IN A JOB OTHER THAN FARMING)
(IF NO OTHER BLUE COLLAR WORKERS, GO TO Q.19)

B2. Approximately what hourly wage rate are they now paid?	Under $3.00 an hour $3.00–$3.99 an hour $4.00–$4.99 an hour $5.00–$5.49 an hour $5.50–$5.99 an hour $6.00–$6.49 an hour $6.50–$6.99 an hour $7.00–$7.49 an hour $7.50–$7.99 an hour $8.00–$8.99 an hour $9.00–$9.99 an hour $10.00 or more an hour Don't know Refused/NA	01 02 03 04 05 06 07 08 09 10 11 12 98 99	15–16

B3. What shift do they currently work on?	Days Afternoons Nights Don't know Refused/NA	1 2 3 8 9	17

B4. Is there another blue collar worker in your household?	Yes (GO TO NEXT PAGE) No (GO TO Q.19) Don't know (GO TO Q.19) Refused/NA (GO TO Q.19)	1 2 8 9	18

C1. What is their job title? (PROBE FOR TITLE OR DESCRIPTION OF WORK)	_____ (RECORD TITLE) Don't know Refused/NA	01 98 99	19–20

(IF FARMER, ASK TO TALK ABOUT SOMEONE WHO IS EMPLOYED IN A JOB OTHER THAN FARMING)
(IF NO OTHER BLUE COLLAR WORKERS, GO TO Q.19)

36 INTERVIEWING

FIGURE 3.1. Telephone Interview Questionnaire (continued)

C2. Approximately what hourly wage rate are they now paid?	Under $3.00 an hour	01	
	$3.00–$3.99 an hour	02	
	$4.00–$4.99 an hour	03	
	$5.00–$5.49 an hour	04	
	$5.50–$5.99 an hour	05	
	$6.00–$6.49 an hour	06	
	$6.50–$6.99 an hour	07	
	$7.00–$7.49 an hour	08	21–22
	$7.50–$7.99 an hour	09	
	$8.00–$8.99 an hour	10	
	$9.00–$9.99 an hour	11	
	$10.00 or more an hour	12	
	Don't know	98	
	Refused/NA	99	

C3. What shift do they currently work on?	Days	1	
	Afternoons	2	
	Nights	3	
	Don't know	8	23
	Refused/NA	9	

19. Do you currently belong to a labor union?	Yes	1	
	No	2	
	Don't know (GO TO Q.20)	8	24
	Refused/NA (GO TO Q.20)	9	

a. About how many years have you been a member of *any* labor union?

Under 1 year	1	
1–3 years	2	
4–5 years	3	
6–10 years	4	
11–15 years	5	25
16–20 years	6	
Over 20 years	7	
Don't know	8	
Refused/NA	9	

aa. Would you prefer to work in a unionized company, or in a non-unionized company?

Prefer unionized	1	
No preference (VOLUNTEERED) (GO TO Q.20)	2	
Prefer non-unionized (GO TO Q.20)	3	37
Don't know (GO TO Q.20)	8	
Refused/NA (GO TO Q.20)	9	

b. Would you be willing to work for a new non-unionized company if the wages and benefits were the same as you receive now?

Yes	1	
No	2	
Don't know	8	26
Refused/NA	9	

bb. Would you be willing to work for a new non-unionized company if the wages and benefits were the same as you receive now?

Yes	1	
No	2	
Don't know	8	38
Refused/NA	9	
(GO TO Q.20)		

FIGURE 3.1. Telephone Interview Questionnaire (continued)

c. (IF "NO" TO Q.19b) Could you briefly comment on why you would not work for a non-unionized company? (ASK AS OPEN END)	Other _____ (SPECIFY) Better working conditions with union Don't trust management Like having a union Better wages and/or benefits with union Don't know Refused/NA	01 02 03 04 27-28 29-30 05 31-32 98 33-34 99 35-36
20. Would you be in favor of a new *heavy* industry locating in this area if it met all environmental standards?	Yes ─ No Don't know Refused/NA	1 2 8 39 9
a. Why not? (ASK AS OPEN END)	Too much pollution Too crowded already Not enough housing Would require too many utility services Too much traffic Other _____ (SPECIFY) Don't know Refused/NA	1 2 3 4 40 5 41 6 42 8 43 9 44
21. Would you be willing to work in Georgia if the employer was located within five miles of the bridge?	Yes ─ No Don't know Refused/NA	1 2 4 8 9
a. Why not? (ASK AS OPEN END)	Prefer current job Tax reasons Distance to work Traffic Other _____ (SPECIFY) Don't know Refused/NA	1 2 3 46 4 47 5 48 8 49 9 50

FIGURE 3.2. External Management Training Survey Questionnaire[2]

COMPANY: _____   DATE: _____

INTERVIEWEE (AND TITLE):   INTERVIEWER:

_____   _____

EXTERNAL MANAGEMENT TRAINING SURVEY

I. **Organizational Structure**

   1. How many employees in total corporation?

   2. How many managers in total corporation?

   3. What is the size of your internal (Corporate) training staff?

   4. What is the approximate make-up of this staff (e.g., instructors _____, managers _____, support people _____, etc.)? Other staff (specify).

   5. How is the management training function organized (centralized vs. decentralized, number of training units, etc.)? (Have organization chart?)
      a. Corporate and Company-wide.

      b. Total number of full-time non-Corporate training people.

   6. What role(s) does the corporate management training group play in servicing:
      a. Other training groups?

      b. Staff groups (e.g., Employee Relations)?

II. **Determining Training Needs**

   7. How are management training needs determined?
      a. Organization/Divisional level (Strategic/Manpower Planning vs. Divisional deficiencies)

FIGURE 3.2. External Management Training Survey Questionnaire (continued)

II. **Determining Training Needs** (continued)

    b. Individual level

    c. What instruments/techniques are used?

  8. How do managers find out about your programs/services?

III. **Program Offerings**

  9. How many corporate management training programs do you offer in a year? (May I have a copy of the brochure, schedule or program listing—something with descriptions and specifications?)

  10. How many participants have attended your corporate management training programs this year? _____ Last year? _____ (or average in a year).

  11. How are program offerings grouped/clustered (i.e., major headings of management training programs)?

  12. In developing your managers from a new manager to an experienced one, what, if any, *sequence* of programs is *recommended* for a manager to take (i.e., any suggested or required curricula)?

  13. a. What management training programs or activities are *required*?

    b. How long has this policy been in effect?

  14. To whom do these management training requirements apply?

  15. How would you describe the direction that your management training function will be taking in the future (What are you/will you be changing, adding or deleting?)

IV. **Inside vs. Outside Programs**

  16. What percentage of your programs are:

    a. developed in-house?

FIGURE 3.2. External Management Training Survey Questionnaire (continued)

IV. **Inside vs. Outside Programs** (continued)

      b. run in-house?

  17. Do you have a list of outside programs that you use and/or recommend?

  18. Of all the management training programs that managers in your organization attend, what are the percentages of in-house vs. outside programs?

V. **Training and Development Resources**

  19. What special management training equipment/hardware does your department have? (e.g., computer-assisted instruction terminals)

  20. Approximately what is the size of your corporate management training budget? Revenues? (Confidential)

VI. **Training "Culture"**

  21. To what extent does top management (e.g., CEOs, COOs, SVPs, etc.) support/endorse management training? Please give some examples.

VII. **Philosophy/Assumptions**

  22. How would you describe the general attitude of managers toward management training?

  23. What is your organization's management training philosophy? (Probe, if necessary: What assumptions (if any) underlie your approach to management *development*?)

VIII. **Evaluation**

  24. a. How do you evaluate the programs your managers attend?

      b. What do you evaluate?
- Participant reaction (have form?)
- Learning
- Behavior
- Results (e.g., increased effectiveness)

FIGURE 3.2. External Management Training Survey Questionnaire (continued)

VIII. **Evaluation** (continued)

25. What, if any, cost effectiveness or return on investment measures have you used?

26. Overall, what do you think of your management training programs?

FIGURE 3.3. Communication Audit Survey Instrument: General Interview Questionnaire[3]

INTERVIEWEE'S DEPT. (UNIT) _____   INTERVIEWERS _____

INTERVIEWEE'S POSITION _____   TIME OF DAY _____

GENERAL INTERVIEW QUESTIONNAIRE

EXEMPT ____   NON-EXEMPT ____   SEX __
(NO OVERTIME)   (ELIGIBLE FOR OVERTIME)

1. Describe your job (duties, functions). _____

   Does this match the official description of your job? _____
   If not, what are the differences? _____

2. What decisions do you usually make in your job? _____

RECEIVING INFORMATION

3. What information do you need to make these decisions? _____

FIGURE 3.3. Communication Audit Survey Instrument: General Interview Questionnaire (continued)

4. Do you agree or disagree with the following statement? "I receive enough information to make necessary decisions." Agree ☐ Disagree ☐
   If Disagree:
   What *specific* type of information is lacking? _____
   _____
   _____
   _____

   Does this lack of information affect your job? _____

   What actions could be taken to ensure that you *would* receive enough information to do your job effectively?
   _____
   _____
   _____
   _____

   Categorize above: Formal (written) Channels   Informal Channels

   _____   _____
   _____   _____
   _____   _____
   _____   _____

5. Is it particularly difficult to receive certain types of information important to your job? Yes ☐ No ☐
   If Yes:
   What type of information? _____
   _____
   _____

   Is this information from within your Department or another (which)?
   _____

   What could be done about this problem? _____
   _____
   _____
   _____

6. Do you agree or disagree with the following statement? "I receive a satisfactory amount of information regarding my job performance."
   Agree ☐ Disagree ☐

FIGURE 3.3. Communication Audit Survey Instrument: General Interview Questionnaire (continued)

If Disagree:
What can be done to ensure that you receive a satisfactory amount of information concerning your job performance?

_____
_____
_____

What specific information areas are lacking? _____
_____
_____

7. How effectively is your Department (Unit) performing? _____
_____

   How do you know? _____
   _____

   Any suggestions? _____
   _____

8. How are other Departments (Units) performing? _____
_____
_____

   How do you know? _____
   _____

   Any suggestions? _____
   _____

9. What is your best source for receiving information on each of the following topics?

Topic	Best Source of Information (Be specific)
Employee Benefits	_____
Promotion Opportunities	_____
Work Schedules	_____
Department Objectives	_____

44 INTERVIEWING

FIGURE 3.3. Communication Audit Survey Instrument: General Interview Questionnaire (continued)

    Management Objectives _____

    Department Progress _____

SENDING INFORMATION

10. How could the system of sharing information between and among Departments (Units) be improved?

11. What problems do you have in sending information to others about your job (its requirements, needs, problems, complaints)?

ACTION AND FOLLOW-UP

12. Do you supervise any people? Yes _____ How many _____ No _____
If Yes:
What could be done to improve the level of performance of those who work for you?

What could *your* supervisor do to increase *your* level of performance?

13. When you make inquiries or suggestions to persons within the organization do you feel you get a satisfactory response? Yes ☐ No ☐ Sometimes ☐
If No or Sometimes:
Can you give me an example? _____

What could be done to improve an unsatisfactory response? _____

FIGURE 3.3. Communication Audit Survey Instrument: General Interview Questionnaire (continued)

14. Do you agree or disagree with the following statement? "I feel comfortable making suggestions upward concerning company related policy."
Agree ☐   Disagree ☐   Sometimes ☐
If Disagree or Sometimes:
Why don't you feel comfortable making upward directed suggestions?

_____
_____
_____
_____

Any suggestions for improving the situation? _____
_____

SOURCES AND CHANNELS OF INFORMATION

15. Describe the formal (written) channels through which you typically receive information about the organization. (Interviewer list these specific channels below.)

_____
_____
_____
_____

What kinds of information do you receive? _____
_____

How often? _____
_____

16. Describe the informal channels through which you typically receive information about this organization. (List these specific channels below.)

_____
_____
_____

What kinds of information do you receive? _____
_____

How often? _____
_____

FIGURE 3.3. Communication Audit Survey Instrument: General Interview Questionnaire (continued)

TIMELINESS

17. How often, if ever, do you receive information about this organization which is of low value or of little use to you on your job?

   _____
   _____

   If and when this happens, what kind of information is it? Be specific. Also, from whom (or what Department) do you receive this "low value" information?

   _____
   _____

18. What would you like to see done to improve information flow in this organization?

   _____
   _____

   Why hasn't it been done already? _____
   _____

19. In response to a previous question, you named the following channels as sources of your information. Now—please rank them from *most* helpful to *least* helpful by assigning 1st, 2nd, 3rd, 4th, 5th, 6th, etc. until through the entire list.

   _____ Face to Face (Supervisor)   _____ Telephone   _____ Report
   _____ Face to Face (Colleague)   _____ Memos/Letters   _____ Update
   _____ Face to Face (Other)   _____ Bulletin Boards   _____ Annual Report
   _____ Office News   _____ Meetings   _____ Newsletter
   _____ Grapevine   _____ Personnel Dept.   _____ Forward Times
   _____ Posters   _____ Quarterly Report
                                           to Stockholders

ORGANIZATIONAL COMMUNICATION RELATIONSHIPS

(*Note:* Encourage Interviewee to be specific and to give examples. Leave EXPERIENCES Form with those having most vivid recall. Conclude each category with their evaluation of "Good", "Adequate", or "Poor.")

20. Describe your communication relationships (level of trust, honesty, openness, etc.) with—

FIGURE 3.3. Communication Audit Survey Instrument: General Interview Questionnaire (continued)

Your immediate supervisor _____

_____ Good ☐ Adequate ☐ Poor ☐

Your co-workers _____

_____ Good ☐ Adequate ☐ Poor ☐

Middle management _____

_____ Good ☐ Adequate ☐ Poor ☐

Top management _____

_____ Good ☐ Adequate ☐ Poor ☐

Your subordinates _____

_____ Good ☐ Adequate ☐ Poor ☐

21. When you get information from others in the organization, do you generally feel free to comment about it? Yes ☐ No ☐ Sometimes ☐

    If No or Sometimes:
    What kinds of information do you feel most comfortable commenting about?

    _____
    _____

    What kinds of information do you feel least comfortable commenting about?

    _____
    _____

ORGANIZATIONAL SATISFACTIONS

22. What are the major communication strengths of this organization? Be specific.

23. What are the major communication weaknesses of this organization? Be specific.

48   INTERVIEWING

FIGURE 3.3. Communication Audit Survey Instrument: General Interview Questionnaire (continued)

24. What do you feel to be the major cause of conflict within the organization?

25. How is conflict within this organization typically resolved?

26. How do you know when this organization has done a good or bad job in accomplishing its goals?

27. If you could tell the company President anything about the communication in this building, what would it be?

28. Is there anything else that you feel you should bring up at this time?

---

the community. When this questionnaire was used, the respondents were contacted by phone at random and without advance warning. Approximately 60 percent of those contacted gave the interviewer the information requested. Note that this particular questionnaire requires that the interviewer proceed sequentially and follow explicitly the written directions based on the interviewee's responses.

Figure 3.2 shows an external management training survey questionnaire designed for face-to-face use by a high-level executive for discussions with his or her peers in other organizations. Unlike the highly structured telephone interview questionnaire in Figure 3.1, the management training survey was used as a guide and as a memory-jogging device for the interviewer. The interviewer covered the points required during each interview in the manner most appropriate to the flow of the conversation. Because the respondents were known to the interviewer and because they had advance warning and had agreed to participate, the response rate was nearly 100 percent.

Figure 3.3 shows a general interview questionnaire for use in a face-to-face situation. In addition to providing basic demographic characteristics, the respondent is asked to react to the following topics: receiving information, sending information, action and follow-up, sources and channels of information, timeliness, organizational communication relationships, and organizational satisfactions. In the organization in which this communication audit instrument was used, the response rate to the general interview questionnaire was nearly 100 percent.

SUMMARY

Survey interviewing is a type of self-report device used extensively in research in a variety of settings and for a variety of purposes. Questionnaire guides are typically used to help the interviewer ask questions and record responses accurately and consistently. Constructing the interview guide is a task to be taken very seriously, as the quality of the information gathered will depend on the quality of the guide itself, as well as on the representativeness of the sample selected.

When conducting survey interviews, care should be taken to avoid biasing the answers of the respondents, both in how the questions are asked and how the responses are recorded. The more open-ended and probing the questions are, the greater the probability will be that the interviewer's interpretation of those responses will cause inaccuracies in recording them. In addition to general interviewing skills, the effective survey interviewer needs to understand and appreciate the importance of interviewing to the research process.

EXERCISES

1. Construct a telephone interview questionnaire based on that in Figure 3.1. (The content of the questionnaire should be of interest to you.) Interview ten respondents, and evaluate your success according to the criteria discussed in this chapter.
2. Construct a face-to-face interview questionnaire based on that in Figure 3.2. (The content of the questionnaire should be of interest to you.) Interview ten respondents, and evaluate your success according to the criteria discussed in this chapter.

NOTES

1. Used by joint permission of the Lynchburg Foundry Company, Lynchburg, Virginia, and Market Opinion Research, Detroit, Michigan.
2. Used by permission of the Corporate Management Development Department, Union Carbide Corporation, Danbury, Connecticut.
3. Used by permission of the Corporate Communications Department, The Mead Corporation, Dayton, Ohio. This instrument was developed jointly by researchers from The Ohio State University and representatives from The Mead Corporation under the direction of the latter. The instrument is patterned closely after the original Communication Audit Survey Instrumentation developed by, and under the auspices of, the International Communication Association.

ADDITIONAL READINGS

Babbie, E. R. *Survey Research Methods.* Belmont, Calif.: Wadsworth, 1973.

Cannell, C. F., and R. L. Kahn. "Interviewing." In *The Handbook of Social Psychology,* vol. 2, edited by G. Lindzey and E. Aronson, pp. 526–595. Reading, Mass.: Addison-Wesley, 1968.

Kish, L. *Survey Sampling.* New York: John Wiley, 1965.

Warwick, D. P., and C. A. Lininger. *The Sample Survey: Theory and Practice.* New York: McGraw-Hill, 1975.

Weisberg, H. F., and B. D. Bowen. *An Introduction to Survey Research and Data Analysis.* San Francisco: W. H. Freeman & Company Publishers, 1977.

4

Persuasive Interviewing

CHAPTER OBJECTIVES

1. Define "persuasion."
2. Differentiate between persuasion and coercion.
3. Explain how respondent perception relates to persuasion.
4. Explain the ethical dimensions of persuasion.
5. Identify and describe the components of problem analysis.
6. Identify and describe the components of participant analysis.
7. Conduct a problem and participant analysis.
8. Explain the purposes of the opening, body, and close of the persuasive interview.
9. Demonstrate the use of "yes-response" as a persuasive technique.
10. Conduct a persuasive interview.

Introduction

As emphasized in Chapter 2, information is a necessary and basic ingredient of interviewing. Often, however, simply the exchange of information (giving it and receiving it) is not the primary reason for having an interview; rather, the main reason is to alter the behaviors (mental and/or physical) of the interviewee in a way consistent with the intent of the interviewer. Changing behavior by means of external influence occurs in one of two ways: (1) either we perceive that we are being forced to behave in a given way (coercion), or (2) we perceive that we have a choice of feasible behaviors and thus consciously decide to behave in a given way (persuasion). Coercion depends for its effectiveness upon the use or threat of force or duress that is imposed upon one individual by another; persuasion, on the other hand, depends for its effectiveness upon the appeals (rational and emotional) that the persuadee evaluates in terms of personal goals and experiences, thus leading to a selected course of action.

Although both forms of influence can be effective, both experience and research suggest that decisions resulting from perceptions of choice and involving the genuine and willing consent of the persuadee produce much more lasting and satisfying results than those made by means of coercion.[1] Accordingly, for centuries those processes that result in persuasion have been systematically observed. This chapter will consider some of the elements of persuasion with particular reference to the interview.

Persuasion Defined

Persuasion is defined as the process through which a participant in an interview purposefully induces a voluntary change of behavior (mental and/or physical) in the other participant, by using appeals to both feeling and intellect. Note that there are several elements in this definition:

1. Persuasion involves a process; that is, it involves activity and interaction, as opposed merely to a static or passive environment. In an interviewing context this means that both parties contribute to the final outcome through active participation. Indeed, both parties often have different secondary goals, although the overall objective of the interview is substantially the same. For example, two persons may agree on the need for a change; yet each may favor different ways of implementing the change.

2. Persuasion reflects purpose and direction by the persuader. This purpose exists in degrees of intensity and probably will be obvious to some extent to both participants. In every interviewing situation primarily involving persuasion, the R, by definition, has a preconceived goal regarding the change expected in the behavior of the E (of which E may or may not be aware). And as indicated in the first item, the E also may have persuasive goals that become apparent as the interview progresses. As the initiative shifts from one party to the other during the interview, the roles of R and E as identified at the beginning of the interview also shift accordingly.

3. Persuasion is the result of voluntary decision-making by the persuadee. As mentioned in the first section of this chapter, this point reflects the essence of persuasion, as contrasted with coercion. If E makes a decision voluntarily and without duress from external sources, then persuasion has occurred. Note that the persuadee's perceptions are the critical ones. Thus, if Participant A in the interview believes (rightly or wrongly) that coercion is being used by Participant B, then for all practical purposes, Participant A is being coerced, regardless of Participant B's intent or belief. In such a situation it is necessary that Participant B offer Participant A viable and legitimate choices or courses of action to be followed.

As Goyer, Redding, and Rickey pointed out, a person is persuaded only when the proposed change in behavior (1) satisfies a felt need (solves a problem, overcomes a difficulty, removes something "painful,") or (2) satisfies a desire (fulfills a wish, gains a desired benefit, improves one's position).[2] The key notion here is that the person being persuaded must perceive the information and appeals as being true. Indeed, it is sometimes argued that persuadees really persuade themselves according to their own perceptions of ideas and events.

Although needs and desires may be the bases of persuasion, the persuadee is not apt to respond positively to a proposal unless it is consistent with (1) the facts and logic as the persuadee understands them and (2) the persuadee's values, ethical and moral standards, and cultural assumptions. In other words, the more the persuader's proposal agrees with (is congruent with) the persuadee's point of view, the more likely it is that the persuadee will be won over voluntarily.

4. Participants in the interview may use appeals to both feeling and intellect in their persuasive efforts. Note that both kinds of appeals may be either good or bad, pertinent or nonpertinent, strong or weak, and so on. Although many people believe that extreme emotional appeals are always bad and that purely intellectual appeals are always good, such a position is a gross oversimplification of reality. In communicative behaviors generally, it is highly improbable that one kind of appeal is found in the complete absence of the other, which is not surprising if one recognizes that humans are creatures of both emotion and reason. This means that in a given situation and within the moral and ethical limitations of that situation, one or the other of these means of appeal is probably more effective. The use (and possible misuse) of appeals to either emotion or reason depends on the user. Persuasion is neither good nor bad; it is amoral, and its goodness or badness depends on the ethical and moral values of the participants.

Ethical Dimensions of Persuasion

In the above section defining persuasion, mention was made of the persuader's need to make a proposal consistent with the persuadee's ethical and moral standards. Since ethical issues are inherent in almost all decisions affecting interpersonal relationships, and since the latter depend heavily on the communicative behaviors of the individual parties, it is not surprising that ethical dimensions of such behaviors have generated much soul-searching and comment during mankind's recorded history.

Because all interviews by definition are goal-oriented, and because the goals of the participants are not always compatible, differences of opinion may arise concerning what constitutes ethical words and actions to achieve a given goal. Particularly in persuasive interviewing, the ethical responsibility of one participant who consciously attempts to influence another participant is of practical concern, because of the future effects of current actions.

Ethics deals with what is good and bad in terms of moral principles and values, and therefore by extension with the behaviors that reflect those principles and values. In the persuasive interview we expect participants who have been raised in similar cultural and social settings to have similar norms and values, and to act accordingly. When one participant violates a given norm or value (e.g., deliberately misleading the other participant by word or action in order to force a decision not in the best interests of the other participant), he or she is accused of behaving unethically, with the practical effect that the credibility of that participant suffers in terms of future interactions between the two parties.

In persuasive interviews involving persons of different cultural or social backgrounds, it is essential that both parties be sensitive to possible differences in the ethical and moral value systems of the other, including the relative importance of individual values within systems. Ignorance of the others' system of ethics may be an accurate description of why an interview fails, but it is a failure nevertheless, and is apt to be perceived as a poor excuse, particularly by the affected party.

In the last analysis, ethics inevitably are a matter of individual judgment. Persuasion per se is neither good nor bad in an ethical sense; it is the people who attempt to be persuasive, and those who are the targets for persuasive efforts, who impose an ethical dimension upon the process. As a result, ethical dimensions in persuasion tend to be situational, since different parties may behave on the basis of different ethical systems.

Problem and Participant Analysis

If one assumes that a person has a "felt need" that involves or is contingent on certain favorable decisions (actions, behaviors) by another person, then the necessary ingredients for a persuasive interview exist. Felt need is another way of saying that the R has a problem that cannot be solved satisfactorily without involving at least one other person in the decision-making process. The more difficult the problem is, the greater will be the necessity to examine systematically its various determinants and possible consequences. When problems develop that require interviewing to resolve them, one should make every effort to analyze the problems and their ramifications well in advance of the interviews themselves. Such an analysis should be directed first at the problem, followed by an analysis of the pertinent relationships between the components of the problem and the characteristics of the interview partners.

Problem Analysis

The first requirement in analyzing the problem is to gather all pertinent information. Be thorough and dispassionate in gathering this information, as your success in the interview will depend on this step. It may be easier to look at the problem from an emotional rather than from an unemotional point of view and to be illogical rather than logical. Nevertheless, there is no substitute for a thorough knowledge of the available facts in the case. Additionally, thoroughness implies anticipation of possible new data and contingency arguments in the interview itself.

The following is a general pattern for systematically examining a problem:

1. *Define the problem.* This means more than merely thinking about the problem. Write it down, as precisely and accurately as possible, and rewrite it until it is thoroughly stated. Next, construct one declarative goal sentence that indicates the principal action that the persuadee should take as a result of the interview.

The following problem statements and goal sentences are examples:

Problem Statement: As chair of the house committee of the athletic club, I need to find a way to raise, in six months, $10,000 to redecorate and upgrade the locker room facilities.

Goal Sentence: At the next regular monthly meeting, persuade the executive committee of the athletic club that the fairest and surest way of raising the needed funds is to assess each of our three hundred members $25, with the balance of $2,500 to be allocated from the "unrestricted gifts" account of our annual budget.

Problem Statement: As manager of internal communication for the Notnats Company, I need to improve the lateral flow of information among middle-management personnel in the organization.

Goal Sentence: Persuade Mr. Blarney, the president of the company, to conduct a communication audit involving all employees, as a basis for identifying strengths and weaknesses in the present procedures of information diffusion and collection.

The material presented and developed in the persuasive interview should support the goal sentence. In effect, as you define the problem you should be answering this question: "What action do I want the E to take?"

2. *What is the background of the problem?* Based on all of the information available, identify the origins and causes of the problem. The more complex the problem is, the greater the likelihood will be that the problem will have multiple determinants, suggesting that it may be helpful to outline the causes of the problem in some detail so as not to overlook any probable causes. Some problems may be "future" oriented, requiring the gathering of different kinds of information (i.e., instead of focusing on past and present constraints and causes, it may be more useful to predict probable future constraints and causes of problems).

A useful way to identify the relationships of causes to problems is to ask:

1. Does A (the cause) always occur before B (the problem)?
2. Does B (the problem) occur only after the occurrence of A (the cause)?
3. Can C (a different causal stimulus) cause B (the problem) to occur in the absence of A?

Even though it may be impossible to make an absolute judgment concerning a problem and its causes, if the necessary relationships prevail with more than chance frequency, you can make probability statements about the cause-problem relationship. For example: Cigarette smoking does not always occur before the onset of lung cancer; lung cancer is not the only result that occurs after cigarette smoking; other stimuli can cause lung cancer. Nevertheless, repeated, controlled observation (evidence) indicates a high probability (much greater than a chance occurrence) that there is a causal link between cigarette smoking and lung cancer.

3. *What conditions (criteria) must be satisfied before the problem can be considered resolved?* Ater identifying the events that may have caused the problem, you are in a position to identify, at least tentatively, the conditions or criteria that will be required before you can consider the problem resolved. This "criterion approach" to persuasion presumes that consciously or unconsciously, a persuadee evaluates a persuasive proposal in regard to how well that proposal appears to meet the various criteria in the persuadee's mind. Because a logical process of decision-making by a persuadee is largely comparing the proposal with as many criteria as possible, it is necessary for both parties in the persuasive interview to identify and agree on the criteria to be used in evaluating the proposals. These criteria will be derived from both rational and irrational bases. Admittedly, there are many situations—especially those involving sensitive interpersonal relationships, such as those between boss and subordinate or between parent and child—in which an explicit statement of criteria may be psychologically awkward or difficult to manage.[3] Note that these criteria are not the same as solutions; they

simply provide a common yardstick against which each possible solution can be measured in order to select the best available solution.

For example, let us assume that Patricia is a high school senior who has decided to enter the nursing profession. She has taken the time and effort to gather a variety of pertinent information (e.g., aptitude tests, job-interest inventories, mental abilities tests, financial resources, romantic involvements, career opportunities, information about nursing schools), and now must decide where to go to get the necessary professional training. Before she considers any possible solutions (i.e., what school to attend), she systematically lists the requirements that she believes must be satisfied before she can consider any source of her training as suitable. These requirements might include such things as (1) low annual cost of tuition and fees, (2) low living expenses, (3) high quality of instruction, (4) short distance from home and boyfriend, (5) special training availability, (6) short time requirements for alternative degree programs, (7) institutional assistance available in job placement, and (8) highly regarded reputation of school selected. After identifying all the relevant criteria, Patricia then ranks them according to her priorities. Assume that these eight conditions are already in her preferred sequence, beginning with the most important. Patricia is now ready for the next step in problem analysis.

4. *Identify and evaluate all possible solutions.* If Patricia knows ten schools that, based on her information search, can prepare her for the career she seeks, she will have ten possible solutions already in hand. Her task then is to evaluate each of the solutions independently against these criteria and to decide which institution will best satisfy her criteria.

Participant Analysis

At this point, Patricia finds it necessary to engage in some persuasive interviewing, because she cannot implement her solution without involving one or more additional persons who must make contributory decisions on her behalf. Accordingly, she concludes that she must have an interview with her father, with the purpose of persuading him to accept her choice of school and to support her financially through the period of her training.

In planning for the interview, Patricia now needs to engage in a different kind of preparation than she did in analyzing the problem. She needs to assess both her interview partner and herself, in terms of (1) general personal characteristics, (2) interpersonal relationships and attitudes between her father and herself, and (3) her father's opinions of and attitudes toward the proposal being made.

1. *Personal characteristics.* In developing an information base for the interview, a knowledge of the participants' general demographic and background characteristics often provides some ideas and insights concerning likely points of agreement or disagreement on topics to be discussed in the interview. These can be categorized according to biological factors (e.g., age, sex, race, physical characteristics) and psychological factors (e.g., attitudes, personality characteristics, intelligence, motives, value systems, habits of thinking).[4]

Although information on such items in regard to yourself should be quite obvious, there nevertheless is merit in systematically reviewing it. But such information about the interview partner may not be so obvious and may be difficult to discover. Patricia should have a relatively easy time analyzing the personal characteristics of her father and herself. As a basis for the next step in the process, however, each participant should gather as much information about the interview partner as is ethically and legally possible, in the time available.

2. *Interpersonal relationships.* Knowledge of demographic facts about your interview partner is of limited value unless used as a basis for analyzing the interpersonal relationships that will exist (or are expected to exist) between you and your interview partner in the proposed interview. How you perceive the role of your fellow participant and how your interview partner probably will perceive you will greatly affect the interpersonal behaviors that will occur during the interview. The amount of respect, affection, suspicion, concern, and the like that the interview partners have for each other when the interview is initiated may well determine whether the interview is doomed to failure before it even starts. It is also evident that the interpersonal relationships between the two parties can change (improve or deteriorate) as the interview progresses, as a function of the attitudes and behaviors that both participants reveal. Patricia knows her father's demographic characteristics well, and she knows that she and her father have a very positive relationship.

3. *Probable attitudes of the partner toward the proposal.* A final point of analysis involving the participants is directed toward the interview partner's predicted reactions to the persuader's proposal. Based on the total preparation thus far, as the persuader you should be able to make some better-than-chance judgments about the probability that your partner will agree to part or all of your proposal. As a persuader, you should now be able to predict (1) whether your proposal is apt to be received with approval, apathy, or opposition; (2) whether you should expect attitudes of cooperation, condescension, or contentiousness; and (3) whether an alternative solution you have considered and rejected is likely to be preferred by your interview partner—and why.

In Patricia's case, she knows that her father wants her to enter the medical profession, not as a nurse, but as a physician specializing in family practice. He would like her to go into premed, enter the medical school from which he graduated, and then join him in his established practice. Furthermore, he believes that she will appreciate her degree(s) and profession more if she has to finance a large portion of her college expenses herself.

Do not forget that no matter how thorough and careful your analyses of the problem and the participants are, it is still possible for the interview to fail to achieve a desired goal. The more thorough your preparation is, however, the less likely it will be that you will fail. Remember, too, that persuasion often requires more than one interview in order to achieve your goal, and that the persuasive goals of one or both parties are likely to change as time passes and the participants influence each other. For Patricia, a series of persuasive interviews is likely to be more successful than a one-shot interview would be.

Structuring the Interview

The ability to adapt to the interview partner, to agree on a mutual goal, and to achieve agreement on the means for achieving that goal is the task of the persuader. Given adequate preparation, the interview itself will depend on the various kinds of behaviors previously discussed in Chapters 1 and 2.

The amount of structure present in a given interview will vary according to the participants' purposes, role relationships, and time constraints. In informational interviewing that uses a standardized interview questionnaire (e.g., consumer research), the purpose may be limited, the role relationships clearly defined and relatively unchanging, and the time limits severe; accordingly, the interview structure will probably be rigid and the procedures inflexible (see Figure 3.1). In persuasive interviewing, however, much more adaptability and permissiveness are usually necessary because of the nature of the task itself.

Regardless of the specific persuasive purposes of the interview, it is convenient to divide it into three parts: the opening, the body, and the close. The *opening* of the interview includes that portion devoted to establishing rapport between the partners, identifying or confirming the topic and purpose of the interview, and agreeing on a common ground ("frame of reference") and the procedures that the interaction should follow. It is probably true that more interviews (particularly persuasive ones) fail because of inadequate and neglected openings than because of any other single reason. The R often assumes that the E's readiness (motivation) to participate in an interview is high, which may be wrong. That the R is prepared is ordinarily assumed, but you should not assume that the E shares the R's knowledge, enthusiasm, interests, or frame of reference concerning the topic of the interview. In fact, it is precisely these kinds of things that you, as the R, should try to establish in the opening, based on your knowledge of the problem and your interview partner. Take as much care and time as necessary to do this well, for this is the base on which the remainder of the interview will rest. Encouraging the E to want to participate in the interview is the object of the opening. This may require not only that you arouse the E's interest in the topic but also that you provide (or expand) the E's information base by referring to the background of the problem, defining terms, or whatever. Make the opening a positive experience for the E by reflecting the E's desired goals, sincerely requesting advice or assistance (which itself is flattering), referring to a third party who is respected by the E, and/or referring to activities and interests that both you and the E share. At the very least, the opening should be neutral and businesslike, and you should be sensitive to the E's role expectations of you.

The body of the interview will be the major portion in both time and content. In the body you should (1) define the particular problem systematically, sensitively, and in detail; (2) discover the interests of the E in relation to you so as to help resolve the problem; (3) suggest, modify as necessary, and secure agreement on the conditions to be met in satisfying the problem; (4) jointly propose alternative solutions to the problem; (5) jointly evaluate the proposed solutions according to the conditions to be met; and (6) agree on the best available solution. The quality of the logic, the relevance of the evidence, the ability to listen, and the willingness to modify beliefs and attitudes will be evident to both participants during this section of the interview.

It is also in the body of interview that you will be most apt to use particular types of questioning techniques designed to produce a particular kind of response. The discussion of "Types of Questions" in Chapter 2 is entirely applicable to the persuasive interview, which builds on an informational base. One of the question types mentioned in that section is especially applicable to persuasive interviewing: the "reinforcing" question, which induces and supports a specific response (referred to as the yes-response technique). Although this type of question must be used with care, it can reinforce the E's response behavior when used in a logical, supportive sequence. It depends for its effectiveness on (the R's) ability to ask a series of logically related questions, the highly probable answers to which will agree with your position. The result is to build in the E a habit of responding, which will increase the chances of the E's agreeing to your final appeal. The following is a simplified example of the application of the yes-response technique:

1. R: Wouldn't you agree that this organization is not equal to others of its type with regard to employee salary scales?
2. E: Yes, I certainly would.
3. R: And you must have noticed, as I have, that our employee morale leaves something to be desired?
4. E: Yes, I've noticed that too.
5. R: Don't you think these two problems might be related?
6. E: Yes, it seems reasonable.
7. R: And isn't it true that our inventory report shows that our organization has a lot of unused and unneeded equipment?
8. E: That's true.
9. R: Since we agree on these points, wouldn't it be a good idea at least to explore the possibility of selling our surplus equipment and using the proceeds to give bonuses to our employees in order to alleviate the low pay and low morale problems until a long-range solution can be determined?
10. E: I think the idea is worth exploring, and I'll look into it right away.

Note that in this example the interviewee has been led to a position consistent with the one that the persuader wants to reach. But suppose the response in the sixth line had been different:

6. E: No, I don't think the two problems are related. First, in line with company policy we have agreed to compensate our employees at a level below the industry median. Second, I think our low morale is due to poor supervision practices rather than low pay.

If this had been the reply, the rest of the series would have been disrupted. In this latter case, the respondent did not accept being led and had a point of view (and the desire to express it) strong enough to overcome the lead.

The close of the interview should give coherence and unity to all that has just occurred. The R should plan on summarizing what has been accomplished, identifying the points of disagreement and agreement (emphasizing the latter), and indicating what will come next. Both participants should agree on what has been done and what should be done (e.g., get more information, implement agreed-upon action plan). Do not make assumptions about these items. Both participants should take whatever initiative is necessary to secure overt expressions from each other on these matters. Always keep in mind that the results of this interview may very well be the basis of yet another interview (i.e., agreements secured in this interview may be referred to in later interviews between the same two parties). When an interview terminates with good rapport between the participants, a positive base has been established for future interaction.

SUMMARY

Persuasion is the process through which a participant in an interview purposefully induces a voluntary change of behavior in the other participant by using appeals to both feeling and intellect. The probabilities of successful persuasive interviewing are increased when the persuader thoroughly and systematically analyzes the problem itself, the personal characteristics of both participants, and the pertinent relationships among the aspects of the problem and the interview partners. In the interests of both efficiency and effectiveness, it is important to establish a common ground with the interview partner in the opening minutes of the interview, to be sensitive and systematic in offering information and making appeals in the body of the interview, and to be skillful in summarizing the results and identifying agreements in the close.

In persuasive interviewing, you always should try to protect the ego of your interview partner. Avoid contentiousness, unnecessary argument, blame, and ridicule of your partner. Instead, be positive, thoughtful, and emphasize points of mutual agreement. Be willing to listen at least as much as you talk, and demonstrate a sincere interest in your fellow participant.

Figure 4.1 is a model of a systematic and detailed plan of preparation for a persuasive interview that covers all the points discussed in this chapter. Notice particularly its thoroughness with regard to both problem and participant analysis.

EXERCISES

1. Conduct an in-class persuasive interview with a classmate on a controversial topic on which you and the interviewee disagree. You should attempt to change either the direction or the intensity of the E's attitudes or behaviors about the topic. Make thorough analyses of the topic, yourself, and your partner, including an interview plan.
2. Conduct an in-class persuasive interview with a classmate that requires both of you to play the participants in a case provided by your instructor. Prepare your analyses and plans as if you really are the person whose role you are playing.
3. Conduct an out-of-class persuasive interview on a topic or problem that is of particular concern to you, and prepare a written report describing your preparation, the actual conduct of the interview, and your evaluation of the results (see Figure 4.1 for a report model).

NOTES

1. Wallace C. Fotheringham, *Perspectives on Persuasion* (Boston: Allyn & Bacon, 1966), pp. 75–104.
2. Robert S. Goyer, W. Charles Redding, and John T. Rickey, *Interviewing Principles and Techniques* (Dubuque, Ia.: Wm. C. Brown, 1964), pp. 49–50.
3. Goyer, Redding, and Rickey, pp. 50–51.
4. Robert S. Goyer and Michael Z. Sincoff, *Interviewing Methods* (Dubuque, Ia.: Kendall/Hunt, 1977).

FIGURE 4.1. Persuasion Case: Problem and Participant Analysis

---

I (Susan J.) am Activities Chairman of my sorority. As such, it is my job to promote campus activities within the sorority house. I'm responsible for getting the pledges started in activities which appeal to them, seeing that they put in the required number of activity hours, and helping them with any problems they have relating to campus activities or their participation therein. I also advise on, and promote activities within, the active chapter.

Criteria for the successful execution on my job and the success of the house in campus activities include: the number of girls participating in campus activities, their personal feelings of satisfaction and achievement within their activities, and the number of girls holding offices of "junior and senior jobs" in campus activities.

A campus activity may be defined as any extracurricular organization or event in which students participate individually and not as part of a residence unit (such as in Varsity Varieties or University Sing). Examples of such campus activities and organizations are the Office of Student Services, Forensics, Y.W.C.A., Panhellenic, Cheerleading Squad, the Student Union, and the student newspaper and yearbook.

Amy L. is a sophomore in the house and has been a worker at the Office of Student Services since February. This organization will be holding its annual officer elections next March, and Amy will be eligible for the position of a junior officer. She would like to have the "junior job," but is wary of the time involved in the execution of its responsibilities. Amy is afraid that her grades will be damaged by holding this office, and they aren't very high now (about a C plus accumulative average). She is also apprehensive concerning her chances of getting the job and doesn't want to waste time preparing the necessary petition and interview if there isn't a chance of her election. There will be approximately 25 students petitioning for 12 junior positions. About 18 of these are very capable people, Amy included.

The Office of Student Services (OSS) is the administrative branch of student government and is directly responsible to the Student Senate. OSS is a service organization for the students. It operates through 15 committees headed by 12 junior officers. A Senior Executive Board composed of five seniors directs the organization and supervises the activities of the junior officers.

Amy is interested mainly in the Publicity Committee, but would also be interested in directing the Elections Committee. The duties of these committees include:

Publicity:
1. Publicize all OSS activities, events, and committees.
2. Publicize all Student Senate and Student Court projects.
3. Act as a public relations agent for OSS and student government.

Elections:
1. Plan and direct the Freshman Elections held in October.
2. Plan and direct the All-Campus Student Government Elections held in the spring.

Amy has worked on both of these committees extensively and has done an excellent and efficient job. She shows leadership abilities and in my opinion would be a good junior officer. As one of the Senior Board members, I will be involved in selecting the new junior officers.

FIGURE 4.1. Persuasion Case: Problem and Participant Analysis (continued)

Analysis of the Problem

I. *Proposal.*
   A. *Maximum*—To persuade Amy to petition for the junior officer position with the Office of Student Services.
   B. *Minimum*—To persuade Amy to think about the situation and *agree to another discussion of it later on.* Set definite date for this further discussion, if necessary.

II. *Reasons.*
   A. My personal motives.
      1. My duty as Activities Chairman.
      2. "Reflected glory" or prestige involved in being a successful Activities Chairman (refer to paragraph 2).
      3. My concern for the house's prestige and success.
      4. My liking for Amy and the desire to see her capabilities put to good use.
   B. Reasons why Amy should consent.
      1. She would be contributing her efforts to student government.
         a. Student government needs capable people.
         b. Every student should be interested in the school's student governmental organization.
         c. To contribute is a duty and a privilege.
      2. Being a junior officer of OSS will help her in her teaching.
         a. Gain greater knowledge of how to handle different types of people.
         b. Gain leadership abilities.
         c. Gain poise, experience in handling herself in various situations.
         d. Learn tact and diplomacy.
         e. Gain organizational experience.
         f. Will be better able to advise her students with problems and also help advise in high school activities. This will result in more personal success for her.
         g. Possible employers will give great weight to her experience in college activities.
         h. Experience in working with publicity would help her in English major and vice-versa.
      3. Being a junior officer will actually *help* her grades.
         a. Learn to budget time better.
         b. The busiest people get the most done.
         c. Gain knowledge of abstract things which help in class—group discussion, ability to think quickly in an emergency, etc.
      4. Will help develop her social personality.
         a. Work with all types of people. Learn to get along with them.
         b. Working with people is stimulating and fun!
      5. Will contribute to the house's success and prestige as generally viewed by campus.
      6. Will result in personal prestige for her.
         a. Viewed as a success or "big wheel."
         b. Opportunity to meet important people—Dean of Men, Dean of Women, etc.

FIGURE 4.1. Persuasion Case: Problem and Participant Analysis (continued)

Analysis of the Problem (continued)
- C. Why Amy might not want to consent.
    1. The job would take too much time.
    2. Holding the office might damage her grades.
    3. Doesn't think she has a good chance of getting the job and doesn't want to waste her time preparing the petition and interview.
    4. Wouldn't give her enough time to participate in house activities.
- D. Amy's motives behind possible refusal.
    1. Lack of confidence in her ability to maintain grades and this activity.
    2. Feels inferior to her co-workers at OSS.
    3. May be slightly afraid of the added responsibility.
    4. Enjoys being very active in house functions.

III. *Background.*
  A. Origin of problem.
    1. OSS needs capable junior officers.
    2. The house needs girls participating in activities and holding offices.
    3. I wish to have the girls I've helped be successful, for their development and my own prestige.
  B. Immediate cause: OSS offices elections in one month.

IV. *Occasion.*
  A. Time and date: 12:30 P.M. Dec. 12.
  B. Place.
    1. Amy's room.
    2. Chi Delta house.
  C. Setting.
    1. Amy will be expecting me. Will not know why I wish to talk with her, but will suspect.
    2. I will have had previous preparation; Amy will not.
    3. Reception will likely be friendly, though she will be on guard.
    4. Mood—probably good. Might be tired.

V. *Criteria.*
  A. Needs/desires.
    1. Amy's
        a. To contribute something to her school.
        b. To contribute something to her sorority.
        c. To further develop her capabilities and personality.
        d. To gain experience in something similar to an actual job.
        e. To learn to budget her time.
        f. For prestige and recognition.
    2. Mine
        a. To fulfill my office's duties.
        b. Prestige of having done my job successfully.
        c. To see Amy get the recognition and prestige she deserves.
  B. Practical considerations and forseeable difficulties.
    1. How she can manage the job and maintain good grades at the same time.
    2. Budgeting of time.
    3. Increasing her self-confidence.

FIGURE 4.1. Persuasion Case: Problem and Participant Analysis (continued)

Analysis of the Problem (continued)

VI. *Advantages.*
   A. My proposal meets the criteria:
      1. Will be helping student government and the university.
         a. OSS is service organization for students.
         b. Administrative branch of student government.
      2. Sorority will gain prestige from having one of its members hold an OSS junior job.
      3. Amy will develop her leadership abilities, capabilities, social poise, tact, etc., by working in such a group with various types of people.
      4. Will provide valuable experience for teaching since employers look for college activities in a prospective employee.
      5. Amy will have to learn to budget her time.
   B. Bonus benefits: Personal prestige for Amy.

VII. *Possible objections.*
   A. "The job will take too much time."
      1. Ans.—Not if the work is organized and delegated to committee members as it should be. Mention the organizational ability she has shown. Will increase her self-confidence and refute this objection.
   B. "Holding the office will damage my grades."
      1. Ans.—Not necessarily. Will help as you will have to budget your time better. The busiest people get the most accomplished. Cite examples of people in the house (or out) who are very active in campus activities and point out that most of them have good grades. Repeat statistics in opening question (interview plan). Mention that she will gain knowledge of certain matters that will help her in class, such as experience in leading group discussions, ability to think quickly in an emergency, etc.
   C. "I don't have a good chance of getting the job."
      1. Ans.—Show her that she has. Have advantage of being on the "inside track" in this matter, and she knows it. Will help in convincing her. Mention her past sophomore chairmanships and how well she has done with them. Tell her about the good comments she's received from other Senior Board members. Mention that her good background in English will be to her advantage concerning the Publicity Committee.
   D. "I won't have time for house activities."
      1. Ans.—You will have time for all activities except the major house offices. Must make decision whether to work for house on campus or within house. Have enough people working in house. Takes more ability to be successful in campus activities. More difficult to succeed and more of a challenge. Elaborate.

VIII. *Possible counterproposals.*
   A. Continue in campus activities, but only in University Choir and as a counselor.
      1. Advantages.
         a. Still would be helping the house, school, and herself.
         b. Wouldn't require as much time.
      2. Disadvantages.
         a. Less opportunity for developing personality and capabilities.
         b. Don't come into contact with as many types of people.
         c. Less prestige for house.

FIGURE 4.1. Persuasion Case: Problem and Participant Analysis (continued)

Analysis of the Problem (continued)
        d. Less prestige for herself.
        e. Less opportunity for job experience.
  B. Work only with house activities.
    1. Advantages.
        a. Working for something for which she has a very great loyalty.
        b. See results of helping house more directly.
        c. Less time involved (debatable).
    2. Disadvantages.
        a. Same as for counterproposal A plus the fact that the time involved won't necessarily be less. Also, won't have opportunity of working with people outside of house.

Personal Analysis of the E

Persuadee: Amy L.

Occupation: Student (sophomore) at the University, majoring in secondary education. Emphases: English and French.

Age: 19.

Mental abilities: Slightly above average, based on an accumulative grade average of C plus. Grasps ideas slowly, but thoroughly. Interested in wide variety of academic subjects. Likes to generalize from specific points.

Membership in groups: Belongs to Chi Delta sorority. Is very loyal and interested in success and prestige of this group. Actively participates in all house functions. Is also a freshman counselor and a member of University Choir. Likes to "belong."

Attitude toward persuader: Well acquainted. Good friends. She has respect for me and my status as a Senior Officer of OSS. Will be slightly on guard, as she knows I will be trying to persuade her to do something she's not sure she wants to do. Is also a *bit* "afraid" of me, because I was strict with her pledge class concerning activity hours.

Attitude toward topic and purpose of interview: Interested in having the junior job, but wary of the time involved and her chances of getting it. Likes working with OSS. Interested in welfare of student government and the house's success in activities. Will not know specifically of interview's purpose beforehand, but will suspect it.

Knowledge of topic: Fairly comprehensive concerning OSS. Realizes the need for house representation in campus activities.

Possible interview habits and peculiarities: Will tend to remain passive in the discussion. Would like to let me do all the talking and then say "she'll think about it."

Principal wants and interests: Concerned about maintaining good grades and good relationships with people both inside and outside of the house. Very sociable. Likes to work with people. Would like prestige of junior job. Wants to be a "somebody."

Possible motive appeals:
1. Her desire to be "somebody."
2. Her interest in student government.
3. Her concern for the house's prestige.
4. Her social nature.
5. Her interest in teaching.

FIGURE 4.1. Persuasion Case: Problem and Participant Analysis (continued)

Personal Analysis of the E (continued)

6. Her concern for her grades.
7. Her liking for applying specific points to general situations.

Things to avoid in the interview: Don't get overly pushy. Amy is already wary of persuading her to do this, and might get resentful. Does not like being interrupted. Doesn't like smoking around her as it irritates her eyes. Dislikes a formal atmosphere.

Personal Analysis of the R (Susan J.)

Persuader: Susan J.

Occupation: Student (senior) at the University, majoring in communication. Emphasis: Organizational Communication.

Age: 21.

Mental abilities: Above average, based on an accumulative grade average of B plus. Interested in courses dealing with human behavior in various organizations, and associated research.

Membership in groups: Belongs to Chi Delta sorority, and very active in supporting its goals and functions. In addition to OSS, I have been moderately active in Forensics and Panhellenic.

Attitude toward persuadee: We're good friends, and have many common interests not related to the sorority (e.g., music, and books).

Attitude toward topic and purpose of interview: I want very much for Amy to apply for the position because I really believe it will be good experience for her and a real benefit for the sorority and the university. In addition, it is my responsibility as Activities Chairman to encourage Amy's involvement.

Knowledge of topic: I'm thoroughly knowledgeable about the position because of my previous and current experience.

Possible interview habits and peculiarities: I know I tend to talk too much in situations like this, and I tend to be too impatient and aggressive at times. Also have a bad habit of overusing the phrase "you know. . . . "

Principal wants and interests: I like authority and positions of leadership. Also like to be with people and to work with people. Tend to be very goal-oriented, and to work hard.

Outline of Interview Plan

I. Opening.
   A. Direct.
      1. Question:
         Did you know that of the 15 Chi Delta's holding junior and senior jobs, 12 of them have at least a C plus accumulative grade? And of these 12, 6 have at least a B.
      2. Explain purpose of interview or proposal. Act as transition into major parts of discussion.

FIGURE 4.1. Persuasion Case: Problem and Participant Analysis (continued)

Outline of Interview Plan (continued)

II. Body.
    A. Criteria—discuss in terms of things she wants to do and be.
    B. Reasons for and advantages of petitioning for an OSS junior job. Show how they fulfill her wants (criteria).
    C. Objections—refute!
    D. Counterproposals, if she brings them up.

III. Closing.
    A. Summarize principal advantages of proposal.
        1. Help student government, the university, herself, and sorority.
        2. Greater respect and prestige for her.
        3. Good experience for future jobs.
        4. Will help to budget time, and grades should improve.
    B. Secure her consent to petition.

ADDITIONAL READINGS

Fishbein, Martin, and Icek Ajzen. *Belief, Attitude, Intention, and Behavior.* Reading, Mass.: Addison-Wesley, 1975.

Fotheringham, Wallace C. *Perspectives on Persuasion.* Boston: Allyn & Bacon, 1966.

King, Stephen W. *Communication and Social Influence.* Reading, Mass.: Addison-Wesley, 1975.

McGill, V. J. *Emotions and Reason.* Springfield, Ill.: Chas. C Thomas, 1954.

Zimbardo, Philip, Ebbe B. Ebbesen, and Cristna Maslach. *Influencing Attitudes and Changing Behavior.* Reading, Mass.: Addison-Wesley, 1977.

5

The Legal Environment of the Employment Process

CHAPTER OBJECTIVES

1. Explain the impact on the employment process of Title VII of the Civil Rights Act of 1964.
2. Explain the major provisions of Title VII of the Civil Rights Act of 1964.
3. Describe generally the role of the Uniform Guidelines of Employee Selection Procedures (1978).
4. Identify four federal acts affecting equal employment opportunity and describe their primary thrusts.
5. Define and differentiate disparate treatment, adverse impact, perpetuation of past discrimination, and lack of reasonable accommodation.
6. Distinguish between "fair discrimination" and "unfair discrimination."
7. Explain the "job-related" criterion.
8. Identify and explain three types of selection criteria validity.
9. Identify and describe four types of employment tests.
10. Define "bona fide occupational qualification."
11. Understand differences between lawful and unlawful questions.
12. Identify and describe eight strategies of responding to questions that are probably unlawful.

Introduction

When President Lyndon B. Johnson signed the Civil Rights Act of 1964, he was translating his political crusade into legal authority in support of one of America's most important pieces of legislation. Although the act was damned by some and praised by others, its impact was profound. Implementation of and compliance with its provisions as stated originally (and as amended) have had widespread ramifications, especially in the area of equal employment opportunity.

Title VII of the Civil Rights Act of 1964 is one of eleven titles.[1] It became effective on July 2, 1965, prohibiting discrimination in employment based on race, color, religion, sex, or national origin in all industries engaged in interstate commerce. Since 1973 its provisions have applied to all such businesses that employ fifteen or more people. Title VII extends coverage to all aspects of employment, including hiring, promotion, termination, and layoffs.

President Richard M. Nixon issued Executive Order 11478, effective August 8, 1969, extending Title VII to federal employees and protecting them also against discrimination on grounds of race, color, religion, sex, or national origin. Title VII also prohibits discrimination by employment agencies (including both public and private agencies and college and university placement offices) and by labor unions.

Under the provisions of Title VII, the president of the United States is authorized to appoint the five-member Equal Employment Opportunity Commission (EEOC). It is charged with administering the provisions of Title VII. By 1976, differences of interpretation of Title VII had emerged as a result of various court cases and the involvement of several federal agencies. Because of these differences in interpreting Title VII and at the urging of the administration of President Jimmy Carter, the EEOC, the Civil Service Commission, the Department of Justice, and the Department of Labor adopted the "Uniform Guidelines on Employee Selection Procedures (1978)," which became effective on September 25, 1978.[2] Because of their importance to the entire area of employment practices, their direct impact on selection procedures from the point of view of both the employer and the applicant, and their effect on the employment interview, Title VII of the Civil Rights Act of 1964 (as amended) and the Uniform Guidelines on Employee Selection Procedures (1978) are reprinted in their entirety in Appendices A and B. We urge you to read them now.

The remainder of this chapter will discuss certain aspects of Equal Employment Opportunity, lawful and unlawful interview topics and questions, and strategies for responding to questions that you believe are unlawful.

Equal Employment Opportunity

Title VII of the Civil Rights Act of 1964 (as amended) prohibits discrimination in employment on the grounds of race, color, religion, sex, or national origin. Organizations covered by the provisions of Title VII include those engaged in interstate commerce employing fifteen or more people, the federal government, labor unions, public and private employment agencies, and college and university placement services.

In addition, the Age Discrimination in Employment act of 1967 as amended in 1978 has as its purpose "to promote employment of older persons based on their ability rather than age; to prohibit arbitrary age discrimination in employment; to help employers and workers find ways of meeting problems arising from the impact of age on employment."[3] This act prohibits discrimination based on age against individuals who are between forty and seventy years old.

The Rehabilitation Act of 1973 as amended in 1974 forbids those employers with federal contracts of $2,500 or more to discriminate against the handicapped or those with a history of disability and requires them to use affirmative action to provide employment opportunities for the handicapped and those with a history of disability.[4]

Even though there are no requirements for goals and timetables under this act, companies often fulfill their obligations under the act by engaging in special outreach programs and/or by upgrading programs for handicapped persons. Companies may also make modifications in buildings to provide improved access to them for handicapped persons.

The Employment Provisions of the Vietnam Era Veterans' Readjustment Assistance Act of 1974 as amended in 1980 require affirmative action by federal contractors to employ and advance in employment qualified special disabled veterans and veterans of the Vietnam era.[5] In complying with this act, companies may post job openings with their state employment service, using that service as a source of candidate recruitment.

The "Uniform Guidelines on Employee Selection Procedures (1978)" (see Appendix B) describe how Title VII is to be applied, not only in the hiring of new employees, but also in the treatment of current employees. In addition, more than half of the states and hundreds of cities, counties, and municipalities have adopted fair employment practices and antidiscrimination legislation that circumscribe even more specific boundaries than does the federal legislation. Typically, these extensions include all that is encompassed in the federal interpretations and preclude discrimination based on other factors as well. As an example, some states extend protection against age discrimination to persons between the ages of eighteen and seventy.

To ensure legal compliance, prospective employers should obtain clear opinions from their legal counsel as to what subjects can be legally inquired about, and how, and/or how questions should be phrased so as to comply with federal, state, and local laws.

Any applicant has the legal right to charge a prospective employer with discriminatory hiring practices. In some cases, the individual is correct in the accusation, and a court will uphold the complaint. In other cases, when the applicant has been rejected for employment for proper and legal reasons, the court will decide in favor of the employer. When enforcing Title VII, the EEOC will consider nearly all complaints, whether right or wrong, but a ruling against the prospective employer will usually be rendered only in cases in which the facts presented conform with one or more of the following four principles.

1. *Disparate Treatment.* You receive treatment that is different from the treatment received by another person solely because you are of a different race, color, religion, sex, or national origin.

2. *Adverse Impact.* The employer does not hire you because of factors that clearly are not job related but that statistically have a disproportionately negative effect on certain groups of people. For example, suppose that an employer requires that its plant security guards be at least six feet tall and weigh 185 pounds. The company must be able to prove that these height and weight requirements are necessary for the successful performance of the work to be done. Otherwise, this practice may be found to be discriminatory (and illegal) against women and possibly Hispanics, Asians, and others as well.

3. *Perpetuating Past Discrimination.* At first glance, an employer's current employment practices may seem nondiscriminatory; yet, the current practices may have a discriminatory effect when they are examined in the context of past discriminatory practices. As an example, suppose that a company usually hires from

a pool of applicants made up of people referred by current employees. This practice may not seem discriminatory unless the entire current work force is black (or white) because of past discriminatory hiring practices. An all-black (or all-white) work force is likely to refer a steady supply of applicants that are all black (or all white).

4. *Lack of Reasonable Accommodation.* Discrimination may occur if an employer refuses to try to find a reasonable solution to problems that pose minor obstacles to employability because of a person's religion, handicap, or disability. (The meaning of the term *reasonable* is not always clear and may depend on a variety of factors, such as collective-bargaining agreements or costs of solving the problem.) Suppose that for religious reasons an applicant is unable to work on Sundays. In most cases the employer could arrange a work schedule for the other six days of the week. But if the employer refused to hire the applicant on the basis of his or her refusal to work on Sunday, a court might uphold a charge of religious discrimination. Employment candidates who believe that they have been subjected to discriminatory treatment by prospective employers should contact their state Labor Department or local Equal Employment Opportunity Office to file a complaint or to request an inquiry. Such an action should not be taken lightly and should be based on belief rather than sour grapes.

Most professional recruiters (whether employed by the company or by a search firm), as well as the five-member Equal Employment Opportunity Commission established under Title VII, believe that organizations are more susceptible to discrimination charges stemming from the selection process than from any other area of employment practice. The implication here is that every manager, every supervisor, every recruiter—anyone—who interviews an applicant or candidate before hiring must be conscious of areas in which even seemingly innocent questions, asked openly and in good faith, can leave the organization open to expensive, time-consuming charges of discrimination.[6]

The purpose of the various antidiscrimination acts, statutes, legislation, guidelines, orders, and laws is to force the prospective employer to base the hiring decision on the candidate's ability to do the job. The applicant's skills, knowledge, experience, and employment record are the principal legal criteria on which the applicant should be hired—not some abstract or discriminatory criteria (such as those prohibited by Title VII).

Three rules govern the kinds of questions the employer may ask in the employment interview. First, the basis for any question asked must be to measure the person for the job. Second, no question may have an adverse impact on any person or class of persons. Third, the questioner must be able to prove that the question is job related. In short, questions should not violate federal, state, or local laws that prohibit discrimination. The burden is on the employer to ensure legal compliance. Usually, discrimination applies to unfair or unequal treatment in employment practices (violations of the Uniform Guidelines), including hiring, promotion, transfer, or termination based on factors other than the person's ability to perform the job. But the distinction between "unfair discrimination" and "fair discrimination" should be noted.

Unfair discrimination occurs when individuals who have equal probabilities of success have unequal probabilities of being hired for a given job.[7] Fair discrimination refers to the use of selection criteria and procedures to differentiate among those applicants more likely to perform in a satisfactory manner and those less likely to perform in a satisfactory manner.[8] Note also that it is not unlawful to treat people unfairly as long as all persons are treated the same way.[9]

One purpose of the employment interview is to screen applicants and, based on that screening process, to select those considered most likely to succeed. In the general hiring process, other screening procedures are used in addition to the interview. Commonly used screens include written applications, paper-and-pencil tests, reference checks, and a physical examination. If any of these can be shown to have an adverse effect on any class of people protected by Title VII, then the employer must prove that the screen is legitimately job related. This means that the employer must show that the adverse effect (negative or discriminatory impact) on employment opportunity for any class protected by Title VII is justified by business necessity. Phrased another way, there must be a valid relationship between the selection criteria used and the eventual job performance.[10]

Three techniques of selection criteria validation are acceptable under the Uniform Guidelines on Employee Selection Procedures (1978).[11] First, *criterion-related validity* is based on the statistical relationship between test scores (the interview is viewed as a test) and quantitative measures of job performance. Second, *content validity* is based on representative samples of parts of the actual job to be performed (for example, actual typing performance on a typing test by an individual applying for a job as a typist). Third, *construct validity* is based on a psychological construct or trait needed for successful job performance and devises an appropriate selection procedure to measure the presence and extent of that construct. An example of construct validity would be to use an "in-basket" exercise (a test devised to determine how people react to items normally found in an office in-basket) to measure the construct judgment.

Tests used in employment generally will be of four types: ability, aptitude, dexterity, and intelligence. *Ability* tests measure the capacity of the individual to perform the required work (e.g., to lift a seventy-five pound bag of sand or to demonstrate proofreading skills). *Aptitude* tests measure the individual's mental inclination or talent to pursue certain vocations (e.g., interests or motivational level). *Dexterity* tests measure mechanical ability or mechanical aptitude (e.g., eye-hand coordination). *Intelligence* tests measure mental capacity or potential. Intelligence tests often are criticized as being culture-bound (using language and examples specific to one culture, such as that of white middle-class Americans). In recent years many tests have been made "culture-fair" (nonspecific to a particular group). Successful scores no longer depend on particular verbal or arithmetic skills or specific life experiences. Rather, they depend on so-called generic examples, pictures, and nonreading materials.

Because there are many complicated laws and guidelines with many amendments, revisions, and interpretations, legal compliance in employment is a difficult and complex achievement. As the law has evolved, one part remains constant: selection procedures must be job related; that is, they must meet what are called Bona Fide Occupational Qualifications (BFOQ). For example, under the provisions of Title VII, it is unlawful to discriminate against someone on the basis of race, color, religion, sex, or national origin. Nevertheless, if any one of these characteristics can be shown to be a BFOQ, then it can be used to discriminate in a lawful manner. At the extreme, some would argue, that one can discriminate lawfully on the basis of sex only if the position opening is for a wet nurse or a donor to a sperm bank. But it would be difficult to use sex as a BFOQ for discriminating between two applicants (one male, one female) for the job of secretary. There is no job-related reason, under most circumstances, that a female would be more qualified than a male would be (or vice versa) for a secretarial position. Although one could argue that sex is a BFOQ for the position of "modeler of women's dresses," a female impersonator might have grounds for charging discrimination if denied the position. By the same token, one might argue more successfully that sex was a BFOQ for the position of "modeler of women's bathing suits," the female impersonator notwithstanding. Other jobs for which sex discrimination might be upheld as being a BFOQ would be to hire a woman instead of a man as an attendant in a women's rest room, to hire an actor instead of an actress to play Vince Lombardi, or to hire an actress instead of an actor to play Marilyn Monroe. In these instances, one can demonstrate successfully that business necessity (a job-related criterion) is the reason for sex discrimination.

The foregoing examples of Bona Fide Occupational Qualifications are meant to suggest some of the ambiguities and complexities encountered when interpreting EEO laws and guidelines. There are few clear-cut, unambiguous laws and guidelines. Again, the questions asked in the selection process must be job related. If the job-related criterion cannot be demonstrated, then the hiring organization can be subjected to litigation. Attorney's fees, expenses of a court trial, and adverse publicity for the organization's image can endanger the organization's financial position.[12]

Lawful and Unlawful Questions[13]

At any phase of the hiring process, but especially during the screening and selection interviews, many topics are likely to be probed appropriately and lawfully by the knowledgeable and skilled employer. In an interview, however, the employer is legally prevented from raising certain issues or asking certain kinds of content in questions. (Note: This restraint is removed in many instances once the applicant is hired.) Within the context of Equal Employment Opportunity, the following interpretations can be used as general ground rules for questioning. Keep in mind that the law allows exceptions to each of these ground rules *if* the employer can demonstrate (prove) that the subject or questions represent a Bona Fide Occupational Qualification (BFOQ). The following are some of the topics that may come up during the interview, topics about which the employer may or may not ask the applicant questions and questions that can be arguably lawful or unlawful (again, the test is whether the question is representative of a Bona Fide Occupational Qualification).

Address. The employer may ask the applicant for his or her current address and length of residency at that address and for previous addresses and length of time at each. It is probably lawful (note here and in the rest of this section the qualification "probably" is based on the test for BFOQ) to ask: "What is your current address?" "How long have you lived at your current address?" "Where have you lived previously, and how long did you live there?"

The employer may not ask about an address in order to determine whether the applicant owns or rents or to determine race, color, religion, sex, creed, or national origin. It is probably unlawful to ask: "Isn't that address in a predominantly black (Catholic, Jewish, Protestant) section of town?" "When you lived in Holland, was that at your parent's residence?" "Did you live in Holland from birth?" "Did you ever live in a coed dormitory?" "Did you ever live in a residence for foreign students?" "Don't most of the radical thinkers live in that neighborhood?"

Age. The employer may ask for a birth certificate or other proof of age *after hiring*. The employer may ask the applicant's birth date. It is probably lawful to ask: "If you are hired, will you give us a birth certificate or other proof of age?" "What is your date of birth?"

The employer may not ask for the applicant's birth certificate or proof of age *before hiring* or for the applicant's age. It is probably unlawful to ask: "How old are you?" "In what year will you be old enough to retire?"

Arrest or conviction record. The employer may ask about the applicant's conviction record. It is probably lawful to ask: "Have you ever been convicted of a crime other than a minor traffic violation?" "Have you ever been convicted of a felony?"

The employer may not ask about the applicant's arrest record. It is probably unlawful to ask: "Have you ever been arrested for a crime?" "Have you ever been charged with a crime?" "How many times have you been arrested?" "How many times have you been charged with a crime?"

Birth certificate (proof of age). The employer may ask for a birth certificate (or copy thereof) or for proof of age, to be supplied by the applicant after hiring. This applies to any other certification or affirmation of birth date. It is probably lawful to ask: "Will you be able to give us a copy of your birth certificate if you are hired?"

The employer may not use the birth certificate before hiring to determine the applicant's age or national origin. The employer may not use other proof of age before hiring to determine the applicant's age, race, color, sex, or national origin. It is probably unlawful to ask: "Is your mother's maiden name on your birth certificate?" "May I see your passport?" (The photograph in a passport combined with the passport itself might indicate age, race, sex, color, or national origin.)

Citizenship. The employer may ask if the applicant is a citizen of the United States or intends to become a citizen. The employer may ask if the applicant is a legal resident of the United States. After hiring, the employer may require the applicant to provide proof of citizenship. It is probably lawful to ask: "Are you a citizen of the United States?" "Will you become a citizen of the United States?" "What is your resident status in the United States?"

The employer may not ask if the applicant is a native-born citizen of the United States or one of its territories that automatically confer U.S. citizenship at birth (e.g., American Samoa, Puerto Rico, or the Virgin Islands). The employer may not ask if the applicant's parents (or other relatives) are citizens of the United States (whether native-born or naturalized). It is probably unlawful to ask: "Where were you born?" "Where were your parents born?" "You speak with a foreign accent. Where is it from?" "Are you a native-born citizen of the United States, or are you naturalized?" "May I see your birth certificate now?" "Is English your native language?"

Color or race. Although in most instances color or race will be apparent on sight, this will not always be the case, and even if it is, color or race may not be used to discriminate against an applicant. The employer may not ask questions that would cause the applicant to state his or her color or race or indicate national origin or ancestry. It is probably unlawful to ask: "Are you a native American?" "Is your ancestry Chinese, Japanese, or Vietnamese?"

Educational background. The employer may ask what schools the applicant attended, the major area of study, courses taken, grade point average, and date of graduation (in order to obtain transcripts). It is probably lawful to ask: "What high school did you attend?" "Did you graduate from high school?" "Where did you receive your MBA?" "What was your undergraduate major?" "After studying Spanish for two years, are you conversational in it?" "In addition to your formal degree(s), do you have any other educational certifications?" "Are you certified in cardiopulmonary resuscitation?"

The employer may not ask about the religious affiliation or racial composition of the applicant's schools, about the applicant's attendance at religious schools, or about the applicant's national origin. It is probably unlawful to ask: "Did you go to a Catholic high school?" "Isn't Manhattan College sectarian?" "Wasn't Central State the first member school in the United Negro College Fund?" "As a child did you attend Hebrew school daily after public school?" "Did you learn Spanish at home because it was your parent's native tongue?"

Extracurricular activities. The employer may ask about collegiate or community-related extracurricular activities in which the applicant participated in order to obtain a picture of the applicant's diversity and interests. It is probably lawful to ask: "In what extra curricular activities did you participate?" "Tell me about your extracurricular activities." "Have you ever held an office in any club or organization?"

The employer may not ask the applicant about extracurricular activities in order to determine the applicant's race, color, religion, sex, creed, national origin, or ancestry. It is probably unlawful to ask: "Are you a member of a fraternity?" "Were you a member of any campus religious organizations?" "Did you participate in the Black Student Caucus?" "Were you a member of the German Students Club?"

Financial position. The employer may ask questions about the applicant's finances. It is probably lawful to ask: "What is your current salary?" "What is your total compensation, including salary, fringe benefits, and perquisites?" "For what percentage of your college education did you pay?"

The employer may not ask financial questions in order to determine race, religion, or national origin of the applicant. It is probably unlawful to ask: "Do you contribute regularly at church?" "What portion of your charitable contributions goes to the National Association for the Advancement of Colored People (United Jewish Appeal? Catholic Relief Fund)?" "How much do you earn from your investments?"

Friends and associates. The employer may ask if the applicant has friends or associates working for the employer's organization. It is probably lawful to ask: "Do you have any friends who are currently employed by us?" "Do you know anyone who has ever worked for us?"

The employer may not ask about the applicant's friends or associates for the purpose of determining the applicant's race, religion, creed, or national origin. It is probably unlawful to ask: "Do you associate with the student leader of the Students for a Democratic Society?" "With whom do you usually sit when you attend meetings of the Slavic Descendants Club?" "Are you a member of the county Republican Committee?" "Would you consider yourself a member of the Moral Majority?"

Handicaps or disabilities. The employer may ask if the applicant has any physical or mental handicap or disability that would prevent the applicant from being able to perform the duties associated with the job. It is probably lawful to ask: "What kinds of work does your blindness prevent you from performing efficiently?" "Do you have any physical disabilities that would prevent you from doing the job that we are discussing?" "How well do you manage stress-inducing situations?"

The employer may not ask about specific handicaps or physical or mental diseases. It is probably unlawful to ask: "What caused your blindness?" "Do you have an artificial limb?" "Do you have asthma?" "Have you ever had a nervous breakdown?" "Have you ever been confined to a mental institution?"

Health. The employer may ask about the applicant's general health and may require that the applicant pass a physical examination as a hiring contingency once the job offer has been extended. It is probably lawful to ask: "Are you in good health?" "Will you take a physical examination from your family physician at our expense and forward the results to us before your employment offer with us becomes official?"

The employer may not ask questions that pertain to the applicant's health problems or the applicant's physical characteristics, even though the answers to these questions would be reflected later in the results of a thorough physical examination. It is probably unlawful to ask: "How much do you weigh?" "How tall are you?" "Have any of your adult teeth been pulled?" "How long have your symptoms of skin cancer been in remission?"

Honors or awards received. The employer may ask the applicant about honors or awards if they are job related. It is probably lawful to ask: "Did you graduate with honors?" "Did you win any scholastic awards while in school?" "Have you held any scholarships or fellowships?" "Have you been honored by any professional societies to which you belong?"

The employer may not ask the applicant about honors or awards if such questions will lead to a determination of the applicant's race, religion, national origin, or ancestry. It is probably unlawful to ask: "Isn't it unusual for a Catholic student to receive a scholarship to Yeshiva University?" "Were you the first black to be so honored?"

Housing preference. The employer may ask the applicant if he or she has any preference for type of housing or location of housing in order to help the applicant get settled in a new community. It is probably lawful to ask: "Would you like us to put you in touch with a local realtor?" "Would you like us to assist you in obtaining a mortgage loan?" "Would you like a house, apartment, or condominium?" "How important is it for you to live near public transportation?"

The employer may not ask about housing preference in order to direct the applicant to a particular geographical location within the community for purposes of discriminating against the applicant on the basis of race, religion, creed, or national origin. It is probably unlawful to ask: "Do you want to live in an all-white neighborhood?" "Do you want to live near a Baptist church?"

Marital status. The employer may not question the applicant's marital status or ask about the applicant's spouse or children. It is probably unlawful to ask: "Are you married?" "Do you have children?" "Do your college-age children live with you?" "Which career is more important to your family—yours or your spouse's?" "Do you use Mrs., Miss, or Ms.?"

Military service background. The employer may ask if the applicant has served in the U.S. armed forces, which branch, when, type of discharge received, and last rank attained. It is probably lawful to ask: "Did you ever serve in the armed forces of the United States?" "Where were you stationed?" "While in the Air Force, were you a pilot?" "What was your rank when discharged?" "What type of discharge were you given?" "What was your M-O-S (Military Occupational Specialty)?"

The employer may not ask the applicant for military service records or ask about military service for countries other than the United States. It is probably unlawful to ask: "As a citizen of the United States, how did you become a pilot in the Royal Air Force?" "May we see your service records?" "Did you ever serve in the military service of a country other than the United States?"

Name. The employer may ask for the applicant's full name. It is probably lawful to ask: "What is your legal name as you want it to appear in your employment record with us?" "What would you like me to call you?" "May I call you Bob?"

The employer may not question the applicant's name for purposes of determining the applicant's race, religion, national origin, or ancestry. It is probably unlawful to ask: "Aren't most people named 'Mohammed' members of a Muslim sect?" "Your last name, Poulos, is Greek, isn't it?"

National origin. The employer may not ask any questions about the applicant's national origin or for proof of birth for purposes of determining national origin. It is probably unlawful to ask: "Where were you born?" "Where were your parents born?" "Are you a first-generation American?" "May I see your birth certificate now?"

Organizational or professional memberships. The employer may ask if the applicant is a member of any organizations or professional associations and if the applicant now holds or has held office(s) in them. It is probably lawful to ask: "What business organizations do you belong to?" "What offices have you held in professional associations?" "Are you a member of the American Society for Personnel Administration?"

The employer may not ask for memberships that would identify the applicant's race, religion, sex, national origin, or ancestry. The employer may not ask the applicant to name each one of his or her organizational or professional memberships. It is probably unlawful to ask: "Do you belong to B'nai B'rith?" "Are you a member of a Masonic lodge?" "Have you held office in a religious organization?" "Are you a lay minister in your church?" "What sorority were you in?"

Photograph. The employer may request the applicant to supply a photograph after being hired and/or require the applicant to be photographed by the company for security identification purposes after being hired. It is probably lawful to ask: "If we hire you, will you supply us with four 4 × 6 black and white glossy photographs?" "Once hired, do you have any objection to being photographed by our plant security office?"

The employer may not ask for a photograph before the applicant is hired. It is probably unlawful to ask: "Will you send us a photograph to accompany your résumé when it is distributed to the people who will interview you during your plant visit?"

Physical characteristics. The employer may question the applicant about physical disabilities that might prevent the applicant from performing the job. The employer may require the applicant to perform on a physical test such as lifting, hoisting, and physical dexterity if moving heavy weights or physical dexterity is required to perform the job. It is probably lawful to ask: "Do you have any physical disabilities that would prevent you from performing the job we have just discussed?" "The warehouse job requires that you stack forty, seventy-five-pound sacks of grain on each wooden pallet. Let's go out to the warehouse so that you can show me that you're able to fill up a pallet."

The employer may not ask about the applicant's physical characteristics, such as height, weight, color, or sex or about any physical characteristics for purposes of determining national origin. It is probably unlawful to ask: "How tall are you?" "How much do you weigh?" "Most women who want to work in the warehouse can't lift seventy-five pounds. Would you find that hard to do?"

Publications. The employer may ask if the applicant has any publications (articles; books; a portfolio of sketches, drawings, or paintings; audiotapes or videotapes of creative work products). It is probably lawful to ask: "How many journal articles and books have you published in the past two years?" "What research are you now engaged in that will lead to publication?" "May I see your portfolio of newsletters you've edited?" "I'd like to look at some of your photographic work." "When you come to the station, will you bring an audition tape that we can listen to?"

The employer may not ask the applicant questions to determine race, religion, color, sex, creed, or national origin. It is probably unlawful to ask: "Why did you submit that article to the *Black Business Journal* instead of to the *Business Journal?*" "Your article on 'Techniques of Zen in the Reduction of Personal Stress' looks interesting, but doesn't the title suggest that you don't believe in God?"

References. The employer may ask the applicant for references from people who can attest to the applicant's knowledge, skill, ability, and work habits or from people who have a personal and work-related association with the applicant. It is probably lawful to ask: "May I speak with your current employer?" "Please give me the names of two people who can tell me about your educational background." "Will you send us three letters of recommendation—one from someone who knows your education, one from someone who knows your job-related skills, and one who knows your general personal characteristics like honesty and integrity?"

The employer may not ask the applicant for references that relate to or identify the applicant's race, color, sex, creed, national origin, or ancestry. It is probably unlawful to ask: "Will you ask your minister (priest, rabbi) to send us a letter attesting to your personal characteristics like honesty and integrity?" "Will you have a recommendation sent to us from someone who knows your family background and history?"

Relatives and family. The employer may ask the applicant for the name of the nearest relative to notify in case of emergency, including that person's relationship to the applicant, address, and telephone number. It is probably lawful to ask: "Whom shall we notify in case of emergency?" "What is your relationship to that person?" "What is that person's address and phone number?"

The employer may not ask the applicant about relatives or family for purposes of identifying race, religion, creed, sex, national origin, or ancestry. It is probably unlawful to ask: "You say we should notify your brother, Mr. Keyzciouzsko, in case of emergency. Was that your name also before it became 'Key'?" "In case of emergency, is there a minister whom we should notify?"

Religion. The employer may not ask any questions about the applicant's religion, religious beliefs, or creed. It is probably unlawful to ask: "Do you believe in God?" "Does it bother you that this job is located in the hard-core Bible Belt?" "Are there any religious reasons why you can't work on Saturdays?" "Do you attend church regularly?"

Sex. The employer may not ask any questions related to the applicant's sex, sexual preferences, or sexual habits. It is probably unlawful to ask: "I'm pleased to meet you. Because you used only your initials on your résumé, I couldn't tell if you were male or female." "Are your best friends male or female?" "Have you ever contracted a venereal disease?" "As a man, how would you react to working for a female supervisor?"

Work experience. The employer may question the applicant's work-related knowledge, skills, experience, or habits (e.g., punctuality, absenteeism, reasons for wanting this job). It is probably lawful to ask: "What are three major work accomplishments that qualify you for this job?" "What's the most positive, satisfying work experience you have had?" "How many times have you been absent during the past year for reasons other than health?" "Will you work the midnight to 8:00 A.M. shift?" "Why do you want to leave your current job?"

The employer may not ask the applicant any questions for the purpose of determining the applicant's race, religion, sex, creed, national origin, or ancestry. It is probably unlawful to ask: "Have you ever worked for a religious organization?" "Has physical discomfort during your menstrual period ever caused you to miss work?" "Will you work on Christmas Day?" "Have you ever taken the day off to commemorate Martin Luther King's birthday?"

Keep in mind that many of these "probably unlawful" questions may be lawful if the employer can demonstrate that they are Bona Fide Occupational Qualifications. Also note that even if the employer does not ask a specific question of the applicant, the applicant may legally volunteer any information. For example, the employer may lawfully ask "Do you speak French?" but not "Were you born in France?" or "Are you of French ancestry?" The applicant may respond to the first question only by saying "Yes, I speak French." or the response may be expanded to include "I was born in Belgium of French-speaking parents, and I have spoken French ever since I began to talk." Similarly, the employer may not lawfully ask about the applicant's religion or national origin, but the applicant may volunteer, "I attended the University of Dayton, the tenth largest Catholic university in the United States. While there, I was president of the Polish-American Student Association."

Responding to Questions That You Believe Are Unlawful

Any applicant may encounter questions that may be unlawful. If you think you have been asked such a question, your response probably will depend on such factors as your interest in the position, how the answer affects you personally (i.e., your emotional reaction to the question), and your ability to recognize the question as unlawful.

Assume that you are asked, "How old are you?" There are at least eight response strategies that you can use when responding to this probably unlawful question.

1. *Acceptance without comment:* Answer the question, even though you know it is probably unlawful: "I'm forty-seven."
2. *Acceptance with comment:* Point out that the question is probably unlawful but answer it anyway: "I don't think the law allows you to ask me my age, but I'm forty-seven."
3. *Confrontation:* Meet the interviewer head-on by asking about the question's appropriateness. "Why did you ask me that?" "Does my age have anything to do with whether I will be hired?"
4. *Rationalization:* Ignore a direct response to the question and point out your qualifications for the position. "My age has nothing to do with my ability to perform the job as described. As you have presented it to me, I have the education, experience, track record, attitude, and desire to excel in this position."
5. *Challenge:* Make the interviewer tell you why this question is a BFOQ. "Please explain to me why age is a criterion for this job."
6. *Redirection:* Refer to an antecedent (something that has come before) to shift the focus of the interview away from your age toward the requirements of the position itself. "What you've said so far suggests that age is not as important for this position as is willingness to travel. Can you tell me more about the travel requirement?"
7. *Refusal:* Say that you will not provide the information requested. "I'm not going to answer that question now, but if I'm hired, I'll be happy to tell you."
8. *Withdrawal:* Physically remove yourself from the interview. End the interview immediately and leave.

Obviously, only you can decide which of these strategies is most appropriate for you in a given situation.

SUMMARY

This chapter described the legal environment of the employment interview, citing relevant legislation and federal laws and stressing the need to ask questions that represent Bona Fide Occupational Qualifications. We discussed many employment interview topics, including what subjects are probably lawful and probably unlawful, as well as strategies for responding to probably unlawful questions. The key point to remember from this chapter is that there is federal legislation that legally restrains employers from nonjob-related discrimination in hiring practices.

EXERCISES

1. Interview a person who does employment interviewing, finding out his or her organization's policies concerning how it conducts employment interviews and what techniques the interviewer uses to obtain sensitive information from an applicant.
2. Assume that as a prospective employer you are going to interview someone for a job. Choose ten topics, and prepare a list of probably lawful and probably unlawful questions to ask.
3. List ten questions that you think would be probably unlawful to ask in an employment interview. Using the response strategies discussed in this chapter, write out how you would feel (what your emotional reaction would be) and how you would respond to each of them.

NOTES

1. Title VII of the Civil Rights Act of 1964 (42 U.S.C. Section 2000e, 78 Stat.253) As Amended (effective October 1, 1980), *Fair Employment Practices Manual* (Washington, D.C.: Bureau of National Affairs, Inc., 1982), pp. 401:11–401:27.
2. Uniform Guidelines on Employee Selection Procedures (1978), *Fair Employment Practices Manual* (Washington, D.C.: Bureau of National Affairs, Inc., 1982), pp. 401:2231–401:2278.
3. Age Discrimination in Employment Act of 1967 (P.L. 90–202, effective June 12, 1968) As Amended (P.L. 95–256, effective April 6, 1978).
4. Rehabilitation Act of 1973 (P.L. 93–112) As Amended (P.L. 93–516, effective February 6, 1975).
5. Vietnam Era Veterans' Readjustment Assistance Act of 1974 As Amended (P.L. 96–466, effective October 1, 1980).
6. *Conducting the Lawful Employment Interview* (New York: Executive Enterprises Publications, 1974), p. 5.
7. R. M. Guion, "Employment Tests and Discriminatory Hiring," *Industrial Relations* 5 (1966):20–37.

8. C. H. Stone, and F. L. Ruch, "Selection, Interviewing, and Testing," in D. Yoder and H. G. Heneman, Jr., *ASPA Handbook of Personnel and Industrial Relations* (Washington, D.C.: Bureau of National Affairs, 1979), pp. 4:418–4:458.
9. *International Brotherhood of Teamsters* v. *United States*, 431 U.S. 324.
10. "Adoption by Four Agencies of Uniform Guidelines on Employee Selection Procedures" (1978).
11. "Adoption."
12. C. H. Stone and F. L. Ruch, p. 4:119.
13. Material in this section is based in part on information compiled from the "Pre-Employment Inquiries Guidelines" found in the *Fair Employment Practices Manual* (Washington, D.C.: Bureau of National Affairs, Inc., 1982), pp. 453:575–453:577 (Arizona), 453:935–453:939 (California), 453:1475–453:1476 (Delaware), 453:2335–453:2340 (Hawaii), 453:3351–453:3353 (Kansas), 455:1149–455:1153 (Michigan), 455:1721–455:1722 (Missouri), 455:2501–455:2502 (New Hampshire), 455:2731–455:2734 (New Jersey), 455:3151–455:3155 (New York), 457:325–457:326 (Ohio), 457:1279–457:1281 (Rhode Island), and 457:2331–457:2332 (Utah).

ADDITIONAL READINGS

Title VII of the Civil Rights Act of 1964 (42 U.S.C. Section 2000e, 78 Stat.253) As Amended (effective October 1, 1980). See Appendix A.

Uniform Guidelines on Employee Selection Procedures (1978). See Appendix B.

Day, Virgil B., Frank Erwin, and Alan M. Koral, eds. *A Professional and Legal Analysis of the Uniform Guidelines on Employee Selection Procedures*. Berea, Ohio: American Society for Personnel Administration, 1981.

6

Preparing for the Employment Interview

CHAPTER OBJECTIVES

1. Identify and describe steps in the employment process.
2. Understand components found in a "position specifications" form.
3. Identify sources for finding potential employers.
4. Perform an appraisal of your interests, abilities, and competencies.
5. Understand how to locate organizations that may be prospective employers.
6. Understand roles played in the employment process by search firms and employment agencies.
7. Recognize the importance of the job application.
8. Identify and describe steps in a typical internal organizational job posting system.
9. Recognize information found on a typical résumé.
10. Prepare your own résumé.
11. Prepare a one-page cover letter to accompany your résumé.
12. Understand the role of references and how to use them in the employment process.

Introduction

Employment interviewing is the term often used to identify the entire process of employment hiring from the perspectives of both the employer and the applicant. As an employer, the issue is that you have a job opening. Your solution is to fill it with a candidate who will be successful. Your method is to generate a pool of applicants, screen and select those who are likely to have the necessary qualifications for the job, evaluate each of them according to the requirements of the job, determine who will be offered the job, make the necessary reference checks, persuade the best qualified person to accept your offer without offending those applicants who are rejected, and follow up after the new employee reports to work. The hiring process is designed to attract, at reasonable wages, the most desirable employees who are able to perform the work capably and who have the potential for growth and advancement.

Conversely, as an applicant, the issue is that you are looking for a job. Your solution is to convince a potential employer to offer you a job. Your method is to assess your background; get your name, face, and qualifications in front of those with positions to fill; impress the screening interviewer enough so that you will be invited back for a more in-depth discussion; convince the decision maker(s) that you are the best qualified person available to do the job; notify your references to expect an inquiry about you; and obtain and accept a job offer.

The hiring process includes at least five areas of activity—recruiting, screening, selection, placement, and training and development. (Depending on the organization and the job(s) in question, there may be additional categories.) Recruiting is the first area. In some organizations, recruiting is one of the general duties of the personnel or human resources departments. In other organizations, specific persons may be designated as college recruiters, executive recruiters, technical recruiters, minority recruiters, and so forth. Organizations may use these persons alone, in combination with one another, or in conjunction with professional search firms or employment agencies. No matter what the title of the individual or organizational affiliation, the recruiter's purpose is to develop a pool of potentially qualified candidates. Before beginning the search, the recruiter obtains a written description of the job's duties and necessary candidate characteristics (Figure 6.1). These are discussed with the person or persons who have issued the position requisition to ensure that the recruiter understands the nature of the opening to be filled and the characteristics of the person being sought. Based on the specifications, the recruiter uses a marketing approach to canvass all potential candidates in order to generate the applicant pool.

Among the marketing techniques the recruiter (the employer) uses are (1) the general public media such as the classified advertising sections of daily newspapers or radio or television announcements; (2) specialized public media such as magazines like *Black Enterprise* and *Business World Women* that are directed toward a minority or female readership or the *Wall Street Journal* or the *Chronicle of Higher Education* that are directed toward a specific group or a group with similar interests (businesspeople, academicians); (3) trade journals such as the *Personnel Journal* or *Training,* both of which list openings in the personnel field; (4) professional media such as the *Job Placement Bulletin* of the Academy of Management, the CMP Publications' *Information Systems News,* or the *Placement Bulletin* of the American Compensation Association; (5) executive search firms or commercial employment agencies, some of which specialize in particular types of jobs (engineering only, scientific research only, personnel only, finance and accounting only), many of which list all types of jobs, and all of which require a placement fee to be paid either by the employer or by the applicant if hired; (6) government employment agencies funded by public tax dollars and operated by the appropriate state or local jurisdictions; (7) college or university employment offices that post jobs and also arrange for on-campus screening interviews; and (8) word of mouth. It is not uncommon for an employer to contact a friend or associate and tell him or her, "We are looking for a bright civil engineer with two or three years of experience, a bachelor's degree, and a willingness to relocate to Albuquerque. The salary is in the high twenties. Do you know of anyone

FIGURE 6.1. Position Specifications

Title: Personnel Coordinator.

Reports To: Manager, Division Personnel.

Supervises: One personnel trainee, one nonexempt secretarial support person.

The Company: A $45MM division of a *Fortune* 500 chemical company headquartered in the Southwest. The company has a reputation for profitability and management excellence.

Function: To coordinate nonexempt and low-level exempt compensation and benefits; to maintain high level of professional interaction with the union leadership as well as the rank and file; to assist in developing labor relations strategy.

Major Duties:
1. Suggest and implement revisions to nonexempt salary structure.
2. Continually survey and make recommendations concerning low-level exempt benefit packages.
3. Develop preliminary strike-prevention strategy to be implemented within six months after hiring and eight months before current union contract expires.
4. Maintain all divisional personnel records for all employees at and below Pay Level 8.
5. Supervise a staff of two (one entry-level professional).

Minimum Background Needed:
1. Bachelor's degree in personnel, business administration, or closely related field; master's degree helpful; related experience helpful.
2. Three years experience as either compensation-and-benefits or labor relations professional.
3. Knowledge of personnel generalist activities.

Personal Characteristics:
1. Strong interpersonal skills; ability to express self well orally and in writing.
2. Ability to deal maturely with all levels of divisional and corporate management.
3. Potential to advance to higher-level personnel position within three years — probably to another division or corporate staff.
4. Capability to lead, supervise, and develop others.

Salary: Mid-to-upper twenties; possibly low thirties if exceptionally strong.

---

who might fit that description?" Once the position has been advertised and the candidate search undertaken, the screening process begins.

Just as the employer composes a list of position specifications and determines the best ways in which to generate an applicant pool, the applicant also prepares to enter the job market. In doing so, there are four preliminary steps the applicant needs to take. First, the applicant should make an honest self-appraisal. This is much more difficult to do than it seems, especially if the applicant is either young (a recent or soon-to-be college graduate) or reeling from the shock of termination. (Refer to Chapter 8 for a discussion of career planning.) Essentially, the applicant should answer questions such as: What am I qualified to do in accordance with my formal education, training, and experience? What do I want to do? What additional training do I need to be able to do what I want to do? What are my assets and strengths? What are my liabilities and weaknesses? What do I value? Who would be willing to give me an honest appraisal of my capabilities?

Questions such as these can be answered at two levels. The applicant can respond with socially acceptable, superficial, nonthreatening answers or else undertake some intensive self-examination and introspection and face what may be some unpleasant realities. One way to resolve the issues raised by these questions is to talk them over with relatives, friends, or co-workers; teachers; counselors; or employment agencies. An applicant may find it desirable to take a battery of vocational interest and aptitude tests, followed by appropriate vocational counseling by professionally trained counselors. The costs of tests and counseling vary considerably—ranging from $50–75 at a university counseling center (even here, the expense may be part of the student's general fee payment) to thousands of dollars at some assessment centers. In addition to seeking help from others, the individual can use self-help exercises. Many books are now on the market that offer techniques of self-guidance in vocational and career choice. (See also Exercise 5 at the end of Chapter 8.) Among the self-guidance books are the best sellers from Richard N. Bolles: *What Color Is Your Parachute? Where Do I Go from Here with the Rest of My Life? The Three Boxes of Life.* Additional representative reference material is Barry Gale's and Linda Gale's *Discover What You're Best At*; Lester Schwartz's and Irv Brechner's *The Career Finder*; Beatrice Nivens's *The Black Woman's Career Guide*; and Catalyst's *What to Do with the Rest of Your Life*. (Catalyst is a nonprofit organization dedicated solely to women and their careers.)

Once the applicant has obtained a clearer picture of personal preferences and vocational interests and direction, he or she should look at some of the environmental characteristics of employment. Questions to be asked include: What is my most important criterion in selecting an employer? The organization itself? The industry it is in? The kind of work to be done? The geographic location? The compensation package (salary and benefits)? Something else? In one instance known to us, a senior at a university located in Washington, D.C., assured the prospective employer that job location was not an important consideration for her, that she had no geographic constraint. After a lengthy series of interviews she was offered a position in Baltimore, Maryland, (approximately thirty-five miles from Washington). She declined the offer, giving as her reason that the work place was too distant. Apparently "no geographic constraint" actually meant to her "any location is acceptable as long as it's in the city where I live now." Had she been willing to acknowledge that location was going to be an important determinant in her employment decision, she could have saved the company and herself both time and money. The point here is that people have preferences that they should recognize and consider honestly during the employment process if they want to make "good" decisions. A second point is that no employment decision is irrevocable. If the applicant makes a mistake about an organization, it is possible to change one's mind, just as the organization can change its mind about the applicant.

After completing a self-assessment and ranking employment priorities, the applicant's third step should be to learn about those organizations that appear to fit his or her needs. Excellent sources of information include company publications such as the annual report, the 10-K financial statement, recruiting brochures, product description brochures, and internal newsletters and other house organs. These documents can be obtained by writing to the company itself. Also, brief descriptions of most companies can be found in reference books and magazines, all of which should be available at a university or public library, as well as in most company libraries: the *College Placement Annual,* the Dun & Bradstreet *Reference Book,* Moody's *Manual,* Standard and Poor's *Corporate Records,* and *Fortune* magazine.

Fortune magazine, for example, annually publishes lists of organizations: the largest 500 industrial corporations in the United States (ranked 1 to 500), the second 500 largest industrial corporations in the United States (501 to 1,000), the 500 largest companies outside the United States, the 100 largest commercial banking companies outside the United States, the 50 leading U.S. exporters, and the 50 largest industrial companies in the world. In addition, *Fortune* publishes its so-called *Fortune* 50's lists that include seven sublists of 350 of the largest nonindustrial companies in the United States, including diversified services, commercial banking, life insurance, diversified financial, retailing, transportation, and utilities.

Another excellent, but often overlooked, source of information about a company is word of mouth. The applicant should talk to people who work for the organization. Although anyone may give a biased view (either positive or negative), the composite view should give a fairly accurate impression of what it would be like to work for that organization.

Fourth, the applicant should be aware of and make use of any combination of recruitment methods mentioned at the outset of this chapter. Finally, the time and place of the preliminary screening interview are arranged, and then the screening process begins.

Screening is the second major step in the hiring process. Here the employer begins to differentiate among the persons in the applicant pool, separating out those who exceed the minimum qualifications from those who are clearly unacceptable. The purpose of screening is to find those applicants who seem to meet the general specifications of the position. As the applicant progresses through the screening process, the screening becomes finer and finer—more demanding, more precise, more difficult—making it harder and harder for the applicant to remain a viable job candidate.

Usually the screening process includes a review of the applicant's qualifications and experience as expressed in his or her résumé, on an application form, or as an outcome of an initial telephone contact inquiry about the applicant's interest. Applicants who pass the initial screens usually are offered preliminary face-to-face screening interviews. These interviews will take place at a placement office, at the company location, at the office of the executive search firm, or at another mutually agreed-upon site. For the college student being recruited, this interview usually will be conducted at a college placement office; for the experienced applicant, this interview will usually take place at a neutral location away from the applicant's current place of work.

A well-conducted preliminary screening interview is more than a casual thirty-minute conversation between an applicant and a prospective employer. Rather, it is a critical period when both parties must be at their best, when they must be alert, responsive, and communicative. If this interview is a failure, the applicant will probably not be given a second chance by this particular hiring organization. The interview should be taken seriously, remembering that a positive impression left in this interview will set the applicant apart and above other applicants and increase the chances of an invitation for further interviews. Similarly, the employer must use interviewing skill, knowledge, and insight to judge whether this particular applicant should be invited for a more intensive follow-up interview. The employer is responsible for instilling in the applicant positive feelings about the organization and the interview.

Selection is the third step in the hiring process, the stage in which the employer makes a series of key decisions about the applicants who have been screened: who will be given follow-up interviews, who will receive detailed reference checks, and who seems to be the best qualified person for the job. At the same time, it is the stage in which the applicants make a series of key decisions about the organization: whether they want to work for this organization, whether they like the person who will be their immediate supervisor, whether they like those who will probably be their co-workers, and whether they like the activities that the organization is asking them to perform. More often than not, any employer with a position to fill is looking at many applicants. Likewise, any applicant in the job market is looking at several potential employers. By the time both parties reach the selection stage, there is almost a kind of courtship ritual taking place as each tries to determine whether the other is the ideal partner.

After one or many rounds of in-depth follow-up interviews, an offer of employment will be made to the candidate considered the strongest. (If no strong candidate emerges, the candidate selection process may start over.) The offer may be made by phone, face to face, or in writing. If by phone or face to face, it should be confirmed in writing, as should the candidate's acceptance or rejection of the offer.

Placement is the fourth step in the hiring process. In the past few years, hiring organizations have been paying more attention to candidates after they have reported for work, and there is now research indicating the importance of giving appropriate information, guidance, supervision, and orientation to ensure the employee's contribution to the organization and the organization's contribution to the employee. Clarification of the employee's role and duties and initial accomplishments should be made early in the employee's tenure. The relationship with co-workers and, most importantly, a supportive attitude by the immediate supervisor are essential to the successful placement of the new employee. A new employee's introduction to the organization should be divided into the induction and the orientation. The *induction* is the period during which the supervisor informs the new worker about work hours, general rules and policies, work location (the office, the place on the manufacturing floor), and other routine items; and the employee is introduced to his or her co-workers. The induction is thus relatively brief, usually taking less than an hour and normally occurring on the new employee's first working day. The *orientation* is more comprehensive and includes induction. The new employee may travel to other company facilities, have lengthy informational interviews and meetings with key people, be introduced to the service and/or product line(s), learn how the company is organized, and become acquainted with other long-range issues. The orientation may last from a few days to many months.

Training and development represents the fifth step in the hiring process and is the step that is most frequently overlooked. Typically, organizations think of training and development as applying to experienced employees rather than to new employees (exclusive of some sort of orientation training). But the fact is that both need appropriate training and development opportunities, ranging from university-sponsored executive development courses to special in-house education experiences to daily discussions with the immediate supervisor on work progress.

Retention is sometimes considered as part of the hiring process. Presumably, once you are employed by an organization, you will want to stay with it and advance upward through it. Although tenure with an organization and promotion potential are important, we do not include retention as part of the employment-hiring or employment-interviewing processes. Rather, we view it as more closely related to the work performance appraisal and career-planning processes discussed in Chapter 8.

In the remainder of this chapter, although we shall refer to the entire employment-hiring process, we shall mainly consider the preliminary screening and selection functions, particularly information gathering and giving, persuasion by both parties, and mutual assessment.

Search Firms and Employment Agencies

As either an employer or an applicant, you may choose to use the services of a search firm or an employment agency. Employers contract with search firms to source (find) and present qualified candidates. The search firms' services are paid for by the employer, not by the candidate. Usually, the fee paid is a percentage (e.g., 30 percent) of the successful candidate's first year's salary. As such, search firms usually represent the employer and not the individual candidate (even though they will maintain an active candidate list). Many search firms recruit in all employment areas, but some specialize and recruit in a particular functional area (e.g., engineering), a particular industry (e.g., retailing, construction, hospital administration, high technology), or at a particular level (e.g., executive). Search firms usually source for relatively high paying positions.

Employment agencies may contract with either the employer or the candidate. In either case, as with search firms, the fee paid usually represents an agreed-upon percentage of the first year's salary (although some employment agencies charge a flat rate for their services). When using an employment agency, it is a good idea to determine at the outset who will pay what. In comparison with search firms, employment agencies usually source for relatively lower paying positions.

The Job Application Form

The job application form is used in two ways by the employer. First, it is used to give the employer a sense of the applicant's personality and his or her background and qualifications. Second, the application is used as an enabling and verification document, authorizing the employer to inquire into the applicant's background, to make reference checks, and to verify that the applicant knows that a physical examination and proof of age or citizenship will be required after a job offer is extended but before employment is secured.

In its background and qualification function, the applicant should try to obtain the organization's job application form as far in advance of the preliminary screening interview as possible. For some jobs, such as those that are nonexempt or hourly, the employer may require a completed application as the initial step in preliminary screening. For other jobs, especially those that are salaried exempt, the application form may not be requested until very late (if ever) in the selection stage of the hiring process.

The applicant should first read through the application form without putting any marks on it and then type in, if possible, the information requested; otherwise, use ink, not pencil. Even though decisions to hire should not be made solely on the basis of the application form, a neatly completed form may set it apart from others and enhance the applicant's chances of moving ahead in the screening stage. Conversely, an applicant may sometimes be eliminated from consideration if the application form is sloppy or incomplete.

All parts of the application form should be completed. For example, if the applicant is asked for his or her current address, the information given should include street address, apartment number, rural route, post office box, the designation "street" ("avenue," "boulevard," or whatever is appropriate), city, state, and zip code. But note that, for example, listing only "Manhattan" is insufficient, as the applicant could live in either Kansas or New York City. Similarly, the city of "Athens" can be found in Alabama, Arkansas, Georgia, Greece, Illinois, Kentucky, Maine, Michigan, Ohio, Tennessee, Texas, and elsewhere. Telephone numbers should include area codes, especially if the applicant is from an area outside that of the hiring organization or is from a state, province, or country having more than one area code. As a rule, abbreviations should be avoided, but if used, they should be generally accepted abbreviations. For example, "Kentucky" is abbreviated as KY or Ky., not as Kent. The post office has a list of standard abbreviations for street names and states. If an item on the application form does not apply, the applicant should insert "not applicable" (or the standard abbreviation "NA"). The word "none" can be used if appropriate. Remember that neatness, thoroughness, clarity, and common sense should dictate how the job application form is completed, and no space should be left empty, as a blank may be interpreted as an oversight. Figure 6.2 shows an employment ap-

FIGURE 6.2. Employment Application Form[1]

Personal Data

Name: _____
　　　　　(Last)　　　　　　　　　　　(First)　　　　　　　　　　　(Middle)

Current Address: _____
　　　　　　　　　(Street)　　　　　　　　　　(City)　　　　(State)　　(Zip Code)

Previous Address: _____
　　　　　　　　　(Street)　　　　　　　　　　(City)　　　　(State)　　(Zip Code)

Current Telephone: _____ Social Security Number: _____

On what date will you be available for employment? _____

Are you a United States citizen or a registered alien? _____

Are you currently on leave of absence or layoff from another company? _____

Have you ever applied for employment with this company? _____

　If yes: _____
　　　　　(when)　　　　　　　　　　　　　(location)

Have you ever been convicted of a felony? _____

　If yes, explain: _____
　_____
　_____
　_____
　_____
　_____

Education

　Elementary School (circle highest grade completed):　1　2　3　4　5　6　7　8

　High School: _____
　　　　　　　　(name and location)

　Circle highest grade completed:　　　　　　　　　　　　　9　10　11　12

　Did you graduate? _____

College/Location	Date From	Date To	Date Graduated	Date Degree Received/Expected	Type of Degree	Major/Minor

FIGURE 6.2. Employment Application Form (continued)

Employment Data

Company Name and Address	Date From	Date To	Full-time/ Part-time	Salary	Name of Supervisor	Type of Work	Reason for Leaving

References

List three responsible persons who have a knowledge of your past work experiences. (Do not include relatives or former employers.)

Name: _____ Address: _____

Phone: _____ Occupation: _____

Name: _____ Address: _____

Phone: _____ Occupation: _____

Name: _____ Address: _____

Phone: _____ Occupation: _____

Work Preferences:

What type of employment are you seeking? ☐ Full-time ☐ Part-time ☐ Summer

For what position are you applying? _____

Are you willing to travel? _____ What percentage of time? _____

What is your minimum salary requirement? _____ Will you relocate? _____

Will you work shifts? _____

This company will not discriminate against any applicant for employment or any employee because of age (as defined by applicable law), religion, sex, race, color, national origin, or because such person is handicapped, a disabled veteran or a Vietnam era veteran. Answers to the questions above will be used for applicable, job-related reasons only.

This application form will remain active for 90 days. If you are hired by the company within that time, it will be transferred to your personnel file. If you are not hired by the company within 90 days, this application will be considered inactive and you will have to reapply if you want to be considered for employment by the company. All information you provide on this form is subject to verification. Any falsification or misrepresentation of information requested here will be cause for rejection of this application or for subsequent discipline up to and including dismissal from employment. The company may require that you submit to a prehiring physical examination in order for your physical ability to perform on the job to be determined.

FIGURE 6.2. Employment Application Form (continued)

I understand that if my application for employment is accepted, the effective date of my employment shall be the time I actually begin to work. If I am employed, I agree to be bound by and comply with the safety and patent rules of the company, as well as by any other applicable rules and regulations of the company. I understand further that if I am employed, my employment will be subject to the conditions of any applicable probationary period established by labor agreement or company policy.

Signature: _____ Date: _____

---

plication form typical of those used by major companies. Appendix C shows the application form used by the federal government: Standard Form 171, Personal Qualifications Statement.

Job-Posting Systems

Some companies have "promote from within" policies, and in order to implement such policies, they have what are called "job-posting" systems. The following comments apply generally to job-posting systems.

Policy. The company encourages internal promotions so as to encourage individual career development. The posting systems ensure the fair and equitable treatment of all employees by providing information regarding advancement opportunity.

Policy administration. The senior line officer or senior staff officer is responsible for administration.

Employee eligibility. All full-time exempt and nonexempt salaried employees with a minimum of twelve months tenure in their present positions are eligible to participate in job posting. Eligibility exceptions will be considered on a case-by-case basis in consultation with the employee, the employee's current supervisor, and the personnel department.

Procedure. When an internal job vacancy occurs, the appropriate department manager will complete a "job-opening" requisition that includes a brief summary of the position, its requirements, its reporting relationship, and its salary range. The completed requisition will be forwarded to the personnel department for processing. The requisition will be posted on bulletin boards for five working days.

Current employees who are interested in a position and who have met eligibility requirements should complete an internal job application form and submit it to the personnel department for screening (see Figure 6.3).

Employees not selected for interviews will be so notified and informed why they were not given further consideration. When appropriate, individual career counseling will be offered. Employees selected for interviews should contact the

94   INTERVIEWING

FIGURE 6.3.   Internal Job Application Form[2]

Applicant for position titled: _____

Name: _____ Application Date: _____

Current Position Title: _____ Current Salary: _____

Current Department: _____ Telephone Extension: _____

Current Supervisor's Name: _____ Time on Current Job: _____

Why are you qualified for this position (be specific)? _____

_____

_____

_____

_____

_____

_____

I have discussed this position with my current supervisor: ☐ Yes   ☐ No

If no, I understand I must do so before interviewing: ☐ Yes   ☐ No

---

To be completed by the Personnel Department

Hiring Manager: _____

Candidate selected/not selected (reason): _____

_____

_____

_____

Screening Date: _____   Interview Date: _____

Person Screening: _____   Person Interviewing: _____

---

personnel department for further details and inform their supervisors before the interview that they are being considered for another position. The hiring manager will interview and evaluate each candidate selected for an interview. The hiring manager will contact each unsuccessful candidate to explain why he or she was unsuccessful and then will notify the successful candidate. The current manager will release employees for new positions within three weeks after selection and acceptance.

The Résumé

There are many points of view regarding the résumé, its use, content, and appearance. Generally, the differences pertain to how much data it should contain and how the information should be displayed. Basically, the résumé should highlight the applicant's background and suitability for employment. It should be brief and succinct, yet thorough in providing a capsule summary (as opposed to a detailed autobiography). If possible, the résumé should be no longer than two pages (prospective employers simply do not want to read more) and should contain the following information (note that not all of the information applies to each person):

1. The individual's formal name.
2. Address and telephone number (the applicant may want to include a permanent contact address as well as a temporary address and the dates of when it applies).
3. A brief statement (twenty-five to thirty words) of job and professional goals.
4. High school name, location, type of degree, date of degree.
5. Colleges or universities, locations, degrees, dates of degrees, major and minor areas of concentration.
6. Professional certifications or courses completed.
7. Work experience (a chronology of most recent to least recent, including names of employers, job titles, addresses of each organization, dates of employment).
8. A statement that additional information is available on request.

This information is considered minimal for most résumés. Although it is not always necessary to include more, many résumés do contain additional information about the applicant, including some that is probably unlawful for the prospective employer to ask about but that the applicant is free to divulge:

9. Date and place of birth.
10. Height and weight.
11. Health status.
12. Marital status.
13. Professional memberships (including offices held).
14. Names of two or three work-related references who can attest to the applicant's work effectiveness (include full name, title, address, and phone number).
15. Names of two or three personal references who can attest to the applicant's character (include full name, title, address, and phone number).

Note that with regard to items 14 and 15, the applicant should contact each reference and ask whether the reference will be a positive one. Avoid listing names of references on a résumé or in a cover letter without first having obtained the individuals' permission. This will help improve the quality of references and reduce the likelihood of persons' being contacted without your knowledge. Avoid asking parents or other relatives for references.

There is the possibility that the applicant may be discriminated against on the basis of information included in the résumé, although most (not all) prospective employers will act in good faith and in a nondiscriminatory manner when reviewing data pertaining to the applicant. Nevertheless, providing certain dates and age, height, weight, marital status, and possibly other items as well, may mean that you will be discriminated against before you have the opportunity to be evaluated in accordance with your qualifications for a position.

Depending on the applicant's background and the general nature of the job (the type of organization, the industry), the applicant may include other kinds of information on the résumé. Moreover, the applicant may prepare two or three different résumés, each containing essentially the same information but highlighting it differently. A new college graduate might include, for example:

16. Grade point average and class standing.
17. Collegiate memberships (including offices held).
18. Academic honors and awards received (including sponsorship of the award and date presented).
19. Part-time summer employment.
20. Extracurricular activities (including offices held in campus organizations).
21. Internship experiences.
22. A list of courses taken in the major and/or minor areas of concentration.

An experienced person out of school for ten years might omit items 14 through 21 but instead might give more details about:

23. Work accomplishments.

A person interested in a job in government service might list:

24. Community service activities.
25. Work as a political campaign staff member.

A person applying for a job as a college or university faculty member might list:

26. Publications (articles, books, reprints).
27. Papers presented at conventions or conferences.
28. University service activities (committees, sponsor activities).

The list of possible items on a résumé is infinite. The important point is that the résumé should contain all pertinent information to cast the applicant in the most positive light.

One further word about the résumé: occasionally the recommendation is made that a résumé be professionally printed, that it be on pastel or off-white paper, that it be of unusual size (for example, on 8 x 10 instead of 8½ x 11 paper), or that it have a nonstandard typeface, such as italics). In most cases, as long as the résumé is neat and readable, it does not matter if it is typeset, originally typed, or photocopied. In fact, many employers view colored paper, oddly sized paper, or italics as "gimicky," and rather than helping the applicant, these gimmicks often serve as a hindrance.

Figures 6.4, 6.5, 6.6, and 6.7 show four different types of résumés: the chronological, the functional or results-oriented, the directed, and the letter.[3] Each

FIGURE 6.4. The Chronological Résumé

Personal:
Tyrone M. Scott, Jr.
2509 Silverwood Trail
Louisville, Kentucky 40228
Home Phone: (502) 716-2633

Born: March 24, 1953
Health: Excellent
Marital Status: Married
Office Phone: (502) 774-6937

Educational:
University of Kentucky, Lexington, Kentucky, BS, Marketing, 1974
University of Louisville, Louisville, Kentucky, 21 hours toward MBA
Harvard University, Cambridge, Massachusetts, 3-week course in strategic planning

Objective:
A responsible position in the marketing organization of a $25MM to $50MM company or division, with the possibility of moving to a functional vice-presidency.

Location:
No restrictions but would prefer eastern or southeastern United States.

Work Experience:

1982 to Present: Marketing Systems, Inc., Louisville, Kentucky
August 1983–present, Marketing Director. Responsible for supervising corporate marketing function, including market research, product planning, advertising and sales promotion, inside and outside sales, product and customer service, and marketing planning. Report to Vice-President, Marketing. Supervise 20 technically trained professionals and 5 support staff. The business has grown 25 percent during this period (from $10MM to $12.5MM) while maintaining an operating budget of $1MM. Developed cutting-edge system for market penetration analysis that accounted for 28 percent of new sales.

FIGURE 6.4. The Chronological Résumé (continued)

April 1982–August 1983, Sales Manager, Mid-South Region, Nashville, Tennessee. Responsible for sales of technical marketing systems. Recruited, trained, and supervised sales personnel in 7-state region. Doubled sales in 16 months.

1979–1982: Diversified Marketing Company, Nashville, Tennessee
February 1979–April 1982, Sales Manager. Responsible for developing sales incentive programs for clients and for penetrating new client organizations. Also established new sales territories and developed new sales organization.

1974–1979: Weaver and Webb, Covington, Kentucky
June 1974–February 1979. Held various positions, including Sales Trainee, Sales Representative, and Sales Manager. Eventually responsible for sales force of 16. Developed Northern Kentucky and Southwest Ohio sales territories.

Organizational Memberships:
   Society of Marketing Analysts (Member, Budget and Finance Committee); Toastmaster's International (Chairman, Membership Committee); Mayor's Council on Economic Development, Louisville, Kentucky.

Publications:
   "Forecasting Market Penetration," *Journal of Technological Forecasting,* June 1983.
   "Client Consultation Skills," *Journal of the American Management Association,* September 1978.

Additional Information: Available on Request.

FIGURE 6.5. The Functional or Results-Oriented Résumé

Tyrone M. Scott, Jr. 　　　　　　　　　　Home Phone: (502) 716-2633
2509 Silverwood Trail 　　　　　　　　　Office Phone: (502) 774-6937
Louisville, Kentucky 40228

Marketing Director

Summary: Corporate Marketing Director experienced in all facets of sales and marketing organizations, including research, product planning, advertising, sales promotion, product and customer service, and planning. Have supervised sales, marketing, and technical personnel. Thirty-one years old, married, with two children.

Experience and Accomplishments

Marketing: Responsible for $12.5MM corporate marketing function supervising staff of 20 technical professionals and 5 support staff. Developed cutting-edge system for market penetration analysis. Developed new sales organizations. Developed new sales territories.

Management: Recruited, selected, and trained sales and marketing personnel in corporate and regional offices. While maintaining fixed operating budget of $1MM, increased sales 25 percent from $10MM to $12.5MM.

Leadership: Selected for "fast track" program by current employer. Selected to attend strategic planning course at Harvard. Member of corporate Job Evaluation Committee.

Education

BS, Marketing, University of Kentucky, Lexington, Kentucky, 1974.
MBA, University of Louisville, Louisville, Kentucky, 21 hours completed, degree expected within one year.
Strategic Planning, 3-week course, Harvard University, Cambridge, Massachusetts, 1983.

Company Affiliations

Marketing Systems, Inc., Louisville, Kentucky, 1982–present.
Diversified Marketing Company, Nashville, Tennessee, 1979–1982.
Weaver and Webb, Covington, Kentucky, 1974–1979.

Organizational Memberships

Society of Marketing Analysts (Member, Budget and Finance Committee).
Toastmaster's International (Chairman, Membership Committee).
Mayor's Council on Economic Development, Louisville, Kentucky.

Publications

"Forecasting and Market Penetration," *Journal of Technological Forecasting,* June 1983.
"Client Consultation Skills," *Journal of the American Management Association,* September 1978.

Personal Data

Born March 24, 1953, in Shelbyville, Kentucky; 5'11", 180 lbs, in excellent health.

References available on request.

FIGURE 6.6. The Directed Résumé

Tyrone M. Scott, Jr.
2509 Silverwood Trail
Louisville, Kentucky 40228

Home Phone: (502) 716-2633
Office Phone: (502) 774-6937

Objective: Vice-President, Marketing

Currently, Director of Marketing with experience since 1974 in sales and sales and marketing management. Have background in marketing research, product planning, advertising, sales promotion, product and customer service, and planning. Experienced in personnel function as it relates to marketing.

Marketing Director: With Marketing Systems, Inc., Louisville, Kentucky, 1982 to present.

Responsible for entire marketing function, including all activities identified above.

Supervise 20 technically trained professionals, 5 support staff. Increased sales from $10MM to $12.5MM since taking this assignment, while holding operating budget at $1MM. Developed cutting-edge system for market penetration analysis that accounted for 28 percent of new sales.

Regional Sales Manager: Also with Marketing Systems, Inc. Recruited, trained, and supervised sales personnel in 7-state region. Doubled sales in 16 months.

Sales Manager: With Diversified Marketing Company, Nashville, Tennessee, 1979–1982. Responsible for developing sales incentive programs for clients and for penetrating new client organizations. Also established new sales territories and developed new sales organization.

Sales Supervisor: With Weaver and Webb, Covington, Kentucky, 1974–1979. Held various positions, including Sales Trainee, Sales Representative, and Sales Manager. Eventually responsible for sales force of 16. Developed Northern Kentucky and Southwest Ohio sales territories.

Education:

BS, Marketing, University of Kentucky, Lexington, Kentucky, 1974. Completed 21 hours toward MBA at University of Louisville, Louisville, Kentucky. Completed 3-week course on strategic planning, Harvard University, Cambridge, Massachusetts, 1983.

Professional Memberships/Affiliations:

Society of Marketing Analysts (Member, Budget and Finance Committee).
Toastmaster's International (Chairman, Membership Committee).
Mayor's Council on Economic Development, Louisville, Kentucky.

Publications

"Forecasting and Market Penetration," *Journal of Technological Forecasting,* June 1983. "Client Consultation Skills," *Journal of the American Management Association,* September 1978.

References furnished on request.

FIGURE 6.7. The Letter Résumé

2509 Silverwood Trail
Louisville, Kentucky 40228

December ___, 19__

Ms. Kathleen M. McDonough
Vice President, Human Resources
Michaelson Corporation
Michaelson Plaza
Washington, D.C. 20202

Dear Ms. McDonough:

Barbara Ross suggested that I contact you concerning my desire to make a career change. As Director of Marketing for Marketing Systems, Inc., I believe my skills, knowledge, and abilities would allow me to make a significant contribution to Michaelson. My accomplishments include

- Increasing sales 25 percent in twelve months while maintaining a stable operating budget.
- Doubling sales during the preceding twelve months.
- Developing a cutting-edge system for market penetration analysis.
- Establishing a new sales organization.
- Developing new sales territories.
- Supervising steadily increasing numbers of technically trained marketing personnel.
- Recruitment, selection, and training of sales and marketing personnel.

My education includes a BS in Marketing from the University of Kentucky, completion of strategic planning course at Harvard University, and 21 hours of course work toward an MBA at the University of Louisville.

I am active in professional and community organizations, married with two children, and in excellent health.

I am confident that I can be a valuable addition to your marketing organization and would appreciate the opportunity to meet with you. I will take the opportunity to call your secretary in two weeks to arrange a convenient time.

Sincerely,

Tyrone M. Scott, Jr.

assumes that the applicant has had some work experience. Figures 6.8 and 6.9 illustrate the kinds of information that may be on the résumé of a recent (or soon-to-be) college graduate.

Cover Letters

Once you have prepared your résumé, you will have to get it to the person(s) who will want to interview you (and, ideally, who will hire you). Assuming that you are not standing face to face with the interviewer, the best way to present your résumé is with a cover letter, a letter that accompanies your résumé and, in effect, introduces it (and you) to the prospective employer.

In this section, we shall present examples of information found in cover letters. Good cover letters have the following characteristics, each of which should be tailored to your specific needs and situation and to the prospective employer's specific needs and situation. One company we know of estimates that it annually receives more than twelve thousand unsolicited employment inquiries (cover letters and résumés). If you are to have any chance against that much competition, the quality of your letter must stand out from the pack. Basically, a good cover letter has these characteristics:

1. It is short—less than one page.
2. It highlights information on the résumé (highlights, not summarizes) but does not repeat that information in detail.
3. It indicates why you are "special."
4. It refers to the specific company and, if known, the specific job.
5. It expresses your level of interest.
6. It indicates the nature of the follow-up.

The cover letter should be typed on standard-sized paper in a standard-sized and standard-appearing typeface (avoid italics and boldface type) and should follow a businesslike format (e.g., placement of inside addresses, margins, salutation, and closing). Pay attention to sentence structure and paragraphing. If any of these items is incorrect, you will probably eliminate yourself from further consideration. In addition, avoid sending your résumé in fancy packages (e.g., a folder with your cover letter and résumé inside), as they tend to frustrate the person who opens the mail for the person who will read your material.

Despite these cautions, however, there are times when deviating from standard may help you. We know of a woman who hand printed her résumé and cover letter and was subsequently hired by a drafting firm that was interested in someone with lettering skills. We know of another person who was interested in a computer-oriented position and whose cover letter was printed by a computer on watermelon (light green and white computer printout) paper. He got the job. But for every success like these, there are countless failures, and so remember that usually these gimmicks will wind up in the trash.

Representative Excerpts from Cover Letters

The following are real, representative excerpts from cover letters. Only the information that identifies the sender or the recipient has been eliminated. These examples are provided to give you ideas of what to say and what not to say in

FIGURE 6.8. Recent College Graduate Résumé

Résumé: Gary W. Green

Address: 4092 Waving Willow Drive
Cochise, Iowa 52160
Phone: (712) 555-4352

Citizenship: United States
Health: Excellent
Date of Birth: November 7, 1962

Objective: Desire an entry-level position specializing in the design and application of digital electronics and microprocessors. Position should lead to general management or technical management responsibilities.

Education: BS, Iowa State University, Ames, Iowa, June 1983. Major: Electrical Engineering (emphasis on digital electronics, microprocessor design, network analysis). Minor: Computer Programming (emphasis FORTRAN, COBOL, BASIC, Pascal). 3.8 of 4.0 grade point average.

East Cochise High School, Cochise, Iowa, June 1979. College Preparatory Degree. Graduated third in class of 277.

Work Experience:
Summers 1982 and 1981: Engineering Designs, Inc., Oak Brook, Illinois. Employed as co-op intern. Assigned to 16K silicon chip project. Worked closely with project engineers, preparing detailed parts layouts from their sketches during first year. Second-year project was to apply the newly developed chip to robot control arm application.

Summer 1980: Reliance Printing Company, West Cochise, Iowa. Employed as Mark-up Assistant. Devised method for automatic computer loading of customers' texts from either disc or magnetic tape. This system was IBM, Wang, Four-Phase compatible.

Summers 1979 and 1978: Parks Department, Cochise, Iowa. Employed as Recreation Instructor. Duties included management of 1 summer recreation center and supervision of 2 staff members and approximately 75 children ages 5 to 15. Responsible for all recreation activity at the center during the 8-week summer session.

University Honors: Hewlett-Packard Engineering Scholarship; Phi Beta Kappa; Outstanding Senior Engineering Paper presented by College of Engineering; Dean's List (Four Years); Outstanding Debater, Best Humorous Speaker, Iowa State Forensics Society (awarded in junior and senior years); Most Improved Wrestler, Iowa State Wrestling Team Award (senior year).

High School Honors: National Merit Scholar; Iowa Board of Regents Scholar; National Honor Society; Quill and Scroll Writing Honor Society; National Forensics League (President); Commencement Speaker; Student Government Vice-President; Fellowship of Christian Athletes (Secretary); Football, Wrestling (Conference Champion, State Runner-up), Baseball teams.

Memberships: American Society for Engineering Education; Institute of Electrical and Electronics Engineers.

References and Additional Information: Available on request.

FIGURE 6.9. Soon-to-Be College Graduate Résumé

Résumé: Barbara E. Redd

Home Address and Phone
8646 11th Avenue
Las Vegas, Nevada 89763
(702) 555-5972

School Address and Phone (until 5/27/84)
Box 5500, University Station
Salt Lake City, Utah 84407
(801) 555-3116

Objective: I am seeking a summer position in a major company (either corporate staff or division) that will allow me to work with participative management and employee involvement programs.

Education: BA, Organizational Communication, University of Utah, Salt Lake City, Utah, expected June 1985. (Course emphasis through junior year has included organizational behavior, leadership, management, small-group process, speaking and listening skills, survey research methods, interviewing, finance, and accounting.)

Las Vegas High School, Las Vegas, Nevada. College Preparatory Degree. Completed four years of English, math, science, and French; three years of social science (psychology and sociology), Spanish, and Latin. Also took elective courses in journalism, automobile mechanics, computer science, public speaking, and woodworking.

Work Experience:
Summer 1982: Department of Communication, University of Utah. Worked on special project to install quality circles in 3 small businesses in the Salt Lake City area. As part of steering committee, helped train facilitators and circle-group members in theories underlying circles and in participative techniques and skills.

Summer 1981: Katana's Clothing Store, Las Vegas, Nevada. Worked as salesperson and cashier. Waited on customers, handled customer complaints, maintained inventory in my area, opened and closed the store, arranged clothing displays.

Summer 1980 and part-time in high school: Redd's Service Station. Worked in family gas station, pumping gas, doing minor automobile maintenance (e.g., oil changes for customers), handling customer inquiries, preparing and handling correspondence to national product supplier.

References:
Dr. Wilson Teacher, Professor of Communication, University of Utah, Salt Lake City, Utah 84112.

Mr. Sam Katana, Owner, Katana's Clothing Store, 4002 West Casino Street, Las Vegas, Nevada 89765.

Rev. James Pfeiffer, Pastor, Las Vegas Lutheran Church, 26th Avenue at Main, Las Vegas, Nevada 89763.

Dr. Janice Strock, Professor of Management, University of Utah, Salt Lake City, Utah 84112.

Additional Information Available on Request.

PREPARING FOR THE EMPLOYMENT INTERVIEW   105

your cover letter. We have made a brief editorial comment in the brackets at the end of each excerpt.

Example 1
". . . Corporation is a successful company with a fine reputation. Based on information I have received from several sources, I am contacting you regarding entry level management, supervisory, production or related operations management positions within your firm." [Weak, opening sentence unnecessary. Second sentence vague, too broad and indecisive.]

Example 2
"This letter is accompanied by a copy of my résumé for employment with your company. I will graduate from the University of _____ with a degree in _____ in June _____ [Opening sentence weak. Why is the letter being sent? Need to state company name. Second sentence good, as it begins to highlight résumé.]

Example 3
"Having studied marketing concepts for four years and having applied these concepts to various leadership positions, I could be the difference between a good sales representative and a great one for the _____ Corporation." [Sounds like bull: too pompous. Good that the sender mentioned the corporation's name.]

Example 4
"As a senior at _____ University majoring in _____, I am looking forward to a career in the field of systems analysis. I am writting [sic] to express my interest in an entry level position with the _____ Corporation." [Good: person begins to highlight résumé, states objective, mentions company. Bad: misspells a word. Correctly or not, the company will assume that this person has poor language skills and pays little attention to detail.]

Example 5
"Enclosed is a copy of my personal résumé that you requested during our recent telephone conversation.
I appreciated the opportunity to talk with you regarding possible career opportunities with _____ Corporation." [Good: referral to previous personal contact and what it was. Second sentence reminds recipient about telephone discussion.]

Example 6
"A friend of mine, [name], of [organization], recently mentioned that you were adding staff in the organizational development and training area. He spoke so highly about your company and the caliber of people working there that I am writing to pursue the matter further. Enclosed is a copy of my résumé for your consideration. I would welcome the opportunity to discuss with you my qualifications and to explore ways in which I can contribute to _____ Company." [Writer is given credibility by referring to a mutually known individual. Writer suggests follow-up. Company is mentioned.]

Example 7
"Thank you for taking the opportunity to review this résumé of my credentials and experience. I am submitting this paperwork in an effort to secure a career-directed professional position functioning in an account development capacity in affiliation with a company providing for visible contribution." [Thanking the recipient is appropriate. The rest of this is jargon and gibberish and is overwritten.]

Example 8
"I am a master's candidate in _____ at _____ University. I will receive my degree in December 19 _, and I am interested in applying for permanent employment with _____ Corporation upon graduation." [Good: gets to the point.]

Example 9
"I have owned and programmed microcomputers for over three years and have significant exposure to both the Z-80 and 6502 based CPUs. Owning an Apple II microcomputer and modem has enabled me to dial into _____ University's Mainframe (Amdahl 470/V: IBM 370 compatible: operating in the CMS environment)." [Applicant is expanding information in the résumé and illustrating interests. But unless the recipient of the letter knows computers, this may be over his or her head.]

Example 10
"Specifically, I am seeking a position as a sales trainee in the _____ Division, but I am open to other opportunities. . . . if you remember, I came to talk with you in November 19__ while I was on a retail internship program with _____ Department Store. At your suggestion, I took a class in professional selling. It involved spending time in the field with a marketing representative. In addition, I developed an actual sales presentation. Overall, I gained invaluable insight and experience in sales. . . ." [Applicant is direct in identifying what position is being sought but shows flexibility. Recipient is reminded of previous meeting and told that advice was followed. Recipient may feel a psychological obligation to follow up.]

Example 11
"As my résumé shows, I am a highly motivated individual who achieves his goals. I believe the communication and analytical skills I learned in school, combined with the leadership and sales abilities I developed while running my own business, prepare me to make a positive contribution to _____ Corporation." [A little pat on the back is okay.]

Example 12
"I understand _____ Company will be recruiting through the _____ University Placement Office in October. I would appreciate an invitation to interview with you or the appropriate representative of your environmental management department at that time. If that is not possible, I would like to schedule an interview at your convenience. I can be reached at [phone number] or at the above address. If there is any additional information you would like, please ask. I look forward to hearing from you." [Good: applicant is using a placement office lead to arrange an interview; area of interest is indicated; alternate methods of contact are given; flexibility is shown.]

Example 13
". . . I returned to school to finish my degree. I would like to call special attention to my grade point averages since returning to school. Including summer school, my averages have been: 4.0, 3.3, 3.5, 2.0, 3.0, 2.8, 4.0, 3.0. My overall grade point average is 2.5 due to problems from my first enrollment in which I now feel I've been able to overcome." [For this person, grade point average is a topic best left undiscussed in the cover letter. Last sentence is not grammatically correct.]

Example 14
"I am very enthusiastic about the possibility of further discussing my qualifications with you. I will be contacting you on Wednesday, February 9, to see if an interview may be set up in [city] at a mutually convenient time. Thank you for your time and consideration." [Good: motivation comes through; follow up noted; courtesy is observed. But applicant should be prepared to have the request for an interview rejected—a company will not set up twelve thousand interviews with unsolicited applicants.]

Example 15
"Enclosed is my résumé which I would greatly appreciate your reviewing in consideration of my employment with your fine company. Having just completed my college education this past December, I am naturally willing to be trained in any program for any position which you feel would be appropriate with my academic background." [First sentence is ingratiating; second is presumptuous and nonspecific.]

Example 16
"This letter is written in response to your recent advertisement in [paper] announcing the opening, [position title]. I am most interested in being considered for this position." [Indicates how applicant became aware of the job; the specific job; interest in the job.]

Example 17
". . . I am dedicated to hard work and consider myself a leader with the ability to motivate others. I enjoy taking responsibility for completing jobs efficiently. . . . I have proven myself in the past by being promoted in every job that I have held. You may also be interested to know that I have financed my education entirely on my own." [Suggests industriousness, responsibility, successful employment track record.]

Example 18
". . . I believe my greatest asset to your sales force would be my communication skills. The various activities I pursued and participated in at _____ University represent my ability to communicate effectively with a wide spectrum of people. Furthermore, each activity required its own element of developing, planning, and organizing. And a great deal of creativity was required to tailor each communication attempt, much as one would for each different account." [Applicant highlights one particular strength that, as it happens, is important to the functional area of prospective employment.]

Recommendations, References, and Background Checks

At some point during the hiring process, usually in the selection stage before you are tendered an offer, the employer will ask you to provide names of persons who can be contacted as references. In preparing for this eventuality, you already should have spoken to those who will serve as references, alerting them that they are being listed as references, reviewing your background with them, highlighting areas to cover, and asking them directly if they will give you a favorable recommendation. If the person says yes, fine; if the person says no, extend your thanks and withdraw your request. Normally, an applicant should not ask for a reference or letter of recommendation from a relative. Another reason for alerting your references is that many people simply do not remember the particulars of a given individual. Early contact helps your references gather their thoughts about you and helps you control what they will say.

In checking references, the prospective employer may make telephone inquiries or request the information in writing. In either case, the kinds of information the prospective employer will want include:

1. Verification of previous employment (or dates of school attendance, academic transcript).
2. Context in which the applicant is known.
3. Positions held with previous employer.

4. Reasons for leaving previous job(s).
5. Overall assessment of quality of work performed.
6. Overall assessment of quantity of work performed.
7. Applicant's competencies.
8. Personal characteristics like initiative, dependability, leadership, and honesty.
9. Ability to get along with work group—supervisor, peers, subordinates, faculty, other students.
10. Major strengths.
11. Major weaknesses.
12. Any reasons why this applicant should not be hired.
13. Communication skills—speaking, writing, grammar, vocabulary, listening, comprehension, recall, demeanor, mannerisms.
14. Potential for advancement.
15. Almost anything else you can think of.

The basic purpose of the reference check is to verify information contained in the applicant's résumé (or on the application blank) or obtained during the various interviews. The reference can verify hard data (e.g., dates of employment) or soft data (e.g., the prospective employer's "impression" that the applicant will take initiative and follow through on a project to its completion).

Some employers pay less attention to what is not said in the recommendation than to what is said. For example, if a recent college graduate uses a former professor as a reference and in the recommendation the professor fails to mention the student's academic ability, that failure will create in the prospective employer's mind questions about the student's ability or willingness to learn, intelligence, and general academic preparation. Similarly, if an experienced applicant uses a former employer as a reference and in the recommendation the former employer fails to mention the applicant's ability to get along with people in the work setting, that failure will create questions about the applicant's work habits, teamwork, abrasiveness, or other possibly disruptive characteristics. A rule of thumb to remember is that the reference should smooth the way, not hinder the way, to employment.

One additional caution should be noted by the employer when making reference checks. Even if an applicant has given written authorization to a previous employing organization to disclose personal information, the previous employer may not be able to do so as a matter of policy. Because of the current interest in privacy legislation, many organizations refuse to divulge information other than verification that the applicant was employed and the dates of employment. Disclosure of other information about the applicant, even that which is positive—but especially that which is negative, although it may be accurate and can be documented—may not be forthcoming.

SUMMARY

In this chapter we discussed methods of preparing for the employment interview, including recruiting, screening, selection, placement, and training and development, as well as commentary on and examples of application forms, résumés, cover letters, recommendations, references, and background checks.

EXERCISES

1. Prepare a one-page résumé and an accompanying cover letter to be used in applying for a real job as listed in the classified section of your local newspaper.
2. Prepare a summary of your entire employment history. A good model to follow is the application form used for the employment of most civilians in the United States government (see Appendix C). This form can be obtained from most post offices. Few corporate application forms will ask for more information than you will provide on this form. For your records, regularly update the data on the form.

NOTES

1. Based on an employment application form used by a *Fortune* 500 company.
2. Based on an internal job-posting form used by a *Fortune* 500 company.
3. These résumé classifications and the four figures identified are based on examples found in the *Job Hunting Guide,* Rev. VI, 1978, prepared by the Corporate Employment Department of The Celanese Corporation. Used by permission of the Corporate Employment Department, The Celanese Corporation, New York, New York.

ADDITIONAL READINGS

Fear, Richard A. *The Evaluation Interview*. 2nd ed., rev. New York: McGraw-Hill, 1978. Chapter 2, pp. 14–30.

7

Conducting the Employment Interview

CHAPTER OBJECTIVES

1. Understand the purposes of the employment interview.
2. Understand the different roles of the prospective employer and of the applicant.
3. Describe techniques used in the opening, body, and close of the employment interview.
4. Describe content often covered in the opening, body, and close of the employment interview.
5. Understand the role of physical behaviors and cues in the employment interview.
6. Identify questions you are likely to ask in the employment interview.
7. Provide answers to questions you are likely to be asked in the employment interview.
8. Ask employment-related questions without suggesting the answers at the same time.
9. Identify "trade" questions.
10. Give and get information about compensation.
11. Describe panel interviewing.
12. Determine if an employment offer is "good" for you.
13. Conduct an employment interview.

Introduction

In Chapters 5 and 6 we discussed the legal environment of the employment interview and how to prepare for it. In this chapter we shall examine the interview itself—the behaviors that normally take place and the kinds of questions that should be expected.

The Employment Interview

Nearly all interviews conducted in the screening and selection phases of the hiring process have similar characteristics. For that reason, we shall combine the separate screening and selection interviews and refer to them together as the employment interview in our discussion.

The primary purpose of the employment interview is for the employer and the applicant to get to know each other through an exchange of information. When the job applicant refuses to reveal pertinent personal information and thus remains psychologically distant from the employer, the former's candidacy is likely to be terminated. When the employer is reticent, displays ignorance about the job to be filled or the organization, or is not responsive to the applicant's questions, the applicant is likely to be discouraged from further pursuit of employment with that organization. Both parties should feel comfortable talking with each other, but because of the serious purpose of the interview, they should expect the tone to be somewhat more formal than that of casual conversation.

Because of the inherent nature of the employment interview, more than information exchange is involved. Both the applicant and the employer are trying to convince the other of a particular point of view and decision. The applicant seeks to persuade the employer of his or her qualifications and potential value, and the employer seeks to persuade the outstanding applicant that the former's organization is the best available.

Often, the smallest thing an employer may say or do will create an impression so positive (or negative) that nothing else will become as important to the applicant. The director of selection and placement for a major manufacturing company told us that after an applicant was hired, the applicant said that he accepted the company's offer because of the courteous way in which he had been treated during his first company visit—the director of selection and placement had offered to hang up his coat and get him a cup of coffee! Similarly, in the same company, a casual comment by the director of executive search early in the recruitment process was one of the principal reasons an applicant accepted the company's offer. The applicant had been told, "Our CEO wants to make this a great company," and she wanted to be part of building such an organization.

On the opposite side, we know of an executive applicant who was being sought by a major medical and pharmaceutical firm. During his first (and only) visit to their corporate headquarters he was scheduled to meet six different people for a series of interviews. Each person kept him waiting (one even missed the interview appointment entirely). Each apologized for being tardy with the same words, "I'm sorry I'm late. It's not usually this hectic around here." During each delay and as he was being escorted from one interview to the next, the applicant had the chance to talk to several support personnel, each of whom echoed the same thought. The applicant decided that based on the way he was treated, he did not want to be part of an organization whose guiding principle seemed to be "It's not usually this hectic around here."

These examples are not exaggerations. If anything, they are understated reports of what kinds of experiences affect applicants. As a recruiter, you will be an important salesperson for your company, and so even your most neutral word or action may have a substantial impact on how an applicant comes to view your organization.

Generally, for the employer, the first 50 to 75 percent of the employment interview is devoted to eliciting information from the applicant. Providing information is the principal task of the applicant during this period, and this information should be presented so as to convince the employer that the applicant should be hired (a persuasive function). During the remainder of the interview, the employer will usually shift to being a giver of information in response to the applicant's questions. In the last few minutes of the interview, the employer should summarize, secure agreements, and indicate how this interview will be followed up. If the employer has decided to hire the applicant, he or she will encourage the applicant to accept employment with the organization. In actuality, the information gathering and giving and the persuasive attempts by both parties will probably take place over the course of several interviews.

Throughout the interview, the employer should demonstrate a trustworthy, concerned attitude toward the applicant, indicating responsiveness to the applicant's needs and giving the applicant a favorable impression of the interview itself, the interviewer, and the organization, whether the eventual employment decision is positive or negative for the applicant. From the employer's viewpoint, this persuasive function is desirable whether in a tight or a loose labor market. When there are many more jobs than applicants to fill them (a tight labor market), however, the employer must convince the applicant that this particular organization will provide the best organization-applicant match.

One should remember that the employer is (or should be) in control in the employment interview. Although behavioral roles will shift periodically during the interview, it is the employer who initiates the interview, creates the psychological climate in which it will take place, determines its location, governs the topics to be covered, establishes its length, and determines the moment of its conclusion. Within these boundaries, the applicant will have relatively little opportunity to change the course of the interview.

The Employer's Behavior in the Employment Interview

Immediately before the interview, the employer should review the available paperwork on the applicant—letter of application, résumé, completed job application form, letters of recommendation, and any other documents in the applicant's file—to ensure sufficient familiarity with the applicant to allow the interview to be profitable.

The employer should receive the applicant with a warm greeting and a firm handshake, a name, a smile, and some words and behaviors that will begin to build rapport. Simply asking the applicant to be seated and motioning to a chair often will eliminate some of the awkwardness that accompanies the opening moments of the employment interview. Though sometimes overused and occasionally substituted for a more substantive opening, phrases such as "I'm going to have a cup of coffee. Would you like one too?" or "I'm very pleased to meet you. How was your trip?" can help put the applicant at ease. Other techniques include beginning with apparent (but not necessarily) casual talk about one or more of the applicant's qualifications or interests. Such an approach allows a smooth transition into a statement of the reason(s) for and direction of the interview: "Now that you've had a chance to relax and get comfortable, let me explain the purpose of this interview. I'd like us to spend some time expanding on the information on your application form and résumé, give you a chance to ask me any questions you may have about our organization, and generally use the next thirty minutes to give us both a chance to get to know each other."

If this interview takes place during the selection process, the applicant probably will be at the employer's location, and this will be one of several different interviews to be conducted during the applicant's visit. In that case, the opening statement could be something like: "Your experience in private industry and government has given you wide exposure to two very different types of organizations. In my role as corporate director of Washington relations, I'd like to spend the time we've been allotted discussing your perceptions of the relationship between those two institutions and how you, with your background, could help us improve it if you joined our company." Or perhaps the interviewer will take a more novel approach: "Mike, before we take our scheduled walk through the manufacturing operation at 11 o'clock, step over to the window with me and let me describe the buildings in our mill complex [the interviewer describes the buildings and what is manufactured in them]. What do you think some of our manufacturing (capital equipment, financial, human, labor, and the like) problems might be in a plant this size?"

Note that in all three of these examples, the employer, at the outset, indicated some knowledge of the applicant's background, delineated the purpose of the immediate interview, noted its timing, and stated the behavioral roles each person is expected to exhibit. In the opening moments of the employment interview, the applicant should be asked for easy, nonstressful material. Liberal use should be made of open-ended questions; relatively few closed-ended questions should be asked. The applicant's individuality should be acknowledged: here and elsewhere during the interview, the applicant's name should be used, a good way of showing interest in a stranger.

In the body of the interview, the employer should move freely (smoothly, fluently, and without fear) to more difficult material. In an orderly progression of topics and questions, the employer should cover the applicant's education, professional training, work experience, goals and objectives, job qualifications, interest and motivation in this job or in this company, integrity and character, and other topics as time allows or as need requires. For example, if appropriate and job related, the employer could use stress-inducing questions and techniques, although normally they would be avoided.

The employer should be prepared to provide information about the job itself, how it fits into the organization's structure, the duties and tasks associated with it, performance expectations of the person filling the job, compensation (salary, bonus) and fringe benefits, opportunities for personal growth and career advancement, and the company's historical growth patterns and anticipated growth directions. The applicant should be given ample opportunity to interject questions, request clarification, or make comments. During the interview, the employer should assess the applicant's work-related educational and experiential qualifications.

At the close of the interview, the employer should summarize briefly what has transpired and explain to the applicant what will come next. For example, the applicant may be told the outcome of the interview or be told how and by what method he or she will be notified: "Based on our conversation today, I'm going to recommend that you be invited to our home office to meet some other people. I'll phone you next Thursday morning between nine and ten to arrange for your visit." Equally plausible would be: "Thank you for taking the time to meet with me today. Currently, I don't see a match between your qualifications and the positions we have open; however, we'll keep your résumé and the results of this interview on file, and should any positions requiring your particular skills become available in the next ninety days, I'll be back in touch with you by letter to your home address."

Finally, the employer should escort the applicant toward the exit (or to the next interview), shake hands, and refer to him or her by name while parting with whatever words are appropriate: "Sandy, this is Dr. Pat Jones, our manager of computer services. You'll be with her for the next hour," or "Bill, again thanks for visiting with us today. It was a pleasure to meet you."

The Applicant's Behavior in the Employment Interview

To help ensure that the employer is familiar with the applicant's background, the applicant should bring additional copies of his or her résumé to the employment interview. There is always the possibility that the interviewer has not received or has misplaced the applicant's credentials file or that more than one interviewer will be present. Or there may be many applicants for this particular position, and the employer may have confused you and your credentials with those of another applicant. In one instance we know of, the executive recruiter for a Chicago-area company said to an applicant, "I know that you really want this job because you're unemployed." The applicant replied, "That's not true. I'm currently employed by _____, and I am secure in my position." Along with the desire to correct misinformation about herself, the applicant needed to make the point that as a gainfully employed person secure in her employment (i.e., she was not about to be terminated) that she had a bargaining position of strength in negotiating with the company, rather than a position of weakness that might require her to accept any offer of employment. Although it is the responsibility of the employer to be informed about the applicant, the applicant is responsible for making sure that is the case.

The employment interview begins with the reception by the employer and ends when the applicant is escorted from the interview room. During the initial greeting, the applicant should make sure of the interviewer's name, and use it during the interview. There is nothing wrong with asking the employer to pronounce his or her name again or to spell it. Often during the interview, especially during the opening moments, the applicant may experience and exhibit physical signs of nervousness. This is a natural occurrence that should be expected. Few people have learned to prevent their palms from becoming sweaty or their mouths from becoming dry. Such physiological changes will occur in normal people, and the applicant should realize this. An experienced interviewer will recognize that the applicant might be nervous and should do whatever possible to put him or her at ease.

In the early moments of the interview, the applicant should follow the lead of the employer. The interview typically will stay in its introductory stage until the employer, not the applicant, progresses the body. In the body of the interview (as well as in the other phases), the applicant should answer the employer's questions completely but not become verbose. The applicant should anticipate the questions likely to be asked (or at least the topics to be covered) and prepare pertinent and concise answers. Admittedly, one cannot prepare for every question or topic, but with some advance planning, one can reduce the element of surprise. The applicant should also prepare a portfolio of drawings, photographs, or articles, an audition tape, or any other materials that might be required to show evidence of training, ability, aptitude, or accomplishments.

In the body of the interview, the applicant should be able to describe clearly and forcefully (*not* antagonistically) his or her background, experience, education, preparation, personal goals and objectives, and general suitability for the position. Although you as an applicant should be concerned with what the organization can offer, your emphasis should be on what you can contribute to the organization. The applicant should stress his or her own personal qualifications and strengths, yet be prepared to acknowledge (and perhaps discuss) personal weaknesses. Remember that even if you, as an applicant, decide that the interview is not going well—that you may not fit the position for which you are being interviewed or that you are having a "personality" conflict with the interviewer—if you handle yourself well during the remainder of the interview, the prospective employer may still submit your name for another interview or as a candidate for a different position within the same organization.

At the close of the interview the applicant should have a clear idea of how and when he or she will be notified of its outcome. Among the final remarks to the employer, the applicant should verify what comes next: "Thank you for your time today. I'm excited about the possibility of working for your company, and look forward to your phone call between nine and ten next Thursday morning" or "Although I'm disappointed that my qualifications are not the right ones for the job, I hope a better match will come up in the next ninety days" or "I just want to verify that I'll receive the results of this interview by mail in the next seven to ten days."

Approximately two or three days after the interview, the applicant should write a short note to the interviewer thanking him or her for the interview, reiterating interest in the position, and reconfirming the follow-up agreed upon. Even if the applicant was rejected by the organization at the close of the interview, some sort of polite follow-up letter is appropriate. There is always a possibility that at some future date the positive feeling created by the follow-up letter will benefit the applicant.

Physical Behaviors and Cues

It is difficult and probably not very productive for our needs to draw rigid, precise conclusions from the research on the effects of physical behaviors (intended or otherwise) in interview situations; however, for our use here we shall examine some of the principal findings and opinions as they relate to the employment interview.

Generally, you should try to conform to the likely mode of dress and the behavior of the interviewer.[1] Because you probably will not have met the interviewer, you will have to make some commonsense guesses about the appropriate attire. For most business positions (e.g., a company headquarters, a bank, a government office, or the like) you should dress conservatively. Men should wear conservative blue, gray, or pinstripe suits, white or blue shirts, dark socks, and dark shoes. Women likewise should dress conservatively, avoiding tight, form-

116 INTERVIEWING

fitting clothing. Both sexes should avoid gaudy stripes and bold patterns, as well as overpowering after-shave lotions, colognes, or perfumes. For an interview for an office position in a factory, men should wear a sportcoat and slacks; women a dress or skirt and blouse. For an on-line job in the same factory, similar or even more casual clothing would be appropriate. Here, you may discover that jeans, a T-shirt, and work boots are just the ticket for a successful interview. These suggestions should be considered as guidelines, not as absolutes chiseled in stone. Use your common sense in matching your clothing and grooming to what is expected in an interview.

As an employer, you may find that the candidate's physical behaviors indicate areas that need further investigation. If your questions cause the applicant's behavior to deviate from what you have observed it to be normally, take note. If you see a sudden tapping of the fingers, eyes that look away, or a hand over the mouth, you may have touched a subject the applicant is trying to hide. Similarly, if, for no apparent reason, the applicant's speech pattern increases or decreases in rate of volume, you may want to probe that content area. As an applicant, you should look and listen for the same kinds of reactions in the interviewer. Just as an applicant may have something to hide, so may the prospective employer.

Employer's Questions in the Employment Interview

In the employment interview, the applicant should be prepared to respond to the following types of questions or to provide the information voluntarily without being asked the question itself. Remember, the only questions the employer may lawfully ask are those that meet the Bona Fide Occupational Qualification Test (see Chapter 5 for a detailed discussion of BFOQ).

Questions About the Applicant's Previous Work Experience:
1. Which of your previous jobs did you like (dislike) the most? Why? (Preferences are normal and expected, and the applicant should have some.)
2. How do you think your previous work experience will help you on the job for which you are applying? (Some attempt should be made by the applicant to link previous work experience with this job.)
3. How did you obtain the jobs you have held? (The applicant can demonstrate initiative and creativity, desire, and motivation to work.)
4. Have you ever had problems working with other people? (The applicant can show interpersonal sensitivity and ability to get along with others, as well as honesty by being willing to talk about negative information.)
5. What has been your most rewarding work-related experience? (This will highlight the applicant's strengths and work values and give some insight into his or her character.)

Questions About the Applicant's Education:
1. Tell me about your major. (The applicant is able to show his or her strengths and educational suitability for the position. If the applicant responds as though the question were "Why did you choose your major?" he or she can demonstrate interest and motivation.)

2. To what extent is your grade point average a valid indicator of your college training? (The applicant is allowed to justify a low accumulative average, stress how hard he or she worked to achieve a high average, and/or mention scholastic honors received.)
3. What types of courses did you prefer? Dislike? Why? (The applicant can indicate preferences and reveal his or her interests, strengths, and weaknesses.)
4. How much of your educational expenses did you earn while in college? (The applicant can indicate drive and financial responsibility, as well as personal resourcefulness.)
5. What has been your most important academic success? Failure? Why? (The applicant can indicate what is rewarding, not rewarding, and the kinds of things that are personally satisfying.)

Questions About the Applicant's Personal and Job-Related Goals:
1. Why are you interested in this job with this organization? (The applicant can reveal knowledge about the organization, the specific job, and perceptions of growth potential and is given the opportunity to state what he or she can do for the organization and how the organization can help meet his or her personal objectives.)
2. If you went to work with our organization today, what type of position would you like to hold in three to five years? (The applicant can demonstrate that he or she has considered his or her future and personal growth.)
3. What kinds of additional training or development experiences do you think you need to meet your occupational/vocational objectives? (This allows the applicant to discuss strengths and weaknesses and to demonstrate that he or she recognizes the need for further education and experience; further, he or she can inquire about company training and development opportunities and/or educational assistance programs.)
4. If you had the opportunity to work in an environment that was very structured but led to concrete results or one that was loosely structured with hard-to-measure results, which would you prefer? Why? (This gives the applicant the chance to express his or her tolerance of or need for structure; it give insight into the applicant's ability to manage by authority or through influence strategies; it suggests to the employer whether placement should be in a staff role or a line role.)
5. What would you do if you were fired by this organization after two years? (The applicant can demonstrate resourcefulness, naiveté, flexibility, and perseverance.)

General Questions:
1. What are your salary requirements? (This allows the applicant to show that he or she is aware of realistic and representative salaries for similar kinds of work.)
2. In what geographic location do you prefer to work? (This allows the applicant to state a preference for a city or a region of the country and also to rule out certain locations.)
3. What three adjectives would your friends use to describe you? Your ene-

mies? Which three would be correct? (The applicant is able to present his or her strengths and weaknesses, attributing them to a neutral third-party.)
4. Is there anything I haven't asked you that you want me to ask you? (The applicant is given the chance to point out again his or her strong characteristics or to reemphasize a previous point.)
5. To what extent have you behaved in this interview the way you normally behave? (The applicant can describe his or her nervousness, indicating openness or apprehension, or can reconfirm that "what you see is what you get.")

Two additional comments are necessary concerning the kinds of questions that the employer may ask. First, the employer should not indicate early in the interview that certain information is "correct" or that a particular answer should be given to a question later in the interview. For example, if travel is an important element of the job, the employer should not say, "We're looking for someone who likes to travel. Do you like to travel?" An applicant who is not altogether honest or who may simply want to appear agreeable is apt to respond affirmatively to the question, whether or not the response is honest. A better approach for the employer is to ask first if the applicant is free to travel, willing to do so, and how much travel is acceptable; then, as appropriate, divulge that the desire to travel and willingness to do so are important elements of the job.

Second, another type of question that the applicant should be prepared for is the "trade" question, a special question designed to elicit specific kinds of job knowledge. For example, if you are applying for a position as an assistant director of a youth center for delinquent and borderline delinquent teenagers, you may be asked, "What would you do if a participant at this center walked into your office brandishing a knife and said, 'I'm going to kill somebody!'?" If asked such a question, you would be required to demonstrate knowledge of crisis intervention techniques, levelheadedness and maturity, and an awareness of social support agencies to contact in such an emergency. Because you would not actually be employed by the youth center when the question was asked, you would not be expected to know specific center policies governing such incidents. Nevertheless, your general approach in responding to this trade question would be used to judge your suitability for employment.

Trade questions come in many forms, but their common purpose is to test the applicant's ability to apply his or her knowledge to real, work-related situations. The following examples demonstrate this point for a job in the indicated fields:

1. Labor relations: "What elements would you put in a prenegotiation strategy document?" or "If you were trying to keep a union out of your organization, what actions would you take?"
2. Marketing: "How would you introduce composite-structure leaf springs into the light truck industry?" or "If you wanted to know whether a community would welcome a new manufacturing plant that would employ six hundred people, what kind of population sample would you select and how would you select it?"
3. Accounting: "React to this statement. To be a plant controller you should be a CPA." or "Under what circumstances do you think it's necessary to 'qualify' the annual financial audit of a major corporation?"

Applicant's Questions in the Employment Interview

Just as the applicant should be prepared to respond to all of the questions noted earlier in this chapter, so should the employer be ready to answer the following types of questions or to provide the information sought before it is requested.

Questions About the Job:
1. In what location will I work?
2. How often can I expect to be transferred from one geographical location to another?
3. What is a typical career path for someone who enters the organization in this job?
4. Why did the previous encumbent leave the position for which I am now applying?
5. What is the annual turnover rate for professionals in the company?
6. Does the position require that I join a union?
7. How well are women, blacks, and other minorities represented in your exempt work force?
8. How often will my performance be evaluated?
9. What is my starting salary, and when will it be reviewed?
10. Do you have a dental benefit plan?
11. If I'm hired, when will you expect me to report to work?
12. To whom does this position report? May I meet him or her?
13. Why aren't you promoting someone from within?
14. Tell me about the background of others who work here.

Questions About Financial Matters:
1. How much do you pay for work-related travel, meal, and lodging expenses?
2. Does this position qualify for stock options?
3. How much does the organization pay for moving and relocation expenses?
4. What other benefits come with the position?
5. How are salary increases determined?
6. What is the company's policy on positioning salaries at the industry median?
7. What will my total compensation be—salary plus benefits?
8. What staff support services will be provided? Secretarial? Research? Computer? Library?

Questions About Individual Development:
1. What will my first two weeks on the job be like?
2. What kinds of training will be provided by the organization?
3. If I decide to get my MBA, will the company reimburse me for tuition and books under your educational assistance plan?
4. What kinds of experience do I need to be considered for a middle- or upper-level position in line management?
5. What criteria does the organization use to determine potential for advancement?
6. How much of a voice will I have in planning my career moves within the organization?

120 INTERVIEWING

7. What percentage of the people in your organization is promoted from within?
8. Do you have an internal job-posting system?

General Questions:
1. Your annual report from last year indicates that your organization has sustained a five-year compounded growth rate of 47 percent. How rapidly do you expect to grow over the next five years?
2. I was once arrested for shoplifting, but I wasn't convicted. Will that affect my chances for employment with your organization?"
3. What do you like about working for this organization? Dislike?
4. Tell me about the working relationship you have with your immediate supervisor.
5. When will the results of this interview be made known to me?
6. If you hire me, will you help me find housing?
7. If I'm hired, when should I expect to report for work?

The questions in this chapter are not meant to be an exhaustive list of possible questions that can be asked in an employment interview. Depending on the interviewer, the applicant, the characteristics of the job in question, the organization, and other factors, these questions can be modified or exchanged for others.

A Word About Salary Questions

You also can expect questions about salary during the interview—either party may ask them. The employer will want to know if the applicant's salary demands are in the range offered by the position, and the applicant will want to have a salary figure that is commensurate with others in the same position who have the applicant's same experience.

An employer is likely to ask an applicant the following kinds of questions:

1. "This position pays between $13,000 and $15,000 to start, depending on your qualifications and the geographic location to which you're assigned. Is that acceptable to you?" [The applicant should position a response indicating yes but should indicate that the offer be between the bottom ($13,000) and the midpoint ($14,000). This gives both parties some flexibility in negotiating the starting salary.]

2. "What is the minimum salary offer you'll accept?" [Unless you have done your homework, you won't know what answer to give. If your preparation has been adequate, you'll have an approximate idea of what others make in this position who have your level of experience. If you're just starting out (and you have no idea what this position is worth), give a salary number in the teens ("I think twelve hundred a month is fair to start."), or better yet, beg the question ("I'd be willing to accept an offer that is competitive with others I receive.").]

3. An experienced candidate (one who is already working) may be asked, "What is your salary now?" [The employer wants to know how you are currently positioned relative to the new job. Your reply may be specific ("I'm at $22,000"), somewhat more general ("I'm in the mid-twenties"), or very general, even vague ("I'm where you'd expect"). You might also try the tactic of giving the inter-

viewer your bottom acceptable figure in order to force the issue. Suppose that your current salary is $20,000. You might respond with "I won't move for less than $24,000" and thus avoid a direct response to the question while indicating that there is no point in continuing the interview unless the prospective employer is willing to meet your minimum salary demand.]

In addition to specific questions about salary, the issue of total compensation may come up. Both parties should be prepared to discuss incentive compensation (bonus), relocation allowance, travel expenses (total reimbursement, per diem), use of a company car, stock options, club memberships, and the other items identified in the earlier section entitled "Questions About Financial Matters."

Panel Interviewing

Although the employment interview usually involves only the applicant and one interviewer, sometimes two or more interviewers will be present. This is a panel interview. The panel interview is rarely found during the screening phase of the hiring process but, rather, during the selection phase when the applicant makes an on-site visit to the organization. The usual purpose of the panel is to probe the applicant's qualifications in the shortest amount of time and from the most perspectives. If an organization brings in more than one applicant for the position to be filled, the panel interview will allow increased objectivity and reliability and hence higher validity in its decision to offer the job to a particular applicant.

The presence of several interviewers can intimidate an applicant, especially one who is inexperienced. Sometimes the panel technique is used purposely to put pressure on the applicant in order to observe how he or she performs under stress or in an environment of conflict or ambiguity. In this situation, different members of the panel will assume conflicting roles in order to trap or confuse the applicant or to make him or her feel uncomfortable. But unless there is some required job-related reason to put the applicant under excessive stress and discomfort, the stress-inducing function of the panel interview should be avoided.

The panel should be made up of two to five people who are knowledgeable about the job and the organization. If possible, someone on the panel should have firsthand experience with the job in question. Often the members on the panel will be part of the applicant's new work group if he or she is hired. Obviously, the composition of the panel depends on the type of job and its level in the organization. The following are representative types of panels:

1. For a technical or highly skilled position: three people from the technical or skill area, one department manager, and one person from personnel.
2. For a major operations position: four people with operations experience and one person from personnel.
3. For a clerical position: one current clerical person, one functional manager, and one person from personnel.
4. For a second-level position in a manufacturing plant: one manager (probably the prospective immediate supervisor), two prospective co-workers, and one person from personnel.

The applicant should be told in advance that the interview will be a panel interview, the reason for having many interviewers, and the panelists and their job titles. In other respects, the panel interview is like any one-on-one employment interview, except that it probably will go into more detail. The applicant should be able to demonstrate his or her job knowledge (experience, education, know-how), skills, and abilities. The panelists should be sufficiently familiar with the job and the applicant's credentials so that they can ask intelligent questions whose answers will tell them whether the applicant can perform the job duties effectively.

The Employment Offer[2]

For most people, the employment interview and job hunting processes are negative experiences. Someone is trying to screen you out rather than let you in. You are likely to be rejected more often than you will be accepted, even when you think you are the most qualified candidate. Try not to let the rejections discourage you because some day you will receive an offer of employment, and then all you will have to do is accept it. Right? Wrong. At this point you will need to ask yourself some additional questions. Some of them you can answer yourself, but others may require follow-up contact with the company making the offer or with the friends that you can use as a sounding board.

Receiving an employment offer is a great ego boost. But unless it is the right offer, you may have no reason to accept it. The offer should be evaluated thoughtfully. Although your decision to accept (or reject) the offer is not irrevocable, some serious thinking now may save you trouble later on. To evaluate the offer, you will want to address these issues:

1. Is this the job you really want? Will it give you the kinds of personal and financial satisfactions you need? Will it allow you to do the kinds of things you want to do? Will the organization support your efforts to accomplish your objectives?
2. What is the organization's reputation in its industry? In its treatment of its people? In its innovation and creativeness? In its responsibility as a corporate citizen? In its integrity?
3. What are its human resources policies and practices relative to promotion from within? Internal training programs? External training programs? Educational assistance plans and benefits? Basis for performance appraisals? Potential for advancement and greater accountability?
4. What does your intuition tell you about the company? How were you treated during the interview process? What do you think about the personalities of the people you met? Their attitudes? Their behavior? Do you want to associate with them on a regular basis?
5. What are the company's compensation and benefits practices? Are they competitive with those of similar companies in the industry? In the geographical area? Will you qualify for profit sharing? For bonuses or other incentive compensation? For employee investment opportunities? What

health and dental plans will you receive? Who pays for what? Does the company have legal insurance (protection against suit) for you? Paid or unpaid vacations? Holidays? Sick leave? Disability insurance? Pension plan? If you leave the organization, what benefits can you take with you?
6. What is the organization's relocation policy? Who pays for what? How many house-hunting trips can you take? Can your spouse accompany you? Who will pay the closing costs? Will the company pay the difference between your current mortgage interest rate and the new higher (presumably) rate you will receive?
7. Reexamine the organization's "public" personality. Review handbooks, reports, internal newspapers, and other documents you may have been given. Do you like what you see? Does your experience with the company to date reinforce what the documents say? Do you find contradictions between the documents and your experience with the company?
8. Consider geography. Do you like the geographical area in which you will be located? Does the community offer the kind of cultural and recreational activities you like? Is the weather to your taste? Can you find affordable housing that is consistent with your style of living? Is public transportation satisfactory within (and to and from) the city? Are community attitudes similar to yours?
9. Overall, how does this organization compare with others with which you are familiar or at which you interviewed?

Here are some additional tips that should become part of your decision-making process:

1. Decide for yourself. Avoid letting someone else push you into this decision. Ask questions until you have the answers you need.
2. Evaluate the job offer on the basis of your criteria. What is important to you (work environment, salary, bonuses, benefits, people you work with, what your friends think you should do, where the job is located, advancement opportunities, and the like)?
3. Should you negotiate once you receive an offer? The higher you go in an organization, the greater will be your opportunity for negotiation. Executive positions have more negotiation flexibility than do entry-level positions. You should raise issues of concern to you or demands that must be met once a mutual interest has been established between you and the company. Tell the company early about your concerns. If it really wants you, it will try to meet your needs.

SUMMARY

This chapter provided an overview of the typical employment or initial screening interview, including examples of questions likely to be encountered. We emphasized the kinds of questions and topics that both the applicant and the employer should be prepared to address, including salary issues, panel interviewing, and responding to the employment offer.

EXERCISES

1. You are a sales manager in a local department store. You need additional help to replace an individual who left to return to college. You want a person who is dependable and who has advancement potential. An applicant is coming in this afternoon for an interview. Her credentials are as follows:

   Name: Peggy Romano
   Age: 23
   Hometown: Tulsa, Oklahoma
   Marital Status: Married
   Education: Associate of Arts Degree, Oklahoma City Community College
   Work Experience: Currently employed full time as a secretary and an administrative aide in a local company

   Mrs. Romano will be in your office in thirty minutes. This is all that you know about her. What else do you want to know? Why? Prepare a list of questions that you will ask her. (Note: This exercise may be used in class with students role playing Peggy Romano and the sales manager.)
2. If Exercise 1 was role played in class, why would you hire or not hire Mrs. Romano as a result of the interview? Write a critique of each participant in the interview, commenting on the opening, body, and close, as well as on the questions and probes used.
3. Prepare a one-page résumé and an accompanying cover letter to be used in applying for a real job as listed in the classified section of your local newspaper. While you are doing this, another person should find out as much as possible about the job (and the organization) for which you are applying. Conduct an interview, with you as the applicant and the other person as the prospective employer. Critique the interview.
4. Complete this in-class interview assignment:
   a. Obtain an employment application from an organization in your community and fill it out.
   b. Prepare a one-page résumé.
   c. Prepare a one-page cover letter to accompany your résumé.
   d. Outline the position specifications of the job for which you are applying.
   e. Give items a, b, c, and d to a classmate, who will role play the prospective employer.
   f. Conduct an in-class interview with your classmate. When the interview is completed, give your instructor all of the documents you prepared for evaluation.
   g. After the interview, prepare a follow-up letter to be sent to the person who interviewed you. This letter should be given to your instructor for evaluation.
   h. Prepare for the interview by gathering data on the organization to which you are applying. Even if the job and the organization are imaginary, you should be able to create "facts" about both.

NOTES

1. John T. Malloy has written two books that, to date, have sold nearly three million copies: *Dress for Success* and *Women's Dress for Success Book*. The combined sales figures suggest that somebody out there (the purchasers) thinks that dress is quite important.
2. Some of the information in this section can be found in the *Job Hunting Guide*, Rev. VI, 1978, prepared by the Corporate Employment Department of the Celanese Corporation. Used by permission of the Corporate Employment Department, Celanese Corporation, New York, New York.

ADDITIONAL READINGS

Fear, Richard A. *The Evaluation Interview*. 2nd ed., rev. New York: McGraw-Hill, 1978. Chapter 6 (pp. 105–122) and Chapter 13 (pp. 262–273).

Genua, Robert L. *The Employer's Guide to Interviewing: Strategy and Tactics for Picking a Winner*. Englewood Cliffs, N.J.: Prentice-Hall, 1979.

Robertson, Jason. *How to Win in a Job Interview*. Englewood Cliffs, N.J.: Prentice-Hall, 1978.

Rogers, Donald P., and Michael Z. Sincoff. "Favorable Impression Characteristics of the Recruitment Interviewer." *Personnel Psychology* 31 (Autumn 1978): 495–504.

8

Appraisal Interviewing

CHAPTER OBJECTIVES

1. Explain various appraisal situations.
2. Identify and describe the objectives of a typical performance appraisal system.
3. Identify and describe the objectives of a typical performance appraisal interview.
4. Identify and describe ways of handling situations likely to occur in a performance appraisal interview.
5. Identify and describe uses of various questioning techniques.
6. Understand factors to be considered in preparing for the performance appraisal interview.
7. Give both positive and negative criticism.
8. Explain alternative activities found in a development plan.
9. Prepare a development plan.
10. Explain the importance of timing, mental set, language choice, and environment in the performance appraisal interview.
11. Conduct a performance appraisal interview.
12. Recognize questions likely to be encountered in a performance appraisal interview.
13. Understand the role of career planning in appraisal.
14. Understand the relationships between and among self-assessment, testing, and counseling.
15. Identify the steps in career planning.
16. Perform a detailed self-assessment.
17. Devise a career plan.

Introduction

Most organizations have some sort of human resources appraisal system, either formal or informal, announced or unannounced (i.e., one that the members of the organization may not be aware of). A wide-ranging human resources appraisal system will account not only for the actual job-related assessment of an employee's performance, potential, personal development needs, and career path but also for overall organizational human resources planning, management depth assessment and succession, compensation, training, development, and work force skill mix. Although we shall not discuss this in detail, you should be aware that this is how an organization uses the data generated through the performance appraisal process.

The appraisal interview itself is a part of a broader, organizationally sanctioned yet individually focused performance review process that usually incorporates assessment and evaluation of performance; problem solving requiring judgmental, coaching, and counseling behaviors; and career planning. A successful performance review process will be characterized by (1) candor, trust, and openness in the discussion between the supervisor and subordinate about performance and career planning; (2) clarification for the employee of his or her performance measurement, career alternatives, and career planning; and (3) structured training for managers in performance assessment and career planning counseling so that they can advise their subordinates.

There are many kinds of performance appraisal systems. In a business setting you are judged on how well your work performance has conformed to overall organizational goals, the central mission of your individual department, your own business objectives as agreed to with your immediate supervisor, and the type and quality of your interpersonal interactions with others. Performance appraisal judgments are used to make decisions affecting current job performance, expansion of job responsibilities, promotional opportunity, transfer, training programs, development activities, merit pay increases, performance bonuses, advancement readiness, or termination.

In an academic environment, faculty and administrative appraisal systems are used to determine an individual's effectiveness in teaching, administering, committee service, university governance, student advising and counseling, publications, and professional society participation and involvement. The judgments rendered affect promotion, tenure, merit pay increases, and other opportunities for professional growth and development. For students, learning is evaluated through examinations, term papers, or special project assignments, each representing an interim performance appraisal and leading to a final course appraisal in the form of a grade. Individual course grades, combined to yield an overall accumulative grade point average, constitute a long-term appraisal by faculty members of a student's work. Grades, coupled with appraisals of the quantity and quality of extracurricular activities, determine career choices (e.g., a particular job or graduate school after graduation).

In the political sector, an incumbent may be judged by the electorate on the extent to which he or she met its expectations created when a candidate for elective office. If the performance appraisal is favorable, that candidate will be reelected; if unfavorable, the officeholder will not be reelected. In cases of extreme negative performance appraisal, the incumbent will be removed from public office or encouraged to resign before the term expires.

Long-term appraisal systems—preparing and updating descriptions of job requirements, developing and using organization-specific appraisal forms (checklists of employee attributes with space for brief comments or a series of open-ended questions calling for a lengthy response), and conducting one or more actual appraisal interviews—are common to most large organizations. These are elaborately conducted, formal systems carried out according to specific guidelines and procedures.

Smaller organizations may have appraisal systems with some of the attributes of those found in larger organizations, but usually they will be maintained in a much less formal and much less structured manner. Finally, in some organizations, with the exception of an occasional pat on the back or reprimand, there is no appraisal system evident until the employee receives a pay increase or is terminated.

Appraisal System Objectives

Generally, performance appraisal systems are designed to allow an organization to use human resources more efficiently and effectively, by providing an opportunity for the organization to achieve its objectives while enabling the individual to achieve personal fulfillment. Though not always carried out to the degree that the organization or the person would like, most performance appraisal systems have objectives similar to the following:

1. To enable the manager and employee to conduct regular and systematic assessments of employee performance in an open and candid environment.
2. To clarify the employee's self-perceptions about job responsibilities and performance expectations, as compared with the supervisor's, in order to help the employee become more successful.
3. To provide data that will enable the manager to evaluate the employee's training and development needs, promotion potential, and increases in compensation and to provide feedback about these issues to the employee.
4. To improve the manager's appraisal and counseling skills so that the manager can become the key professional career development resource for the employee and be able to participate in the development of subordinates.
5. To enable the organization to conduct improved management needs assessments and management succession planning as part of its overall human resources appraisal system.

Appraisal Interview Objectives

The appraisal interview itself has many purposes that usually relate to improving individual performance, increasing individual productivity, and raising profitability. In theory, these purposes are accomplished through early problem identification and resolution, creation of improved manager-employee communication, and reinforced employee commitment to the tasks at hand and to the organization. In practice, these purposes are accomplished by successful conduct of the appraisal interview.

Among the specific objectives of the performance appraisal interview are to:

1. Review and discuss the employee's present job performance in relation to previously agreed-upon job responsibilities, goals, and performance standards.
2. Allow both the manager and the employee to discuss specific strengths and weaknesses in the employee's work performance during the appraisal period.
3. Allow the employee to discuss and obtain assistance in solving day-to-day job problems and to give the employee the opportunity to suggest methods of improving work performance.
4. Allow the employee to express feelings about personal and work-related variables affecting performance and career direction.
5. Allow the manager and the employee to modify the employee's job responsibilities, goals, and performance indicators.
6. Develop jointly between the manager and employee plans for improvement, their implementation schedule, and expected milestones to be noted as the improvement plans are accomplished.
7. Determine the employee's needs for long-term training and development leading to improved performance in the present position, to promotion, or to transfer.
8. Provide a basis for subsequent salary reviews and promotion decisions.

If conducted properly, the appraisal interview becomes a powerful tool for determining variables in job effectiveness, approaches to evaluating performance, employee counseling, and individual and organizational growth. Positive outcomes will be more likely if performance feedback is constructive, positive, specific, and job oriented. Most organizations provide little or no training for managers in conducting a proper appraisal interview. Additionally, most organizations fail to ensure that the supervisor recognizes the emotionally charged, stress-inducing nature of the appraisal interview. But even if all goes well, the appraisal interview is probably one of the most emotional interactions that takes place between a manager and an employee. Indeed, appraisals often fail because the manager does not recognize the emotional overtones in the interview or because the actual appraisal itself is vague—not job-related or oriented toward the individual's personal or physical characteristics (over which the person may have no control)—lacks planning for corrective action, does not allow enough time for its completion, is interrupted, or has not been prepared for by the manager.

The remainder of this chapter will examine some of the variables related to job effectiveness and performance evaluation that should be considered when conducting a performance appraisal interview.

Common Performance Appraisal Situations

The performance appraisal interview is likely to include correction, problem-area identification, criticism of the supervisor, goal setting, counseling, and anger.

Correction. Supervisors often are reluctant to provide negative performance feedback, as it is uncomfortable for them to do. They are embarrassed, or they are not prepared to deal with specific faults or corrective actions. Nevertheless, correcting subordinates is a supervisory function, and when discussing correction, the supervisor should be instructive, giving specific examples of incorrect behavior and describing correct behaviors. As a supervisor, you should avoid making personal attacks against the subordinate but, rather, attack the performance and suggest ways of improving it. Explain why the behavior is incorrect, indicate the consequences of continued incorrect action, and reach an agreement with the subordinate on how the action will be corrected. Treat the employee like an adult, maintaining his or her dignity and sense of self-worth.

Problem area identification. You will need to identify specific problem areas that need to be improved. These may include the individual's work attitudes, productivity, and/or work habits. Work attitudes can produce behaviors such as being uncooperative, disruptive, inattentive, or belligerent—in general, undermining the efforts of others in the organization. Productivity problems include insufficient quantity of work and/or work of low quality. Poor work habits include insufficient attention to detail, a lack of thoroughness in performing assignments, missed deadlines, delays, inattention to work hours (tardiness in reporting to work, extended lunch hours, leaving early), or excessive absences. As the appraiser, your task is to describe the deviant behavior, give examples of when and how it occurred, what its consequences will be, and how it can be corrected. You will need to reach an agreement with the employee about solutions and their implementation. Probe for the reasons for the deviant behavior to see if the causes of it can be eliminated.

Criticism of the supervisor. Supervisors may encourage criticism from their subordinates, and although most supervisors who ask for criticism are sincere in their request, others are not. You may want to consider the following guidelines if your supervisor ever asks you for criticism.

1. Verify the request. Does the supervisor want both negative and positive criticism, or is this just the supervisor's way of giving you a chance to say something? Rely on your past experience with your supervisor. Do you have an open relationship and talk freely with each other? Does the work environment allow you to say what is on your mind without being penalized?

2. Use tact. Your supervisor is your supervisor. Avoid claiming that you are always right and your supervisor is always wrong. You want to avoid a power struggle. Instead of saying, "Boss, your decision on the maintenance contract was the worst I've ever seen," try "Boss, your decision on the maintenance contract caused me a lot of difficulty." The first statement allows little room for maneuvering and sets up a win-lose situation (with you as the loser); the latter gives some freedom for discussion and an opportunity for problem solving.

3. Suggest solutions. When you describe a problem or a fault, also indicate what you think should or can be done to resolve it. Make your complaint, then give your solution. This should defuse a possibly explosive situation, by focusing it on methods of improvement.

4. Make your criticism valid, and offer specific examples. Support the examples with hard data from reliable sources (the maintenance supervisor, downtime records, labor-cost increases, and so forth). This lets the supervisor evaluate objective information rather than subjective criticism from you alone. It also reveals your preparation and thus your concern.

5. Get the supervisor on your side. Ask for help in resolving problems. This will flatter your supervisor.

Your supervisor probably will be receptive to negative criticism if (1) his or her actions and decisions have something to do with the issues you raise and (2) the criticism is a source of information for subsequent decision making rather than an emotional attack. It has become popular in many organizations to use terms like employee *involvement* and *participation.* Although there is merit in these concepts and although many supervisors mouth the words "Tell me what you think," they really want to hear only the positives. Bearers of negative information run the risk of being cast as nay-sayers or troublemakers rather than as employees expressing the truth as they see it and/or honestly disagreeing. You often will run a risk when you respond in a negative way to a request for information, but nevertheless, we recommend truthfulness expressed with tact and diplomacy.

Goal setting. Goal setting encourages and leads to improved performance. Through negotiation, goal setting can result in a mutual commitment to and involvement in agreed-upon goals. Dictating and ordering should be eliminated, as they are less productive than discussing and achieving agreement. When setting goals, try using the following process:

1. Explain the goal of the strategic business unit (work group, company, division, department, assembly line, project team, as appropriate).

2. Describe preliminary goals (function—what is to be done; scope—generally where is it to be done; time—within what time period it is to be done, e.g., units per hour, by September 30).

3. Request clarification of what is needed to reach the goal (e.g., materials, guidance, supervision, human resources, money).

4. Set standards against which the results will be measured.

5. Determine how the results will be measured.

6. Negotiate agreements.

7. Inform other employees in the work group of the agreements reached so that each person in the work group will be aware of what the others are supposed to be doing.

8. Review the progress toward accomplishing goals (monthly, quarterly, semiannually, annually, as appropriate). Discuss barriers to completion and how to overcome them. Determine where deviations from plan occur, what causes them, and how they can be corrected.

9. Renegotiate goals as required (priorities may shift, business conditions may change).

Counseling. The appraisal interview has several elements in common with counseling interviews (see Chapter 9), particularly as counseling techniques can be used to create a coequal atmosphere for discussion, to elicit information from the employee, and to encourage the employee to suggest his or her own solutions to performance problems. Using counseling techniques will demonstrate the interviewer's interest in and understanding of the employee's point of view and the employee's performance problems.

Creating a coequal atmosphere. To demonstrate coequality in the appraisal interview, the appraiser should (1) state the purpose of the interview, (2) use the employee's first name (or nickname if appropriate), (3) position the furniture so that both parties have an unimpeded view of each other, and (4) provide a comfortable physical interview setting in which both parties can relax. The employee often will be anxious, and so a clear statement of the purpose of the interview, its format, its uses, its expected outcome, as well as thoughtful responses to the employee's questions will help put him or her at ease. The main purpose of the appraisal interview is evaluation, and both the supervisor and the employee should know that. Nevertheless, the supervisor should avoid making evaluative comments (either positive or negative) after each of the employee's utterances. By making periodic, relatively neutral, nonevaluative responses (such as uh-huh or hmm-mm), the supervisor does not place any psychological constraint on what the employee might say. Of course, after a given problem or area of work performance has been discussed or after the entire interview has taken place, evaluative comments *must* be made.

Eliciting information. Especially in the early stages of the appraisal interview and into its body, the supervisor should use the following techniques:

1. Open-ended questions, those requiring an expansive answer by the employee, such as "What particular reasons can you think of for missing that production quota?" or "How might the problem be resolved?"

2. Silence, simply keeping your mouth shut. If the supervisor asks a question, there will be a psychological pressure on the employee to respond; therefore, the supervisor should keep quiet to allow the employee to respond. If the employee makes a declarative statement and then pauses, there will be a psychological pressure on the employee to continue talking; therefore, the supervisor should remain quiet. By using silence, the supervisor is likely to get answers to his or her questions and better organized responses from the employee.

3. Guggles, sounds or words that encourage one to keep speaking, such as uh-huh, hmm-mm, yeah, I see, right. Sometimes guggles are actual words, though they mean only, "Yes, I understand you, keep talking."

4. Mirrors or restatement, repeating either the exact words or tone that the employee has used. If the employee says, "I seem to have been having a little trouble with my job lately," the supervisor can emphasize either the entire sentence by repeating it verbatim or particular phrases by repeating them:

> "You seem to have been having a little trouble with your job lately?" (the supervisor is saying, "I heard the words you said, now give me more information.")
> "A *little* trouble?" (asking for magnitude).
> "*Trouble!*" (indicating that the employee is up to his neck in trouble).
> "*With your job?*" (asking if there might be some other problem).
> "*Lately!*" (indicating that the trouble has been around for some time).

By using the exact words of the employee, the supervisor can elicit more information about the problem.

Another form of mirroring occurs when just the tone is repeated, without necessarily using the employee's words. The employee says, "I seem to have been having a little trouble with my job lately." The supervisor can say, simply, "Tell me more about it." In this instance, the probe is more general than those in the preceding paragraph; yet it can still yield valuable information, as the likely response will be for the employee to describe the problem.

Self-solution. As in the counseling interview, in the appraisal interview the interviewer will encourage the employee to suggest solutions himself or herself. One way to do this is for the supervisor to summarize the problem (or to encourage the employee to do so). Encouraging the employee to suggest solutions himself or herself will create a stronger commitment to them.

Anger. If the appraisal is likely to be negative, the employee will probably be angry. Usually, it will be one of two types: anger at you specifically or anger that is generalized to the situation. In either case, the steps for handling it are the same. First, listen. Let the employee vent his or her feelings. Second, ask about the causes of the anger. Third, summarize the employee's point of view. Fourth, give your point of view, in a calm, even tone. Fifth, ask the employee how the issue(s) should be resolved. Sixth, negotiate an acceptable solution and the action required to implement the solution. Seventh, agree on the items negotiated. Finally, arrange follow-up interviews to ensure that the problem is being resolved.

Preparing for the Appraisal Interview

The appraisal process should begin with a preliminary meeting between the supervisor and the employee. At this meeting, the supervisor should discuss the review process and give the employee any necessary information and forms to be completed. This brief discussion should review the objectives or work plans toward which the employee has been working during the year; remind the employee of any events, incidents, or discussions that have occurred and that would help assess performance; and offer instructions for completing any forms. (Some organizations require that the employee complete a self-appraisal form and submit it to the supervisor before the actual performance appraisal interview.)

To prepare for the actual appraisal interview itself, the supervisor should evaluate the employee's performance and document it with specific examples that reflect the basis of the assessment. Ideally, this is done before receiving any information from the employee. The employee should evaluate his or her own performance and submit it in writing to the supervisor. In both instances, the supervisor and the employee should comment on the employee's performance in accordance with objectives and the way the entire job was accomplished (e.g., productivity was above average, but the employee's attitude and behavior alienated almost everyone); the employee's career interests and readiness for promotion or transfer to another position; and planned development activities that will add to the employee's strengths and overcome weaknesses.

Before the appraisal interview, each party should consider the employee's performance, personal characteristics, capacities and attitudes, supervisory skills (if appropriate), interactions with others, and performance potential. Possible development plans should be considered also.

Employee's Performance:
1. Major accomplishments in meeting all facets of job performance.
2. Major areas of performance in need of improvement.
3. Performance areas in which the employee regularly receives praise.
4. Performance areas in which the employee regularly receives criticism.

5. Performance areas in which the employee works best as a team player.
6. Performance areas in which the employee works best as an individual contributor.
7. Strengths and weaknesses in performing basic management tasks such as planning, organizing, staffing, directing, controlling, counseling, guiding, and appraising.
8. How well the employee keeps others informed and seeks out information pertinent to the job.

Employee's Personal Characteristics:
1. adaptability
2. caution
3. cheerfulness
4. conformity
5. conservatism
6. cooperation
7. creativity
8. dependability
9. dominance
10. emotionality
11. empathy
12. energy
13. enthusiasm
14. flexibility
15. forcefulness
16. impatience
17. impulsivity
18. imagination
19. individuality
20. inhibition
21. interests
22. maturity
23. optimism
24. persistence
25. self-confidence
26. self-reliance
27. sense of humor
28. sensitivity
29. supportiveness
30. trustworthiness
31. other characteristics

Employee's Capacities and Attitudes:
1. aloofness
2. amount of time the employee is willing to spend on the job
3. amount of compensation the employee wants
4. ability to organize own work
5. ambition
6. conscientiousness
7. competitiveness

8. diplomacy
9. enjoyment of hard work
10. ability to concentrate
11. initiative
12. authority and responsibility
13. organization
14. originality
15. procrastination
16. reliability
17. resistance
18. capacity for criticism
19. self-expression
20. leadership
21. other

Employee's Supervisory Skills:
1. Encourages subordinates.
2. Delegates tasks and authority effectively.
3. Creates positive work climate, characterized by high productivity, high quality, and high morale.
4. Requires high performance standards of subordinates and self.
5. Treats subordinates fairly.
6. Represents subordinates fairly and objectively to others.
7. Accomplishes group tasks effectively.
8. Has influence upward and horizontally in the organization.

Employee's Interactions with Others:
1. establishes rapport easily
2. pleasant
3. leads conversations
4. cooperative
5. easily annoyed
6. excitable
7. easygoing
8. listens well
9. has sense of humor
10. loyal
11. is team player
12. good-natured
13. reserved
14. encourages others
15. responsive
16. retiring
17. socially skilled
18. other

Employee's Performance Potential:
1. Demonstrates problem-solving ability (defines clearly, solves quickly, shows good judgment, generates imaginative solutions, analyzes thoroughly, shows insight, and so on).

2. Provides accurate, complete, and timely information.
3. Reaches conclusions and shows insights usually found at higher organizational levels.
4. Reacts favorably to negative criticism (corrects weaknesses and builds on strengths).
5. Demonstrates ability and willingness to assume responsibility usually reserved for higher organizational levels.
6. Resolves differences through negotiation and persuasion without having to involve others needlessly.
7. Contributes in ways not normally seen at this organizational level.
8. As a supervisor, has demonstrated ability to plan, organize, staff, direct, control, counsel, guide, appraise.
9. Performs current job in high-level manner, demonstrating effectiveness.

Possible Development Plans. Factors to be considered here include determination of characteristics that the employee has currently (integrity, interpersonal skills, job skills, job knowledge, good performance) and those that the employee needs to develop to be considered for promotion, transfer, or job enlargement (knowledge or skills in a new functional area, adaptability, analytical skills, business understanding, creativity, motivation, professional relationships or exposure to others in the organization, leadership, problem-solving, development of subordinates).

Development Methods:
1. Coaching by the supervisor on the job.
   Rationale:
   to develop the employee's knowledge and skills in performing activities related to the current job.
   Method:
   a. goal setting.
   b. development of work plans.
   c. instruction by the supervisor.
   d. regularly scheduled discussions with supervisor.
   e. direct guidance by supervisor.
2. Attendance at regularly scheduled staff meetings to discuss current business issues.
   Rationale:
   a. to develop a sense of participation in and sharing of business decisions.
   b. to develop and practice problem-solving techniques.
   c. to identify solution(s) to current problems.
   Method:
   a. to learn conference leadership, group discussion, and conduct techniques.
   b. to learn how to participate (to give and to receive information).
3. Special projects and special task force assignments.
   Rationale:
   a. to develop knowledge, skills, or ability in a specific area.
   b. to build on strengths or to correct weaknesses.

c. to develop ability to lead and participate in group activities.
   d. to develop premanagerial skills.
   e. to develop communication skills.
   Method:
   a. to be assigned full authority and to accept responsibility for the special project.
   b. to assign authority while accepting responsibility for task force results.
   c. to participate as a task force leader or member or to be a consultant to the task force.
   d. to present the written or oral project or task force report.
4. Job reassignment.
   Rationale:
   a. to provide added perspective.
   b. to build on strengths or to correct weaknesses.
   c. to test potential.
   d. to uncover latent or dormant abilities.
   e. to determine versatility and flexibility.
   f. to broaden knowledge of the organization.
   g. to screen for possible promotion.
   Method:
   a. to put the employee in the new position.
   b. to assign authority as appropriate.
5. Course work.
   Rationale:
   to develop knowledge and skills applicable to specific development needs.
   Method:
   a. attendance at classes taught by in-house instructors, outside schools, or vendors.
   b. correspondence courses.
6. Directed reading programs.
   Rationale:
   a. to expose the employee to the current literature.
   b. to develop knowledge and skills applicable to specific development needs.
   Method:
   a. to use the organization's (or other) library.
   b. to read materials listed on a prepared bibliography.
   c. to route selected articles, reports, and books to the employee.
 7. Teaching or instructing.
    Rationale:
    a. to develop knowledge and skills relevant to the subjects being taught.
    b. to develop or improve presentation skills.
    c. to develop ability of the employee to "think on his or her feet" when responding to questions.
    Method:
    a. to teach course(s).
    b. to prepare course materials.
    c. to engage in question-and-answer sessions.
    d. to speak before groups.

8. Counseling.
   Rationale:
   to identify handicaps, barriers, and solutions to personal and career development needs.
   Method:
   a. personal or group counseling.
   b. professional counseling assistance.
9. Outside activities.
   Rationale:
   a. to develop leadership and followership abilities and knowledge in areas not directly related to the work place.
   b. to develop outside interests and well-rounded experience.
   Method:
   a. participation in community organizations.
   b. election to local office.
   c. voluntary committee work.
   d. participation in hobbies.

In general, all of these items should be considered before the appraisal interview. In some instances, some of the items will be deleted from consideration, and others will be added. If nothing else, your decision to delete or add should be consciously planned and not be left to chance. In addition, several other factors should be considered by the supervisor before the appraisal interview: timing, mental set, language choice, and environment.

Timing. Timing refers to the selection of the specific time of the interview and the length of time needed for its completion. The supervisor should pick a mutually acceptable time for both people and should allow time for preparation, without either party feeling hurried. If possible, the interview should be scheduled at the close of a natural work cycle (an accounting period, at the end of a project) and at a time of the day and week that will not conflict or interfere with other activities (travel, meetings with customers, other projects). The length of time needed for the interview should be decided in advance; usually, from one to three hours is an acceptable length. If the interview will extend beyond three hours, several short interviews should be scheduled, rather than one long one.

Mental set. Each party in the interview will bring a preconceived mental frame of reference. The supervisor may be more concerned about performance in only one area of the employee's job, and the employee may be concerned that the supervisor will overlook other areas of positive performance. The supervisor may believe the interview is routine and not fear provoking, and the employee may view it as extremely stressful. Conversely, there may be significant discrepancies between the supervisor's evaluation of the employee's performance and the employee's self-evaluation: the supervisor may be ready to initiate termination procedures by putting the employee on a ninety-day notice that performance must improve, and the employee may be ready to substantiate above-average performance during the appraisal period.

Language choice. One's choice of words can affect the outcome of the appraisal interview. The supervisor who says, "All right, you eight ball, you've really messed up over the last three months," has established an acrimonious tone that will make the employee defensive and probably yield few beneficial results. On the other hand, the supervisor who is tactful throughout the interview will have a much more positive outcome.

Environment. An acceptable location for the appraisal interview is one free from interruption and distraction from third parties, either in person or by telephone. For the appraisal interview, the supervisor will usually want to create evidence of authority and indicate nonverbally that he or she is in control, and so the interview should be conducted in the supervisor's office. But when the supervisor wants to deemphasize his or her authority and control, the interview can be held in a neutral location (a conference room) or even the employee's home territory. The location often depends on the relationship of the supervisor and the employee, as well as the expected tone of the interview. With proper preparation, the timing of the interview will be appropriate; discrepant mental sets can be brought into some semblance of similarity; and attention to the kinds of statements to be made, questions to be asked, and tone to be developed should yield a productive interview outcome.

Conducting the Appraisal Interview

As noted in the previous section, the appraisal interview begins with preparation. Independently, the supervisor and the employee should review the employee's performance during the appraisal period. All appropriate data—specific examples, papers, reports, files, or other material—should be gathered and studied so that each party will be familiar with the employee's performance.

At the outset of the interview, the employee should be greeted politely, and an attempt should be made to build rapport. The supervisor should state the purpose of the interview clearly and succinctly and outline the procedure to be followed, progressing logically through the appraisal and including the topics to be covered. A good opening statement after the initial greeting would be:

> *Andy, as part of our ongoing system of labor planning, this is your semiannual performance review. As you know from the homework we've done, its purpose is for us to discuss the strengths and weaknesses of your work performance and to determine how we can work together to maintain and strengthen those areas in which you have done well and to improve those areas in which your performance has been below our expectations, as agreed upon in your last appraisal. I'd also like to talk with you about some specific development plans and get a better idea of what you see as your career direction. Let's begin by your telling me about the maintenance project you've been working on."*

Note that this statement indicates that the supervisor wants to have a dialogue with the employee, rather than just make a series of one-way comments about the employee's performance. Note also that this statement mentions that this is a routine interview required as part of a broader companywide program (the end use of the information discussed), not a special interview designed to single out one employee.

The supervisor could have been more direct in the opening. Instead of saying,

"Let's begin by your telling me about the maintenance project you've been working on," the supervisor could have substituted, "Let's begin by your reading the performance evaluation I'm giving you. After you've read it, we can discuss each point I've made." In this case, a discussion is still possible, even though it will be more focused. Our experience indicates that the second approach is more common in most organizations than the first is, although the first is more desirable.

The body of the interview allows for a detailed discussion of the employee's performance, career interests, and development plans. The supervisor should be sensitive to information that the employee has not stated overtly but that seems to be suggested by the employee's remarks and explore the employee's comments with follow-up questions. The burden is also on the supervisor to create a cooperative atmosphere by adapting to the employee, to use evidence and reasoning skillfully, to show maturity in dealing with emotional topics, to be firm yet supportive, to identify problem areas and discuss them, to be sensitive and empathetic, to be organized, to use appropriate question-and-answer techniques, and to listen well. Perhaps the supervisor's most important tasks in the body of the interview are to explain how the employee's performance was evaluated, to encourage the employee to initiate possible performance improvement plans, and to set a timetable for their achievement. An employee is more likely to work toward a self-established goal than one set by the supervisor.

At the close of the interview, the supervisor should summarize the pertinent information discussed, including areas agreed upon in which strengths are to be maintained and enhanced, in which improvements in performance are necessary, the kinds of changes that should take place, and new goals (or job duties) that will affect those changes. Development plans and the purpose(s) of the interview should be reviewed, and the time and place of the next follow-up discussion (if necessary) should be determined. The employee should be asked if there are any questions, doubts, or confusion about what has transpired. If so, these concerns should be addressed and/or clarified. After the interview has been concluded, the supervisor should prepare a written summary of topics covered, agreements secured, and follow-up action. Copies of the summary should be signed by both the supervisor and the employee and contain any comments by the employee (in some organizations, the supervisor's supervisor will also sign the summary document). Copies of the summary should be given to the supervisor and the employee and added to the employee's personnel file. The content of the interview itself and the summary should be treated as confidential.

Job Variables Discussed in the Appraisal Interview

Job variables frequently discussed in the appraisal interview include:

1. Verification of demographic data about the employee (title, length of time in position, and the like).
2. Time covered by the current appraisal period (annual, semiannual).
3. Discussion of the employee's overall work environment (what the employee does, where, relationships with co-workers).

4. Current work performance evaluation.
5. Proposals for building on strengths.
6. Proposals for correcting deficiencies.
7. Review of job duties, indicators of performance, goals and objectives.
8. Types of training and development needed.
9. Readiness for promotion.

Environmental Variables Discussed in the Appraisal Interview

Environmental variables include those events not directly connected to job duties but that could affect the employee's performance. Some environmental variables are highly personal, and so care should be taken when discussing them. Some supervisors may decide to avoid such issues altogether because of the discomfort they may feel in dealing with them. Other environmental variables are concerned with working conditions and consequently are much less personal. Environmental variables include:

1. Employee's insecurity and anxiety.
2. Outside (nonwork) pressure or other stress-inducing events.
3. Working conditions.
4. Conflict between the employee's personal goals and those of the job or the organization.

Representative Questions in the Appraisal Interview

To elicit information about job and environmental variables, the following questions and statements can be used. Adapt them to fit the individual and the job under discussion.

1. Have you completed the refresher course you were taking to qualify for your real estate broker's license?
2. What additional courses do you have to take before receiving your bachelor's degree?
3. I want to verify that this appraisal covers the period from April 1 to March 31.
4. How would you evaluate your overall performance over the last twelve months?
5. Tell me what difficulties you've had over the past twelve months.
6. What do you think is the problem?
7. Have we defined the problem accurately?
8. How can your performance be improved?
9. What steps will you take to improve your performance?
10. How can I help you overcome the problem?
11. Why is the turnover in your department 20 percent higher than the company average?

12. Last August when the reorganization took place, your department performed exceptionally well. What did you do to effect such a smooth transition?
13. How has your daughter's illness affected your performance?
14. Were you able to consolidate your debts by getting a bank loan?
15. Have you noted any side effects from the medication you've been taking that might be affecting your performance?
16. What are the chances you'll be leaving us to enter graduate school?
17. How will the new bidding system affect quality control in your department?
18. What part of your current job do you like? Dislike? Would you like to get rid of?
19. What do you think of your career progress to date?
20. What do you see as your next job with this company?
21. How do your personal goals mesh with those that the company has for you?
22. What self-development activities have you initiated in the past year?
23. We're thinking about moving you to the planning department. Would that interest you?
24. What do you want to be doing in five years?
25. In the foreseeable future there is no promotion for you, but you can stay as long as you want in your current job.
26. We have agreed that these are the areas in which you should improve your performance and on the dates by which the items listed are to be completed. What else needs to be done?

Career Planning

Career planning is often part of the performance appraisal process and is a natural topic to be discussed during the appraisal interview. We shall treat career planning as separate from the appraisal interview, even though almost everything mentioned can and does apply to the performance appraisal.

The responsibility for formulating and achieving your career plan rests with you. You are the architect of your career. Even though others may counsel you or advise you, you alone must make the decisions about your interests, goals, career choices, and occupation, as well as the significance of any barriers that might prevent you from selecting a particular career. To do so requires thoughtful, realistic self-assessment and self-evaluation, along with careful planning to achieve your needs and reach your personal and job-related goals. Few people achieve success by accident or luck alone. Those who are successful ("success" is however *you* define it) probably considered the kinds of issues raised in this section.

You may know people who spend more time planning their vacations than their careers. We know them, too; however, we think that career planning is a full-time activity. Our purpose is not to tell you what you should be or how you should get there. Rather, we shall offer a set of tools and instructions on how to use them. How you do use them is up to you, but we recommend that you, first, respond frankly to the issues raised; second, annually review the material in this chapter to make sure you are on what you consider to be the right career path; and finally, review these materials if you ever find yourself looking for employment.

Many events trigger career-planning activity. Some of you will undertake career planning because of negative circumstances: you have lost your job, your self-confidence has been shaken, you have lost faith in your abilities, your former colleagues ignore you, you have lost control of your old support systems, and you question your future. For others of you, the activity is a positive one: your career is just beginning, your schooling is almost completed, and you are ready to enter the work force for the first time in a capacity other than through a temporary or part-time job. Perhaps you are currently employed and have decided to change jobs or change companies. You send out a few résumés to test the market. A headhunter (search firm) calls. Suddenly new career opportunities are presented.

It is unusual to select a career early in life and stick with it to retirement. You may take the first job offered (or any subsequent job as well). The career path that you are on, though possibly satisfying initially, may no longer be exciting after five (or fifteen or twenty-five) years. New challenges are needed. When that happens, you are ready to reexamine your career-planning tools and processes. There are five steps to take: assessment, analysis and insight, decision making, change, and reassessment.

Assessment

There are many sources of assessment data that you can use: evaluations from others with whom you work (peers, your supervisor); written and oral performance evaluations (data from the appraisal interview); opinions from friends, relatives, and others whom you value; career testing and counseling; and your own thoughts and perceptions. We shall be concerned here with career testing and counseling and self-assessment.

Career Testing and Counseling. Career testing and counseling are not necessary for everyone, but if you have never before used this service, you may want to consider it. Testing and counseling programs are conducted by companies, universities, and private licensed psychologists. Typically, the program will consist of a general assessment test battery of three to five tests taken over a four- to six-hour period. When the tests are scored and charted (sometimes on the same day), there is a follow-up session (one or more hours as necessary) during which a trained counselor reviews your test results and profiles and helps you interpret and understand what they mean for you. Additional testing and/or counseling may be suggested. Unless agreed otherwise, the results of the testing and counseling are confidential between you and the counselor.

Frequently the testing and counseling will tell you things about yourself that you had never known before, and you will need to decide if you want to pursue them further. Some people report that the testing and counseling programs in which they have participated have provided no new information but just confirmed what they already knew about themselves. If you give that some thought, you will realize that confirmation alone is useful, as it suggests that you already have a pretty good idea about who you are and where you want to go.

There are many kinds of career tests available, and the good ones are valid and reliable measures. But in all cases, the truest test of a test's "goodness" is the task itself. Technically, a bumblebee cannot fly—its body is too big and heavy for its wings. Yet, if you have ever been chased by a bumblebee, you will know that it was flying, not sprinting. Thus the flying-test results are wrong. Similarly, sometimes counseling test results are incorrect as they apply to you. Do not accept the results as gospel, but rather accept them as additional information about yourself, and apply them as you think appropriate. Here, the trained career counselor can help.

A representative career-counseling test battery (a series or combination of examinations) includes tests that measure a variety of characteristics. As an example, The Strong-Campbell Interest Inventory measures your interests and how they compare with those of others in particular vocations. The California Test of Mental Maturity measures intelligence. The Nelson-Denny Reading Test measures reading aptitude, comprehension, and recall. The Guilford-Zimmerman Temperament Survey measures personality. Other tests may be substituted, and additional tests may be added if warranted by the general testing. Specific aptitude tests can be selected if they are relevant to your interests, temperament, and abilities.

Basically, career testing and counseling will provide objective data about your personal characteristics, what makes you tick, and what is likely to give you personal satisfaction. The information will suggest career directions that are consistent with your interests, aptitudes, abilities, and temperament. Your task is to relate the new or confirming testing and counseling information to what you already know about yourself.

Self-assessment. The purpose of self-assessment is to allow you to confront your own perceptions of yourself. Your goal is to identify and evaluate your skills, abilities, strengths, weaknesses, accomplishments, objectives—just about anything you know about yourself—so that you can make thoughtful career judgments. Although you may seek counseling to help you with the self-assessment, we recommend that you start with a series of self-report questions that will help reveal insights into your personal motives, needs, and characteristic behaviors. Write out the information requested and keep it as a permanent record so that you can refer to it at a later date (see the career planning questionnaire in Figure 8.1 at the end of this chapter. This questionnaire is similar to one used by several *Fortune* 500 industrial companies to aid their managers in self-assessment and career-assessment.)

Analysis and Insight

Once you have completed the assessment phase, you will need to analyze what you have learned. Review your test results and your self-assessment responses. How does each compare with the other? What new information have you uncovered about yourself? What were you able to confirm about yourself? What discrepancies did you find between the test data and the self-report data? What patterns seem to be emerging (or have emerged), not only in regard to your motivations, interests, aptitudes, behaviors, likes, dislikes, strengths, and weaknesses, but also in regard to anything else that is important to you? Do you agree or disagree with what you have learned? Why? What do you want to know more about? In trying to analyze and gain insight, you may want to bounce findings and ideas off another person. Pick a counselor or someone else you trust (a friend, relative, supervisor, teacher, spouse) who can assume that role for you. You may also want to consider other sources of information about yourself. Everything is fair game, from current performance appraisal data to old elementary school report cards.

Decision Making

You have now assessed and analyzed all your information. Select the two or three principal themes or trends that have emerged. What do you want to do about them? Can you identify strengths you want to build on? Weaknesses you want to correct? Potential you want to achieve? At this stage you will want to begin to develop a plan of action. Try to determine what you want to do, what is under your control, what requires the help of others, and the approximate length of your timetable. Probably the most important question you can answer here is "Is it realistic?"

Ron is a friend of ours. When he was twenty-one, he decided to become a physician. His wife and parents agreed to support him, and so his wife left school to work as a secretary. They prepared to take out a loan. Ron switched majors from psychology to biology, learned advanced first-aid techniques and taught classes for the Red Cross. He applied for but was denied admission to medical school and so became a paramedic and for two years made emergency runs with a local rescue squad. Through perseverance and some remedial course work Ron was finally admitted to medical school. Today, at the age of thirty-two he is a practicing physician specializing in emergency medicine. Ron's wife returned to school, graduated, and has been admitted for graduate work, and Ron has begun to reimburse his parents.

Bill is also a friend of ours, who joined the marines after high school. After returning from Vietnam, he went to work in a factory in his hometown. Ten years later, even though he had been promoted to supervisor, he was bored with his work. He had always wanted to own a fast-food restaurant and was saving money to do so when he retired (in the year 2003). But after self-assessment and analysis, he decided to open the restaurant earlier, and at age thirty-five, he left his factory job to open a restaurant in Missouri.

Steve is a business acquaintance. He is fifty-one and has been with his company for seventeen years. He is fed up with his boss and with the amount of ambiguity and uncertainty he has to deal with in his job. Unlike Ron or Bill, Steve does not think he is mobile. He is the sole support for his parents, both of whom are in their eighties and are confined to a constant-care nursing home. Steve also has three children in college. It is unrealistic for him to change companies or to relocate, and he does not think that he can meet his financial obligations on a lower salary. Currently, he plans to use his next performance review to discuss a lateral transfer to another job in the same company.

Change

When considering your decisions, evaluate their practicality in terms of your present life circumstances. Do you have the time, education, experience, background, psychological support system, and financing to implement your decision? Can you afford the worst-case risk? Will the benefit of your decisions and the satisfactions experienced when achieving your goals outweigh the risks associated with the change (Bill)? If you cannot now make the changes you want, start planning to make them at a later date (Steve). Also try to make alternative plans to enable you to achieve small increments toward your ultimate objective (Ron).

Reassessment

As indicated earlier, career planning is a full-time activity. Reevaluate your situation regularly, especially before a performance appraisal. As necessary, work through the earlier steps in the career-planning process. How can you build upon what you do well and what you like to do, while improving what you do poorly and eliminating what you do not like to do? Change does not have to be radical. Incremental shifts can help you toward where you want to be. An ancient saying is applicable to career planning: a journey of a thousand miles begins with the first step.

SUMMARY

This chapter described the appraisal interview as it relates to the long-term appraisal system of an organization and to individual career planning and development. We discussed the purposes of the appraisal interview, common situations encountered during the appraisal interview, preparation for the appraisal interview, conduct of the appraisal interview, personal and environmental variables that affect performance, and career and life planning.

EXERCISES

1. Conduct an appraisal interview in which you appraise a classmate's performance in this course.
2. Contact an employer or supervisor of others. Conduct an interview in which you elicit information about the kinds of characteristics that that person looks for when appraising the performance of others. Determine what kind of appraisal system the organization has, how often appraisal interviews are conducted, and how the interview data are used for career planning.
3. Jerry Warner, one of your subordinates, has you puzzled. You would like him to take over your position in the near future, but he does not seem to have the necessary prerequisites for promotion—at least, this is your perception. Jerry is twenty-seven years old. He has had three years of college

and seems to be intellectually capable. He is pleasant and generally admired by most of his fellow employees. He handles himself well under stress, and his attitude toward hard work is excellent. When he is working on the job, his attention to detail is precise but sadly lacking in the area of administrative reports and corporate procedures. His attitude toward reports and procedures is recognized by his subordinates. You have spoken to him several times, and although he seems to understand your reasoning, his response is one of diminishing effectiveness. Jerry is single but has recently started seeing a woman he dated in college. He has a younger brother enrolled at State University and an older sister married and living in British Columbia. Jerry seems to be in good health, to have no special financial worries, and to be generally well adjusted.

You be the appraiser; a classmate will be Jerry. Given only this much information, conduct an interview in which your goal is to develop a specific course of action necessary to groom Jerry for promotion within the next two years.

4. Prepare a case of approximately three hundred words in which you are the appraisee. The case may be similar in form to the one in Exercise 3. The case should be a brief description of your job—a statement of your current performance relative to your job duties, the goals of your performance, and your attitudes toward your work. The case may be real, based on a job or jobs you have held, or it may be imaginary.
   a. Give the case to a classmate who has been assigned as the appraiser. You will be the appraisee.
   b. Conduct the interview in class. When the interview is over, give the case to your instructor for evaluation.
5. Complete the career planning questionnaire that follows (see Figure 8.1). Develop a realistic plan to get you to where you want to be in three years (or in five years).

NOTE

1. This questionnaire is similar to those used by the authors as consultants to several major business organizations in the United States and Europe. The questionnaire is used to help middle- and senior-level executives assess their career progress to date, potential, and related subjects.

ADDITIONAL READINGS

Loughary, John W., and Theresa M. Ripley. *Career & Life Planning Guide*. Chicago: Follett, 1976.

Maier, Norman R. F. *The Appraisal Interview: Three Basic Approaches*. La Jolla, Calif.: University Associates, 1976.

Performance Appraisal Series. Reprints from *Harvard Business Review*, no. 21143 (1972).

148   INTERVIEWING

FIGURE 8.1. Career Planning Questionnaire[1]

[*Directions:* Complete this questionnaire honestly and in detail. Take as much time and space as you need to be thorough.]

1. Name:
2. Age and birth date:
3. Marital status:
4. Spouse's name:
5. Names and ages of children:

6. Education—degree(s) held, school(s), date(s), major(s), minor(s):

7. Special certification(s):

8. Current job title, length of time in position, major duties:

9. Work history (List all jobs held, with most recent job first):
    Title   Company   Dates   Duties

10. Which of your jobs did you like the best? Why?

11. Which of your jobs did you like the least? Why?

12. What were you able to accomplish in each job you listed? (List five to ten accomplishments for each job.)

13. What five adjectives would your friends use to describe you?

14. What five adjectives would your enemies use to describe you?

FIGURE 8.1. Career Planning Questionnaire (continued)

15. Which set of five adjectives in Questions 13 and 14 is correct? Why?

16. What three things do you like best about your current job? Why?

17. What three things do you dislike most about your current job? Why?

18. Of the things you like and dislike in your current job, which ones are under your control?

19. What single thing would make you more satisfied in your current job?

20. What are your strengths?

21. What are your weaknesses?

22. In what geographical location would you prefer to live? Why?

23. What causes you to be under pressure at work?

24. What causes you to be under pressure at home?

25. What do you see as your next job (in one to three years)? How do you intend to get there?

26. What do you see as your job in four to six years? What do you need to do to get there?

FIGURE 8.1. Career Planning Questionnaire (continued)

27. Without regard to your current knowledge or skills, what would you really like to be doing in five years? Why?

28. What do you do in your spare time? Why?

29. Are you satisfied with yourself? Why?

30. What are the key "make" or "break" elements in your current job?

31. Write a job description of your "ideal" position.

32. How effectively can you lead without arousing hostility in others? Explain.

33. What impression do you make on others? Why?

34. How well do you perceive behavioral cues in others? Give an example.

35. How likely are you to solve a management problem in a novel way? Give an example.

36. How realistic are your insights into your own abilities?

37. How easy is it for you to modify your behavior in order to accomplish a goal? Give an example.

38. To what extent are you emotionally dependent on others? Give an example.

FIGURE 8.1. Career Planning Questionnaire (continued)

39. Would you rather be around higher-status people or lower-status people? Why?

40. How do you react to authority figures? Give a positive and a negative example.

41. How well does your performance stand up in the face of stress? Give an example.

42. Give three examples of your good communication skills.

43. Give three examples of your bad communication skills.

44. Which skills in Questions 42 and 43 are most representative of you? Why?

45. Are you willing to trust others with sensitive information? Give examples.

46. Can you discuss objectively with someone else things that that person does not want to hear? Give examples.

47. When you give a performance appraisal, give examples of your being candid:

    honest:

    positive:

    negative:

48. How comfortable were you in each of the situations identified in Question 47?

FIGURE 8.1. Career Planning Questionnaire (continued)

49. Describe yourself as a manager (researcher, individual contributor, teacher, and so on, as appropriate).

50. Give three work examples of when you have been a team player.

51. Give three work examples of when you have been a loner.

52. Which situations in Questions 50 and 51 did you prefer? Why?

53. What was the last thing you did extraordinarily well at work? Why did you do it so well?

54. What was the last thing you did poorly at work? Why did you do it so poorly?

55. What can you start doing (that you do not do now) to help you in the future?

56. What can you stop doing (that you do do now) to help you in the future?

57. What can you continue doing (that you do do now) to help you in the future?

58. What do you need to do now so that in six months you can say, "I'm better at _____ than I was six months ago."

59. Evaluate your knowledge, skills, or ability in the following areas, and also indicate how much you like or dislike doing the activity:
technical skills (in specialty):

FIGURE 8.1. Career Planning Questionnaire (continued)

ability to apply technical information (in specialty):
problem solving:
decision making:
creativity:
interpersonal sensitivity:
listening:
reading skills:
writing:
public speaking:
conversation:
leading meetings:
participating in meetings:
giving instructions:
receiving instructions:
handling discipline:
giving evaluations:
planning:
organizing:
staffing:
directing:
controlling:
counseling:
coaching:
appraising:
developing others:

60. How much time, effort, and money are you willing to commit to achieve your career goals and objectives?

61. Rank the following career items (1-most important to you, 2-second most important, and so on), and explain your ranking:

Company/organization size:	Dental insurance:
Type of industry/product/service:	Life insurance:
Geographic location:	Disability insurance:
Organizational climate/ management style:	Liability insurance:
	Vacations and holidays:
Unionized/nonunionized:	Pension:
Your title:	Club memberships:
Prestige:	Company car:
Advancement/growth opportunity:	Parking at work:
Amount of authority:	Housing:
Your reporting relationship:	School system:
Personal relationship with co-workers:	Public transportation:
	Recreational activities:
Salary:	Cultural activities:
Incentive compensation:	Community tax base:
Health Insurance:	

FIGURE 8.1. Career Planning Questionnaire (continued)

Religious activities: Other:

62. What family (or other) considerations will affect your career planning?

63. What is your plan for advancing your career? How will you implement it?

64. When you review your responses to Questions 1 through 63, what consistent or contradictory patterns do you find?

65. Have you been honest in completing this questionnaire? If not, do it again.

66. Have you answered this questionnaire completely? If not, do it again.

9

The Exit Interview

CHAPTER OBJECTIVES

1. Explain the purposes of the exit interview.
2. Identify circumstances when exit interviews are appropriate.
3. Explain the benefits of conducting exit interviews.
4. Identify questions likely to be asked in the exit interview.
5. Identify two pitfalls likely to be encountered by the interviewer in the exit interview.
6. Describe the role of outplacement in the exiting process.
7. Conduct an exit interview.

Introduction

We know of a situation that plagued a major American corporation several years ago. The company had a reputation within its industry for having an excellent human resources department that developed superb programs and functioned with strong support from the senior operating management in the areas of individual development, organizational development, and organizational design. It was seen as being on the cutting edge of human technology. But within a period of eighteen months, following a change of chief executive officer (CEO), the company lost by resignation over 90 percent of its training and development specialists.

We know of another situation involving a small manufacturing plant employing 300 people in North Central Texas. The turnover among the hourly workers in the plant was running at nearly 150 percent annually. (This meant that each year, in order to maintain an hourly work force of 250 employees, the plant had to hire 375 new employees!) The plant's goal was to reduce the turnover to 60 percent (i.e., to hire 150 new employees each year).

These employee turnover levels are excessive, and so both organizations undertook studies to determine the causes. In the first case, the principal cause was found to be a shift of support at the CEO level, away from the internal training and development function. The change was so subtle that most of the corporation's management did not notice it. But the training and development staff did see it and quickly left the organization to accept employment with other companies. This finding was uncovered by piecing together bits of information obtained in the exit interviews with those who were leaving.

In the second case (the manufacturing plant), exit interview data were not always available, as many employees simply left their jobs and never returned. But, from the data obtained from those exit interviews that were held, the plant management was able to determine that the dominant characteristic of the work force was its migratory nature. Workers would accept employment for a few months, long enough to save a few dollars, and then they would move on. Furthermore, the exit interviewers found that some of the employees had worked for the plant on three or more occasions, for at least three months each time, over the preceding ten years. (As an interesting aside, in the plant situation, many of the exit interviews were "gate" interviews—actually held at the plant's main gate as the employees who had quit were leaving.) These two findings from the exit interviews prompted a study of the employment records of all of the plant's employees with more than one year of service, in an effort to determine what caused people to stay, rather than what caused them to leave. That study revealed that long-term employees had either "roots" (family or property) in the community or family or friends also working in the plant. To the extent that the law allowed, these factors became part of the applicant-screening process.

During the late 1970s and early 1980s many organizations in both the public and private sectors were forced by poor economic conditions to reduce their work forces. In many instances, organizations planned their turnover (unlike the unplanned cases above). They identified departments to be consolidated, product lines to be eliminated, services to be discontinued, and individuals to be terminated. If these organizations were generating their own turnover, what did they have to gain from exit interviews? First, they could still obtain valuable information from terminated employees about their perceptions of management, financial, growth, and other organizational practices. Second, and more important in this context, they could gain the goodwill of the terminated employees by providing outplacement assistance.

Turnover is a problem, whether planned or unplanned, voluntary or involuntary. First, when trained people leave, it costs money to replace the human investment they represent. One executive recruiter we know estimated that his company spends over $40,000 in direct recruiting and relocation costs for each new executive hired. This reflects none of the hidden costs, such as the recruiter's time; the time it takes for the new executive to "get up to speed" in his or her new job (perhaps six months before comfort and knowledge levels are reached); or the knowledge, talent, and skills that terminated employees often take with them when they leave the organization.

Second, a high rate of attrition often indicates that something is wrong with the company. Management and reward systems may not be working properly. Persons currently being recruited may have second thoughts about accepting job offers with the company. Current employees may lose morale and begin to look elsewhere for employment when they see their co-workers leaving.

Third, high turnover may give competitors an edge. Employees who leave your company and who are hired by competitors often are familiar with your strategic directions, plans, and approaches to achieving them. They know the vulnerabilities of your organization. Although most will not take unfair or unethical advantage of their position, some will.

Ideally, the conditions that might lead to unplanned turnover should be addressed long before exit interviews are needed, though conditions and circumstances are seldom ideal. But in any condition of attrition, whether planned or unplanned, the exit interview is likely to have outcomes beneficial to both the organization and the terminated employee.

Company Benefits

From the company viewpoint, there are three reasons for conducting exit interviews.

1. To obtain perceptions of the company from employees who have "nothing to lose." Typically, this information will concern the employee's perceptions of salary, wages, benefits, and management style; the employee's supervisor, co-workers, and work relationships; the extent to which the employee was challenged on the job; organizational climate; growth and development; clarity of career paths and advancement potential; and specific reasons why the employee is leaving (see Figure 9.1). But you should be aware that many employees will avoid being too frank, as they do not want their comments used against them later.
2. To create goodwill for the company by informing the employee about severance pay and benefits (if applicable), company support (if appropriate) in helping the employee find a new job, and to indicate what the company will confirm about the employee's employment history and reasons for leaving if the company is asked for a reference by a prospective new employer.
3. To complete processing of the terminating employee. This includes such items as recording a forwarding address and phone number, returning credit cards, processing final expense reports, collecting expense advances, sending notification of the termination to the personnel department, returning other company property (such as calculators), and verifying how various company benefits will be handled (see Figures 9.2 and 9.3).

Terminating Employee Benefits

From the viewpoint of the employee who has terminated either voluntarily (the employee is leaving of his or her own choice) or involuntarily (the employee has been fired or laid off), the benefits of participating in the exit interview tend to be the flip side of those for the company.

1. To provide perceptions of the company for the record, typically in the areas of salary, wages, benefits, management style, supervision, co-workers, work relationships, on-the-job challenges, organizational climate, growth and advancement opportunity, and specific reasons for leaving.

158   INTERVIEWING

FIGURE 9.1. Employee Termination Notice[1]

Employee Data

Name: _____ Department: _____

Title: _____ Classification (E/N–E): _____

Effective Termination Date: _____ Last Day Worked: _____

Vacation Pay Due: _____ Severance Pay Due: _____

New Employer: _____
                  (address)   (phone)

Reason for Termination

Voluntary:
___ other work, better wages
___ other work, better conditions
___ other work, more interest
___ other work, personality conflict
___ relocation outside area
___ spouse transferred
___ marriage
___ family obligations
___ illness
___ pregnancy
___ inadequate public transportation
___ resume education
___ refused similar work
___ retirement (paid)
___ retirement (unpaid)
___ travel
___ other

Involuntary:
___ assignment over
___ contract expired
___ reduction in force
___ displaced by senior employee
___ reorganization
___ total disability
___ other

Discharge:
___ absenteeism
___ tardiness
___ dishonesty
___ rule violations
___ insubordination
___ incompetence
___ alcoholism
___ drug use
___ will not follow instructions
___ other

Recommended for Future Employment
☐ Yes ☐ No

Performance Evaluation (use reverse side)

Signature and Date: _____

2. To determine what, if any, severance pay and benefits will be forthcoming, what company support in finding new employment will be provided, and what information the company will release to prospective new employers.
3. To complete termination processing, including not only the items discussed for the employer but also the arrangements for receipt of the last paycheck and what it will include, insurance conversion, and items covered under the stock purchase plan, vested retirement benefits and options, savings

FIGURE 9.2. Supervisor Checklist for Terminating Employees[2]

Employee Name: _____ Department: _____
Supervisor: _____

___ Employee's last workday: _____
___ Employee's last benefits day: _____
___ Employee's last payday: _____
___ Final expense report processed.
___ Written termination notice forwarded to personnel department.
___ Employee's expense and/or salary advances returned.
___ Forwarding address and phone number recorded.
___ Company property returned (keys, calculator, etc.):
_____
_____
___ Company credit cards returned (air travel, automobile, telephone, etc.).
___ Other.

FIGURE 9.3. Personnel Department Checklist for Terminating Employees[3]

Employee Name: _____ Interviewer: _____
___ Termination notice given in writing.
___ Exit interview schedule: time: _____ location: _____
___ Benefits department notified.
___ All paper work processed, including notification of last day worked, last day paid, last day of benefits, vacation pay owed, forwarding address and telephone.
___ Identification card and credit cards collected.
___ Final expense report processed.
___ Arrangements made for handling:
  ___ Return of company property (calculators, dictation equipment, etc.)
  ___ Stock purchase plan
  ___ Health (and other) insurance conversion
  ___ Vested retirement benefits and options
  ___ U.S. Savings Bonds
  ___ Credit union account
  ___ Employee stock ownership plan
  ___ Other
___ Date for receiving last paycheck and what will be included.

plans (credit union, savings bonds, and stock ownership plan). In addition, the employee should make sure that all expense reimbursement forms for money owed to him or her have been processed.

Conducting the Exit Interview

The exit interview includes information gathering, information giving, and counseling. Information is elicited by each party from the other in an open and supportive environment. The interviewer, however, makes no effort to help the interviewee solve problems. Rather, the interviewer probes for information and records it for later analysis. In general, the exit interview should be conducted as a controlled nondirective interview in which the interviewer (the company representative) controls the general categories to be discussed, but the terminated employee provides specific information within the categories in whatever fashion it comes to mind (see Chapter 10 for a discussion of the controlled nondirective interview). Categories to be covered may be framed as questions that restrict the general parameters of the answer but that then are followed by questions that allow more wide-ranging responses (see Figure 9.4).

The Opening

The opening of the exit interview sets its tone. Will the interview be supportive and businesslike, or will it be hostile? In the opening, the interviewer outlines the reasons for the interview, how it will progress, and what the psychological contract (the ground rules) will be between the interviewer and the interviewee.

Assuming that the normal courtesies have taken place, the interviewer may begin with an opening remark like:

> *Joe, thank you for taking the time today to talk with me. As you know, I was sorry to learn that you were leaving our company but pleased for you that your new job is a promotion. For the next thirty minutes or so, I would like to explore with you some of your reasons for leaving and your perceptions of this company, as well as review with you your benefit plan options. In addition, I want to make sure all of your paperwork has been processed and to respond to any questions you may have. Everything you say will be treated confidentially. You will not be linked directly with any comments you make.*

This opening suggests that the interviewer and the interviewee know each other and share some degree of respect and trust. In an interview in which the interviewee may be somewhat hostile (having been fired or laid off), a more direct, confrontational approach may be necessary:

> *Joe, thanks for stopping by to see me. I know you're mad as hell at the company for laying you off, and you're probably mad at me, too. But I hope you'll take a few minutes to tell me what went wrong. Whatever you say will be held in confidence. Now, will you talk to me?*

Such an approach carries with it the risk that the interviewee may refuse to participate. But by showing empathy for and understanding of what the interviewee is feeling, the interviewer may get the interviewee to open up and vent

FIGURE 9.4. Exit Interview Form[4]

Name: _____ Position title: _____

Division: _____ City location: _____

Directions: Please complete this form and bring it with you to your exit interview. After the interview, it will be kept in your personnel folder. Any questions you have concerning your company benefits will be answered during the interview.

I. *General*
Do you have a new job? Yes ☐ No ☐

If yes, what is your new title? _____

What is your new company? _____

Do you consider your new job a promotion? Yes ☐ No ☐

Compare your new pay rate with the job you are leaving.
Above ☐ Same ☐ Below ☐

II. *Management*
Do you think company management is partial to some employees and not to others? _____

How could the recruitment and selection process for your position be improved? _____

Were your job responsibilities clearly communicated? _____

III. *Training and Development*
Were you properly trained to do your job? _____

Was the company interested in your personal growth? _____

IV. *Financial*
Is the company pay: high ☐ above average ☐ average ☐ low ☐
Are company benefits: high ☐ above average ☐ average ☐ low ☐
Were your personal pay increases: good ☐ average ☐ poor ☐

V. *Information Flow*
Are company employees kept informed on matters that affect them on the job? _____

FIGURE 9.4. Exit Interview Form (continued)

How can employees be kept better informed? _____

_____

VI. *Other*
Why are you leaving the company? _____

_____

_____

If you could tell your supervisor one thing, what would it be? _____

_____

Would you work for the company in the future if you were offered employment here? _____

_____

What made you start looking for a job outside the company? _____

_____

What advantages does your new job have over the one you are leaving?

_____

_____

VII. What other comments do you want to make for the record? _____

_____

_____

VIII. *Interviewer Comments:* _____

_____

_____

Date: _____ Employee's Signature: _____

Date: _____ Interviewer's Signature: _____

his or her anger and frustration. From what the interviewee says, the adept interviewer will be able to glean useful information. Moreover, once the interviewee begins to talk, the interviewer probably will be able to accomplish most, if not all, of the other purposes of the exit interview.

The Body

In the body, the interviewer will cover the main content categories and provide an opportunity for the interviewee to make additional comments or ask additional questions. Typical questions asked by the interviewer would be:

1. Why are you leaving?
2. What could the company have done to persuade you to stay?
3. Is your new job a promotion?
4. Under what circumstances would you consider returning to work here?
5. How would you describe the supervision you received in your last assignment?
6. Would you recommend this company to a friend?
7. How does this company pay in relation to similar companies with which you are familiar?
8. How would you describe our benefit programs?
9. What other benefits would you like to have?
10. How well did the company prepare you for your current assignment?
11. Which do you think is more important in this company, how well you perform or whom you know? Why?
12. How would you describe your co-workers?
13. Is there anything I haven't asked you that you want to comment on? What?
14. Let me explain the outplacement assistance that will be extended to you.
15. Do you think that others still with this organization share your views?

Typical questions asked by the interviewee would be:

1. What will you do with the information that I give you?
2. What benefits am I entitled to receive?
3. When do I get my last paycheck? What does it include?
4. When do I receive the stock I purchased under the stock purchase plan?
5. What kind of a reference will I receive from the company?
6. Will I qualify for reemployment if business conditions improve?
7. How will the company help me in finding a new job?
8. What do I do with my credit cards (telephone, air travel), keys (to doors, desk), and company identification badge?
9. How do I turn in my company car?
10. You have discriminated against me (age, sex, race, physical handicap, color, religion, national origin), and so you can expect a charge to be filed with the Equal Employment Opportunity Commission!

The Close

The close of the exit interview should reaffirm the positive tone established at the outset. If the interview has been riddled with anger and hostility, a positive note should still be struck. Thank the interviewee for the time spent in the interview, and for the service given to the organization. If you are sorry to see the interviewee leave, say so. Reaffirm that the interviewee's responses and comments will be kept confidential. Summarize what, if anything, has been agreed to during the interview.

A representative ending might be:

> Mary, as neither of us has any more questions or anything else to say, I'd like to thank you once again for your time and for the useful and constructive comments you made. Everything you said will be treated confidentially. I wish you were staying, but I understand your reasons for leaving, and I appreciate them. Good luck on your new job. If I can ever be of help to you, let me know.

Or:

> Mary, even though there were some things you didn't want to talk about, I do understand how you feel at being terminated. I'm going to match up what you said with what others have told me to see what kind of pattern emerges. Maybe we'll be able to prevent this sort of thing from happening to others in the future. Meanwhile, you'll get your last check on Friday. On Monday, report at 9:00 A.M. to the outplacement center we've set up in the bank building next door. Good luck to you.

Pitfalls

Two pitfalls are likely to be encountered in the exit interview. The first, confrontation leading to an unwillingness to participate, has already been mentioned. The interviewer's primary purpose is to gather information, even from the most reluctant interviewee, and nothing will be gained if the interviewee walks out. An even temperament, courtesy, good listening skills, and open-ended questioning techniques will be the interviewer's strongest allies.

The second pitfall is the tendency of the interviewer to lapse into a counseling mode, especially with employees who have been terminated involuntarily. When an individual is released from a company, emotions usually run high on both sides. The individual will feel ego damage, anger, and shock. There may be a tendency to wallow in self-pity, to deny the fact of termination, or to make accusations against the supervisor or the company. For the company representative who conducts the exit interview, there may be feelings of guilt, a desire to avoid confrontation, and a desire to be helpful. Both parties should keep counseling separate from the exit interview.

Outplacement

Although in existence for many years, since the late 1970s the provision of outplacement assistance has mushroomed in American organizations. Whether offered by outside consultants or internal specialists, terminated employees are helped to assess their skills and abilities, given guidance on résumé preparation and job interviewing, and assisted in making potential employment contacts.

But probably the most important aspect of outplacement assistance is that it helps the ex-employee put unemployment in perspective.

Although the company may gain goodwill from it, the primary function of outplacement is to enable terminated employees to obtain new jobs. This is a time for the employee to come to grips with the termination and why it has taken place. Appraisals and counseling are often helpful here. It is a time for the individual to assess personal aptitudes (What do I do well?), attitudes (Do I like to do what I do well?), aspirations (What do I want to become?), education (What am I formally educated to do?), experiences (What am I qualified to do by the personal experiences I have had?), needs (What will satisfy me?), and outside influences (What impact will my family and friends have on my decision(s)?).

SUMMARY

This chapter reviewed the purposes of the exit interview, including its benefits for both the organization and the employee. We also discussed representative information gathered and given and pitfalls likely to be encountered, and we reviewed the organization of the interview, the kinds of questions asked, and the role of outplacement.

EXERCISES

1. Find a company in your community that conducts exit interviews for terminating employees. Interview someone who administers them regularly. Find out what kind of information the company obtains and how the information is used, including what new programs, practices, or procedures have been implemented within the company as a result of exit interview data.
2. You may know of someone who has been an interviewee in an exit interview. Interview that person to find out his or her opinions of it.
3. In-class assignment:
   a. Conduct an exit interview with a classmate who is role-playing a person who has been fired. Secretly you are happy the person is leaving. The interviewee is angry. Your goal is to defuse the situation and create goodwill for the company.
   b. Conduct an exit interview with a classmate who is role-playing a person who has resigned to accept employment with a competitor. Your primary interest is to learn why the person is leaving and what your company can do to keep employees. You have heard that your company may have some "attitude" problems, and you want to check that, too.

NOTES

1. Based on the employee termination notice form used by a *Fortune* 500 company.
2. Based on a form used by a *Fortune* 500 company. This form is given to the supervisor of the terminating employees.

3. Based on a form used by a *Fortune* 500 company. This form is given to terminating employees who then bring it to the exit interview.
4. Based on a exit interview form used by a *Fortune* 500 company.

ADDITIONAL READINGS

Jablonski, Walter A. "How Useful Are Exit Interviews?" in Stewart Ferguson and Sherry Devereaux Ferguson, *INTERCOM: Readings in Organizational Communication.* Rochelle Park, N.J.: Hayden Book Company, 1980. Chapter 25, pp. 271–276.

Lopez, Felix M. *Personnel Interviewing: Theory and Practice.* 2nd ed. New York: McGraw-Hill, 1975. Chapter 17, pp. 317–334.

10

Counseling

CHAPTER OBJECTIVES

1. Describe the "helping relationship."
2. Differentiate between directive and nondirective interviewing.
3. Describe the supportive counseling environment.
4. Explain the role of listening in the counseling interview.
5. Identify and describe purposes of the opening, body, and close of the counseling interview.
6. Identify and describe specific questioning techniques useful in the counseling interview.
7. Conduct a counseling interview.

Introduction

The counseling interview typifies the "helping" relationship. Its main objective is to change the counselee's behavior or the attitudes that motivate the behavior. For either of these objectives to be reached, there are two conditions that must be met. First, the counselee must want to change and must seek help in order to do so. Second, the counselor must want to help and, after agreeing to do so, must demonstrate excellent listening and probing skills and empathy in order for the counselee to resolve the issues that initially caused him or her to seek help.

Counseling activity takes place in many forms and is practiced by people in many different occupations: you may be in a counseling situation without recognizing it. The important point to remember is that the techniques used in counseling are common to all types of counseling interviews. From the standpoint of technique, it really does not matter whether the interview is between a psychiatrist and a patient, a priest and a congregant, a lawyer and a client, a teacher and a student, a manager and a subordinate, two roommates, a parent and a child, or a husband and wife. Of course, the more complex the issues are, the greater will be the necessity for competent professional help.

Directive Versus Nondirective Counseling

Directive counseling is advisory in nature and assumes that the counselor knows the answers. The directive counselor follows a problem-solution format in conducting the interview, gathering data from the counselee, defining and analyzing the problem, providing and evaluating solutions, and, in effect, telling the counselee what to do. Criminal lawyers and financial and academic advisers usually are directive counselors.

Nondirective counseling centers on the counselee's motivations, perceptions, and feelings. It assumes that by creating the proper emotional environment and interpersonal trust levels, the counselor can help the counselee resolve the problem. The nondirective counselor aids the counselee in defining and analyzing the problem, generating and evaluating solutions, and implementing them. Psychiatrists and psychologists, career counselors, and social workers usually are nondirective counselors.

Neither the directive nor the nondirective counseling approach occurs in the absence of the other. In practice, there will be elements of nondirection in predominantly directive interviews and elements of direction in predominantly nondirective interviews. Moreover, a counselor who usually uses a directive interviewing approach sometimes may use a nondirective format (and vice versa).

The history of the nondirective interviewing approach can be traced to two different sources. In 1927, a group of researchers from Harvard University initiated a series of studies at the Hawthorne Plant of the Western Electric Company. Two of these interviewing pioneers, Fritz J. Roethlisberger and William J. Dickson, described the development of their theory:

> It was finally decided . . . to adopt a new interviewing technique, which at that time was called the indirect approach. . . . As long as the employee talked spontaneously, the interviewer was to follow the employee's ideas, displaying a real interest in what the employee had to say. . . . While the employee continued to talk, no attempt was made to change the subject. The interviewer was not to interrupt or try to change the topic to one he thought more important. He was to listen attentively to anything the worker had to say about any topic and take part in the conversation only so far as it was necessary in order to keep the employee talking. If he did ask questions, they were to be phrased in a noncommittal manner and certainly not in the form, previously, which suggested answers.[1]

Roethlisberger and Dickson formulated five rules for the conduct of their "indirect approach" interviews:

1. The interviewer should listen to the speaker in a patient and friendly manner.
2. The interviewer should not display any kind of authority.
3. The interviewer should not give advice or moral admonition.
4. The interviewer should not argue with the speaker.
5. The interviewer should talk or ask questions only under certain conditions.
    a. To help the person talk.
    b. To relieve . . . fears or anxieties on the part of the speaker. . . .

c. To praise.
  d. To veer the discussion to some topic which has been omitted or neglected.
  e. To discuss implicit assumptions, if this is advisable.[2]

At just about the same time Roethlisberger's and Dickson's indirect approach was being developed and used as part of the Hawthorne Studies, a nearly identical set of techniques was being developed in the field of clinical psychology by Carl Rogers. Rogers described his interviewing rules:

> . . . *counseling of the non-directive sort is characterized by a preponderance of client activity, the client doing most of the talking about his problems. The counselor's primary techniques are those which help the client more clearly to recognize and understand his feelings, attitudes, and reaction patterns, and which encourage the client to talk about them.*
>
> *The Counselor may further achieve his aim by restating or clarifying the subject content of the client's conversation. Not infrequently he gives the client opportunity to express his feelings on specified topics. Less infrequently he asks specific questions of an information-getting sort. Occasionally he gives information or explanations related to the client's situation.*[3]

In addition to the directive and nondirective approaches, there is one other counseling approach that we want to mention. It is the *controlled nondirective* approach. Recall that the directive interviewer takes responsibility for gathering data, defining the problem, providing and evaluating solutions, and telling the counselee what to do. The nondirective counselor takes no responsibility for these events but rather provides an environment that encourages the counselee to work out his or her own problems. The controlled nondirective approach requires that the counselor maintain control over the major topic(s) to be discussed, but once they are raised, nondirective techniques such as those offered by Roethlisberger, Dickson, and Rogers are used.[4]

The Supportive Counseling Climate

A skilled counselor can create a supportive psychological climate for the interview. The counselor's manner of listening should encourage the counselee to speak, and the counselor's postural, facial, and verbal cues should draw out the counselee. Probably the best general discussion of ways to reduce defensiveness, while at the same time creating supportiveness, is one by Jack Gibb.[5] Gibb suggested six pairs of defensive and supportive behavioral categories:

Defensive Climate	*Supportive Climate*
1. Evaluation	1. Description
2. Control	2. Problem-orientation
3. Strategy	3. Spontaneity
4. Neutrality	4. Empathy
5. Superiority	5. Equality
6. Certainty	6. Provisionalism

As postulated by Gibb, "evaluation" is making value judgments about the content of messages being sent or about the individual who is sending them. "Description" is a request for information with no evaluative penalty. The counselor attempts to characterize the attitudes and feelings of the counselee or a situation or issue without judging its "goodness" or "badness."

"Control" is the counselor's attempt to make the counselee adopt another specified position or behavior. (Notice that this is a directive technique.) By exhibiting "problem-orientation," the counselor shows no predetermined solutions or attitudes, but rather a mutuality between the counselor and counselee in defining the problem and generating the solutions. There is a sense of "we are in this together."

"Strategy" refers to the counselee's perception that the counselor is attempting to manipulate him or her. "Spontaneity" on the part of the counselor shows a straightforward and honest disposition to explore whatever comes up in the interview, free of the perception of devious stratagems.

"Neutrality" (as manifested in speech with little emotional tone that communicates limited warmth and caring), according to Gibb, indicates the counselor's lack of concern for, or an implicit communicative rejection of, the counselee. "Empathy" requires that the counselor identify with and share the feelings of the counselee.

"Superiority" refers to that circumstance in which the counselor is perceived by the counselee as occupying a higher-status level, with the result that the counselee develops a feeling of inadequacy or inferiority. "Equality" implies that in the interview the participants perceive each other as peers, with mutual respect and trust.

"Certainty" represents rigidity in thinking and action and the impression that the counselor believes himself or herself to be right in all circumstances. It implies a rejection of new ideas or of new or different ways of thinking or action. "Provisionalism" represents an open willingness by the counselor to experiment with his or her own ideas, behavior, or attitudes. The counselor remains flexible in regard to the needs and perspective of the counselee.

In essence, when creating a supportive climate, the counselor uses many of the techniques suggested in the nondirective approach, attempts to withhold judgment and evaluation of what the counselee is saying, listens without overt involvement, and tries to understand the counselee's particular biases and attitudes. In addition, the counselor avoids interjecting personal perceptions of the subject being discussed and tries to view neutrally the information being presented.

Several behaviors common to all counseling interviews can be used to generate a supportive climate. One of these is to focus on the counselee's comments or feelings by repeating (in similar terms or tone) what has been expressed. Such mirror questions avoid evaluation and demonstrate permissiveness: "It's okay, keep talking, tell me more." Additionally, by using verbatim restatements of the counselee's exact words and vocal and tonal inflections, the counselor will clarify, expand, and elaborate on the ideas that have been expressed. Examples of reflections and mirrors and situations in which they can be used will be provided later in this chapter.

Listening and Counseling

There are four primary verbal communication skills: writing, reading, speaking, and listening. While at The Ohio State University in the late 1920s, Paul Rankin conducted what is believed to be the first contemporary study on listening.[6] Rankin asked eighty-eight adults to record, every fifteen minutes during their waking hours, in which of the four primary skills they had engaged during the last fifteen minutes. Rankin found that the adults in his study spent approximately 70 percent of their waking hours using one of the four primary verbal communication skills. Of the time spent using the communication skills, approximately 9 percent was in writing, 16 percent in reading, 30 percent in speaking, and 45 percent in listening. (Incidentally, these percentages showing use of the skills are in inverse proportion to the amount of time we spend in our schools learning how to use these skills.) Over the years, several studies have replicated Rankin's findings, yielding approximately the same proportional relationships among the four skills and demonstrating the importance of listening as a communicative tool.

For our purposes, listening will be considered as an activity that is a function of hearing acuity and the ability to focus attention. In the counseling interview, this means that to be effective the counselor must have the intellectual capacity and the emotional willingness to listen and must exhibit good listening practices. As a counselor, whether as a trained professional or a layperson, you must want to become a sounding board for one who is troubled and must learn how to use the tools available to you.

Ralph Nichols has had significant and continuing impact on the study of listening and listening behavior. In *Are You Listening?* written with Leonard Stevens, Nichols first popularized listening as a subject for discussion and a topic for study. In regard to nondirective listening, Nichols suggested:

1. Take the time to listen whenever you sense that someone is disturbed, is ready to "explode," or just needs to talk.
2. Be attentive and make every effort you can to understand what is being said. Empathize.
3. Employ guggles [Nichols called them "eloquent and encouraging grunts"], use silence, and use mirrors and restatement.
4. Probe to help the counselee understand rather than to meet your own needs for inquisitiveness.
5. Withhold evaluations until the whole story has been heard.
6. Strive to provide the environment that allows the counselee to work things out for himself.[7]

We all have been in counseling situations, whether with a friend or in a professional circumstance—whether as the counselor or the counselee. Even if we use all of the preceding suggestions, it is unusual for a counselee to unburden all of his or her problems in a single interview. Counseling, like persuasion, is rarely a single event; rather, it takes place over many exposures, as problems are often solved only in small increments.

Conducting the Counseling Interview

Counseling takes place over time. The keys to successful counseling are creating a supportive environment, using open-ended questioning techniques, and taking the time to listen.

Preparation

If the counseling session is initiated by the counselee, you may have little time to prepare. When that is the case, try to assess the situation. Is there undue urgency in the counselee? Is the counselee rational? A person who says to you, "I have nothing to live for. I'm thinking about killing myself" is in far greater need of your help (and referral to a qualified professional) than is someone who comes to you and says, "When you have some free time in the next couple of days, I'd like to talk to you about a problem I'm having at work." In the former case, the need for help is immediate. You should probe and listen (and get professional help). In the latter case, you have the time to get a few preliminary facts, set up an appointment, and plan how you will conduct the interview.

If you, the counselor, initiate the counseling session ("It seems to me that you've been on edge lately. I'd like to talk to you about what I've seen and heard from others about your behavior. Let's talk when you're ready."), you should have sufficient time to plan for the interview—its time, place, and the approach you want to take. In addition, you will be able to focus on your purpose and the outcomes you expect from the interview. Ideally, the counseling session should be conducted in a location where both parties will feel psychologically and physically comfortable. The location should be private (no third parties listening in), with no distractions and no chance for interruptions. If you are not a trained counselor, the chances are good that a steady stream of people will not be coming to you for counseling assistance. The chances are good, however, that some of your friends or acquaintances may seek your help. In other instances, you may observe that someone you know seems to be troubled, and you may offer your help.

The Opening

At the outset of the interview, try to put the counselee at ease. Indicate that you want to help. Try to make the counselee comfortable enough and trusting enough to want to disclose his or her thoughts to you. Depending on your relationship with the counselee, you may need to indicate the purpose of the interview, what you and the counselee should gain from it, and how much time is available for the counseling session. Show by your words and actions that you support the counselee, that what is said will be held in confidence, and that you empathize with—and are sensitive to—the counselee's needs. If you are distracted by other pressures or are emotionally upset by something, try to delay the start of the interview until you are relaxed and calmed down. Specific techniques used to "open up" the counselee will be described in the next section and are useful throughout the counseling interview.

The Body

Your primary counseling tools will be open questions, silence, guggles, direct and indirect mirrors, and listening. Open questions will often have antecedents that connect what the counselee has just said to some previous comment.

Open Questions. Remember that an open question cannot be answered logically by yes or no, as they contain words like "who," "what," "when," "where," "why," and "how," as well as phrases like "Tell me more about . . . ."

Examples of open questions:

"Tell me what's troubling you."
"How would you describe the problem?"
"What other causes do you see for the problem?"
"How can I help you?"
"Why do you think that?"

Silences. Silences are just that. You say nothing. The rule for using them is that if the counselee is making a declarative statement, use silence. If the counselee makes an interrogative statement, respond to it. When using silence, its length should not be allowed to become so long as to cause awkwardness.

Examples of silence:

Counselee: "Yesterday, I really ran into a problem with my son."
Counselor: Silence (showing that you want the counselee to keep talking).

Counselee: "Guess what happened to my son yesterday?"
Counselor: "What?" (Using an open question shows interest. Had silence been used here, it could have indicated disinterest and proved awkward.)

Guggles. Guggles are vocal pauses or words used to encourage the interviewee to keep talking. They show understanding and interest.

Examples of guggles:

Counselee: "Yesterday, I really ran into a problem with my son."
Counselor: "Hmm." (Keep talking.)
Counselee: "It all began when my new neighbor, you know, the big guy with the gray hair. . . ."
Counselor: "Uh-huh." (Yes, keep talking.)
Counselee: "Well, he came over to tell me that somebody had knocked down his fence. . . .

Direct Mirrors. Direct mirrors are exact repetitions of what the counselee has said, using the counselee's own words.

Examples of direct mirrors:

Counselee: "Yesterday, I really ran into a problem with my son."
Counselor: "You ran into a problem with your son?" (These are your words, tell me more.)
Counselee: "Yeah, he got into trouble with a neighbor."

Indirect Mirrors. Indirect mirrors reflect the sense of what the counselee said, or its tone, but they do not use the exact words.

Examples of indirect mirrors:

Counselee: "Yesterday, I really ran into a problem with my son."
Counselor: "He caused you some difficulty?" (Understanding shown and effort made to probe cause.)

Counselee: "Yeah, he got into a fight with my new neighbor."
Counselor: "Your neighbor was upset?" (Tell me about it.)
Counselee: "Yeah, you see his fence. . . ."

Antecedents. Antecedents are used when the counselor wants to connect what the counselee has just said with something said previously.

Examples of antecedents:

Counselee: "Yesterday, I really ran into a problem with my son."
Counselor: "Your son?" (Mirror: tell me more.)
Counselee: "Yeah, he got into a fight with my new neighbor. . . ."
Counselor: "That's an interesting story. It reminds me of the situation you told me about last week—you know, your son and his teacher. What common thread do you see between the two situations?" (I listened last week and I remember what you said. Explore the connection between the two similar situations.)

You should spend most of your time in the counseling interview listening rather than speaking. Listen for tone as well as words. Listen between the lines. What is the counselee *not* saying? Listen to understand the emotion and intensity of the counselee, and be able to demonstrate that you do understand. Avoid evaluating the counselee's comments. Questioning techniques that should be avoided (or used sparingly, at most) include closed questions, leading questions, loaded questions, and phrases that produce confrontation or withdrawal.

Closed Questions. Closed questions are those that can be answered with yes or no. Using them excessively will cut off the counselee and will discourage the free flow of words and feelings.

Examples of closed questions:

Counselee: "Yesterday, I really ran into a problem with my son."
Counselor: "Isn't he the one who was arrested six months ago?"
Counselee: "Yes."
Counselor: "I thought so. There's always one rotten apple in the basket, isn't there?"

Leading Questions. Leading questions are those that prompt the resondent to say what the questioner wants to hear. The second response of the counselor in the preceding example is a leading question. The counselor wants to hear the answer yes. You can infer from the example that the counselor has already formed a picture of the problem, even in the absence of information about it.

Loaded Questions. Loaded questions contain information on which the answer to them is based. Frequently, they are invalid, requiring clarifying answers.

Examples of loaded questions:

Counselee: "Yesterday, I really ran into a problem with my son."
Counselor: "Isn't he the one who was arrested six months ago?"
Counselee: "Yes."
Counselor: "I thought so. He's the one rotten apple in the basket. When will you be placing him in the youth home?"
Counselee: "First, he's staying with me and his father. Second, six months ago he was arrested, but he wasn't convicted of anything—in fact, we got an apology from the police. Third, the problem yesterday was caused by one of my son's friends whom the new neighbor mistook for my son."

Confrontation Phrases. Confrontation phrases are those that challenge or attack the counselee, offending the counselee or causing him or her to withdraw. Examples of confrontation phrases:

"Only an idiot would say that."
"That's the silliest thing I ever heard."
"What's wrong with you is. . . ."
"You know what you can do with that idea. . . ."
"Yes, but. . . ."
"When that happened to me, I. . . ."

Not only will you be asking questions in the body of the counseling interview, but also you will be trying to get the counselee to define the problem, examine its causes, select the best solution from among alternatives, and finally, implement the solution. Remember that you must enable the counselee to accept "ownership" of the problem, its causes, and its solutions. You cannot change the counselee's behavior; only the counselee can do that. You cannot change the counselee's attitudes; the counselee must be the one to decide to change. But what you can do is to help the counselee identify the problem and its causes and embark on a plan of action to resolve it. You can help the counselee develop solutions, but you cannot tell the counselee what to do or solve the problem yourself. But by showing your support, you can reinforce the actions that the counselee wishes to take and by discussing the counselee's ideas, you can show the wisdom of those actions.

The Close

The close of the counseling interview has three purposes: (1) to summarize the counselee's point of view, (2) to reaffirm what has been agreed to, and (3) to indicate what will happen next. Review objectively and unemotionally what has transpired. Restate the points raised and the conclusions reached by the counselee. Restate actions that the counselee has agreed to take. Schedule a follow-up interview if necessary. Determine what role, if any, you will have in subsequent actions that the counselee will take. Reaffirm your interest in the counselee's well-being and your role as a helper.

SUMMARY

This chapter described counseling as a "helping" relationship, differentiating between directive and nondirective approaches. We also suggested ways of creating a supportive climate and emphasized the importance of listening behaviors in counseling and specific aspects of organizing and conducting the counseling interview.

EXERCISES

1. Interview a counselor in your community. Find out what counseling techniques the counselor uses, how the counselor prepares for an interview, how the counselor puts the counselee at ease, and how the counselor generally conducts the interview.

2. List five situations you experienced in the last few weeks in which you engaged in counseling behaviors. What were the general circumstances? What techniques did you use? What outcomes did you achieve?
3. In-class assignment:
    a. Agree with a classmate that he or she will bring a real problem to a counseling interview, in which you will be the counselor.
    b. Without knowing the actual problem, prepare for the interview in the best way you can. How will you put the counselee at ease, draw out the problem, get the counselee to accept ownership of the problem, and help the counselee reach a solution?
    c. Conduct the interview. When it is over, write a critique of your behavior during the interview, including an analysis of your degree of success. What would you do again? What would you do differently?
4. Read Appendix D, "The Joe Hatton Situation: An Action Maze." You will be asked to record your decisions and the reasons for them on the decision path record sheet. When the exercise is over, analyze your behavior. What would you do differently? What would stay the same? How could you have improved your counseling behavior with Joe Hatton?

NOTES

1. F. J. Roethlisberger and William J. Dickson, *Management and the Worker* (Cambridge, Mass.: Harvard University Press, 1939), p. 203.
2. Roethlisberger and Dickson, p. 287.
3. Carl R. Rogers, *Counseling and Psychotherapy* (Boston: Houghton Mifflin, 1942), pp. 124–125.
4. Robert L. Kahn and Charles F. Cannell, *The Dynamics of Interviewing* (New York: John Wiley, 1957), pp. 208–210.
5. Jack R. Gibb, "Defensive Communication," *Journal of Communication* 11 (1961): 141–148.
6. See Paul T. Rankin, "The Measurement of the Ability to Understand Spoken Language," *Dissertation Abstracts* 12 (1926):847; "Listening Ability," *Proceedings of the Ohio State Educational Conference's Ninth Annual Session* (Columbus: The Ohio State University, 1929), pp. 172–183; "Listening Ability: Its Importance, Measurement and Development," *Chicago Schools Journal* 12 (1930):177. For a recent summary of listening, see Andrew R. Wolvin and Carolyn G. Coakley, *Listening* (Dubuque, Ia.: Wm. C. Brown, 1982).
7. Ralph G. Nichols and Leonard A. Stevens, *Are You Listening?* New York: McGraw-Hill, 1957), pp. 53–54.

ADDITIONAL READINGS

Dickson, William J., and F. J. Roethlisberger. *Counseling in an Organization: A Sequel to the Hawthorne Studies.* Cambridge, Mass.: Division of Research, Graduate School of Business Administration, Harvard University, 1966.

Edinburg, Golda M., Norman E. Zinberg, and Wendy Kelman. *Clinical Interviewing & Counseling: Principles and Techniques.* New York: Appleton-Century-Crofts, 1975.

Eriksen, Karen. *Communications Skills for the Human Services.* Reston, Va.: Reston, 1979.

APPENDIX A
Title VII of the Civil Rights Act of 1964[1]

[1] Title VII of the Civil Rights Act of 1964 (42 U.S.C. Section 2000e, 78 Stat.253) As Amended (effective October 1, 1980), *Fair Employment Practices Manual* (Washington, D.C.: Bureau of National Affairs, Inc., pp. 401:11–401:27). Reprinted by permission from *Fair Employment Practices Manual*, copyright 1982, by The Bureau of National Affairs, Inc., Washington, D.C.

Title VII of the Civil Rights Act of 1964

Following is the text of Title VII of the 1964 Civil Rights Act (42 U.S.C. § 2000e, 78 Stat. 253), Public Law 88-352, signed by President Johnson on July 2, 1964, amended by Public Law 92-261, effective March 24, 1972, by Public Law 93-608 on January 2, 1975, by Public Law 95-251, effective March 27, 1978, by Public Law 95-555, effective October 31, 1978 and by Public Law 96-191, effective October 1, 1980.

DEFINITIONS

Sec. 701. For the purposes of this title—

(a) The term "person" includes one or more individuals, governments, governmental agencies, political subdivisions, labor unions, partnerships, associations, corporations, legal representatives, mutual companies, joint-stock companies, trusts, unincorporated organizations, trustees, trustees in bankruptcy, or receivers.

[**1972 Amendments:** Section 701(a) was amended by P.L. 92-261, effective March 24, 1972, expanding term "person" to include "governments, governmental agencies, political subdivisions..."]

(b) The term "employer" means a person engaged in an industry affecting commerce who has fifteen or more employees for each working day in each of twenty or more calendar weeks in the current or preceding calendar year, and any agent of such a person, but such term does not include (1) the United States, a corporation wholly owned by the Government of the United States, an Indian tribe, or any department or agency of the District of Columbia subject by statute to procedures of the competitive service (as defined in section 2102 of title 5 of the United States Code), or (2) a bona fide private membership club (other than a labor organization) which is exempt from taxation under section 501(c) of the Internal Revenue Code of 1954, except that during the first year after the date of enactment of the Equal Employment Opportunity Act of 1972, persons having fewer than twenty-five employees (and their agents) shall not be considered employers.

[**1972 Amendments:** Section 701(b) was amended by P.L. 92-261, effective March 24, 1972, expanding "employer" to include all state and local "governments, governmental agencies, political subdivisions...", but does not include departments or agencies of the District of Columbia who are subject to competitive service under provisions of 5 U.S.C. Section 2102. Effective March 24, 1973, the number of employees was changed from "twenty-five" to "fifteen".]

(c) The term "employment agency" means any person regularly undertaking with or without compensation to procure employees for an employer or to procure for employees opportunities to work for an employer and includes an agent of such a person.

[**1972 Amendments:** Section 701(c) was amended by P.L. 92-261, effective March 24, 1972, to reflect the changes made in Sections 701(a) and 701(b), and the following language deleted from the end of subsection (c): "... but shall not include an agency of the United States, or an agency of a State or political subdivision of a State, except that such term shall include the United States Employment Service and the system of state and local employment service receiving Federal assistance."]

(d) The term "labor organization" means a labor organization engaged in an industry affecting commerce, and any agent of such an organization, and includes any organization of any kind, any agency, or employee representation committee, group, association, or plan so engaged in which employees participate and which exists for the purpose, in whole or in part, of dealing with employers concerning grievances, labor disputes, wages, rates of pay, hours, or other terms or conditions of employment, and any conference, general committee, joint or system board, or joint council so engaged which is subordinate to a national or international labor organization.

(e) A labor organization shall be deemed to be engaged in an industry affecting commerce if (1) it maintains or operates a hiring hall or hiring office which procures employees for an employer or procures for employees opportunities to work for an employer, or (2) the number of its members (or, where it is a labor organization composed of other labor organizations or their representatives, if the aggregate number of the members of such other labor organization) is (A) twenty-five or more during the first year after the date of enactment of the Equal Employment Opportunity Act of 1972, or (B) fifteen or more thereafter, and such labor organization.

[1972 Amendments: Section 701(e) was amended by P.L. 92-261, effective March 24, 1972, and previously read: "... (A) one hundred or more during the first year after the effective date prescribed in subsection (a) of section 716, (B) seventy-five or more during the second year after such date or fifty or more during the third year, or (C) twenty-five or more thereafter, and such labor organization—".]

(1) is the certified representative of employees under the provisions of the National Labor Relations Act, as amended, or the Railway Labor Act, as amended;

(2) although not certified, is a national or international labor organization or a local labor organization recognized or acting as the representative of employees of an employer or employers engaged in an industry affecting commerce; or

(3) has chartered a local labor organization or subsidiary body which is representing or actively seeking to represent employees of employers within the meaning of paragraph (1) or (2); or

(4) has been chartered by a labor organization representing or actively seeking to represent employees within the meaning of paragraph (1) or (2) as the local or subordinate body through which such employees may enjoy membership or become affiliated with such labor organization; or

(5) is a conference, general committee, joint or system board, or joint council subordinate to a national or international labor organization, which includes a labor organization engaged in an industry affecting commerce within the meaning of any of the preceding paragraphs of this subsection.

(f) The term "employee" means an individual employed by an employer, except that the term "employee" shall not include any person elected to public office in any State or political subdivision of any State by the qualified voters thereof, or any person chosen by such officer to be on such officer's personal staff, or an appointee on the policy making level or an immediate adviser with respect to the exercise of the constitutional or legal powers of the office. The exemption set forth in the preceding sentence shall not include employees subject to the civil service laws of a State government, governmental agency or political subdivision.

[1972 Amendments: Section 701(f) was amended by P.L. 92-261, effective March 24, 1972, and added exceptions and exclusions to term "employee".]

(g) The term "commerce" means trade, traffic, commerce, transportation, transmission, or communication among the several States; or between a State and any place outside thereof; or within the District of Columbia, or a possession of the United States; or between points in the same State but through a point outside thereof.

(h) The term "industry affecting commerce" means any activity, business, or industry in commerce or in which a labor dispute would hinder or obstruct commerce or the free flow of commerce and includes any activity or industry "affecting commerce" within the meaning of the Labor-Management Reporting and Disclosure Act of 1959, and further includes any governmental industry, business, or activity.

[1972 Amendments: Section 701(h) was amended by P.L. 92-261, effective March 24, 1972, and added the following inclusions: "... and further includes any governmental industry, business, or activity.".]

(i) The term "State" includes a State of the United States, the District of Columbia, Puerto Rico, the Virgin Islands, American Samoa, Guam, Wake Island, the Canal Zone, and Outer Continental Shelf lands defined in the Outer Continental Shelf Lands Act.

(j) The term "religion" includes all aspects of religious observance and practice, as well as belief, unless an employer demonstrates that he is unable to reasonably accommodate to an employee's or prospective employee's religious observance or practice without undue hardship on the conduct of the employer's business.

[1972 Amendments: Subsection (j) added to Section 701 by P.L. 92-261, effective March 24, 1972, creating statutory basis for EEOC to form guidelines on religious-based discrimination.]

(k) The terms "because of sex" or "on the basis of sex" include, but are not limited to, because of or on the basis of pregnancy, childbirth or related medical conditions; and women affected by pregnancy, childbirth, or related medical conditions shall be treated the same for all employment-related purposes, including receipt of benefits under fringe benefit programs, as other persons not so affected but similar in their ability or inability to work, and nothing in Section 703 (h) of this title shall be interpreted to permit otherwise. This subsection shall not require an employer to pay for health insurance benefits for abortion, except where the life of the mother would be endangered if the fetus were carried to term, or except where medical complications have arisen from an abortion: **Provided,** That nothing herein shall preclude an employer from providing abortion benefits or otherwise effect bargaining agreements in regard to abortion.

[1978 Amendments: Section 701(k) was added by P.L. 95-555, effective October 31, 1978, except that employers will have until April 29, 1979 to make necessary adjustments in existing fringe benefit or insurance programs. Also, employers must wait until October 31, 1979, or until the expiration of an applicable collective bargaining contract, before they may reduce benefits under a current plan in order to comply with the amendment. EEOC issued interpretive Questions and Answers on P.L. 95-555 as an Appendix to its Sex Discrimination Guidelines (29 CFR 1604.10), 44 FR 1196 (March 2, 1979) effective March 9, 1979.]

EXEMPTION

Sec. 702. This title shall not apply to an employer with respect to the employment of aliens outside any State, or to a religious corporation, association, educational institution, or society with respect to the employment of individuals of a particular religion to perform work connected with the carrying on by such corporation, association, educational institution, or society of its activities.

[1972 Amendments: Section 702 was amended by P.L. 92-261, effective March 24, 1972, and previously read: "Sec. 702. This title shall not apply to an employer with respect to the employment of aliens outside any State, or to a religious corporation, association, or society with respect to the employment of individuals of a particular religion to perform work connected with the carrying on by such corporation, association, or society of its religious activities or to an educational institution with respect to the employment of individuals to perform work connected with the educational activities of such institution."]

DISCRIMINATION BECAUSE OF RACE, COLOR, RELIGION, SEX, OR NATIONAL ORIGIN

Sec. 703 (a) It shall be an unlawful employment practice for an employer—

(1) to fail or refuse to hire or to discharge any individual, or otherwise to discriminate against any individual with respect to his compensation, terms, conditions, or privileges of employment, because of such individual's race, color, religion, sex, or national origin; or

(2) limit, segregate, or classify his employees or applicants for employment in any way which would deprive or tend to deprive any individual of employment opportunities or otherwise adversely affect his status as an employee, because of such individual's race, color, religion, sex, or national origin.

[1972 Amendments: Sec. 703(a)(2) was amended by P.L. 92-261, effective March 24, 1972, and added the words "applicants for employment".]

(b) It shall be an unlawful employment practice for an employment agency to fail or refuse to refer for employment, or otherwise to discriminate against, any individual because of his race, color, religion, sex, or national origin, or to classify or refer for employment any individual on the basis of his race, color, religion, sex, or national origin.

(c) It shall be an unlawful employment practice for a labor organization—

(1) to exclude or to expel from its membership, or otherwise to discriminate against, any individual because of his race, color, religion, sex, or national origin;

(2) to limit, segregate, or classify its membership or applicants for membership or to classify or fail or refuse to refer for employment any individual, in any way which would deprive or tend to deprive any individual of employment opportunities, or would limit such employment opportunities or otherwise adversely affect his status as an employee or as an applicant for employment, because of such individual's race, color, religion, sex, or national origin; or

[1972 Amendments: Sec. 703(c)(2) was amended by P.L. 92-261, effective March 24, 1972, and added the words "applicants for membership".]

(3) to cause or attempt to cause an employer to discriminate against an individual in violation of this section.

(d) It shall be an unlawful employment practice for any employer, labor, organization, or joint labor-management committee controlling apprenticeship or other training or retraining, including on-the-job training programs to discriminate against any individual because of his race, color, religion, sex, or national origin in admission to, or employment in, any program established to provide apprenticeship or other training.

(e) Notwithstanding any other provision of this title, (1) it shall not be an unlawful employment practice for an employer to hire and employ employees, for an employment agency to classify, or refer for employment any individual, for a labor organization to classify its membership or to classify or refer for employment any individual, or for an employer, labor organization, or joint labor-management committee controlling apprenticeship or other training or retraining programs to admit or employ any individual in any such program, on the basis of his religion, sex, or national origin in those certain instances where religion, sex, or national origin is a bona fide occupational qualification reasonably necessary to the normal operation of that particular business or enterprise, and (2) it shall not be an unlawful employment practice for a school, college, university, or other educational institution or institution of learning to hire and employ employees of a particular religion if such school, college, university, or other educational institution or institution of learning is, in whole or in substantial part, owned, supported, controlled, or managed by a particular religion or by a particular religious corporation, association, or society, or if the curriculum of such school, college, university, or other educational institution or institution of learning is directed toward the propagation of a particular religion.

(f) As used in this title, the phrase "unlawful employment practice" shall not be deemed to include any action or measure taken by an employer, labor organization, joint labor-management committee, or employment agency with respect to an individual who is a member of the Communist Party of the United States or of any other organization required to register as a Communist-action or Communist-front organization by final order of the Subversive Activities Control Board pursuant to the Subversive Activities Control Act of 1950.

(g) Notwithstanding any other provision of this title, it shall not be an unlawful employment practice for an employer to fail or refuse to hire and employ any individual for any position, for an employer to discharge an individual from any position, or for an employment agency to fail or refuse to refer any individual for employment in any position, or for a labor organization to fail or refuse to refer any individual for employment in any position, if —

(1) the occupancy of such position, or access to the premises in or upon which any part of the duties of such position is performed or is to be performed, is subject to any requirement imposed in the interest of the national security of the United States under any security program in effect pursuant to or administered under any statute of the United States or any Executive order of the President; and

(2) such individual has not fulfilled or has ceased to fulfill that requirement.

(h) Notwithstanding any other provision of this title, it shall not be an unlawful employment practice for an employer to apply different standards of compensation, or different terms, conditions, or privileges of employment pursuant to a bona fide seniority or merit system, or a system which measures earnings by quantity or quality of production or to employees who work in different locations, provided that such differences are not the result of an intention to discriminate because of race, color, religion, sex, or national origin; nor shall it be an unlawful employment practice for an employer to give and to act upon the results of any professionally developed ability test provided that such test, its administration or action upon the results is not designed, intended, or used to discriminate because of race, color, religion, sex, or national origin. It shall not be an unlawful employment practice under this title for any employer to differentiate upon the basis of sex in determining the amount of the wages or compensation paid or to be paid to employees of such employer if such differentiation is authorized by the provisions of Section 6(d) of the Fair Labor Standards Act of 1938 as amended (29 U.S.C. 206(d)).

(i) Nothing contained in this title shall apply to any business or enterprise on or near an Indian reservation with respect to any publicly announced employment practice of such business or enterprise under which a preferential treatment is given to any individual because he is an Indian living on or near a reservation.

(j) Nothing contained in this title shall be interpreted to require any employer, employment agency, labor organization, or joint labor-management committee subject to this title to grant preferential treatment to any individual or to any group because of the race, color, religion, sex, or national origin of such individual or group on account of an imbalance which may exist with respect to the total number of percentage of persons of any race, color, religion, sex, or national origin employed by any employer, referred or classified for employment by any employment agency or labor organization, admitted to membership or classified by any labor organization, or admitted to, or employed in, any apprenticeship or other training program, in comparison with the total number or percentage of persons of such race, color, religion, sex, or national origin in any community, State, section, or other area, or in the available work force in any community, State, section, or other area.

OTHER UNLAWFUL EMPLOYMENT PRACTICES

Sec. 704. (a) It shall be an unlawful employment practice for an employer to discriminate against any of his employees or applicants for employment, for an employment agency, or joint labor-management committee controlling apprenticeship or other training or retraining, including on-the-job training programs, to discriminate against any individual, or for a labor organization to discriminate against any member thereof or applicant for membership, because he has opposed any practice, made an unlawful employment practice by this title, or because he has made a charge, testified, assisted, or participated in any manner in an investigation, proceeding, or hearing under this title.

[1972 Amendments: Section 704(a) was amended by P.L. 92-261, effective March 24, 1972, reflecting earlier amendments in the Title, and added the following language: "..., or joint labor-management committee controlling apprenticeship or other training or retraining including on-the-job training programs".]

(b) It shall be an unlawful employment practice for an employer, labor organization, employment agency, or joint labor-management committee controlling apprenticeship or other training or retraining, including on-the-job training programs, to print or cause to be printed or published any notice or advertisement relating to employment by such an employer or membership in or any classification or referral for employment by such a labor organization, or relating to any classification or referral for employment by such an employment agency, or relating to admission to, or employment in, any program established to provide apprenticeship or other training by such a joint labor-management committee indicating any preference, limitation, specification, or discrimination, based on race, color, religion sex or national origin, except that such a notice or advertisement may indicate a preference, limitation, specification, or discrimination based on religion, sex or national origin when religion, sex, or national origin is a bona fide occupational qualification for employment.

[1972 Amendments: Section 704(b) was amended by P.L. 92-261, effective March 24, 1972, reflecting earlier amendments in the Title, and added certain language to include other organizations and methods relating to job referrals.]

EQUAL EMPLOYMENT OPPORTUNITY COMMISSION

Sec. 705 (a) There is hereby created a Commission to be known as the Equal Employment Opportunity Commission, which shall be composed of five members, not more than three of whom shall be members of the same political party. Members of the Commission shall be appointed by the President by and with the advice and consent of the Senate for a term of five years. Any individual chosen to fill a vacancy shall be appointed only for the unexpired term of the member whom he shall succeed, and all members of the Commission shall continue to serve until their successors are appointed and qualified, except that no such member of the Commission shall continue to serve (1) for more than sixty days when the Congress is in session unless a nomination to fill such vacancy shall have been submitted to the Senate, or (2) after the adjournment sine die of the session of the Senate in which such nomination was submitted. The President shall designate one member to serve as Chairman of the Commission, and one member to serve as Vice Chairman. The Chairman shall be responsible on behalf of the Commission for the administrative operations of the Commission, and, except as provided in subsection (b), shall appoint, in accordance with the provisions of title 5, United States Code, governing appointments in the competitive service, such officers, agents, attorneys, administrative law judges, and employees as he deems necessary to assist it in the performance of its functions and to fix their compensation in accordance with the provisions of chapter 51 and subchapter III of chapter 53 of title 5, United States Code, relating to classification and General Schedule pay rates: *Provided,* That assignment, removal, and compensation of administrative law judges shall be in accordance with sections 3105, 3344, 5362, and 7521 of title 5, United States Code.

(b)(1) There shall be a General Counsel of the Commission appointed by the President, by and with the advice and consent of the Senate, for a term of four years. The General Counsel shall have responsibility for the conduct of litigation as provided in sections 706 and 707 of this title. The General Counsel shall have such other duties as the Commission may prescribe or as may be provided by law and shall concur with the Chairman of the Commission on the appointment and supervision of regional attorneys. The General Counsel of the Commission on the effective date of this Act shall continue in such position and perform the functions specified in this subsection until a successor is appointed and qualified.

(2) Attorneys appointed under this section may, at the direction of the Commission, appear for and represent the Commission in any case in court, provided that the Attorney General shall conduct all litigation to which the Commission is a party in the Supreme Court pursuant to this title.

[1972 **Amendments:** Subsection (b) added by P.L. 92-261, effective March 24, 1972, providing for the appointment of EEOC General Counsel and representation by its attorneys in all cases to which the Commission is a party.]

[Subsections (3) and (h) repealed by P.L. 92-261.]

[Subsections (b), (c), (d), (i), and (j) redesignated subsections (c), (d), (e), (h), and (i) respectively.]

[1978 **Amendments:** Subsection (a) amended to change hearing examiners to administrative law judges by P.L. 95-251, effective March 27, 1978.]

(c) A vacancy in the Commission shall not impair the right of the remaining members to exercise all the powers of the Commission and three members thereof shall constitute a quorum.

(d) The Commission shall have an official seal which shall be judicially noticed.

(e) The Commission shall at the close of each fiscal year report to the Congress and to the President concerning the action it has taken, and the moneys it has disbursed. It shall make such further reports on the cause of and means of eliminating discrimination and such recommendations for further legislation as may appear desirable.

[1975 Amendments: Section 705(e) was amended by P.L. 93-608, approved January 2, 1975, and previously read: ". . . President concerning the action it has taken; the names, salaries, and duties of all individuals in its employ and the moneys it has disbursed; and shall make such further . . .".]

(f) The principal office of the Commission shall be in or near the District of Columbia, but it may meet or exercise any or all its powers at any other place. The Commission may establish such regional or State offices as it deems necessary to accomplish the purpose of this title.

(g) The Commission shall have power—

(1) to cooperate with and, with their consent, utilize regional, State, local, and other agencies, both public and private, and individuals;

(2) to pay to witnesses whose depositions are taken or who are summoned before the Commission or any of its agents the same witness and mileage fees as are paid to witnesses in the courts of the United States;

(3) to furnish to persons subject to this title such technical assistance as they may request to further their compliance with this title or an order issued thereunder;

(4) upon the request of (i) any employer, whose employees or some of them, or (ii) any labor organization, whose members or some of them, refuse or threaten to refuse to cooperate in effectuating the provisions of this title, to assist in such effectuation by conciliation or such other remedial action as is provided by this title:

(5) to make such technical studies as are appropriate to effectuate the purposes and policies of this title and to make the results of such studies available to the public;

(6) to intervene in a civil action brought under section 706 by an aggrieved party against a respondent other than a government, governmental agency or political subdivision. (As amended by P.L. No. 92-261, eff. March 24, 1972)

(h) The Commission shall, in any of its educational or promotional activities, cooperate with other departments and agencies in the performance of such educational and promotional activities.

(i) All officers, agents, attorneys and employees of the Commission, including the members of the Commission, shall be subject to the provisions of section 9 of the Act of August 2, 1939, as amended (the Hatch Act), notwithstanding any exemption contained in such section.

PREVENTION OF UNLAWFUL EMPLOYMENT PRACTICES

Sec. 706. (a) The Commission is empowered, as hereinafter provided, to prevent any person from engaging in any unlawful employment practice as set forth in section 703 or 704 of this title.

(b) Whenever a charge is filed by or on behalf of a person claiming to be aggrieved, or by a member of the Commission, alleging that an employer, employment agency, labor organization, or joint labor-management committee controlling apprenticeship or other training or retraining, including on-the-job training programs, has engaged in an unlawful employment practice, the Commission shall serve a notice of the charge (including the date, place and circumstances of the alleged unlawful employment practice) on such employer, employment agency, labor organization, or joint labor-management committee (hereinafter referred to as the 'respondent') within ten days and shall make an investigation thereof. Charges shall be in writing under oath or affirmation and shall contain such information and be in such form as the Commission requires. Charges shall not be made public by the Commission. If the Commission determines after such investigation that there is not reasonable cause to believe that the charge is true, it shall dismiss the charge and promptly notify the person claiming to be aggrieved and the respondent of its action. In determining whether reasonable cause exists, the Commission shall accord substantial weight to final findings and orders made by State or local authorities in proceedings commenced under State or local law pursuant to the requirements of subsections (c) and (d). If the Commission determines after such investigation that there is reasonable cause to believe that the charge is true, the Commission shall endeavor to eliminate any such alleged unlawful employment practice by informal methods of conference, conciliation, and persuasion. Nothing said or done during and as a part of such informal endeavors may be made public by the Commission, its officers or employees, or used as evidence in a subsequent proceeding without the written consent of the persons concerned. Any person who makes public information in violation of this subsection shall be fined not more than $1,000 or imprisoned for not more than one year, or both. The Commission shall make its determination on reasonable cause as promptly as possible and, so far as practicable, not later than one hundred and twenty days from the filing of the charge or, where applicable under subsection (c) or (d), from the date upon which the Commission is authorized to take action with respect to the charge.

(c) In the case of an alleged unlawful employment practice occurring in a State, or political subdivision of a State, which has a State or local law prohibiting the unlawful employment practice alleged and establishing or authorizing a State or local authority to grant or seek relief from such practice or to institute criminal proceedings with respect thereto upon receiving notice thereof, no charge may be filed under subsection (a) by the person aggrieved before the expiration of sixty days after proceedings have been commenced under the State or local law, unless such proceedings have been earlier terminated, provided that such sixty-day period shall be extended to one hundred and twenty days during the first year after the effective date of such State or local law. If any requirement for the commencement of such proceedings is imposed by a State or local authority other than a requirement of the filing of a written and signed statement of the facts upon which the proceeding is based, the proceeding shall be deemed to have been commenced for the purposes of this subsection at the time such statement is sent by registered mail to the appropriate State or local authority.

(d) In the case of any charge filed by a member of the Commission alleging an unlawful employment practice occurring in a State or political subdivision of a State which has a State or local law prohibiting the practice alleged and establishing or authorizing a State or local authority to grant or seek relief from such practice or to institute criminal proceedings with respect thereto upon receiving notice thereof, the Commission shall, before taking any action with respect to such charge, notify the appropriate State or local officials and, upon request, afford them a reasonable time, but not less than sixty days (provided that such sixty-day period shall be extended to one hundred and twenty days during the first year after the effective day of such State or local law), unless a shorter period is requested, to act under such State or local law to remedy the practice alleged.

(e) A charge under this section shall be filed within one hundred and eighty days after the alleged unlawful employment practice occurred and notice of the charge (including the date, place and circumstances of the alleged unlawful employment practice) shall be served upon the person against whom such charge is made within ten days thereafter, except that in a case of an unlawful employment practice with respect to which the person aggrieved has initially instituted proceedings with a State or local agency with authority to grant or seek relief from such practice or to institute criminal proceedings with respect thereto upon receiving notice thereof, such charge shall be filed by or on behalf of the person aggrieved within three hundred days after the alleged unlawful employment practice occurred, or within thirty days after receiving notice that the State or local agency has terminated the proceedings under the State or local law, whichever is earlier, and a copy of such charge shall be filed by the Commission with the State or local agency.

(f)(1) If within thirty days after a charge is filed with the Commission or within thirty days after expiration of any period of reference under subsection (c) or (d), the Commission has been unable to secure from the respondent a conciliation agreement acceptable to the Commission, the Commission may bring a civil action against any respondent not a government, governmental agency, or political subdivision named in the charge. In the case of a respondent which is a government, governmental agency, or political subdivision, if the Commission has been unable to secure from the respondent a conciliation agreement acceptable to the Commission, the Commission shall take no further action and shall refer the case to the Attorney General who may bring a civil action against such respondent in the appropriate United States district court. The person or persons aggrieved shall have the right to intervene in a civil action brought by the Commission or the Attorney General in a case involving a government, governmental agency, or political subdivision. If a charge filed with the Commission pursuant to subsection (b) is dismissed by the Commission, or if within one hundred and eighty days from the filing of such charge or the expiration of any period of reference under subsection (c) or (d), whichever is later, the Commission has not filed a civil action under this section or the Attorney General has not filed a civil action in a case involving a government, governmental agency, or political subdivision, or the Commission has not entered into a conciliation agreement to which the person aggrieved is a party, the Commission, or the Attorney General in a case involving a government, governmental agency, or political subdivision, shall so notify the person aggrieved and within ninety days after the giving of such notice a civil action may be brought against the respondent named in the charge (A) by the person claiming to be aggrieved or (B) if such charge was filed by a member of the Commission, by any person whom the charge alleges was aggrieved by the alleged unlawful employment practice. Upon application by the complainant and in such circumstances as the court may deem just, the court may appoint an attorney for such complainant and may authorize the commencement of the action without the payment of fees, costs, or security. Upon timely application, the court may, in its discretion, permit the Commission, or the Attorney General in a case involving a government, governmental agency, or political subdivision, to intervene in such civil action upon certification that the case is of general public importance. Upon request, the court may, in its discretion, stay further proceedings for not more than sixty days pending the termination of State or local proceedings described in subsections (c) or (d) of this section or further efforts of the Commission to obtain voluntary compliance.

(2) Whenever a charge is filed with the Commission and the Commission concludes on the basis of a preliminary investigation that prompt judicial action is necessary to carry out the purposes of this Act, the Commission, or the Attorney General in a case involving a government, governmental agency, or political subdivision, may bring an action for appropriate temporary or preliminary relief pending final disposition of such charge. Any temporary restraining order or other order granting preliminary or temporary relief shall be issued in accordance with rule 65 of the Federal Rules of Civil Procedure. It shall be the duty of a court having jurisdiction over proceedings under this section to assign cases for hearing at the earliest practicable date and to cause such cases to be in every way expedited.

(3) Each United States district court and each United States court of a place subject to the jurisdiction of the United States shall have jurisdiction of actions brought under this title. Such an action may be brought in any judicial district in the State in which the unlawful employment practice is alleged to have been committed, in the judicial district in which the employment records relevant to such practice are maintained and administered, or in the judicial district in which the aggrieved person would have worked but for the alleged unlawful employment practice, but if the respondent is not found within any such district, such an action may be brought within the judicial district in which the respondent has his principal office. For purposes of sections 1404 and 1406 of title 28 of the United States Code, the judicial district in which the respondent has his principal office shall in all cases be considered a district in which the action might have been brought.

(4) It shall be the duty of the chief judge of the district (or in his absence, the acting chief judge) in which the case is pending immediately to designate a judge in such district to hear and determine the case. In the event that no judge in the district is available to hear and determine the case, the chief judge of the district, or the acting chief judge, as the case may be, shall certify this fact to the chief judge of the circuit (or in his absence, the acting chief judge) who shall then designate a district or circuit judge of the circuit to hear and determine the case.

(5) It shall be the duty of the judge designated pursuant to this subsection to assign the case for hearing at the earliest practicable date and to cause the case to be in every way expedited. If such judge has not scheduled the case for trial within one hundred and twenty days after issue has been joined that judge may appoint a master pursuant to rule 53 of the Federal Rules of Civil Procedure

(g) If the court finds that the respondent has intentionally engaged in or is intentionally engaging in an unlawful employment practice charged in the complaint, the court may enjoin the respondent from engaging in such unlawful employment practice, and order such affirmative action as may be appropriate, which may include, but is not limited to, reinstatement or hiring of employees, with or without back pay (payable by the employer, employment agency, or labor organization, as the case may be, responsible for the unlawful employment practice), or any other equitable relief as the court deems appropriate. Back pay liability shall not accrue from a date more than two years prior to the filing of a charge with the Commission. Interim earnings or amounts earnable with reasonable diligence by the person or persons discriminated against shall operate to reduce the back pay otherwise allowable. No order of the court shall require the admission or reinstatement of an individual as a member of a union, or the hiring, reinstatement, or promotion of an individual as an employee, or the payment to him of any back pay, if such individual was refused admission, suspended, or expelled, or was refused employment or advancement or was suspended or discharged for any reason other than discrimination on account of race, color, religion, sex, or national origin or in violation of section 704(a).

[**1972 Amendments:** Subsections (1) through (g) of Section 706 were amended by P.L. 92-261, effective March 24, 1972, empowering the EEOC to prevent any person from engaging in any unlawful employment practice described in Section 703 or 704; extended procedures through conciliation efforts; outlined enforcement procedures where no voluntary compliance; when an action may be brought by Federal Government, and an aggrieved party.]

(h) The provisions of the Act entitled "An Act to amend the Judicial Code and to define and limit the jurisdiction of courts sitting in equity, and for other purposes," approved March 23, 1932 (29 U.S.C. 101-115), shall not apply with respect to civil actions brought under this section.

(i) In any case in which an employer, employment agency, or labor organization fails to comply with an order of a court issued in a civil action brought under this section the Commission may commence proceedings to compel compliance with such order.

(j) Any civil action brought under this section and any proceedings brought under subsection (j) shall be subject to appeal as provided in sections 1291 and 1292, title 28, United States Code.

[**1972 Amendments:** Sections 706(i) and 706(j), amended by P.L. 92-261, effective March 24, 1974, reflecting prior sections' amendments and redesignations.]

(k) In any action or proceeding under this title the court, in its discretion, may allow the prevailing party, other than the Commission or the United States, a reasonable attorney's fee as part of the costs, and the Commission and the United States shall be liable for costs the same as a private person.

Sec. 707. (a) Whenever the Attorney General has reasonable cause to believe that any person or group of persons is engaged in a pattern or practice of resistance to the full enjoyment of any of the rights secured by this title, and that the pattern or practice is of such a nature and is intended to deny the full exercise of the rights herein described, the Attorney General may bring a civil action in the appropriate district court of the United States by filing with it a complaint (1) signed by him (or in his absence the Acting Attorney General), (2) setting forth facts pertaining to such pattern or practice, and (3) requesting such relief, including an application for a permanent or temporary injunction, restraining order or other order against the person or persons responsible for such pattern or practice, as he deems necessary to insure the full enjoyment of the rights herein described.

(b) The district courts of the United States shall have and shall exercise jurisdiction of proceedings instituted pursuant to this section, and in any such proceeding the Attorney General may file with the clerk of such court a request that a court of three judges be convened to hear and determine the case. Such request by the Attorney General shall be accompanied by a certificate that, in his opinion, the case is of general public importance. A copy of the certificate and request for a three-judge court shall be immediately furnished by such clerk to the chief judge of the circuit (or in his absence, the presiding circuit judge of the circuit) in which the case is pending. Upon receipt of such request it shall be the duty of the chief judge of the circuit or the presiding circuit judge, as the case may be, to designate immediately three judges in such circuit, of whom at least one shall be a circuit judge and another of whom shall be a district judge of the court in which the proceeding was instituted, to hear and determine such case, and it shall be the duty of the judges so designated to assign the case for hearing at the earliest practicable date, to participate in the hearing and determination thereof, and to cause the case to be in every way expedited. An appeal from the final judgment of such court will lie to the Supreme Court.

In the event the Attorney General fails to file such a request in any such proceeding, it shall be the duty of the chief judge of the district (or in his absence, the acting chief judge) in which the case is pending immediately to designate a judge in such district to hear and determine the case. In the event that no judge in the district is available to hear and determine the case, the chief judge of the district, or the acting chief judge, as the case may be, shall certify this fact to the chief judge of the circuit (or in his absence, the acting chief judge) who shall then designate a district or circuit judge of the circuit to hear and determine the case.

It shall be the duty of the judge designated pursuant to this section to assign the case for hearing at the earliest practicable date and to cause the case to be in every way expedited.

(c) Effective two years after the date of enactment of the Equal Employment Opportunity Act of 1972, the functions of the Attorney General under this section shall be transferred to the Commission, together with such personnel, property, records, and unexpended balances of appropriations, allocations, and other funds employed, used, held, available, or to be made available in connection with such functions unless the President submits, and neither House of Congress vetoes, a reorganization plan pursuant to chapter 9 of title 5, United States Code, inconsistent with the provisions of this subsection. The Commission shall carry out such functions in accordance with subsections (d) and (e) of this section.

(d) Upon the transfer of functions provided for in subsection (c) of this section, in all suits commenced pursuant to this section prior to the date of such transfer, proceedings shall continue without abatement, all court orders and decrees shall remain in effect, and the Commission shall be substituted as a party for the United States of America, the Attorney General, or the Acting Attorney General, as appropriate.

(e) Subsequent to the date of enactment of the Equal Employment Opportunity Act of 1972, the Commission shall have authority to investigate and act on a charge of a pattern or practice of discrimination, whether filed by or on behalf of a person claiming to be aggrieved or by a member of the Commission. All such actions shall be conducted in accordance with the procedures set forth in section 706 of this Act.

[1972 Amendments: Subsections (c), (d), and (e) were added to Section 707 by P.L. 92-261, effective March 24, 1972.]

EFFECT OF STATE LAWS

Sec. 708. Nothing in this title shall be deemed to exempt or relieve any person from any liability, duty, penalty, or punishment provided by any present or future law of any State or political subdivision of a State, other than any such law which purports to require or permit the doing of any act which would be an unlawful employment practice under this title.

INVESTIGATIONS, INSPECTIONS, RECORDS, STATE AGENCIES

Sec. 709. (a) In connection with any investigation of a charge filed under section 706, the Commission or its designated representative shall at all reasonable times have access to, for the purposes of examination, and the right to copy any evidence of any person being investigated or proceeded against that relates to unlawful employment practices covered by this title and is relevant to the charge under investigation.

(b) The Commission may cooperate with State and local agencies charged with the administration of State fair employment practices laws and, with the consent of such agencies, may, for the purpose of carrying out its functions and duties under this title and within the limitation of funds appropriated specifically for such purpose, engage in and contribute to the cost of research and other projects of mutual interest undertaken by such agencies, and utilize the services of such agencies and their employees, and, notwithstanding any other provision of law, pay by advance or reimbursement such agencies and their employees for services rendered to assist the Commisssion in carrying out this title. In furtherance of such cooperative efforts, the Commission may enter into written agreements with such State or local agencies and such agreements may include provisions under which the Commission shall refrain from processing a charge in any cases or class of cases specified in such agreements or under which the Commission shall relieve any person or class of persons in such State or locality from requirements imposed under this section. The Commission shall rescind any such agreement whenever it determines that the agreement no longer serves the interest of effective enforcement of this title.

(c) Every employer, employment agency, and labor organization subject to this title shall (1) make and keep such records relevant to the determinations of whether unlawful employment practices have been or are being committed, (2) preserve such records for such periods, and (3) make such reports therefrom as the Commission shall prescribe by regulation or order, after public hearing, as reasonable, necessary, or appropriate for the enforcement of this title or the regulations or orders thereunder. The Commission shall, by regulation, require each employer, labor organization, and joint labor-management committee subject to this title which controls an apprenticeship or other training program to maintain such records as are reasonably necessary to carry out the purposes of this title, including, but not limited to, a list of applicants who wish to participate in such program, including the chronological order in which applications were received, and to furnish to the Commission upon request, a detailed description of the manner in which persons are selected to participate in the apprenticeship or other training program. Any employer, employment agency, labor organization, or joint labor-management committee which believes that the application to it of any regulation or order issued under this section would result in undue hardship may apply to the Commission for an exemption from the application of such regulation or order, and, if such application for an exemption is denied, bring a civil action in the United States district court for the district where such records are kept. If the Commission or the court, as the case may be, finds that the application of the regulation or order to the employer, employment agency, or labor organization in question would impose an undue hardship, the Commission or the court, as the case may be, may grant appropriate relief. If any person required to comply with the provisions of this subsection fails or refuses to do so, the United States district court for the district in which such person is found, resides, or transacts business, shall, upon application of the Commission, or the Attorney General in a case involving a government, governmental agency or political subdivision, have jurisdiction to issue to such person an order requiring him to comply.

(d) In prescribing requirements

pursuant to subsection (c) of this section, the Commission shall consult with other interested State and Federal agencies and shall endeavor to coordinate its requirements with those adopted by such agencies. The Commission shall furnish upon request and without cost to any State or local agency charged with the administration of a fair employment practice law information obtained pursuant to subsection (c) of this section from any employer, employment agency, labor organization, or joint labor-management committee subject to the jurisdiction of such agency. Such information shall be furnished on condition that it not be made public by the recipient agency prior to the institution of a proceeding under State or local law involving such information. If this condition is violated by a recipient agency, the Commission may decline to honor subsequent requests pursuant to this subsection.

(e) It shall be unlawful for any officer or employee of the Commission to make public in any manner whatever any information obtained by the Commission pursuant to its authority under this section prior to the institution of any proceeding under this title involving such information. Any officer or employee of the Commission who shall make public in any manner whatever any information in violation of this subsection shall be guilty of a misdemeanor and upon conviction thereof, shall be fined not more than $1,000, or imprisoned not more than one year.

[1972 **Amendments**: As added to, and amended by P.L. 92-261, effective March 24, 1972, Section 709 (c) and (d) were expanded to provide that (1) where an employer fails or refuses to keep required records, the EEOC or Attorney General may bring an action in the district court and (2) EEOC shall endeavor to coordinate its record-keeping requirements with those of other state and Federal agencies.]

INVESTIGATORY POWERS

Sec. 710. For the purpose of all hearings and investigations conducted by the Commission or its duly authorized agents or agencies, section 11 of the National Labor Relations Act (49 Stat. 455; 29 U.S.C. 161) shall apply.

[1972 **Amendments**: Section 710 was amended by P.L. 92-261, effective March 24, 1972, and empowers EEOC to conduct all hearings and investiations under Section 11 of the NLRA.]

NOTICES TO BE POSTED

Sec. 711. (a) Every employer, employment agency and labor organization, as the case may be, shall post and keep posted in conspicuous places upon its premises where notices to employees, applicants for employment, and members are customarily posted a notice to be prepared or approved by the Commission setting forth excerpts from or, summaries of, the pertinent provisions of this title and information pertinent to the filing of a complaint.

(b) A willful violation of this section shall be punishable by a fine of not more than $100 for each separate offense.

VETERANS' PREFERENCE

Sec. 712. Nothing contained in this title shall be construed to repeal or modify any Federal, State, territorial, or local law creating special rights or preference for veterans.

RULES AND REGULATIONS

Sec. 713. (a) The Commission shall have authority from time to time to issue, amend, or rescind suitable procedural regulations to carry out the provisions of this title. Regulations issued under this section shall be in conformity with the standards and limitations of the Administrative Procedure Act.

(b) In any action or proceeding based on any alleged unlawful employment practice, no person shall be subject to any liability or punishment for or on account of (1) the commission by such person of an unlawful employment practice if he pleads and proves that the act or omission complained of was in good faith, in conformity with, and in reliance on any written interpretation or opinion of the Commission, or (2) the failure of such person to publish and file any information required by any provision of this title if he pleads and proves that he failed to publish and file such information in good faith, in conformity with the instructions of the Commission issued under this title regarding the filing of such information. Such a defense, if established, shall be a bar to the action or proceeding, notwithstanding that (A) after such act or omission, such interpretation or opinion is modified or rescinded or is determined by judicial authority to be invalid or of no legal effect, or (B) after publishing or filing the description and annual reports, such publication or filing is determined by judicial authority not to be in conformity with the requirements of this title.

FORCIBLY RESISTING THE COMMISSION OR ITS REPRESENTATIVES

Sec. 714. The provisions of sections 111 and 1114, title 18, United States Code, shall apply to officers, agents, and employees of the Commission in the performance of their official duties. Notwithstanding the provisions of sections 111 and 1114 of title 18, United States Code, whoever in violation of the provisions of section 114 of such title kills a person while engaged in or on account of the performance of his official functions under this Act shall be punished by imprisonment for any term of years or for life. (As amended by P.L. 92-261, effective March 24, 1972)

EQUAL EMPLOYMENT OPPORTUNITY COORDINATION COUNCIL

Sec. 715. There shall be established an Equal Employment Opportunity Coordinating Council (hereinafter referred to in this section as the Council) composed of the Secretary of labor, the Chairman of the Equal Employment Opportunity Commission, the Attorney General, the Chairman of the United States Civil Service Commission, and the Chairman of the United States Civil Rights Commission, or their respective delegates. The Council shall have the responsibility for developing and implementing agreements, policies and practices designed to maximize effort, promote efficiency, and eliminate conflict, competition, duplication and inconsistency among the operations, functions and jurisdictions of the various departments, agencies and branches of the Federal Government responsible for the implementation and enforcement of equal employment opportunity legislation, orders, and policies. On or before July 1 of each year, the Council shall transmit to the President and to the Congress a report of its activities, together with such recommendations for legislative or administrative changes as it concludes are desirable to further promote the purposes of this section.

[**1972 Amendments:** Section 715, previously designated "Special Study by Secretary of Labor", retitled and amended by P.L. No. 92-261, effective March 24, 1972, established the Equal Employment Opportunity Coordinating Council and its function and purpose.]

EFFECTIVE DATE

Sec. 716. (a) This title shall become effective one year after the date of its enactment. *[The effective date thus is July 2, 1965.]*

(b) Notwithstanding subsection (a), sections of this title other than sections 703, 704, 706, and 707 shall become effective immediately.

(c) The President shall, as soon as feasible after the enactment of this title, convene one or more conferences for the purpose of enabling the leaders of groups whose members will be affected by this title to become familiar with the rights afforded and obligations imposed by its provisions, and for the purpose of making plans which will result in the fair and effective administration of this title when all of its provisions become effective. The President shall invite the participation in such conference or conferences of (1) the members of the President's Committee on Equal Employment Opportunity, (2) the members of the Commission on Civil Rights, (3) representatives of State and local agencies engaged in furthering equal employment opportunity, (4) representatives of private agencies engaged in furthering equal employment opportunity, and (5) representatives of employers, labor organizations, and employment agencies who will be subject to this title.

NON DISCRIMINATION IN FEDERAL GOVERNMENT EMPLOYMENT

Sec. 717. (a) All personnel actions affecting employees or applicants for employment (except with regard to aliens employed outside the limits of the United States) in military departments as defined in section 102 of title 5, United States Code in executive agencies as defined in section 105 of title 5, United States Code (including employees and applicants for employment who are paid from nonappropriated funds), in the United States Postal Service and the Postal Rate Commission, in those units of the Government of the District of Columbia having positions in the competitive service, and in those units of the legislative and judicial branches of the Federal Government having positions in the competitive service, and in the Library of Congress shall be made free from any discrimination based on race, color, religion, sex, or national origin.

(b) Except as otherwise provided in this subsection, the Civil Service Commission shall have authority to enforce the provisions of suibsection (a) through appropriate remedies, including reinstatement or hiring of employees with or without back pay, as will effectuate the policies of this section, and shall issue such rules, regulations, orders and instructions as it deems necessary and appropriate to carry out its responsibilities under this section. The Civil Service Commission shall—

(1) be responsible for the annual review and approval of a national and regional equal employment opportunity plan which each department and agency and each appropriate unit referred to in subsection (a) of this section shall submit order to maintain an affirmative program of equal employment opportunity for all such employees and applicants for employment;

(2) be responsible for the review and evaluation of the operation of all agency equal employment opportunity programs, periodically obtaining and publishing (on at least a semi-annual basis) progress reports from each such department, agency, or unit; and

(3) consult with and solicit the recommendations of interested individuals, groups, and organizations relating to equal employment opportunity.

The head of each such department, agency, or unit shall comply with such rules, regulations, orders, and instructions which shall include a provision that an employee or applicant for employment shall be notified of any final action taken on any complaint of discrimination filed by him thereunder. The plan submitted by each department, agency, and unit shall include, but not be limited to—

(1) provision for the establishment of training and education programs designed to provide a maximum opportunity for employees to advance so as to perform at their largest potential; and

(2) a description of the qualifications in terms of training and experience relating to equal employment opportunity for the principal and operating officials of each such department, agency, or unit responsible for carrying out the equal employment opportunity program and of the allocation of personnel and resources proposed by such department, agency, or

unit to carry out its equal employment opportunity program.

With respect to employment in the Library of Congress, authorities granted in this subsection to the Civil Service Commission shall be exercised by the Librarian of Congress.

(c) Within thirty days of receipt of notice of final action taken by a department, agency, or unit referred to in subsection 717(a), or by the Civil Service Commission upon an appeal from a decision or order of such department, agency, or unit on a complaint of discrimination based on race, color, religion, sex or national origin, brought pursuant to subsection (a) of this section, Executive Order 11478 or any succeeding Executive orders, or after one hundred and eighty days from the filing of the initial charge with the department, agency, or unit or with the Civil Service Commission on appeal from a decision or order of such department, agency or unit until such time as final action may be taken by a department, agency, or unit, an employee or applicant for employment, if aggrieved by the final disposition of his complaint, or by the failure to take final action on his complaint, may file a civil action as provided in section 706, in which civil action the head of the department, agency, or unit, as appropriate, shall be the defendant.

(d) The provisions of section 706(f) through (k), as applicable, shall govern civil actions brought hereunder.

(e) Nothing contained in this Act shall relieve any Government agency or official of its or his primary responsibility to assure nondiscrimination in employment as required by the Constitution and statutes or of its or his responsibilities under Executive Order 11478 relating to equal employment opportunity in the Federal Government.

[**1972 Amendments:** As added by P.L. 92-261, effective March 24, 1972, Section 717 provides for (1) "nondiscrimination for employees and applicants for employment in Federal agencies and in competitive service positions in the District of Columbia government, (2) gives the Civil Service Commission authority to enforce Section 717(a), and (3) enables an employee (as defined in Section 717(a)) to file a civil action in court, under the provisions of Section 706.]

[**1980 Amendment:** P.L. 96-191, effective October 1, 1980, removed the provision in Sec. 717(a) excluding the General Accounting Office from coverage of the law.]

SPECIAL PROVISION WITH RESPECT TO DENIAL, TERMINATION AND SUSPENSION OF GOVERNMENT CONTRACTS

Sec. 718. No Government contract, or portion thereof, with any employer, shall be denied, withheld, terminated, or suspended, by any agency or officer of the United States under any equal employment opportunity law or order, where such employer has an affirmative action plan which has previously been accepted by the Government for the same facility within the past twelve months without first according such employer full hearing and adjudication under the provisions of title 5, United States Code, section 554, and the following pertinent section: *Provided*, That if such employer has deviated substantially from such previously agreed to affirmative action plan, this section shall not apply. *Provided further*, That for the purposes of this section an affirmative action plan shall be deemed to have been accepted by the Government at the time the appropriate compliance agency has accepted such plan unless within forty-five days thereafter the Office of Federal Contract Compliance has disapproved such plan.

APPENDIX B

Uniform Guidelines on Employee Selection Procedures (1978) [1]

[1] "Uniform Guidelines on Employee Selection Procedures (1978)," *Fair Employment Practices Manual* (Washington, D.C.: Bureau of National Affairs, Inc., pp. 401:2231–401:2278). Reprinted by permission from *Fair Employment Practices Manual,* copyright 1982, by The Bureau of National Affairs, Inc., Washington, D.C.

Uniform Guidelines on Employee Selection Procedures (1978)

Following is full text of the final version of the Uniform Guidelines on Employee Selection Procedures adopted August 22, 1978 by the four federal equal employment opportunity agencies — The Equal Employment Opportunity Commission, the U.S. Civil Service Commission, and the Departments of Labor and Justice.

The Treasury Department interim regulations adopted the same guidelines, effective September 11, 1978 (See 401:2278). The Treasury Department enforces the revenue sharing act.

The guidelines, effective September 25, 1978, are preceeded by introductory material which will not appear with the Guidelines themselves in the Code of Federal Regulations. However, the introductory material, which was published with the guidelines in the August 25 Federal Register, has been described as "legislative history."

The final guidelines culminated nearly six years of effort and gives employers one set of government requirements to meet in order to avoid discrimination in testing and other employee selection processes. The bulk of the guidelines consist of the government's interpretation of validation standards.

Prior to issuance of the final version of the guidelines, two conflicting sets of guides were in effect. In 1976 the Labor and Justice Departments, and the Civil Service Commission issued guidelines. In response, EEOC re-issued its own revised regulations. In an effort to resolve the conflict, the four agencies agreed to proposed guides, which were issued in December, 1977.

For full text of 90 interpretive "Questions & Answers" on the guidelines, see 401:2301.

Title 29—Labor
CHAPTER XIV—EQUAL EMPLOYMENT OPPORTUNITY COMMISSION
PART 1607—UNIFORM GUIDELINES ON EMPLOYEE SELECTION PROCEDURES (1978)
Title 5—Administrative Personnel
CHAPTER 1—CIVIL SERVICE COMMISSION
PART 300—EMPLOYMENT (GENERAL)
Title 28—Judicial Administration
CHAPTER 1—DEPARTMENT OF JUSTICE
PART 50—STATEMENTS OF POLICY
Title 41—Public Contracts and Property Management
CHAPTER 60—OFFICE OF FEDERAL CONTRACT COMPLIANCE PROGRAMS, DEPARTMENT OF LABOR
PART 60-3—UNIFORM GUIDELINES ON EMPLOYEE SELECTION PROCEDURES (1978)

Adoption of Employee Selection Procedures

AGENCIES: Equal Employment Opportunity Commission, Civil Service Commission, Department of Justice and Department of Labor.

ACTION: Adoption of uniform guidelines on employee selection procedures as final rules by four agencies.

SUMMARY: This document sets forth the uniform guidelines on employee selection procedures adopted by the Equal Employment Opportunity Commission, Civil Service Commission, Department of Justice, and the Department of Labor. At present two different sets of guidelines exist. The guidelines are intended to establish a uniform Federal position in the area of prohibiting discrimination in employment practices on grounds of race, color, religion, sex, or national origin. Cross reference documents are published at 5 CFR 300.103(c) (Civil Service Commission), 28 CFR 50.14 (Department of Justice), 29 CFR Part 1607 (Equal Employment Opportunity Commission), and 41 CFR Part 60-3 (Department of Labor) elsewhere in this issue.

EFFECTIVE DATE: September 25, 1978.

FOR FURTHER INFORMATION CONTACT:

Doris Wooten, Associate Director, Donald J. Schwartz, Staff Psychologist, Office of Federal Contract Compliance Programs, Room C-3324, Department of Labor, 200 Constitution Avenue N.W., Washington, D.C. 20210, 202-523-9426.

Peter C. Robertson, Director, Office of Policy Implementation, Equal Employment Opportunity Commission, 2401 E. Street N.W., Washington, D.C. 20506, 202-634-7060.

David L. Rose, Chief, Employment Section, Civil Rights Division, Department of Justice, 10th Street and Pennsylvania Avenue N.W., Washington, D.C. 20530, 202-739-3831.

A. Diane Graham, Director, Federal Equal Employment Opportunity, Civil Service Commission, 1900 E Street NW., Washington, D.C. 20415, 202-632-4420.

H. Patrick Swygert, Gneral Counsel, Civil Service Commission, 1900 E Street NW., Washington, D.C. 20415, 202-632-4632.

SUPPLEMENTARY INFORMATION:

An Overview of the 1978 Uniform Guidelines on Employee Selection Procedures

I. BACKGROUND

One problem that confronted the Congress which adopted the Civil Rights Act of 1964 involved the effect of written preemployment tests on equal employment opportunity. The use of these test scores frequently denied employment to minorities in many cases without evidence that the tests were related to success on the job. Yet employers wished to continue to use such tests as practical tools to assist in the selection of qualified employees. Congress sought to strike a balance which would proscribe discrimination, but otherwise permit the use of tests in the selection of employees. Thus, in title VII, Congress authorized the use of "any professionally developed ability test provided that such test, its administration or action upon the results is not designed intended or used to discriminate ***".[1]

At first, some employers contended that, under this section, they could use any test which had been developed by a professional so long as they did not intend to exclude minorities, even if such exclusion was the consequence of the use of the test. In 1966, the Equal Employment Opportunity Commission (EEOC) adopted guidelines to advise employers and other users what the law and good industrial psychology practice required.[2] The Department of Labor adopted the same approach in 1968 with respect to tests used by Federal Contractors under Executive Order 11246 in a more detailed regulation. The Government's view was that the employer's intent was irrelevant. If tests or other practices had an adverse impact on protected groups, they were unlawful unless they could be justified. To justify a test which screened out a higher proportion of minorities, the employer would have to show that it fairly measured or predicted performance on the job. Otherwise, it would not be considered to be "professionally developed."

In succeeding years, the EEOC and the Department of Labor provided more extensive guidance which elaborated

[1] Section 703(h), 42 U.S.C. 2000e(2)(h).

[2] See 35 U.S.L.W. 2137 (1966).

upon these principles and expanded the guidelines to emphasize all selection procedures. In 1971 in *Griggs* v. *Duke Power Co.*,[3] the Supreme Court announced the principle that employer practices which had an adverse impact on minorities and were not justified by business necessity constituted illegal discrimination under title VII. Congress confirmed this interpretation in the 1972 amendments to title VII. The elaboration of these principles by courts and agencies continued into the mid-1970's,[4] but differences between the EEOC and the other agencies (Justice, Labor, and Civil Service Commission) produced two different sets of guidelines by the end of 1976.

With the advent of the Carter administration in 1977, efforts were intensified to produce a unified government position. The following document represents the result of that effort. This introduction is intended to assist those not familiar with these matters to understand the basic approach of the uniform guidelines. While the guidelines are complex and technical, they are based upon the principles which have been consistently upheld by the courts, the Congress, and the agencies.

The following discussion will cite the sections of the Guidelines which embody these principles.

II. ADVERSE IMPACT

The fundamental principle underlying the guidelines is that employer policies or practices which have an adverse impact on employment opportunities of any race, sex, or ethnic group are illegal under title VII and the Executive order unless justified by business necessity.[5] A selection procedure which has no adverse impact generally does not violate title VII or the Executive order.[6] This means that an employer may usually avoid the application of the guidelines by use of procedures which have no adverse impact.[7] If adverse impact exists, it must be justified on grounds of business necessity. Normally, this means by validation which demonstrates the relation between the selection procedure and performance on the job.

The guidelines adopt a "rule of thumb" as a practical means of determining adverse impact for use in enforcement proceedings. This rule is known as the "4/5ths" or "80 percent" rule.[8] It is not a legal definition of discrimination, rather it is a practical device to keep the attention of enforcement agencies on serious discrepancies in hire or promotion rates or other employment decisions. To determine whether a selection procedure violates the "4/5ths rule", an employer compares its hiring rates for different groups.[9] But this rule of thumb cannot be applied automatically. An employer who has conducted an extensive recruiting campaign may have a larger than normal pool of applicants, and the "4/5ths rule" might unfairly expose it to enforcement proceedings.[10] On the other hand, an employer's reputation may have discouraged or "chilled" applicants of particular groups from applying because they believed application would be futile. The application of the "4/5ths" rule in that situation would allow an employer to evade scrutiny because of its own discrimination.[11]

III. IS ADVERSE IMPACT TO BE MEASURED BY THE OVERALL PROCESS?

In recent years some employers have eliminated the overall adverse impact of

---

[3] 401 U.S. 424 (1971).
[4] See, *e.g.*, *Albermarle Paper Co.* v. *Moody*, 422 U.S. 405 (1975).
[5] *Griggs*, note 3, supra; uniform guidelines on employee selection procedures (1978), section 3A, (hereinafter cited by section number only).
[6] *Furnco* v. *Waters*, 98 S.Ct. 2943 (1978).
[7] Section 6.
[8] Section 4D.
[9] Section 16R (definition of selection rate).
[10] Section 4D (special recruiting programs).
[11] *Ibid* (user's actions have discouraged applicants).

a selection procedure and employed sufficient numbers of minorities or women to meet this "⅘th's rule of thumb". However, they might continue use of a component which does have an adverse impact. For example, an employer might insist on a minimum passing score on a written test which is not job related and which has an adverse impact on minorities.[12] However, the employer might compensate for this adverse impact by hiring a sufficient proportion of minorities who do meet its standards, so that its overall hiring is on a par with or higher than the applicant flow. Employers have argued that as long as their "bottom line" shows no overall adverse impact, there is no violation at all, regardless of the operation of a particular component of the process.

Employee representatives have argued that rights under equal employment opportunity laws are individual, and the fact that an employer has hired some minorities does not justify discrimination against other minorities. Therefore, they argue that adverse impact is to be determined by examination of each component of the selection procedure, regardless of the "bottom line." This question has not been answered definitively by the courts. There are decisions pointing in both directions.

These guidelines do not address the underlying question of law. They discuss only the exercise of prosecutorial discretion by the Government agencies themselves.[13] The agencies have decided that, generally, their resources to combat discrimination should be used against those respondents whose practices have restricted or excluded the opportunities of minorities and women. If an employer is appropriately including all groups in the workforce, it is not sensible to spend Government time and effort on such a case, when there are so many employers whose practices do have adverse effects which should be challenged. For this reason, the guidelines provide that, in considering whether to take enforcement action, the Government will take into account the general posture of the employer concerning equal employment opportunity, including its affirmative action plan and results achieved under the plan.[14] There are some circumstances where the government may intervene even though the "bottom line" has been satisfied. They include the case where a component of a selection procedure restricts promotional opportunities of minorities or women who were discriminatorily assigned to jobs, and where a component, such as a height requirement, has been declared unlawful in other situations.[15]

What of the individual who is denied the job because of a particular component in a procedure which otherwise meets the "bottom line" standard? The individual retains the right to proceed through the appropriate agencies, and into Federal court.[16]

IV. WHERE ADVERSE IMPACT EXISTS: THE BASIC OPTIONS

Once an employer has established that there is adverse impact, what steps are required by the guidelines? As previously noted, the employer can modify or eliminate the procedure which produces the adverse impact, thus taking the selection procedure from the coverage of these guidelines. If the employer does not do that, then it must justify the use of the procedure on grounds of "business necessity."[17] This normally means that it must show a clear relation between perfor-

[12] See, e.g., Griggs v. Duke Power Co., 401 U.S. 424 (1971).
[13] Section 4C.
[14] Section 4E.
[15] Section 4C.
[16] The processing of individual cases is excluded from the operation of the bottom line concept by the definition of "enforcement action," section 16I. Under section 4C, where adverse impact has existed, the employer must keep records of the effect of each component for 2 years after the adverse effect has dissipated.
[17] A few practices may be used without validation even if they have adverse impact. See, e.g., McDonnell Douglas v. Green, 411 U.S. 792 (1973) and section 6B.

mance on the selection procedure and performance on the job. In the language of industrial psychology, the employer must validate the selection procedure. Thus the bulk of the guidelines consist of the Government's interpretation of standards for validation.

V. VALIDATION: CONSIDERATION OF ALTERNATIVES

The concept of validation as used in personnel psychology involves the establishment of the relationship between a test instrument or other selection procedure and performance on the job. Federal equal employment opportunity law has added a requirement to the process of validation. In conducting a validation study, the employer should consider available alternatives which will achieve its legitimate business purpose with lesser adverse impact.[18] The employer cannot concentrate solely on establishing the validity of the instrument or procedure which it has been using in the past.

This same principle of using the alternative with lesser adverse impact is applicable to the manner in which an employer uses a valid selection procedure.[19] The guidelines assume that there are at least three ways in which an employer can use scores on a selection procedure: (1) To screen out of consideration those who are not likely to be able to perform the job successfully; (2) to group applicants in accordance with the likelihood of their successful performance on the job, and (3) to rank applicants, selecting those with the highest scores for employment.[20]

The setting of a "cutoff score" to determine who will be screened out may have an adverse impact. If so, an employer is required to justify the initial cutoff score by reference to its need for a trustworthy and efficient work force.[21] Similarly, use of results for grouping or for rank ordering is likely to have a greater adverse effect than use of scores solely to screen out unqualified candidates. If the employer chooses to use a rank order method, the evidence of validity must be sufficient to justify that method of use.[22]

VI. TESTING FOR HIGHER LEVEL JOBS

Normally, employers test for the job for which people are hired. However, there are situations where the first job is temporary or transient, and the workers who remain are promoted to work which involves more complex activities. The guidelines restrict testing for higher level jobs to users who promote a majority of the employees who remain with them to the higher level job within a reasonable period of time.[23]

VII. HOW IS VALIDATION TO BE CONDUCTED

Validation has become highly technical and complex, and yet is constantly changing as a set of concepts in industrial psychology. What follows here is a simple introduction to a highly complex field. There are three concepts which can be used to validate a selection procedure. These concepts reflect different approaches to investigating the job relatedness of selection procedures and may be interrelated in practice. They are (1) criterion-related validity,[24] (2) content validity,[25] and (3) construct validity.[26] In criterion-related validity, a selection procedure is justified by a statistical relationship between scores on the test or

---

[18] *Albermarle Paper Co. v. Moody*, 422 U.S. 405 (1975); *Robinson v. Lorillard Corp.*, 444 F.2d 791 (4th Cir. 1971).
[19] Sections 3B; 5G.
[20] *Ibid.*
[21] See sections 3B; 5H. See also sections 14B(6) (criterion-related validity); 14C(9) (content validity); 14D(1) (construct validity).
[22] Sections 5G, 14B(6); 14C(9); 14D(1).
[23] Sections 5I.

[24] Sections 5B, (General Standards); 14B (Technical Standards); 15B (Documentation); 16F (Definition).
[25] Sections 5B (General Standards); 14C (Technical Standards); 15C (Documentation); 16D (Definition).
[26] Sections 5B (General Standards); 14D (Technical Standards); 15D (Documentation); 16E (Definition).

other selection procedure and measures of job performance. In content validity, a selection procedure is justified by showing that it representatively samples significant parts of the job, such as a typing test for a typist. Construct validity involves identifying the psychological trait (the construct) which underlies successful performance on the job and then devising a selection procedure to measure the presence and degree of the construct. An example would be a test of "leadership ability."

The guidelines contain technical standards and documentation requirements for the application of each of the three approaches.[27] One of the problems which the guidelines attempt to meet is the "borderline" between "content validity" and "construct validity." The extreme cases are easy to understand. A secretary, for example, may have to type. Many jobs require the separation of important matters which must be handled immediately from those which can be handled routinely. For the typing function, a typing test is appropriate. It is justifiable on the basis of content validity because it is a sample of an important or critical part of the job. The second function can be viewed as involving a capability to exercise selective judgment in light of the surrounding circumstances, a mental process which is difficult to sample.

In addressing this situation, the guidelines attempt to make it practical to validate the typing test by a content strategy,[28] but do not allow the validation of a test measuring a construct such as "judgment" by a content validity strategy.

The bulk of the guidelines deals with questions such as those discussed in the above paragraphs. Not all such questions can be answered simply, nor can all problems be addressed in the single document. Once the guidelines are issued, they will have to be interpreted in light of changing factual, legal, and professional circumstances.

VIII. SIMPLIFICATION OF REPORTING AND RECORDKEEPING REQUIREMENTS

The reporting and recordkeeping provisions which appeared in the December 30 draft which was published for comment have been carefully reviewed in light of comments received and President Carter's direction to limit paperwork burdens on those regulated by Government to the minimum necessary for effective regulation. As a result of this review, two major changes have been made in the documentation requirements of the guidelines:

(1) A new section 15A(1) provides a simplified recordkeeping option for employers with fewer than 100 employees;

(2) Determinations of the adverse impact of selection procedures need not be made for groups which constitute less than 2 percent of the relevant labor force.

Also, the draft has been changed to make clear that users can assess adverse impact on an annual basis rather than on a continuing basis.

Analysis of comments. The uniform guidelines published today are based upon the proposition that the Federal Government should speak to the public and to those whom it regulates with one voice on this important subject; and that the Federal Government ought to impose upon itself obligations for equal employment opportunity which are at least as demanding as those it seeks to impose on others. These guidelines state a uniform Federal position on this subject, and are intended to protect the rights created by title VII of the Civil Rights Act of 1964, as amended, Executive Order 11246, as amended, and other provisions of Federal law. The uniform guidelines are also intended to represent "professionally

---

[27]Technical standards are in section 14; documentation requirements are in section 15.
[28]Section 14C.

acceptable methods" of the psychological profession for demonstrating whether a selection procedure validly predicts or measures performance for a particular job. *Albemarle Pater Co. v. Moody,* 442 U.S. 405, 425. They are also intended to be consistent with the decisions of the Supreme Court and authoritative decisions of other appellate courts.

Although the development of these guidelines preceded the issuance by President Jimmy Carter of Executive Order 12044 designed to improve the regulatory process, the spirit of his Executive order was followed in their development. Initial agreement among the Federal agencies was reached early in the fall of 1977, and the months from October 1977 until today have been spent in extensive consultation with civil rights groups whose clientele are protected by these guidelines; employers, labor unions, and State and local governments whose employment practices are affected by these guidelines; State and local government antidiscrimination agencies who share with the Federal Government enforcement responsibility for discriminatory practices; and appropriate members of the general public. For example, an earlier draft of these guidelines was circulated informally for comment on October 28, 1977, pursuant to OMB Circular A-85. Many comments were received from representatives of State and local governments, psychologists, private employers, and civil rights groups. Those comments were taken into account in the draft of these guidelines which was published for comment December 30, 1977, 42 FR 66542.

More than 200 organizations and individuals submitted written comments on the December 30, 1977, draft. These comments were from representatives of private industry, public employers, labor organizations, civil rights groups, the American Psychological Association and components thereof, and many individual employers, psychologists, and personnel specialists. On March 3, 1978, notice was given of a public hearing and meeting to be held on April 10, 1978, 42 FR 9131. After preliminary review of the comments, the agencies identified four issues of particular interest, and invited testimony particularly on those issues, 43 FR 11812 (March 21, 1978). In the same notice the agencies published questions and answers on four issues of concern to the commenters. The questions and answers were designed to clarify the intent of the December 30, 1977, draft, so as to provide a sharper focus for the testimony at the hearing.

At a full day of testimony on April 10, 1978, representatives of private industry, State and local governments, labor organizations, and civil rights groups, as well as psychologists, personnel specialists, and others testified at the public hearing and meeting. The written comments, testimony, and views expressed in subsequent informal consultations have been carefully considered by the four agencies. We set forth below a summary of the comments, and the major issues raised in the comments and testimony, and attempt to explain how we have resolved those issues.

The statement submitted by the American Psychological Association (A.P.A) stated that "these guidelines represent a major step forward and with careful interpretation can provide a sound basis for concerned professional work." Most of the A.P.A. comments were directed to clarification and interpretation of the present language of the proposal. However, the A.P.A. recommended substantive change in the construct validity section and in the definition of work behavior.

Similarly, the Division of Industrial and Organizational Psychology (division 14) of the A.P.A. described the technical standards of the guidelines as "superior" in terms of congruence with professional standards to "most previous orders and guidelines but numerous troublesome aspects remain." Division 14 had substantial concerns with a number of the provisions of the general principles of the draft.

Civil rights groups generally found the uniform guidelines far superior to the FEA guidelines, and many urged the adoption, with modifications concerning ranking and documentation. Others raised concerns about the "bottom line" concept and other provisions of the guidelines.

The Ad Hoc Group on Employee Selection Procedures representing many employers in private industry supported the concept of uniform guidelines, but had a number of problems with particular provisions, some of which are described below. The American Society for Personnel Administration (ASPA) and the International Personnel Management Association, which represents State and local governments, generally took the same position as the ad hoc group. Major industrial unions found that the draft guidelines were superior to the FEA guidelines, but they perceived them to be inferior to the EEOC guidelines. They challenged particularly the bottom line concept and the construct validity section.

The building trade unions urged an exclusion of apprenticeship programs from coverage of the guidelines. The American Council on Education found them inappropriate for employment decisions concerning faculty at institutions of higher education. Other particular concerns were articulated by organizations representing the handicapped, licensing and certifying agencies, and college placement offices.

General Principles

1. *Relationship between validation and elimination of adverse impact, and affirmative action.* Federal equal employment opportunity law generally does not require evidence of validity for a selection procedure if there is not adverse impact; e.g., *Griggs* v. *Duke Power Co.*, 401 U.S. 424. Therefore, a user has the choice of complying either by providing evidence of validity (or otherwise justifying use in accord with Federal law), or by eliminating the adverse impact. These options have always been present under Federal law, 29 CFR 1607.3; 41 CFR 60-3.3(a); and the Federal Executive Agency Guidelines, 41 FR 51734 (November 23, 1976). The December 30 draft guidelines, however, clarified the nature of the two options open to users.

Psychologists expressed concern that the December 30 draft of section 6A encouraged the use of invalid procedures as long as there is no adverse impact. Employers added the concern that the section might encourage the use of illegal procedures not having an adverse impact against the groups who have historically suffered discrimination (minorities, women), even if they have an adverse impact on a different group (whites, males).

Section 6A was not so intended, and we have revised it to clarify the fact that illegal acts purporting to be affirmative action are not the goal of the agencies or of the guidelines; and that any employee selection procedure must be lawful and should be as job related as possible. The delineation of examples of alternative procedures was eliminated to avoid the implication that particular procedures are either prescribed or are necessarily appropriate. The basic thrust of section 6A, that elimination of adverse impact is an alternative to validation, is retained.

The inclusion of excerpts from the 1976 Equal Employment Opportunity Coordinating Council Policy Statement on Affirmative Action in section 13B of the December 30 draft was criticized as not belonging in a set of guidelines for the validation of selection procedures. Section 13 has been revised. The general statement of policy in support of voluntary affirmative action, and the reaffirmation of the policy statement have been retained, but this statement itself is now found in the appendix to the guidelines.

2. *The "bottom line" (section 4C).* The guidelines provide that when the overall selection process does not have an adverse impact the Government will usually not examine the individual components of that process for adverse impact or evidence of validity. The concept is based upon the view that the Federal Government should not generally concern itself with individual components of a selection process, if the overall effect of that process is nonexclusionary. Many commenters criticized the ambiguity caused by the word "generally" in the December 30 draft of section 4C which provided, "the Federal enforcement agencies * * * generally will not take enforcement action based upon adverse impact of any component" of a process that does not have an overall adverse impact. Employer groups stated the position that the "bottom line" should be a rule prohibiting enforcement action by Federal agencies with respect to all or any part of a selection process where the bottom line does not show adverse impact. Civil rights and some labor union representatives expressed the opposing concerns that the concept may be too restrictive, of law, and that it might allow certain discriminatory conditions to go unremedied.

The guidelines have been revised to clarify the intent that the bottom line concept is based upon administrative and prosecutorial discretion. The Federal agencies cannot accept the recommendation that they never inquire into or take enforcement action with respect to any component procedure unless the whole process of which it is a part has an adverse impact. The Federal enforcement agencies believe that enforcement action may be warranted in unusual circumstances, such as those involving other discriminatory practices, or particular selection procedures which have no validity and have a clear adverse impact on a national basis. Other unusual circumstances may warrant a high level agency decision to proceed with enforcement actions although the "bottom line" has been satisfied. At the same time the agencies adhere to the bottom line concept of allocating resources primarily to those users whose overall selection processes have an adverse impact. See overview, above, part III.

3. *Investigation of alternative selection procedures and alternative methods of use (section 3B).* The December draft included an obligation on the user, when conduction a validity study, to investigate alternative procedures and uses, in order to determine whether there are other procedures which are substantially equally valid, but which have less adverse impact. The American Psychological Assocation stated:

"We would concur with the drafters of the guidelines that it is appropriate in the determination of a selection strategy to consider carefully a variety of possible procedures and to think carefully about the question of adverse impact with respect to each of those procedures. Nevertheless, we feel it appropriate to note that a rigid enforcement of these sections, particularly for small employers, would impose a substantial and expensive burden on these employers."

Since a reasonable consideration of alternatives is consistent with the underlying principle of minimizing adverse impact consistent with business needs, the provision is retained.

Private employer representatives challenged earlier drafts of these guidelines as being inconsistent with the decision of the Supreme Court in *Albemarle Paper Co.* v. *Moody,* 422 U.S. 405. No such inconsistency was intended. Accordingly, the first sentence of section 3B was revised to paraphrase the opinion in the *Albemarle* decision, so as to make it clear that section 3B is in accord with the principles of the *Albemarle* decision.

Section 3B was further revised to clarify the intent of the guidelines that the obligation to investigate alternative procedures is a part of conducting a validity study, so that alternative procedures should be evaluated in light of validity studies meeting professional standards, and that section 3B does not impose an obligation to search for alternatives if the user is not required to conduct a validity study.

Just as, under section 3B of the guidelines, a user should investigate alternative selection procedures as a part of choosing and validating a procedure, so should the user investigate alternative uses of the selection device chosen to find the use most appropriate to his needs. The validity study should address the question of what method of use (screening, grouping, or rank ordering) is appropriate for a procedure based on the kind and strength of the validity evidence shown, and the degree of adverse impact of the different uses.

4. *Establishment of cutoff scores and rank ordering.* Some commenters from civil rights groups believed that the December 30 draft guidelines did not provide sufficient guidance as to when it was permissible to use a selection procedure on a ranking basis rather than on a pass-fail basis. They also objected to section 5G in terms of setting cutoff scores. Other comments noted a lack of clarity as to how the determination of a cutoff score or the use of a procedure for ranking candidates relates to adverse impact.

As we have noted, users are not required to validate procedures which do not have an adverse impact. However, if one way of using a procedure (e.g., for ranking) results in greater adverse impact than another way (e.g., pass/fail), the procedure must be validated for that use. Similarly, cutoff scores which result in adverse impact should be justified. If the use of a validated procedure for ranking results in greater adverse impact than its use as a screening device, the evidence of validity and utility must be sufficient to warrant use of the procedures as a ranking device.

A new section 5G has been added to clarify these concepts. Section 5H (formerly section 5G) addresses the choice of a cutoff score when a procedure is to be used for ranking.

5. *Scope: Requests for exemptions for certain classes of users.* Some employer groups and labor organizations (e.g., academic institutions, large public employers, apprenticeship councils) argued that they should be exempted from all or some of the provisions of these guidelines because of their special needs. The intent of Congress as expressed in Federal equal employment opportunity law is to apply the same standards to all users, public and private.

These guidelines apply the same principles and standards to all employers. On the other hand, the nature of the procedures which will actually meet those principles and standards may be different for different employers, and the guidelines recognize that fact. Accordingly, the guidelines are applicable to all employers and other users who are covered by Federal equal employment opportunity law.

Organizations of handicapped persons objected to excluding from the scope of these guidelines the enforcement of laws prohibiting discrimination on the basis of handicap, in particular the Rehabilitation Act of 1973, sections 501, 503, and 504. While this issue has not been addressed in the guidelines, nothing precludes the adoption of the principles set forth in these guidelines for other appropriate situations.

Licensing and certification boards raised the question of the applicability of the guidelines to their licensing and certification functions. The guidelines make it clear that licensing and certification are covered "to the extent" that licensing and certification may be covered by Federal equal employment opportunity law.

Voluntary certification boards, where certification is not required by law, are not users as defined in section 16 with respect to their certifying functions and therefore are not subject to these guidelines. If an employer relies upon such certification in making employment decisions, the employer is the user and must be prepared to justify, under Federal law, that reliance as it would any other selection procedure.

6. *The "Four-Fifths Rule of Thumb" (section 4D).* Some representatives of employers and some professionals suggest that the basic test for adverse impact should be a test of statistical significance, rather than the four-fifths rule. Some civil rights groups, on the other hand, still regard the four-fifths rule as permitting some unlawful discrimination.

The Federal agencies believe that neither of these positions is correct. The great majority of employers do not hire, promote, or assign enough employees for most jobs to warrant primary reliance upon statistical significance. Many decisions in day-to-day life are made on the basis of information which does not have the justification of a test of statistical significance. Courts have found adverse impact without a showing of statistical significance. *Griggs* v. *Duke Power Co.,* supra; *Vulcan Society of New York* v. *CSC of N.Y.,* 490 F.2d 387, 393 (2d Cir. 1973); *Kirkland* v. *New York St. Dept. of Corr. Serv.,* 520 F.2d 420, 425 (2d Cir. 1975).

Accordingly, the undersigned believe that while the four-fifths rule does not define discrimination and does not apply in all cases, it is appropriate as a rule of thumb in identifying adverse impact.

Technical Standards

7. *Criterion-related validity (section 14B).* This section of the guidelines found general support among the commenters from the psychological profession and, except for the provisions concerning test fairness (sometimes mistakenly equated with differential prediction or differential validity), generated relatively little comment.

The provisions of the guidelines concerning criterion-related validity studies call for studies of fairness of selections procedures where technically feasible.

Section 14B(8). Some psychologists and employer groups objected that the concept of test fairness or unfairness has been discredited by professionals and pointed out that the term is commonly misused. We recognize that there is serious debate on the question of test fairness; however, it is accepted professionally that fairness should be examined where feasible. The A.P.A. standards for educational and psychological tests, for example, direct users to explore the question of fairness on finding a difference in group performances (section E9, pp. 43-44). Similarly the concept of test fairness is one which is closely related to the basic thrust of Federal equal employment opportunity law; and that concept was endorsed by the Supreme Court in *Albemarle Paper Co.* v. *Moody,* 422 U.S. 405.

Accordingly, we have retained in the guidelines the obligation upon users to investigate test fairness where it is technically feasible to do so.

8. *Content validity.* The Division of Industrial and Organizational Psychology of A.P.A. correctly perceived that the provisions of the draft guidelines concerning content validity, with their emphasis on observable work behaviors or work products, were "greatly concerned with minimizing the inferential leap between test and performance." That division expressed the view that the draft guidelines neglected situations where a knowledge, skill or ability is necessary to an outcome but where the work behavior

cannot be replicated in a test. They recommended that the section be revised.

We believe that the emphasis on observable work behaviors or observable work products is appropriate; and that in order to show content validity, the gap between the test and performance on the job should be a small one. We recognize, however, that content validity may be appropriate to support a test which measures a knowledge, skill, or ability which is a necessary prerequisite to the performance of the job, even though the test might not be close enough to the work behavior to be considered a work sample, and the guidelines have been revised appropriately. On the other hand, tests of mental processes which are not directly observable and which may be difficult to determine on the basis of observable work behaviors or work products should not be supported by content validity.

Thus, the Principles for the Validation and Use of Personnel Selection Procedures (Division of Industrial and Organizational Psychology, American Psychological Association, 1975, p. 10), discuss the use of content validity to support tests of "specific items of knowledge, or specific job skills," but call attention to the inappropriateness of attempting to justify tests for traits or constructs on a content validity basis.

9. *Construct validity (section 14D)*. Business groups and professionals expressed concern that the construct validity requirements in the December 30 draft were confusing and technically inaccurate. As section 14D indicates, construct validity is a relatively new procedure in the field of personnel selection and there is not yet substantial guidance in the professional literature as to its use in the area of employment practices. The provisions on construct validity have been revised to meet the concerns expressed by the A.P.A. The construct validity section as revised clarifies what is required by the Federal enforcement agencies at this stage in the development of construct validity. The guidelines leave open the possibility that different evidence of construct validity may be accepted in the future, as new methodologies develop and become incorporated in professional standards and other professional literature.

10. *Documentation (section 15)*. Commenters stated that the documentation section did not conform to the technical requirements of the guidelines or was otherwise inadequate. Section 15 has been clarified and two significant changes have been made to minimize the recordkeeping burden (See overview, part VIII.)

11. *Definitions (section 16)*. The definition of work behavior in the December 30, 1977 draft was criticized by the A.P.A. and others as being too vague to provide adequate guidance to those using the guidelines who must identify work behavior as a part of any validation technique. Other comments criticized the absence or inadequacies of other definitions, especially "adverse impact." Substantial revisions of and additions to this section were therefore made.

UNIFORM GUIDELINES ON EMPLOYEE SELECTION PROCEDURES (1978)

Note.—These guidelines are issued jointly by four agencies. Separate official adoptions follow the guidelines in this part IV as follows: Civil Service Commission, Department of Justice, Equal Employment Opportunity Commission, Department of Labor.

For official citation see section 18 of these guidelines.

TABLE OF CONTENTS
GENERAL PRINCIPLES

1. Statement of Purpose
   A. Need for Uniformity—Issuing Agencies
   B. Purpose of Guidelines
   C. Relation to Prior Guidelines
2. Scope
   A. Application of Guidelines
   B. Employment Decisions

No. 353   UNIFORM GUIDELINES ON EMPLOYEE SELECTION   401:2243

  C. Selection Procedures
  D. Limitations
  E. Indian Preference Not Affected
3. Discrimination Defined: Relationship Between Use of Selection Procedures and Discrimination
  A. Procedure Having Adverse Impact Constitutes Discrimination Unless Justified
  B. Consideration of Suitable Alternative Selection Procedures
4. Information on Impact
  A. Records Concerning Impact
  B. Applicable Race, Sex and Ethnic Groups For Record Keeping
  C. Evaluation of Selection Rates. The "Bottom Line"
  D. Adverse Impact And The "Four-Fifths Rule"
  E. Consideration of User's Equal Employment Opportunity Posture
5. General Standards for Validity Studies
  A. Acceptable types of Validity Studies
  B. Criterion-Related, Content, and Construct Validity
  C. Guidelines Are Consistent with Professional Standards
  D. Need For Documentation of Validity
  E. Accuracy and Standardization
  F. Caution Against Selection on Basis of Knowledges, Skills or Abilities Learned in Brief Orientation Period
  G. Method of Use of Selection Procedures
  H. Cutoff Scores
  I. Use of Selection Procedures of Higher Level Jobs
  J. Interim Use of Selection Procedures
  K. Review of Validity Studies for Currency
6. Use of Selection Procedures Which Have Not Been Validated
  A. Use of Alternate Selection Procedures to Eliminate Adverse Impact
  B. Where Validity Studies Cannot or Need Not Be Performed
    (1) Where Informal or Unscored Procedures Are Used
    (2) Where Formal And Scored Procedures Are Used
7. Use of Other Validity Studies
  A. Validity Studies not Conducted by the User
  B. Use of Criterion-Related Validity Evidence from Other Sources
    (1) Vlidity Evidence
    (2) Job Similarity
    (3) Fairness Evidence
  C. Validity Evidence from Multi-Unit Study
  D. Other Significant Variables
8. Cooperative Studies
  A. Encouragement of Cooperative Studies
  B. Standards for Use of Cooperative Studies
9. No Assumption of Validity
  A. Unacceptable Substitutes for Evidence of Validity
  B. Encouragement of Professional Supervision
10. Employment Agencies and Employment Services
  A. Where Selection Procedures Are Devised by Agency
  B. Where Selection Procedures Are Devised Elsewhere
11. Disparate Treatment
12. Retesting of Applicants
13. Affirmative Action
  A. Affirmative Action Obligations
  B. Encouragement of Voluntary Affirmative Action Programs

TECHNICAL STANDARDS

14. Technical Standards for Validity Studies
  A. Validity Studies Should be Based on Review of Information about the Job
  B. Technical Standards for Criterion-Related Validity Studies
    (1) Technical Feasibility
    (2) Analysis of the Job
    (3) Criterion Measures
    (4) Representativeness of the Sample
    (5) Statistical Relationships
    (6) Operational Use of Selection Procedures
    (7) Over-Statement of Validity Findings
    (8) Fairness
    (a) Unfairness Defined
    (b) Investigation of Fairness
    (c) General Considerations in Fairness Investigations
    (d) When Unfairness Is Shown
    (e) Technical Feasibility of Fairness Studies
    (f) Continued Use of Selection Procedures When Fairness Studies not Feasible
  C. Technical Standards for Content Validity Studies
    (1) Appropriateness of Content Validity Studies
    (2) Job Analysis for Content Validity
    (3) Development of Selection Procedure
    (4) Standards For Demonstrating Content Validity
    (5) Reliability
    (6) Prior Training or Experience
    (7) Training Success
    (8) Operational Use
    (9) Ranking Based on Content Validity Studies
  D. Technical Standards For Construct Validity Studies

(1) Appropriateness of Construct Validity Studies
(2) Job Analysis For Construct Validity Studies
(3) Relationship to the Job
(4) Use of Construct Validity Study Without New Criterion-Related Evidence
(a) Standards for Use
(b) Determination of Common Work Behaviors

DOCUMENTATION OF IMPACT AND VALIDITY EVIDENCE

15. Documentation of Impact and Validity Evidence
A. Required Information
(1) Simplified Recordkeeping for Users With Less Than 100 Employees
(2) Information on Impact
(a) Collection of Information on Impact
(b) When Adverse Impact Has Been Eliminated in The Total Selection Process
(c) When Data Insufficient to Determine Impact
(3) Documentation of Validity Evidence
(a) Type of Evidence
(b) Form of Report
(c) Completeness
B. Criterion-Related Validity Studies
(1) User(s), Location(s), and Date(s) of Study
(2) Problem and Setting
(3) Job Analysis or Review of Job Information
(4) Job Titles and Codes
(5) Criterion Measures
(6) Sample Description
(7) Description of Selection Procedure
(8) Techniques and Results
(9) Alternative Procedures Investigated
(10) Uses and Applications
(11) Source Data
(12) Contact Person
(13) Accuracy and Completeness
C. Content Validity Studies
(1) User(s), Location(s), and Date(s) of Study
(2) Problem and Setting
(3) Job Analysis—Content of the Job
(4) Selection Procedure and its Content
(5) Relationship Between Selection Procedure and the Job
(6) Alternative Procedures Investigated
(7) Uses and Applications
(8) Contact Person
(9) Accuracy and Completeness
D. Construct Validity Studies
(1) User(s), Location(s), and Date(s) of Study
(2) Problem and Setting
(3) Construct Definition
(4) Job Analysis
(5) Job Titles and Codes
(6) Selection Procedure
(7) Relationship to Job Performance
(8) Alternative Procedures Investigated
(9) Uses and Applications
(10) Accuracy and Completeness
(11) Source Data
(12) Contact Person
E. Evidence of Validity from Other Studies
(1) Evidence from Criterion-Related Validity Studies
(a) Job Information
(b) Relevance of Criteria
(c) Other Variables
(d) Use of the Selection Procedure
(e) Bibliography
(2) Evidence from Content Validity Studies
(3) Evidence from Construct Validity Studies
F. Evidence of Validity from Cooperative Studies
G. Selection for Higher Level Jobs
H. Interim Use of Selection Procedures

DEFINITIONS

16. Definitions

APPENDIX

17. Policy Statement on Affirmative Action (see Section 13B)
18. Citations

GENERAL PRINCIPLES

SECTION 1. *Statement of purpose.*—A. *Need for uniformity—Issuing agencies.* The Federal Government's need for a uniform set of principles on the question of the use of tests and other selection procedures has long been recognized. The Equal Employment Opportunity Commission, the Civil Service Commission, the Department of Labor, and the Department of Justice jointly have adopted these uniform guidelines to meet that need, and to apply the same principles to the Federal Government as are applied to other employers.

B. *Purpose of guidelines.* These guidelines incorporate a single set of principles which are designed to assist employers, labor organizations, employment agencies, and licensing and certification boards to comply with requirements of Federal law prohibiting employment practices which discriminate on grounds of race, color, religion, sex, and national origin. They are designed to provide a framework for determining the proper use of tests and other selection procedures. These guidelines do not require a user to conduct validity studies of selection procedures where no adverse impact results. However, all users are encouraged to use selection procedures which are valid, especially users operating under merit principles.

C. *Relation to prior guidelines.* These guidelines are based upon and supersede previously issued guidelines on employee selection procedures. These guidelines have been built upon court decisions, the previously issued guidelines of the agencies, and the practical experience of the agencies, as well as the standards of the psychological profession. These guidelines are intended to be consistent with existing law.

Sec. 2. *Scope.*—A. *Application of guidelines.* These guidelines will be applied by the Equal Employment Opportunity Commission in the enforcement of Title VII of the Civil Rights Act of 1964, as amended by the Equal Employment Opportunity Act of 1972 (hereinafter "Title VII"); by the Department of Labor, and the contract compliance agencies until the transfer of authority contemplated by the President's Reorganization Plan No. 1 of 1978, in the administration and enforcement of Executive Order 11246, as amended by Executive Order 11375 (hereinafter "Executive Order 11246"); by the Civil Service Commission and other Federal agencies subject to section 717 of Title VII; by the Civil Service Commission in exercising its responsibilities toward State and local governments under section 208(b)(1) of the Intergovernmental-Personnel Act; by the Department of Justice in exercising its responsibilities under Federal law; by the Office of Revenue Sharing of the Department of the Treasury under the State and Local Fiscal Assistance Act of 1972, as amended; and by any other Federal agency which adopts them.

B. *Employment decisions.* These guidelines apply to tests and other selection procedures which are used as a basis for any employment decision. Employment decisions include but are not limited to hiring, promotion, demotion, membership (for example, in a labor organization), referral, retention, and licensing and certification, to the extent that licensing and certification may be covered by Federal equal employment opportunity law. Other selection decisions, such as selection for training or transfer, may also be considered employment decisions if they lead to any of the decisions listed above.

C. *Selection procedures.* These guidelines apply only to selection procedures which are used as a basis for making employment decisions. For example, the use of recruiting procedures designed to attract members of a particular race, sex, or ethnic group, which were previously denied employment opportunities or which are currently underutilized, may be necessary to bring an employer into compliance with Federal law, and is frequently an essential element of any effective affirmative action program; but recruitment practices are not considered by these guidelines to be selection procedures. Similarly, these guidelines do not pertain to the question of the lawfulness of a seniority system within the meaning of section 703(h), Executive Order 11246 or other provisions of Federal law or regulation, except to the extent that such systems utilize selection procedures to determine qualifications or abilities to perform the job. Nothing in these guidelines is intended or should be interpreted as discouraging the use of a selection procedure for the purpose of determining qualifications or for the purpose of selection on the basis of relative qualifications, if the selection procedure had been validated in accord with these guidelines for each such purpose for which it is to be used.

D. *Limitations.* These guidelines apply only to persons subject to Title VII, Executive Order 11246, or other equal employment opportunity requirements of Federal law. These guidelines do not apply to responsibilities under the Age Discrimination in Employment Act of 1967, as amended, not to discriminate on the basis of age, or under sections 501, 503, and 504 of the Rehabilitation Act of 1973, not to discriminate on the basis of handicap.

E. *Indian preference not affected.* These guidelines do not restrict any obligation imposed or right granted by Federal law to users to extend a preference in employment to Indians living on or near an Indian reservation in connection with employment opportunities on or near an Indian reservation.

Sec. 3. *Discrimination defined: Relationship between use of selection procedures and discrimination.*—A. *Procedure having adverse impact constitutes discrimination unless justified.* The use of any selection procedure which has an adverse impact on the hiring, promotion, or other employment or membership opportunities of members of any race, sex, or ethnic group will be considered to be discriminatory and inconsistent with these guidelines, unless the procedure has been validated in accordance with these guidelines, or the provisions of section 6 below are satisfied.

B. *Consideration of suitable alternative selection procedures.* Where two or more selection procedures are available which serve the user's legitimate interest in efficient and trustworthy workmanship, and which are substantially equally valid for a given purpose, the user should use the procedure which has been demonstrated to have the lesser adverse impact. Accordingly, whenever a validity study is called for by these guidelines, the user should include, as a part of the validity study, an investigation of suitable alternative selection procedures and suitable alternative methods of using the selection procedure which have as little adverse impact as possible, to determine the appropriateness of using or validating them in accord with these guidelines. If a user has made a reasonable effort to become aware of such alternative procedures and validity has been demonstrated in accord with these guidelines, the use of the test or other selection procedure may continue until such time as it should reasonably be reviewed for currency. Whenever the user is shown an alternative selection procedure with evidence of less adverse impact and substantial evidence of validity for the same job in similar circumstances, the user should investigate it to determine the appropriateness of using or validating it in accord with these guidelines. This subsection is not intended to preclude the combination of procedures into a significantly more valid procedure, if the use of such a combination has been shown to be in compliance with the guidelines.

Sec. 4. *Information on impact.*—A. *Records concerning impact.* Each user should maintain and have available for inspection records or other information which will disclose the impact which its tests and other selection procedures have upon employment opportunities of persons by identifiable race, sex, or ethnic group as set forth in subparagraph B below in order to determine compliance with these guidelines. Where there are large numbers of applicants and procedures are administered frequently, such information may be retained on a sample basis, provided that the sample is appropriate in terms of the applicant population and adequate in size.

B. *Applicable race, sex, and ethnic groups for recordkeeping.* The records called for by this section are to be maintained by sex, and the following races and ethnic groups: Blacks (Negroes), American Indians (including Alaskan Natives), Asians (including Pacific Islanders), Hispanic (including persons of Mexican, Puerto Rican, Cuban, Central or South American, or other Spanish origin or culture regardless of race), Whites (Caucasians) other than Hispanic, and totals. The race, sex, and ethnic classifications called for by this section are consistent with the Equal Employment Opportunity Standard Form 100, Employer Information Report EEO-1 series of reports. The user should adopt safeguards to insure that the records required by this paragraph are used for appropriate purposes such as determining adverse impact, or (where required) for developing and monitoring affirmative action programs, and that such records are not used improperly. See sections 4E and 17(4), below.

C. *Evaluation of selection rates. The "bottom line."* If the information called for by sections 4A and B above shows that the total selection process for a job has an adverse impact, the individual components of the selection process should be evaluated for adverse impact. If this information shows that the total selection process does not have an adverse impact, the Federal enforcement agencies, in the exercise of their administrative and prosecutorial discretion, in usual circumstances, will not expect a user to evaluate the individual components for adverse impact, or to validate such individual components, and will not take enforcement action based upon adverse impact of any component of that process, including the separate parts of a multipart selection procedure or any separate procedure that is used as an alternative method of selection. However, in the following circumstances the Federal enforcement agencies will expect a user to evaluate the individual components for adverse impact and may, where appropriate, take enforcement action with respect to the individual components: (1) where the selection procedure is a significant factor in the continuation of patterns of assignments of incumbent employees caused by prior discriminatory employment practices, (2) where the weight of court decisions or administrative interpretations hold that a specific procedure (such as height or weight requirements or no-arrest records) is not job related in the same or similar circumstances. In unusual circumstances, other than those listed in (1) and (2) above, the Federal enforcement agencies may request a user to evaluate the individual components for adverse impact and may, where appropriate, take enforcement action with respect to the individual component.

D. *Adverse impact and the "four-fifths rule."* A selection rate for any race, sex, or ethnic group which is less than four-fifths ($1/5$) (or eighty percent) of the rate for the group with the highest rate will generally be regarded by the Federal enforcement agencies as evidence of adverse impact, while a greater than four-fifths rate will generally not be regarded by Federal enforcement agencies as evidence of adverse impact. Smaller differences in selection rate may nevertheless constitute adverse impact, where they are significant in both statistical and practical terms or where a user's actions have discouraged applicants disproportionately on grounds of race, sex, or ethnic group. Greater differences in selection rate may not constitute adverse impact where the differences are based on small numbers and are not statistically significant, or where special recruiting or other programs cause the pool of minority or female candidates to be atypical of the normal pool of applicants from that group. Where the user's evidence concerning the impact of a selection procedure indicates adverse impact but is based upon numbers which are too small to be reliable, evidence concerning the impact of the procedure over a longer period of time and/or evidence concerning the impact which the selection procedure had when used in the same manner in similar circumstances elsewhere may be considered in determining adverse impact. Where the user has not maintained data on adverse impact as required by the documentation section of applicable guidelines, the Federal enforcement agencies may draw an inference of adverse impact of the selection process from the failure of the user to maintain such data, if the user has an underutilization of a group in the job category, as compared to the group's representation in the relevant labor market or, in the case of jobs filled from within, the applicable work force.

E. *Consideration of user's equal employment opportunity posture.* In carrying out their obligations, the Federal enforcement agencies will consider the general posture of the user with respect to equal employment opportunity for the job or group of jobs in question. Where a user has adopted an affirmative action program, the Federal enforcement agencies will consider the provisions of that program, including the goals and timetables which the user has adopted and the progress which the user has made in carrying out that program and in meeting the goals and timetables. While such affirmative action programs may in design and execution be race, color, sex, or ethnic conscious, selection procedures under such programs should be based upon the ability or relative ability to do the work.

Sec. 5. *General standards for validity studies.*—A. *Acceptable types of validity studies.* For the purposes of satisfying these guidelines, users may rely upon criterion-related validity studies, content validity studies or construct validity studies, in accordance with the standards set forth in the technical standards of these guidelines, section 14 below. New strategies for showing the validity of selection procedures will be evaluated as they become accepted by the psychological profession.

B. *Criterion-related, content, and construct validity.* Evidence of the validity of a test or other selection procedure by a criterion-related validity study should consist of empirical data demonstrating that the selection procedure is predictive of or significantly correlated with important elements of job performance. See section 14B below. Evidence of the validity of a test or other selection procedure by a content validity study should consist of data showing that the content of the selection procedure is representative of important aspects of performance on the job for which the candidates are to be evaluated. See section 14C below. Evidence of the validity of a test or other selection procedure through a construct validity study should consist of data showing that the procedure measures the degree to which candidates have identifiable characteristics which have been determined to be important in successful performance in the job for which the candidates are to be evaluated. See section 14D below.

C. *Guidelines are consistent with professional standards.* The provisions of these guidelines relating to validation of selection procedures are intended to be consistent with generally accepted professional standards for evaluating standardized tests and other selection procedures, such as those described in the Standards for Educational and Psychological Tests prepared by a joint committee of the American Psychological Association, the American Educational Research Association, and the National Council on Measurement in Education (American Psychological Association,

Washington, D.C., 1974) (hereinafter "A.P.A. Standards") and standard textbooks and journals in the field of personnel selection.

D. *Need for documentation of validity.* For any selection procedure which is part of a selection process which has an adverse impact and which selection procedure has an adverse impact, each user should maintain and have available such documentation as is described in section 15 below.

E. Accuracy and standardization. Validity studies should be carried out under conditions which assure insofar as possible the adequacy and accuracy of the research and the report. Selection procedures should be administered and scored under standardized conditions.

F. *Caution against selection on basis of knowledges, skills, or ability learned in brief orientation period.* In general, users should avoid making employment decisions on the basis of measures of knowledges, skills, or abilities which are normally learned in a brief orientation period, and which have an adverse impact.

G. *Method of use of selection procedures.* The evidence of both the validity and utility of a selection procedure should support the method the user chooses for operational use of the procedure, if that method of use has a greater adverse impact than another method of use. Evidence which may be sufficient to support the use of a selection procedure on a pass/fail (screening) basis may be insufficient to support the use of the same procedure on a ranking basis under these guidelines. Thus, if a user decides to use a selection procedure on a ranking basis, and that method of use has a greater adverse impact than use on an appropriate pass/fail basis (see section 5H below), the user should have sufficient evidence of validity and utility to support the use on a ranking basis. See sections 3B, 14B (5) and (6), and 14C (8) and (9).

H. *Cutoff scores.* Where cutoff scores are used, they should normally be set so as to be reasonable and consistent with normal expectations of acceptable proficiency within the work force. Where applicants are ranked on the basis of properly validated selection procedures and those applicants scoring below a higher cutoff score than appropriate in light of such expectations have little or no chance of being selected for employment, the higher cutoff score may be appropriate, but the degree of adverse impact should be considered.

I. *Use of selection procedures for higher level jobs.* If job progression structures are so established that employees will probably, within a reasonable period of time and in a majority of cases, progress to a higher level, it may be considered that the applicants are being evaluated for a job or jobs at the higher level. However, where job progression is not so nearly automatic, or the time span is such that higher level jobs or employees' potential may be expected to change in significant ways, it should be considered that applicants are being evaluated for a job at or near the entry level. A "reasonable period of time" will vary for different jobs and employment situations but will seldom be more than 5 years. Use of selection procedures to evaluate applicants for a higher level job would not be appropriate:

(1) If the majority of those remaining employed do not progress to the higher level job;

(2) If there is a reason to doubt that the higher level job will continue to require essentially similar skills during the progression period; or

(3) If the selection procedures measure knowledges, skills, or abilities required for advancement which would be expected to develop principally from the training or experience on the job.

J. *Interim use of selection procedures.* Users may continue the use of a selection procedure which is not at the moment fully supported by the required evidence of validity, provided: (1) The user has available substantial evidence of validity, and (2) the user has in progress, when technically feasible, a study which is designed to produce the additional evidence required by these guidelines within a reasonable time. If such a study is not technically feasible, see section 6B. If the study does not demonstrate validity, this provision of these guidelines for interim use shall not constitute a defense in any action, nor shall it relieve the user of any obligations arising under Federal law.

K. *Review of validity studies for currency.* Whenever validity has been shown in accord with these guidelines for the use of a particular selection procedure for a job or group of jobs, additional studies need not be performed until such time as the validity study is subject to review as provided in section 3B above. There are no absolutes in the area of determining the currency of a validity study. All circumstances concerning the study, including the validation strategy used, and changes in the relevant labor market and the job should be considered in the determination of when a validity study is outdated.

Sec. 6. *Use of selection procedures which have not been validated.*—A. *Use of alternative selection procedures to eliminate adverse impact.* A user may choose to utilize alternative selection procedures in order to eliminate adverse impact or as part of an affirmative action program. See section 13 below. Such alternative procedures should eliminate the adverse impact in the total selection process, should be lawful and should be as job related as possible.

B. *Where validity studies cannot or need not be performed.* There are circumstances in which a user cannot or need not utilize the validation techniques contemplated by these guidelines. In such circumstances, the user should utilize selection procedures which are as job related as possible and which will minimize or eliminate adverse impact, as set forth below.

(1) *Where informal or unscored procedures are used.* When an informal or unscored selection procedure which has an adverse impact is utilized, the user should eliminate the adverse impact, or modify the procedure to one which is a formal, scored or quantified measure or combination of measures and then validate the procedure in accord with these guidelines, or otherwise justify continued use of the procedure in accord with Federal law.

(2) *Where formal and scored procedures are used.* When a formal and scored selection procedure is used which has an adverse impact, the validation techniques contemplated by these guidelines usually should be followed if technically feasible. Where the user cannot or need not follow the validation techniques anticipated by these guidelines, the user should either modify the procedure to eliminate adverse impact or otherwise justify continued use of the procedure in accord with Federal law.

Sec. 7. *Use of other validity studies.*—A. *Validity studies not conducted by the user.* Users may, under certain circumstances, support the use of selection procedures by validity studies conducted by other users or conducted by test publishers or distributors and described in test manuals. While publishers of selection procedures have a professional obligation to provide evidence of validity which meets generally accepted professional standards (see section 5C above), users are cautioned that they are responsible for compliance with these guidelines. Accordingly, users seeking to obtain selection procedures from publishers and distributors should be careful to determine that, in the event the user becomes subject to the validity requirements of these guidelines, the necessary information to support validity has been determined and will be made available to the user.

B. *Use of criterion-related validity evidence from other sources.* Criterion-related validity studies conducted by one test user, or described in test manuals and the professional literature, will be considered acceptable for use by another user when the following requirements are met:

(1) *Validity evidence.* Evidence from the available studies meeting the standards of section 14B below clearly demonstrates that the selection procedure is valid:

(2) *Job similarity.* The incumbents in the user's job and the incumbents in the job or group of jobs on which the validity study was conducted perform substantially the same major work behaviors, as shown by appropriate job analyses both on the job or group of jobs on which the validity study was performed and on the job for which the selection procedure is to be used; and

(3) *Fairness evidence.* The studies include a study of test fairness for each race, sex, and ethnic group which constitutes a significant factor in the borrowing user's relevant labor market for the job or jobs in question. If the studies under consideration satisfy (1) and (2) above but do not contain an investigation of test fairness, and it is not technically feasible for the borrowing user to conduct an internal study of test fairness, the borrowing user may utilize the study until studies conducted elsewhere meeting the requirements of these guidelines show test unfairness, or until such time as it becomes technically feasible to conduct an internal study of test fairness and the results of that study can be acted upon. Users obtaining selection procedures from publishers should consider, as one factor in the decision to purchase a particular selection procedure, the availability of evidence concerning test fairness.

C. *Validity evidence from multiunit study.* If validity evidence from a study covering more than one unit within an organization satisfies the requirements of section 14B below, evidence of validity specific to each unit will not be required unless there are variables which are likely to affect validity significantly.

D. *Other significant variables.* If there are variables in the other studies which are likely to affect validity significantly, the user may not rely upon such studies, but will be expected either to conduct an internal validity study or to comply with section 6 above.

Sec. 8. *Cooperative studies.*—A. *Encouragement of cooperative studies.* The agencies issuing these guidelines encourage employers, labor organizations, and employment agencies to cooperate in research, development, search for lawful alternatives, and validity studies in order to achieve procedures which are consistent with these guidelines.

B. *Standards for use of cooperative studies.* If validity evidence from a cooperative study satisfies the requirements of section 14 below, evidence of validity specific to each user will not be required unless there are variables in the user's situation which are likely to affect validity significantly.

Sec. 9. *No assumption of validity.*—A. *Unacceptable substitutes for evidence of validity.* Under no circumstances will the general reputation of a test or other selection procedures, its author or its publisher, or casual reports of its validity be accepted in lieu of evidence of validity. Specifically ruled out are: assumptions of validity based on a procedure's name or descriptive labels; all forms of promotional literature; data hearing on the frequency of a procedure's usage; testimonial statements and credentials of sellers, users, or consultants; and other nonempirical or anecdotal accounts of selection practices or selection outcomes.

B. *Encouragement of professional supervision.* Professional supervision of selection activities is encouraged but is not a substitute for documented evidence of validity. The enforcement agencies will take into account the fact that a thorough job analysis was conducted and that careful development and use of a selection procedure in accordance with professional standards enhance the probability that the selection procedure is valid for the job.

Sec. 10. *Employment agencies and employment services.*—A. *Where selection procedures are devised by agency.* An employment agency, including private employment agencies and State employment agencies, which agrees to a request by an employer or labor organization to devise and utilize a selection procedure should follow the standards in these guidelines for determining adverse impact. If adverse impact exists the agency should comply with these guidelines. An employment agency is not relieved of its obligation herein because the user did not request such validation or has requested the use of some lesser standard of validation than is provided in these guidelines. The use of an employment agency does not relieve an employer or labor organization or other user of its responsibilities under Federal law to provide equal employment opportunity or its obligations as a user under these guidelines.

B. *Where selection procedures are devised elsewhere.* Where an employment agency or service is requested to administer a selection procedure which has been devised elsewhere and to make referrals pursuant to the results, the employment agency or service should maintain and have available evidence of the impact of the selection and referral procedures which it administers. If adverse impact results the agency or service should comply with these guidelines. If the agency or service seeks to comply with these guidelines by reliance upon validity studies or other data in the possession of the employer, it should obtain and have available such information.

Sec. 11. *Disparate treatment.* The principles of disparate or unequal treatment must be distinguished from the concepts of validation. A selection procedure—even though validated against job performance in accordance with these guidelines—cannot be imposed upon members of a race, sex, or ethnic group where other employees, applicants, or members have not been subjected to that standard. Disparate treatment occurs where members of a race, sex, or ethnic group have been denied the same employment, promotion, membership, or other employment opportunities as have been available to other employees or applicants. Those employees or applicants who have been denied equal treatment, because of prior discriminatory practices or policies, must at least be afforded the same opportunities as had existed for other employees or applicants during the period of discrimination. Thus, the persons who were in the class of persons discriminated against during the period the user followed the discriminatory practices should be allowed the opportunity to qualify under less stringent selection procedures previously followed, unless the user demonstrates that the increased standards are required by business necessity. This section does not prohibit a user who has not previously followed merit standards from adopting merit standards which are in compliance with these guidelines nor does it preclude a user who has previously used invalid or unvalidated selection procedures from developing and using procedures which are in accord with these guidelines.

Sec. 12. *Retesting of applicants.* Users should provide a reasonable opportunity for retesting and reconsideration. Where examinations are administered periodically with public notice, such reasonable opportunity exists, unless persons who have previously been tested are precluded from retesting. The user may however take reasonable steps to preserve the security of its procedures.

Sec. 13. *Affirmative action.*—A. *Affirmative action obligations.* The use of selection procedures which have been validated pursuant to these guidelines does not relieve users of any obligations they may have to undertake affirmative action to assure equal employment opportunity. Nothing in these guidelines is intended to preclude the use of lawful selection procedures which assist in remedying the effects of prior discriminatory practices, or the achievement of affirmative action objectives.

B. *Encouragement of voluntary affirmative action programs.* These guidelines are also intended to encourage the adoption and implementation of voluntary affirmative action programs by users who have no obligation under Federal law to adopt them; but are not intended to impose any new obligations in that regard. The agencies issuing and endorsing these guidelines endorse for all private employers and reaffirm for all governmental employers the Equal Employment Opportunity Coordinating Council's "Policy Statement on Affirmative Action Programs for State and Local Government Agencies" (41 FR 38814, September 13, 1976). That policy statement is attached hereto as appendix, section 17.

Technical Standards

Sec. 14. *Technical standards for validity studies.* The following minimum standards, as applicable, should be met in conducting a validity study. Nothing in these guidelines is intended to preclude the development and use of other professionally acceptable techniques with respect to validation of selection procedures. Where it is not technically feasible for a user to conduct a validity study, the user has the obligation otherwise to comply with these guidelines. See sections 6 and 7 above.

A. *Validity studies should be based on review of information about the job.* Any validity study should be based upon a review of information about the job for which the selection procedure is to be used. The review should include a job analysis except as provided in section 14B(3) below with respect to criterion-related validity. Any method of job analysis may be used if it provides the information required for the specific validation strategy used.

B. *Technical standards for criterion-related validity studies.*—(1) *Technical feasibility.* Users choosing to validate a selection procedure by a criterion-related validity strategy should determine whether it is technically feasible (as defined in section 16) to conduct such a study in the particular employment context. The determination of the number of persons necessary to permit the conduct of a meaningful criterion-related study should be made by the user on the basis of all relevant information concerning the selection procedure, the potential sample and the employment situation. Where appropriate, jobs with substantially the same major work behaviors may be grouped together for validity studies, in order to obtain an adequate sample. These guidelines do not require a user to hire or promote persons for the purpose of making it possible to conduct a criterion-related study.

(2) *Analysis of the job.* There should be a review of job information to determine measures of work behavior(s) or performance that are relevant to the job or group of jobs in question. These measures or criteria are relevant to the extent that they represent critical or important job duties, work behaviors or work outcomes as developed from the review of job information. The possibility of bias should be considered both in selection of

the criterion measures and their application. In view of the possibility of bias in subjective evaluations, supervisory rating techniques and instructions to raters should be carefully developed. All criterion measures and the methods for gathering data need to be examined for freedom from factors which would unfairly alter scores of members of any group. The relevance of criteria and their freedom from bias are of particular concern when there are significant differences in measures of job performance for different groups.

(3) *Criterion measures.* Proper safeguards should be taken to insure that scores on selection procedures do not enter into any judgments of employee adequacy that are to be used as criterion measures. Whatever criteria are used should represent important or critical work behavior(s) or work outcomes. Certain criteria may be used without a full job analysis if the user can show the importance of the criteria to the particular employment context. These criteria include but are not limited to production rate, error rate, tardiness, absenteeism, and length of service. A standardized rating of overall work performance may be used where a study of the job shows that it is an appropriate criterion. Where performance in training is used as a criterion, success in training should be properly measured and the relevance of the training should be shown either through a comparison of the content of the training program with the critical or important work behavior(s) of the job(s), or through a demonstration of the relationship between measures of performance in training and measures of job performance. Measures of relative success in training include but are not limited to instructor evaluations, performance samples, or tests. Criterion measures consisting of paper and pencil tests will be closely reviewed for job relevance.

(4) *Representativeness of the sample.* Whether the study is predictive or concurrent, the sample subjects should insofar as feasible be representative of the candidates normally available in the relevant labor market for the job or group of jobs in question, and should insofar as feasible include the races, sexes, and ethnic groups normally available in the relevant job market. In determining the representativeness of the sample in a concurrent validity study, the user should take into account the extent to which the specific knowledges or skills which are the primary focus of the test are those which employees learn on the job.

Where samples are combined or compared, attention should be given to see that such samples are comparable in terms of the actual job they perform, the length of time on the job where time on the job is likely to affect performance, and other relevant factors likely to affect validity differences; or that these factors are included in the design of the study and their effects identified.

(5) *Statistical relationships.* The degree of relationship between selection procedure scores and criterion measures should be examined and computed, using professionally acceptable statistical procedures. Generally, a selection procedure is considered related to the criterion, for the purposes of these guidelines, when the relationship between performance on the procedure and performance on the criterion measure is statistically significant at the 0.05 level of significance, which means that it is sufficiently high as to have a probability of no more than one (1) in twenty (20) to have occurred by chance. Absence of a statistically significant relationship between a selection procedure and job performance should not necessarily discourage other investigations of the validity of that selection procedure.

(6) *Operational use of selection procedures.* Users should evaluate each selection procedure to assure that it is appropriate for operational use, including establishment of cutoff scores or rank ordering. Generally, if other factors remain the same, the greater the magnitude of the relationship (e.g., correlation coefficent) between performance on a selection procedure and one or more criteria of performance on the job, and the greater the importance and number of aspects of job performance covered by the criteria, the more likely it is that the procedure will be appropriate for use. Reliance upon a selection procedure which is significantly related to a criterion measure, but which is based upon a study involving a large number of subjects and has a low correlation coefficient will be subject to close review if it has a large adverse impact. Sole reliance upon a single selection instrument which is related to only one of many job duties or aspects of job performance will also be subject to close review. The appropriateness of a selection procedure is best evaluated in each particular situation and there are no minimum correlation coefficients applicable to all employment situations. In determining whether a selection procedure is appropriate for operational use the following considerations should also be taken into account: The degree of adverse impact of the procedure, the availability of other selection procedures of greater or substantially equal validity.

(7) *Overstatement of validity findings.* Users should avoid reliance upon techniques which tend to overestimate validity findings as a result of capitalization on chance unless an appropriate safeguard is taken. Reliance upon a few selection procedures or criteria of successful job performance when many selection procedures or criteria of performance have been studied, or the use of optimal statistical weights for selection procedures computed in one sample, are techniques which tend to inflate validity estimates as a result of chance. Use of a large sample is one safeguard: cross-validation is another.

(8) *Fairness* This section generally calls for studies of unfairness where technically feasible. The concept of fairness or unfairness of selection procedures is a developing concept. In addition, fairness studies generally require substantial numbers of employees in the job or group of jobs being studied. For these reasons, the Federal enforcement agencies recognize that the obligation to conduct studies of fairness imposed by the guidelines generally will be upon users or groups of users with a large number of persons in a job class, or test developers; and that small users utilizing their own selection procedures will generally not be obligated to conduct such studies because it will be technically infeasible for them to do so.

(a) *Unfairness defined.* When members of one race, sex, or ethnic group characteristically obtain lower scores on a selection procedure than members of another group, and the differences in scores are not reflected in differences in a measure of job performance, use of the selection procedure may unfairly deny opportunities to members of the group that obtains the lower scores.

(b) *Investigation of fairness.* Where a selection procedure results in an adverse impact on a race, sex, or ethnic group identified in accordance with the classifications set forth in section 4 above and that group is a significant factor in the relevant labor market, the user generally should investigate the possible existence of unfairness for that group if it is technically feasible to do so. The greater the severity of the adverse impact on a group, the greater the need to investigate the possible existence of unfairness. Where the weight of evidence from other studies shows that the selection procedure predicts fairly for the group in question and for the same or similar jobs, such evidence may be relied on in connection with the selection procedure at issue.

(c) *General consideration in fairness investigations.* Users conducting a study of fairness should review the A.P.A. Standards regarding investigation of possible bias in testing. An investigation of fairness of a selection procedure depends on both evidence of validity and the manner in which the selection procedure is to be used in a particular employment context. Fairness of a selection procedure cannot necessarily be specified in advance without investigating these factors. Investigation of fairness of a selection procedure in samples where the range of scores on selection procedures or criterion measures is severely restricted for any subgroup sample (as compared to other subgroup samples) may produce misleading evidence of unfairness. That factor should accordingly be taken into account in conducting such studies and before reliance is placed on the results.

(d) *When unfairness is shown.* If unfairness is demonstrated through a showing that members of a particular group perform better or poorer on the job than their scores on the selection procedure would indicate through comparison with how members of other groups perform, the user may either revise or replace the selection instrument in accordance with these guidelines, or may continue to use the selection instrument operationally with appropriate revisions in its use to assure compatibility between the probability of successful job performance and the probability of being selected.

(e) *Technical feasibility of fairness studies.* In addition to the general conditions needed for technical feasibility for the conduct of a criterion-related study (see section 16, below) an investigation of fairness requires the following:

(i) An adequate sample of persons in each group available for the study to achieve findings of statistical significance. Guidelines do not require a user to hire or promote persons on the basis of group classifications for the purpose of making it possible to conduct a study of fairness; but the user has the obligation otherwise to comply with these guidelines.

(ii) The samples for each group should be comparable in terms of the actual job they perform, length of time on the job where time on the job is likely to affect performance, and other relevant factors likely to affect validity differences; or such factors should be included in the design of the study and their effects identified.

(f) *Continued use of selection procedures when fairness studies not feasible.* If a study of fairness should otherwise be performed, but is not technically feasible, a selection procedure may be used which has otherwise met the validity standards of these guidelines, unless the technical infeasibility resulted from discriminatory employment practices which are demonstrated by facts other than past failure to conform with requirements for validation of selection procedures. However, when it becomes technically feasible for the user to perform a study of fairness and such a study is otherwise called for, the user should conduct the study of fairness.

C. *Technical standards for content validity studies.* —(1) *Appropriateness of content validity studies.* Users choosing to validate a selection procedure by a content validity strategy should determine whether it is appropriate to conduct such a study in the particular employment context. A selection procedure can be supported by a content validity strategy to the extent that it is a representative sample of the content of the job. Selection procedures which purport to measure knowledges, skills, or abilities may in certain circumstances be justified by content validity, although they may not be representative samples, if the knowledge, skill, or ability measured by the selection procedure can be operationally defined as provided in section 14C(4) below, and if that knowledge, skill, or ability is a necessary prerequisite to successful job performance.

A selection procedure based upon inferences about mental processes cannot be supported solely or primarily on the basis of content validity. Thus, a content strategy is not appropriate for demonstrating the validity of selection procedures which purport to measure traits or constructs, such as intelligence, aptitude, personality, common sense, judgment, leadership, and spatial ability. Content validity is also not an appropriate strategy when the selection procedure involves knowledges, skills, or abilities which an employee will be expected to learn on the job.

(2) *Job analysis for content validity.* There should be a job analysis which includes an analysis of the important work behavior(s) required for successful performance and their relative importance and, if the behavior results in work product(s), an analysis of the work product(s). Any job analysis should focus on the work behavior(s) and the tasks associated with them. If work behavior(s) are not observable, the job analysis should identify and analyze those aspects of the behavior(s) that can be observed and the observed work products. The work behavior(s) selected for measurement should be critical work behavior(s) and/or important work behavior(s) constituting most of the job.

(3) *Development of selection procedures.* A selection procedure designed to measure the work behavior may be developed specifically from the job and job analysis in question, or may have been previously developed by the user, or by other users or by a test publisher.

(4) *Standards for demonstrating content validity.* To demonstrate the content validity of a selection procedure, a user should show that the behavior(s) demonstrated in the selection procedure are a representative sample of the behavior(s) of the job in question or that the selection procedure provides a representative sample of the work product of the job. In the case of a selection procedure measuring a knowledge, skill, or ability, the knowledge, skill, or ability being measured should be operationally defined. In the case of a selection procedure measuring a knowledge, the knowledge being measured should be operationally defined as that body of learned information which is used in and is a necessary prerequisite for observable aspects of work behavior of the job. In the case of skills or abilities, the skill or ability being measured should be operationally defined in terms of observable aspects of work behavior of the job. For any selection procedure measuring a knowledge, skill, or ability the user should show that (a) the selection procedure measures and is a representative sample of that knowledge, skill, or ability; and (b) that knowledge, skill, or ability is used in and is a necessary prerequisite to performance of critical or important work behavior(s). In addition, to be content valid, a selection procedure measuring a skill or ability should either closely approximate an observable work behavior, or its product should closely approximate an observable work product. If a test purports to sample a work behavior or to provide a sample of a work product, the manner and setting of the selection procedure and its level and complexity should closely approximate the work situation. The closer the content and the context of the selection procedure are to work samples or work behaviors, the stronger is the basis for showing content validity. As the content of the selection procedure less resembles a work behavior, or the setting and manner of the administration of the selection procedure less resemble the work situation, or the result less resembles a work product, the less likely the selection procedure is to

be content valid, and the greater the need for other evidence of validity.

(5) *Reliability.* The reliability of selection procedures justified on the basis of content validity should be a matter of concern to the user. Whenever it is feasible, appropriate statistical estimates should be made of the reliability of the selection procedure.

(6) *Prior training or experience.* A requirement for or evaluation of specific prior training or experience based on content validity, including a specification of level or amount of training or experience, should be justified on the basis of the relationship between the content of the training or experience and the content of the job for which the training or experience is to be required or evaluated. The critical consideration is the resemblance between the specific behaviors, products, knowledges, skills, or abilities in the experience or training and the specific behaviors, products, knowledges, skills, or abilities required on the job, whether or not there is close resemblance between the experience or training as a whole and the job as a whole.

(7) *Content validity of training success.* Where a measure of success in a training program is used as a selection procedure and the content of a training program is justified on the basis of content validity, the use should be justified on the relationship between the content of the training program and the content of the job.

(8) *Operational use.* A selection procedure which is supported on the basis of content validity may be used for a job if it represents a critical work behavior (i.e., a behavior which is necessary for performance of the job) or work behaviors which constitute most of the important parts of the job.

(9) *Ranking based on content validity studies.* If a user can show, by a job analysis or otherwise, that a higher score on a content valid selection procedure is likely to result in better job performance, the results may be used to rank persons who score above minimum levels. Where a selection procedure supported solely or primarily by content validity is used to rank job candidates, the selection procedure should measure those aspects of performance which differentiate among levels of job performance.

D. *Technical standards for construct validity studies.*—(1) *Approporiateness of construct validity studies.* Construct validity is a more complex strategy than either criterion-related or content validity. Construct validation is a relatively new and developing procedure in the employment field, and there is at present a lack of substantial literature extending the concept to employment practices. The user should be aware that the effort to obtain sufficient empirical support for construct validity is both an extensive and arduous effort involving a series of research studies, which include criterion related validity studies and which may include content validity studies. Users choosing to justify use of a selection procedure by this strategy should therefore take particular care to assure that the validity study meets the standards set forth below.

(2) *Job analysis for construct validity studies.* There should be a job analysis. This job analysis should show the work behavior(s) required for successful performance of the job, or the groups of jobs being studied, the critical or important work behavior(s) in the job or group of jobs being studied, and an identification of the construct(s) believed to underlie successful performance of these critical or important work behaviors in the job or jobs in question. Each construct should be named and defined, so as to distinguish it from other constructs. If a group of jobs is being studied the jobs should have in common one or more critical or important work behaviors at a comparable level of complexity.

(3) *Relationship to the job.* A selection procedure should then be identified or developed which measures the construct identified in accord with subparagraph (2) above. The user should show by empirical evidence that the selection procedure is validly related to the construct and that the construct is validly related to the performance of critical or important work behavior(s). The relationship between the construct as measured by the selection procedure and the related work behavior(s) should be supported by empirical evidence from one or more criterion-related studies involving the job or jobs in question which satisfy the provisions of section 14B above.

(4) *Use of construct validity study without new criterion-related evidence*— (a) *Standards for use.* Until such time as professional literature provides more guidance on the use of construct validity in employment situations, the Federal agencies will accept a claim of construct validity without a criterion-related study which satisfies section 14B above only when the selection procedure has been used elsewhere in a situation in which a criterion-related study has been conducted and the use of a criterion-related validity study in this context meets the standards for transportability of criterion-related validity studies as set forth above in section 7. However, if a study pertains to a number of jobs having common critical or important work behaviors at a comparable level of complexity, and the evidence satisfies subparagraphs 14B (2) and (3) above for those jobs with criterion-related validity evidence for those jobs, the selection procedure may be used for all the jobs to which the study pertains. If construct validity is to be generalized to other jobs or groups of jobs not in the group studied, the Federal enforcement agencies will expect at a minimum additional empirical research evidence meeting the standards of subparagraphs section 14B (2) and (3) above for the additional jobs or groups of jobs.

(b) *Determination of common work behaviors.* In determining whether two or more jobs have one or more work behavior(s) in common, the user should compare the observed work behavior(s) in each of the jobs and should compare the observed work product(s) in each of the jobs. If neither the observed work behavior(s) in each of the jobs nor the observed work product(s) in each of the jobs are the same, the Federal enforcement agencies will presume that the work behavior(s) in each job are different. If the work behaviors are not observable, then evidence of similarity of work products and any other relevant research evidence will be considered in determining whether the work behavior(s) in the two jobs are the same.

Documentation of Impact and Validity Evidence

Sec. 15. *Documentation of impact and validity evidence.*—A. *Required information.* Users of selection procedures other than those users complying with section 15A(1) below should maintain and have available for each job information on adverse impact of the selection process for that job and, where it is determined a selection process has an adverse impact, evidence of validity as set forth below.

(1) *Simplified recordkeeping for users with less than 100 employees.* In order to minimize recordkeeping burdens on employers who employ one hundred (100) or fewer employees, and other users not required to file EEO-1, et seq., reports, such users may satisify the requirements of this section 15 if they maintain and have available records showing, for each year:

(a) The number of persons hired, promoted, and terminated for each job, by sex, and where appropriate by race and national origin;

(b) The number of applicants for hire and promotion by sex and where appropriate by race and national origin; and

(c) The selection procedures utilized (either standardized or not standardized).

These records should be maintained for each race or national origin group (see section 4 above) constituting more than two percent (2%) of the labor force in the relevant labor area. However, it is not necessary to maintain records by race and/or national origin (see § 4 above) if one race or national origin group in the relevant labor area constitutes more than ninety-eight percent (98%) of the labor force in the area. If the user has reason to believe that a selection procedure has an adverse impact, the user should maintain any available evidence of validity for that procedure (see sections 7A and 8).

(2) *Information on impact*—(a) *Collection of information on impact*. Users of selection procedures other than those complying with section 15A(1) above should maintain and have available for each job records or other information showing whether the total selection process for that job has an adverse impact on any of the groups for which records are called for by sections 4B above. Adverse impact determinations should be made at least annually for each such group which constitutes at least 2 percent of the labor force in the relevant labor area or 2 percent of the applicable workforce. Where a total selection process for a job has an adverse impact, the user should maintain and have available records or other information showing which components have an adverse impact. Where the total selection process for a job does not have an adverse impact, information need not be maintained for individual components except in circumstances set forth in subsection 15A(2)(b) below. If the determination of adverse impact is made using a procedure other than the "four-fifths rule," as defined in the first sentence of section 4D above, a justification, consistent with section 4D above, for the procedure used to determine adverse impact should be available.

(b) *When adverse impact has been eliminated in the total selection process*. Whenever the total selection process for a particular job has had an adverse impact, as defined in section 4 above, in any year, but no longer has an adverse impact, the user should maintain and have available the information on individual components of the selection process required in the preceding paragraph for the period in which there was adverse impact. In addition, the user should continue to collect such information for at least two (2) years after the adverse impact has been eliminated.

(c) *When data insufficient to determine impact*. Where there has been an insufficient number of selections to determine whether there is an adverse impact of the total selection process for a particular job, the user should continue to collect, maintain and have available the information on individual components of the selection process required in section 15(A)(2)(a) above until the information is sufficient to determine that the overall selection process does not have an adverse impact as defined in section 4 above, or until the job has changed substantially.

(3) *Documentation of validity evidence.* —(a) *Types of evidence*. Where a total selection process has an adverse impact (see section 4 above) the user should maintain and have available for each component of that process which has an adverse impact, one or more of the following types of documentation evidence:

(i) Documentation evidence showing criterion-related validity of the selection procedure (see section 15B, below).

(ii) Documentation evidence showing content validity of the selection procedure (see section 15C, below).

(iii) Documentation evidence showing construct validity of the selection procedure (see section 15D, below).

(iv) Documentation evidence from other studies showing validity of the selection procedure in the user's facility (see section 15E, below).

(v) Documentation evidence showing why a validity study cannot or need not be performed and why continued use of the procedure is consistent with Federal law.

(b) *Form of report.* This evidence should be compiled in a reasonably complete and organized manner to permit direct evaluation of the validity of the selection procedure. Previously written employer or consultant reports of validity, or reports describing validity studies completed before the issuance of these guidelines are acceptable if they are complete in regard to the documentation requirements contained in this section, or if they satisfied requirements of guidelines which were in effect when the validity study was completed. If they are not complete, the required additional documentation should be appended. If necessary information is not available the report of the validity study may still be used as documentation, but its adequacy will be evaluated in terms of compliance with the requirements of these guidelines.

(c) *Completeness.* In the event that evidence of validity is reviewed by an enforcement agency, the validation reports completed after the effective date of these guidelines are expected to contain the information set forth below. Evidence denoted by use of the word "(Essential)" is considered critical. If information denoted essential is not included, the report will be considered incomplete unless the user affirmatively demonstrates either its unavailability due to circumstances beyond the user's control or special circumstances of the user's study which make the information irrelevant. Evidence not so denoted is desirable but its absence will not be a basis for considering a report incomplete. The user should maintain and have available the information called for under the heading "Source Data" in section 15B(11) and 15D(11). While it is a necessary part of the study, it need not be submitted with the report. All statistical results should be organized and presented in tabular or graphic form to the extent feasible.

B. *Criterion-related validity studies.* Reports of criterion-related validity for a selection procedure should include the following information:

(1) *User(s), location(s), and date(s) of study.* Dates and location(s) of the job analysis or review of job information, the date(s) and location(s) of the administration of the selection procedures and collection of criterion data, and the time between collection of data on selection procedures and criterion measures should be provided (Essential). If the study was conducted at several locations, the address of each location, including city and state, should be shown.

(2) *Problem and setting.* An explicit definition of the purpose(s) of the study and the circumstances in which the study was conducted should be provided. A description of existing selection procedures and cutoff scores, if any, should be provided.

(3) *Job analysis or review of job information.* A description of the procedure used to analyze the job or group of jobs, or to review the job information should be provided (Essential). Where a review of job information results in criteria which may be used without a full job analysis (see section 14B(3)), the basis for the selection of these criteria should be reported (Essential). Where a job analysis is required a complete description of the work behavior(s) or work outcome(s), and measures of their criticality or importance should be provided (Essential). The report should describe the basis on which

the behavior(s) or outcome(s) were determined to be critical or important, such as the proportion of time spent on the respective behaviors, their level of difficulty, their frequency of performance, the consequences of error, or other appropriate factors (Essential). Where two or more jobs are grouped for a validity study, the information called for in this subsection should be provided for each of the jobs, and the justification for the grouping (see section 14B(1)) should be provided (Essential).

(4) *Job titles and codes*. It is desirable to provide the user's job title(s) for the job(s) in question and the corresponding job title(s) and code(s) from U.S. Employment Service's Dictionary of Occupational Titles.

(5) *Criterion measures*. The bases for the selection of the criterion measures should be provided, together with references to the evidence considered in making the selection of criterion measures (essential). A full description of all criteria on which data were collected and means by which they were observed, recorded, evaluated, and quantified, should be provided (essential). If rating techniques are used as criterion measures, the appraisal form(s) and instructions to the rater(s) should be included as part of the validation evidence, or should be explicitly described and available (essential). All steps taken to insure that criterion measures are free from factors which would unfairly alter the scores of members of any group should be described (essential).

(6) *Sample description*. A description of how the research sample was identified and selected should be included (essential). The race, sex, and ethnic composition of the sample, including those groups set forth in section 4A above, should be described (essential). This description should include the size of each subgroup (essential). A description of how the research sample compares with the relevant labor market or work force, the method by which the relevant labor market or work force was defined, and a discussion of the likely effects on validity of differences between the sample and the relevant labor market or work force, are also desirable. Descriptions of educational levels, length of service, and age are also desirable.

(7) *Description of selection procedures*. Any measure, combination of measures, or procedure studied should be completely and explicitly described or attached (essential). If commercially available selection procedures are studied, they should be described by title, form, and publisher (essential). Reports of reliability estimates and how they were established are desirable.

(8) *Techniques and results*. Methods used in analyzing data should be described (essential). Measures of central tendency (e.g., means) and measures of dispersion (e.g., standard deviations and ranges) for all selection procedures and all criteria should be reported for each race, sex, and ethnic group which constitutes a significant factor in the relevant labor market (essential). The magnitude and direction of all relationships between selection procedures and criterion measures investigated should be reported for each relevant race, sex, and ethnic group and for the total group (essential). Where groups are too small to obtain reliable evidence of the magnitude of the relationship, need not be reported separately. Statements regarding the statistical significance of results should be made (essential). Any statistical adjustments, such as for less then perfect reliability or for restriction of score range in the selection procedure or criterion should be described and explained; and uncorrected correlation coefficients should also be shown (essential). Where the statistical technique categorizes continuous data, such as biserial correlation and the phi coefficient, the categories and the bases

on which they were determined should be described and explained (essential). Studies of test fairness should be included where called for by the requirements of section 14B(8) (essential). These studies should include the rationale by which a selection procedure was determined to be fair to the group(s) in question. Where test fairness or unfairness has been demonstrated on the basis of other studies, a bibliography of the relevant studies should be included (essential). If the bibliography includes unpublished studies, copies of these studies, or adequate abstracts or summaries, should be attached (essential). Where revisions have been made in a selection procedure to assure compatability between successful job performance and the probability of being selected, the studies underlying such revisions should be included (essential). All statistical results should be organized and presented by relevant race, sex, and ethnic group (essential).

(9) *Alternative procedures investigated.* The selection procedures investigated and available evidence of their impact should be identified (essential). The scope, method, and findings of the investigation, and the conclusions reached in light of the findings, should be fully described (essential).

(10) *Uses and applications.* The methods considered for use of the selection procedure (e.g., as a screening device with a cutoff score, for grouping or ranking, or combined with other procedures in a battery) and available evidence of their impact should be described (essential). This description should include the rationale for choosing the method for operational use, and the evidence of the validity and utility of the procedure as it is to be used (essential). The purpose for which the procedure is to be used (e.g., hiring, transfer, promotion) should be described (essential). If weights are assigned to different parts of the selection procedure, these weights and the validity of the weighted composite should be reported (essential). If the selection procedure is used with a cutoff score, the user should describe the way in which normal expectations of proficiency within the work force were determined and the way in which the cutoff score was determined (essential).

(11) *Source data.* Each user should maintain records showing all pertinent information about individual sample members and raters where they are used, in studies involving the validation of selection procedures. These records should be made available upon request of a compliance agency. In the case of individual sample members these data should include scores on the selection procedure(s), scores on criterion measures, age, sex, race, or ethnic group status, and experience on the specific job on which the validation study was conducted, and may also include such things as education, training, and prior job experience, but should not include names and social security numbers. Records should be maintained which show the ratings given to each sample member by each rater.

(12) *Contact person.* The name, mailing address, and telephone number of the person who may be contacted for further information about the validity study should be provided (essential).

(13) *Accuracy and completeness.* The report should describe the steps taken to assure the accuracy and completeness of the collection, analysis, and report of data and results.

C. *Content validity studies.* Reports of content validity for a selection procedure should include the following information:

(1) *User(s), location(s) and date(s) of study.* Dates and location(s) of the job analysis should be shown (essential).

(2) *Problem and setting.* An explicit definition of the purpose(s) of the study and the circumstances in which the study was conducted should be provided. A

description of existing selection procedures and cutoff scores, if any, should be provided.

(3) *Job analysis—Content of the Job.* A description of the method used to analyze the job should be provided (essential). The work behavior(s), the associated tasks, and, if the behavior results in a work product, the work products should be completely described (essential). Measures of criticality and/or importance of the work behavior(s) and the method of determining these measures should be provided (essential). Where the job analysis also identified the knowledges, skills, and abilities used in work behavior(s), an operational definition for each knowledge in terms of a body of learned information and for each skill and ability in terms of observable behaviors and outcomes, and the relationship between each knowledge, skill, or ability and each work behavior, as well as the method used to determine this relationship, should be provided (essential). The work situation should be described, including the setting in which work behavior(s) are performed, and where appropriate, the manner in which knowledges, skills, or abilities are used, and the complexity and difficulty of the knowledge, skill, or ability as used in the work behavior(s).

(4) *Selection procedure and its content.* Selection procedures, including those constructed by or for the user, specific training requirements, composites of selection procedures, and any other procedure supported by content validity, should be completely and explicitly described or attached (essential). If commercially available selection procedures are used, they should be described by title, form, and publisher (essential). The behaviors measured or sampled by the selection procedure should be explicitly described (essential). Where the selection procedure purports to measure a knowledge, skill, or ability, evidence that the selection procedure measures and is a representative sample of the knowledge, skill, or ability should be provided (essential).

(5) *Relationship between the selection procedure and the job.* The evidence demonstrating that the selection procedure is a representative work sample, a representative sample of the work behavior(s), or a representative sample of a knowledge, skill, or ability as used as a part of a work behavior and necessary of that behavior should be provided (essential). The user should identify the work behavior(s) which each item or part of the selection procedure is intended to sample or measure (essential). Where the selection procedure purports to sample a work behavior or to provide a sample of a work product, a comparison should be provided of the manner, setting, and the level of complexity of the selection procedure with those of the work situation (essential). If any steps were taken to reduce adverse impact on a race, sex, or ethnic group in the content of the procedure or in its administration, these steps should be described. Establishment of time limits, if any, and how these limits are related to the speed with which duties must be performed on the job, should be explained. Measures of central tendency (e.g., means) and measures of dispersion (e.g., standard deviations) and estimates of reliability should be reported for all selection procedures if available. Such reports should be made for relevant race, sex, and ethnic subgroups, at least on a statistically reliable sample basis.

(6) *Alternative procedures investigated.* The alternative selection procedures investigated and available evidence of their impact should be identified (essential). The scope, method, and findings of the investigation, and the conclusions reached in light of the findings, should be fully described (essential).

(7) *Uses and applications.* The methods considered for use of the selection procedure (e.g., as a screening device with a

cutoff score, for grouping or ranking, or combined with other procedures in a battery) and available evidence of their impact should be described (essential). This description should include the rationale for choosing the method for operational use, and the evidence of the validity and utility of the procedure as it is to be used (essential). The purpose for which the procedure is to be used (e.g., hiring, transfer, promotion) should be described (essential). If the selection procedure is used with a cutoff score, the user should describe the way in which normal expectations of proficiency within the work force were determined and the way in which the cutoff score was determined (essential). In addition, if the selection procedure is to be used for ranking, the user should specify the evidence showing that a higher score on the selection procedure is likely to result in better job performance.

(8) *Contact person.* The name, mailing address, and telephone number of the person who may be contacted for further information about the validity study should be provided (essential).

(9) *Accuracy and completeness.* The report should describe the steps taken to assure the accuracy and completeness of the collection, analysis, and report of data and results.

D. *Construct validity studies.* Reports of construct validity for a selection procedure should include the following information:

(1) *User(s), location(s), and date(s) of study.* Date(s) and location(s) of the job analysis and the gathering of other evidence called for by these guidelines should be provided (essential).

(2) *Problem and setting.* An explicit definition of the purpose(s) of the study and the circumstances in which the study was conducted should be provided. A description of existing selection procedures and cutoff scores, if any, should be provided.

(3) *Construct definition.* A clear definition of the construct(s) which are believed to underlie successful performance of the critical or important work behavior(s) should be provided (essential). This definition should include the levels of construct performance relevant to the job(s) for which the selection procedure is to be used (essential). There should be a summary of the position of the construct in the psychological literature, or in the absence of such a position, a description of the way in which the definition and measurement of the construct was developed and the psychological theory underlying it (essential). Any quantitative data which identify or define the job constructs, such as factor analyses, should be provided (essential).

(4) *Job analysis.* A description of the method used to analyze the job should be provided (essential). A complete description of the work behavior(s) and, to the extent appropriate, work outcomes and measures of their criticality and/or importance should be provided (essential). The report should also describe the basis on which the behavior(s) or outcomes were determined to be important, such as their level of difficulty, their frequency of performance, the consequences of error or other appropriate factors (essential). Where jobs are grouped or compared for the purposes of generalizing validity evidence, the work behavior(s) and work product(s) for each of the jobs should be described, and conclusions concerning the similarity of the jobs in terms of observable work behaviors or work products should be made (essential).

(5) *Job titles and codes.* It is desirable to provide the selection procedure user's job title(s) for the job(s) in question and the corresponding job title(s) and code(s) from the United States Employment Service's dictionary of occupational titles.

(6) *Selection procedure.* The selection procedure used as a measure of the construct should be completely and ex-

plicitly described or attached (essential). If commercially available selection procedures are used, they should be identified by title, form and publisher (essential). The research evidence of the relationship between the selection procedure and the construct, such as factor structure, should be included (essential). Measures of central tendency, variability and reliability of the selection procedure should be provided (essential). Whenever feasible, these measures should be provided separately for each relevant race, sex and ethnic group.

(7) *Relationship to job performance.* The criterion-related study(ies) and other empirical evidence of the relationship between the construct measured by the selection procedure and the related work behavior(s) for the job or jobs in question should be provided (essential). Documentation of the criterion-related study(ies) should satisfy the provisions of section 15B above or section 15E(1) below, except for studies conducted prior to the effective date of these guidelines (essential). Where a study pertains to a group of jobs, and, on the basis of the study, validity is asserted for a job in the group, the observed work behaviors and the observed work products for each of the jobs should be described (essential). Any other evidence used in determining whether the work behavior(s) in each of the jobs is the same should be fully described (essential).

(8) *Alternative procedures investigated.* The alternative selection procedures investigated and available evidence of their impact should be identified (essential). The scope, method, and findings of the investigation, and the conclusions reached in light of the findings should be fully described (essential).

(9) *Uses and applications.* The methods considered for use of the selection procedure (e.g., as a screening device with a cutoff score, for grouping or ranking, or combined with other procedures in a battery) and available evidence of their impact should be described (essential). This description should include the rationale for choosing the method for operational use, and the evidence of the validity and utility of the procedure as it is to be used (essential). The purpose for which the procedure is to be used (e.g., hiring, transfer, promotion) should be described (essential). If weights are assigned to different parts of the selection procedure, these weights and the validity of the weighted composite should be reported (essential). If the selection procedure is used with a cutoff score, the user should describe the way in which normal expectations of proficiency within the work force were determined and the way in which the cutoff score was determined (essential).

(10) *Accuracy and completeness.* The report should describe the steps taken to assure the accuracy and completeness of the collection, analysis, and report of data and results.

(11) *Source data.* Each user should maintain records showing all pertinent information relating to its study of construct validity.

(12) *Contact person.* The name, mailing address, and telephone number of the individual who may be contacted for further information about the validity study should be provided (essential).

E. *Evidence of validity from other studies.* When validity of a selection procedure is supported by studies not done by the user, the evidence from the original study or studies should be compiled in a manner similar to that required in the appropriate section of this section 15 above. In addition, the following evidence should be supplied:

(1) *Evidence from criterion-related validity studies.*—a. *Job information.* A description of the important job behavior(s) of the user's job and the basis on which the behaviors were determined to be important should be provided (essen-

tial). A full description of the basis for determining that these important work behaviors are the same as those of the job in the original study (or studies) should be provided (essential).

b. *Relevance of criteria.* A full description of the basis on which the criteria used in the original studies are determined to be relevant for the user should be provided (essential).

c. *Other variables.* The similarity of important applicant pool or sample characteristics reported in the original studies to those of the user should be described (essential). A description of the comparison between the race, sex and ethnic composition of the user's relevant labor market and the sample in the original validity studies should be provided (essential).

d. *Use of the selection procedure.* A full description should be provided showing that the use to be made of the selection procedure is consistent with the findings of the original validity studies (essential).

e. *Bibliography.* A bibliography of reports of validity of the selection procedure for the job or jobs in question should be provided (essential). Where any of the studies included an investigation of test fairness, the results of this investigation should be provided (essential). Copies of reports published in journals that are not commonly available should be described in detail or attached (essential). Where a user is relying upon unpublished studies, a reasonable effort should be made to obtain these studies. If these unpublished studies are the sole source of validity evidence they should be described in detail or attached (essential). If these studies are not available, the name and address of the source, an adequate abstract or summary of the validity study and data, and a contact person in the source organization should be provided (essential).

(2) *Evidence from content validity studies.* See section 14C(3) and section 15C above.

(3) *Evidence from construct validity studies.* See sections 14D(2) and 15D above.

F. *Evidence of validity from cooperative studies.* Where a selection procedure has been validated through a cooperative study, evidence that the study satisfies the requirements of sections 7, 8 and 15E should be provided (essential).

G. *Selection for higher level job.* If a selection procedure is used to evaluate candidates for jobs at a higher level than those for which they will initially be employed, the validity evidence should satisfy the documentation provisions of this section 15 for the higher level job or jobs, and in addition, the user should provide: (1) a description of the job progression structure, formal or informal; (2) the data showing how many employees progress to the higher level job and the length of time needed to make this progression; and (3) an identification of any anticipated changes in the higher level job. In addition, if the test measures a knowledge, skill or ability, the user should provide evidence that the knowledge, skill or ability is required for the higher level job and the basis for the conclusion that the knowledge, skill or ability is not expected to develop from the training or experience on the job.

H. *Interim use of selection procedures.* If a selection procedure is being used on an interim basis because the procedure is not fully supported by the required evidence of validity, the user should maintain and have available (1) substantial evidence of validity for the procedure, and (2) a report showing the date on which the study to gather the additional evidence commenced, the estimated completion date of the study, and a description of the data to be collected (essential).

Definitions

Sec. 16. *Definitions.* The following definitions shall apply throughout these guidelines:

A. *Ability.* A present competence to perform an observable behavior or a behavior which results in an observable product.

B. *Adverse impact.* A substantially different rate of selection in hiring, promotion, or other employment decision which works to the disadvantage of members of a race, sex, or ethnic group. See section 4 of these guidelines.

C. *Compliance with these guidelines.* Use of a selection procedure is in compliance with these guidelines if such use has been validated in accord with these guidelines (as defined below), or if such use does not result in adverse impact on any race, sex, or ethnic group (see section 4, above), or, in unusual circumstances, if use of the procedure is otherwise justified in accord with Federal law. See section 6B, above.

D. *Content validity.* Demonstrated by data showing that the content of a selection procedure is representative of important aspects of performance on the job. See section 5B and section 14C.

E. *Construct validity.* Demonstrated by data showing that the selection procedure measures the degree to which candidates have identifiable characteristics which have been determined to be important for successful job performance. See section 5B and section 14D.

F. *Criterion-related validity.* Demonstrated by empirical data showing that the selection procedure is predictive of or significantly correlated with important elements of work behavior. See sections 5B and 14B.

G. *Employer.* Any employer subject to the provisions of the Civil Rights Act of 1964, as amended, including State or local governments and any Federal agency subject to the provisions of section 717 of the Civil Rights Act of 1964, as amended, and any Federal contractor or subcontractor or federally assisted construction contractor or subcontractor covered by Executive Order 11246, as amended.

H. *Employment agency.* Any employment agency subject to the provisions of the Civil Rights Act of 1964, as amended.

I. *Enforcement action.* For the purposes of section 4 a proceeding by a Federal enforcement agency such as a lawsuit or an administrative proceeding leading to debarment from or withholding, suspension, or termination of Federal Government contracts or the suspension or withholding of Federal Government funds; but not a finding of reasonable cause or a conciliation process or the issuance of right to sue letters under title VII or under Executive Order 11246 where such finding, conciliation, or issuance of notice of right to sue is based upon an individual complaint.

J. *Enforcement agency.* Any agency of the executive branch of the Federal Government which adopts these guidelines for purposes of the enforcement of the equal employment opportunity laws or which has responsibility for securing compliance with them.

K. *Job analysis.* A detailed statement of work behaviors and other information relevant to the job.

L. *Job description.* A general statement of job duties and responsibilities.

M. *Knowledge.* A body of information applied directly to the performance of a function.

N. *Labor organization.* Any labor organization subject to the provisions of the Civil Rights Act of 1964, as amended, and any committee subject thereto controlling apprenticeship or other training.

O. *Observable.* Able to be seen, heard, or otherwise perceived by a person other than the person performing the action.

P. *Race, sex, or ethnic group.* Any group of persons identifiable on the grounds of race, color, religion, sex, or national origin.

Q. *Selection procedures.* Any measure, combination of measures, or procedure used as a basis for any employment decision. Selection procedures include the full range of assessment techniques from traditional paper and pencil tests, performance tests, training programs, or probationary periods and physical, educational, and work experience requirements through informal or casual interviews and unscored application forms.

R. *Selection rate.* The proportion of applicants or candidates who are hired, promoted, or otherwise selected.

S. *Should.* The term "should" as used in these guidelines is intended to connote action which is necessary to achieve compliance with the guidelines, while recognizing that there are circumstances where alternative courses of action are open to users.

T. *Skill.* A present, observable competence to perform a learned psychomotor act.

U. *Technical feasibility.* The existence of conditions permitting the conduct of meaningful criterion-related validity studies. These conditions include: (1) An adequate sample of persons available for the study to achieve findings of statistical significance; (2) having or being able to obtain a sufficient range of scores on the selection procedure and job performance measures to produce validity results which can be expected to be representative of the results if the ranges normally expected were utilized; and (3) having or being able to devise unbiased, reliable and relevant measures of job performance or other criteria of employee adequacy. See section 14B(2). With respect to investigation of possible unfairness, the same considerations are applicable to each group for which the study is made. See section 14B(8).

V. *Unfairness of selection procedure.* A condition in which members of one race, sex, or ethnic group characteristically obtain lower scores on a selection procedure than members of another group, and the differences are not reflected in differences in measures of job performance. See section 14B(7).

W. *User.* Any employer, labor organization, employment agency, or licensing or certification board, to the extent it may be covered by Federal equal employment opportunity law, which uses a selection procedure as a basis for any employment decision. Whenever an employer, labor organization, or employment agency is required by law to restrict recruitment for any occupation to those applicants who have met licensing or certification requirements, the licensing or certifying authority to the extent it may be covered by Federal equal employment opportunity law will be considered the user with respect to those licensing or certification requirements. Whenever a State employment agency or service does no more than administer or monitor a procedure as permitted by Department of Labor regulations, and does so without making referrals or taking any other action on the basis of the results, the State employment agency will not be deemed to be a user.

X. *Validated in accord with these guidelines or properly validated.* A demonstration that one or more validity study or studies meeting the standards of these guidelines has been conducted, including investigation and, where appropriate, use of suitable alternative selection procedures as contemplated by section 3B, and has produced evidence of validity sufficient to warrant use of the procedure for the intended purpose under the standards of these guidelines.

Y. *Work behavior.* An activity performed to achieve the objectives of the job. Work behaviors involve observable (physical) components and unobservable (mental) components. A work behavior consists of the performance of one or more tasks. Knowledges, skills, and abilities are not behaviors, although they may be applied in work behaviors.

Appendix

17. *Policy statement on affirmative action* (see section 13B). The Equal Employment Opportunity Coordinating Council was established by act of Congress in 1972, and charged with responsibility for developing and implementing agreements and policies designed, among other things, to eliminate conflict and inconsistency among the agencies of the Federal Government responsible for administering Federal law prohibiting discrimination on grounds of race, color, sex, religion, and national origin. This statement is issued as an initial response to the requests of a number of State and local officials for clarification of the Government's policies concerning the role of affirmative action in the overall equal employment opportunity program. While the Coordinating Council's adoption of this statement expresses only the views of the signatory agencies concerning this important subject, the principles set forth below should serve as policy guidance for other Federal agencies as well.

(1) Equal employment opportunity is the law of the land. In the public sector of our society this means that all persons, regardless of race, color, religion, sex, or national origin shall have equal access to positions in the public service limited only by their ability to do the job. There is ample evidence in all sectors of our society that such equal access frequently has been denied to members of certain groups because of their sex, racial, or ethnic characteristics. The remedy for such past and present discrimination is twofold.

On the one hand, vigorous enforcement of the laws against discrimination is essential. But equally, and perhaps even more important are affirmative, voluntary efforts on the part of public employers to assure that positions in the public service are genuinely and equally accessible to qualified persons, without regard to their sex, racial, or ethnic characteristics. Without such efforts equal employment opportunity is no more than a wish. The importance of voluntary affirmative action on the part of employers is underscored by title VII of the Civil Rights Act of 1964, Executive Order 11246, and related laws and regulations—all of which emphasize voluntary action to achieve equal employment opportunity.

As with most management objectives, a systematic plan based on sound organizational analysis and problem identification is crucial to the accomplishment of affirmative action objectives. For this reason, the Council urges all State and local governments to develop and implement results oriented affirmative action plans which deal with the problems so identified.

The following paragraphs are intended to assist State and local governments by illustrating the kinds of analyses and activities which may be appropriate for a public employer's voluntary affirmative action plan. This statement does not address remedies imposed after a finding of unlawful discrimination

(2) Voluntary affirmative action to assure equal employment opportunity is appropriate at any stage of the employment process. The first step in the construction of any affirmative action plan should be an analysis of the employer's work force to determine whether percentages of sex, race, or ethnic groups in individual job classifications are substantially similar to the percentages of those groups available in the relevant job market who possess the basic job-related qualifications.

When substantial disparities are found through such analyses, each element of the overall selection process should be examined to determine which elements operate to exclude persons on the basis of sex, race, or ethnic group. Such elements include, but are not limited to, recruit-

No. 353 UNIFORM GUIDELINES ON EMPLOYEE SELECTION 401:2271

ment, testing, ranking certification, interview, recommendations for selection, hiring, promotion, etc. The examination of each element of the selection process should at a minimum include a determination of its validity in predicting job performance.

(3) When an employer has reason to believe that its selection procedures have the exclusionary effect described in paragraph 2 above, it should initiate affirmative steps to remedy the situation. Such steps, which in design and execution may be race, color, sex, or ethnic "conscious," include, but are not limited to, the following:

(a) The establishment of a long-term goal, and short-range, interim goals and timetables for the specific job classifications, all of which should take into account the availability of basically qualified persons in the relevant job market;

(b) A recruitment program designed to attract qualified members of the group in question;

(c) A systematic effort to organize work and redesign jobs in ways that provide opportunities for persons lacking "journeyman" level knowledge or skills to enter and, with appropriate training, to progress in a career field;

(d) Revamping selection instruments or procedures which have not yet been validated in order to reduce or eliminate exclusionary effects on particular groups in particular job classifications;

(e) The initiation of measures designed to assure that members of the affected group who are qualified to perform the job are included within the pool of persons from which the selecting official makes the selection;

(f) A systematic effort to provide career advancement training, both classroom and on-the-job, to employees locked into dead end jobs; and

(g) The establishment of a system for regularly monitoring the effectiveness of the particular affirmative action program, and procedures for making timely adjustments in this program where effectiveness is not demonstrated.

(4) The goal of any affirmative action plan should be achievement of genuine equal employment opportunity for all qualified persons. Selection under such plans should be based upon the ability of the applicant(s) to do the work. Such plans should not require the selection of the unqualified, or the unneeded, nor should they require the selection of persons on the basis of race, color, sex, religion, or national origin. Morever, while the Council believes that this statement should serve to assist State and local employers, as well as Federal agencies, it recognizes that affirmative action cannot be viewed as a standardized program which must be accomplished in the same way at all times in all places.

Accordingly, the Council has not attempted to set forth here either the minimum or maximum voluntary steps that employers may take to deal with their respective situations. Rather, the Council recognizes that under applicable authorities, State and local employers have flexibility to formulate affirmative action plans that are best suited to their particular situations. In this manner, the Council believes that affirmative action programs will best serve the goal of equal employment opportunity.

Because of its equal employment opportunity responsibilities under the State and Local Government Fiscal Assistance Act of 1972 (the revenue sharing act), the Department of Treasury was invited to participate in the formulation of this policy statement; and its concurs and joins in the adoption of this policy statement.

Done this 26th day of August 1976.

Section 18. *Citations.* The official title of these guidelines is "Uniform Guidelines on Employee Selection Procedures (1978)". The Uniform Guidelines on Employee Selection Procedures (1978) are intended to establish a uniform Federal position in the area of prohibiting discrimination in employment practices on grounds of race, color, religion, sex, or national origin. These guidelines have been adopted by the Equal Employment Opportunity Commission, the Department of Labor, the Department of Justice, and the Civil Service Commission.

The official citation is:

"Section _____ , Uniform Guidelines on Employee Selection Procedure (1978); 43 FR _____ , (August 25, 1978)."

The short form citation is:

"Section _____ , U.G.E.S.P. (1978); 43 FR _____ (August 25, 1978)."

When the guidelines are cited in connection with the activities of one of the issuing agencies, a specific citation to the regulations of that agency can be added at the end of the above citation. The specific additional citations are as follows:

Equal Employment Opportunity Commission
29 CFR Part 1607
Department of Labor
Office of Federal Contract Compliance Programs
41 CFR Part 60-3
Department of Justice
28 CFR 50.14
Civil Service Commission
5 CFR 300.103(c)

Normally when citing these guidelines, the section number immediately preceding the title of the guidelines will be from these guidelines series 1-18. If a section number from the codification for an individual agency is needed it can also be added at the end of the agency citation. For example, section 6A of these guidelines could be cited for EEOC as follows: "Section 6A, Uniform Guidelines on Employee Selection Procedures (1978); 43 FR _____ , (August 25, 1978); 29 CFR Part 1607, section 6A."

CIVIL SERVICE COMMISSION
Title 5—Administrative Personnel
CHAPTER 1—CIVIL SERVICE COMMISSION
PART 300—EMPLOYMENT (GENERAL)
Uniform Guidelines on Employee Selection Procedures (1978)

The Uniform Guidelines on Employee Selection Procedures (1978) which are printed at the beginning of this part IV in today's Federal Register are adopted by the Civil Service Commission, in conjunction with the Equal Employment Opportunity Commission, Department of Justice, and the Department of Labor to establish uniformity in prohibiting discrimination in employment practices on grounds of race, color, religion, sex, or national origin. Cross reference documents are published at 29 CFR parts 1607 (Equal Employment Opportunity Commission), 29 CFR 50.14 (Department of Justice), and 41 CFR 60-3 (Department of Labor) elsewhere in this issue of the Federal Register.

By virtue of the authority vested in it by sections 3301, 3302, 7151, 7154, and 7301 of title 5 and section 4763(b) of title 42, United States Code, and Executive Order 10577, 3 CFR 1954-58 comp. page 218 and Executive Order 11478, 3 CFR 1959 comp. 133, and section 717 of the Civil Rights Act of 1964, as amended (42 U.S.C. 2000e-16), the Civil Service Commission amends title 5, part 300, subpart A, § 300.103(c) of the Code of Federal Regulations to read as follows:

§ 300.103 Basic Requirements.

"(c) Equal employment opportunity. An employment practice shall not discriminate on the basis of race, color, religion, sex, age, national origin, partisan political affiliation, or other nonmerit factor. Employee selection procedures shall meet the standards established by the "Uniform Guidelines on Employee Selection Procedures (1978), 43 FR _____ (August 25, 1978)."

No. 353   UNIFORM GUIDELINES ON EMPLOYEE SELECTION   401:2273

The Civil Service Commission rescinds the Guidelines on Employee Selection Procedures, 41 FR 51752, Federal Personnel Manual part 900, subpart F and adopts the Uniform Guidelines on Employee Selection Procedures (1978), to be issued as identical supplement appendices to supplements 271-1, Development of Qualification Standards; 271-2, Tests and Other Applicant Appraisal Procedures; 335-1, Evaluation of Employees for Promotion and Internal Placement; and 990-1 (Book III), part 900, subpart F, Administration of Standards for a Merit System of Personnel Administration of the Federal Personnel Manual in order to insure the examining, testing standards, and employment practices are not affected by discrimination on the basis of race, color, religion, sex or national origin.

Effective date: September 25, 1978.

DEPARTMENT OF JUSTICE
Title 28—Judicial Administration
CHAPTER 1—DEPARTMENT OF JUSTICE
PART 50—STATEMENTS OF POLICY

Uniform Guidelines on Employee Selection Procedures (1978)

The Uniform Guidelines on Employee Selection Procedures which are provided at the beginning of this part IV in today's Federal Register are adopted by the Department of Justice, in conjunction with the Civil Service Commission, Equal Employment Opportunity Commission, and the Department of Labor to establish a uniform Federal position in the area of prohibiting discrimination in employment practices on grounds of race, color, religion, sex, or national origin. Cross reference documents are published at 5 CFR 300.103(c), (Civil Service Commission) 29 CFR 1607 (Equal Employment Opportunity Commission), and 41 CFR 60-3 (Department of Labor), elsewhere in this issue of the Federal Register.

By viture of the authority vested in me by 28 U.S.C. 509 and 5 U.S.C. 301, Sec. 50.14 of part 50 of chapter 1 of title 28 of the Code of Federal Regulations is amended by substituting the Uniform Guidelines on Employee Selection Procedures (1978) for part I through part IV.

Effective date: September 25, 1978.

EQUAL EMPLOYMENT OPPORTUNITY COMMISSION
Title 29—Labor
CHAPTER XIV—EQUAL EMPLOYMENT OPPORTUNITY COMMISSION
PART 1607—UNIFORM GUIDELINES ON EMPLOYEE SELECTION PROCEDURES (1978)

The Uniform Guidelines on Employee Selection Procedures which are printed at the beginning of this part IV in today's Federal Register are adopted by the Equal Employment Opportunity Commission, in conjunction with the Civil Service Commission, Department of Justice, and the Department of Labor to establish a uniform Federal position in the area of prohibiting discrimination in employment practices on grounds of race, color, religion, sex, or national origin. Cross reference documents are published at 5 CFR 300.103(c) (Civil Service Commission), 28 CFR 50.14 (Department of Justice) and 41 CFR 60-3 Department of Labor), elsewhere in this issue.

By virtue of the authority vested in it by sections 713 and 709 of title VII of the Civil Rights Act of 1964 (78 Stat. 265), as amended by the Equal Employment Opportunity Act of 1972 (Pub. L. 92-261), (42 U.S.C. 2000e-12 and 2000e-8), the Equal Employment Opportunity Commission hereby revises part 1607 of chapter XIV of title 29 of the Code of Federal Regulations by rescinding the Guidelines on Employee Selection Procedures (see 35 FR 12333, August 1, 1970; and 41 FR 51984, November 24, 1976) and adopting the Uniform Guidelines on Employee Selection Procedures (1978) as a new part 1607.

Effective date: September 25, 1978.

TABLE OF CONTENTS
GENERAL PRINCIPLES

1607.1 Statement of Purpose
  A. Need for Uniformity—Issuing Agencies
  B. Purpose of Guidelines
  C. Relation to Prior Guidelines
1607.2 Scope
  A. Application of Guidelines
  B. Employment Decisions
  C. Selection Procedures
  D. Limitations
  E. Indian Preference Not Affected
1607.3 Discrimination Defined: Relationship Between Use of Selection Procedures and Discrimination
  A. Procedure Having Adverse Impact Constitutes Discrimination Unless Justified
  B. Consideration of Suitable Alternative Selection Procedures
1607.4 Information on Impact
  A. Records Concerning Impact
  B. Applicable Race, Sex, and Ethnic Groups for Recordkeeping
  C. Evaluation of Selection Rates. The "Bottom Line"
  D. Adverse Impact and the "Four-Fifths Rule"
  E. Consideration of User's Equal Employment Opportunity Posture
1607.5 General Standards for Validity Studies
  A. Acceptable Types of Validity Studies
  B. Criterion-Related, Content, and Construct Validity
  C. Guidelines Are Consistent With Professional Standards
  D. Need for Documentation of Validity
  E. Accuracy and Standardization
  F. Caution Against Selection on Basis of Knowledges, Skills, or Abilities Learned in Brief Orientation Period
  G. Method of Use of Selection Procedures
  H. Cutoff Scores
  I. Use of Selection Procedures for Higher Level Jobs
  J. Interim Use of Selection Procedures
  K. Review of Validity Studies for Currency
1607.6 Use of Selection Procedures Which Have Not Been Validated
  A. Use of Alternate Selection Procedures To Eliminate Adverse Impact
  B. Where Validity Studies Cannot or Need Not Be Performed
    (1) Where Informal or Unscored Procedures Are Used
    (2) Where Formal and Scored Procedures Are Used
1607.7 Use of Other Validity Studies
  A. Validity Studies Not Conducted by the User
  B. Use of Criterion-Related Validity Evidence From Other Sources
    (1) Validity Evidence
    (2) Job Similarity
    (3) Fairness Evidence
  C. Validity Evidence From Multi-Unit Study
  D. Other Significant Variables
1607.8 Cooperative Studies
  A. Encouragement of Cooperative Studies
  B. Standards for Use of Cooperative Studies
1607.9 No Assumption of Validity
  A. Unacceptable Substitutes for Evidence of Validity
  B. Encouragement of Professional Supervision
1607.10 Employment Agencies and Employment Services
  A. Where Selection Procedures Are Devised by Agency
  B. Where Selection Procedures are Devised Elsewhere
1607.11 Disparate Treatment
1607.12 Retesting of Applicants
1607.13 Affirmative Action
  A. Affirmative Action Obligations
  B. Encouragement of Voluntary Affirmative Action Programs

TECHNICAL STANDARDS

1607.14 Technical Standards for Validity Studies
  A. Validity Studies Should Be Based on Review of Information About the Job
  B. Technical Standards for Criterion-Related Validity Studies
    (1) Technical Feasibility
    (2) Analysis of the Job
    (3) Criterion Measures
    (4) Representativeness of the Sample
    (5) Statistical Relationships
    (6) Operational Use of Selection Procedures
    (7) Over-Statement of Validity Findings
    (8) Fairness
    (a) Unfairness Defined
    (b) Investigation of Fairness
    (c) General Considerations in Fairness Investigations
    (d) When Unfairness is Shown
    (e) Technical Feasibility of Fairness Studies
    (f) Continued Use of Selection Procedures When Fairness Studies Not Feasible
  C. Technical Standards for Content Validity Studies
    (1) Appropriateness of Content Validity Studies
    (2) Job Analysis for Content Validity

No. 353   UNIFORM GUIDELINES ON EMPLOYEE SELECTION   401:2275

(3) Development of Section Procedure
(4) Standards for Demonstrating Content Validity
(5) Reliability
(6) Prior Training of Experience
(7) Training Success
(8) Operational Use
(9) Ranking Based on Content Validity Studies
D. Technical Standards for Construct Validity Studies
(1) Appropriateness of Construct Validity Studies
(2) Job Analysis Required in Construct Validity Studies
(3) Relationship to the Job
(4) Use of Construct Validity Study Without New Criterion-Related Evidence
(a) Standards for Use
(b) Determination of Common Work Behaviors

DOCUMENTATION OF IMPACT AND VALIDITY EVIDENCE

1607.15 Documentation of Impact and Validity Evidence
A. Required Information
(1) Simplified Recordkeeping for Users With Less Than 100 Employees
(2) Information on Impact
(a) Collection of Information on Impact
(b) When Adverse Impact Has Been Eliminated in the Total Selection Process
(c) When Data Insufficient to Determine Impact
(3) Documentation of Validity Evidence
(a) Type of Evidence
(b) Form of Report
(c) Completeness
B. Criterion-Related Validity Studies
(1) User(s), Location(s), and Date(s) of Study
(2) Problem and Setting
(3) Job Analysis or Review of Job Information
(4) Job Titles and Codes
(5) Criterion Measures
(6) Sample Description
(7) Description of Selection Procedure
(8) Techniques and Results
(9) Alternative Procedures Investigated
(10) Uses and Applications
(11) Source Data
(12) Contact Person
(13) Accuracy and Completeness
C. Content Validity Studies
(1) User(s), Location(s), and Date(s) of Study
(2) Problem and Setting
(3) Job Analysis—Content of the Job
(4) Selection Procedure and Its Content
(5) Relationship Between Selection Procedure and the Job
(6) Alternative Procedures Investigated
(7) Uses and Applications
(8) Contact Person
(9) Accuracy and Completeness
D. Construct Validity Studies
(1) User(s), Location(s), and Date(s) of Study
(2) Problem and Setting
(3) Construct Definition
(4) Job Analysis
(5) Job Titles and Codes
(6) Selection Procedure
(7) Relationship to Job Performance
(8) Alternative Procedures Investigated
(9) Uses and Applications
(10) Accuracy and Completeness
(11) Source Data
(12) Contact Person
E. Evidence of Validity From Other Studies
(1) Evidence From Criterion-Related Validity Studies
(a) Job Information
(b) Relevance of Criteria
(c) Other Variables
(d) Use of the Selection Procedure
(e) Bibliography
(2) Evidence From Content Validity Studies
(3) Evidence From Construct Validity Studies
F. Evidence of Validity From Cooperative Studies
G. Selection for Higher Level Jobs
H. Interim Use of Selection Procedures

DEFINITIONS

1607.16 Definitions

APPENDIX

1607.17 Policy Statement on Affirmative Action (see section 13B)
1607.18 Citations

DEPARTMENT OF LABOR
Title 41—Public Contracts and Property Management
CHAPTER 60—OFFICE OF FEDERAL CONTRACT COMPLIANCE PROGRAMS, DEPARTMENT OF LABOR
PART 60-3—UNIFORM GUIDELINES ON EMPLOYEE SELECTION PROCEDURES (1976)

The Uniform Guidelines on Employee Selection Procedures which are printed at the beginning of this part IV of today's Federal Register are adopted by the Department of Labor, in conjunction with the Civil Service Commission, Department of Justice, and the Equal Employment Opportunity Commission to establish a uniform Federal position in the area of prohibiting discrimination in employment practices on grounds of race, color, religion, sex, or national origin. Cross reference documents are published at 5 CFR 300.103(c) (Civil Service Commission), 28 CFR 50.14 (Department of Justice) and 29 CFR 1607 (Equal Employment Opportunity Commission), elsewhere in this issue of the Federal Register.

By virtue of the authority of sections 201, 202, 203, 203(a), 205, 206(a), 301, 303(b), and 403(b) of Executive Order 11246, as amended, 30 FR 12319; 32 FR 14303; section 60-1.2 of part 60-1 of 41 CFR chapter 60, and section 715 of the Civil Rights Act of 1964, as amended (42 U.S.C. 2000e-14), part 60-3 of chapter 60 of title 41 of the Code of Federal Regulations is revised by rescinding the Guidelines on Employee Selection Procedures (see 41 FR 51744, November 23, 1976) and adopting the Uniform Guidelines on Employee Selection Procedures (1978) as a new part 60-3.

Effective date: September 25, 1978.

Table of Contents
GENERAL PRINCIPLES

60-3.1 Statement of Purpose
  A. Need for Uniformity—Issuing Agencies
  B. Purpose of Guidelines
  C. Relation to Prior Guidelines
60-3.2 Scope
  A. Application of Guidelines
  B. Employment Decisions
  C. Selection Procedures
  D. Limitations
  E. Indian Preference Not Affected
60-3.3 Discrimination Defined: Relationship Between Use of Selection Procedures and Discrimination
  A. Procedure Having Adverse Impact Constitutes Discrimination Unless Justified
  B. Consideration of Suitable Alternative Selection Procedures
60-3.4 Information on Impact
  A. Records Concerning Impact
  B. Applicable Race, Sex, and Ethnic Groups for Recordkeeping
  C. Evaluation of Selection Rates. The "Bottom Line"
  D. Adverse Impact and the "Four-Fifths Rule"
  E. Consideration of User's Equal Employment Opportunity Posture
60-3.5 General Standards for Validity Studies
  A. Acceptable Types of Validity Studies
  B. Criterion-Related, Content, and Construct Validity
  C. Guidelines Are Consistent With Professional Standards
  D. Need for Documentation of Validity
  E. Accuracy and Standardization
  F. Caution Against Selection on Basis of Knowledges, Skills, or Abilities Learned in Brief Orientation Period
  G. Method of Use of Selection Procedures
  H. Cutoff Scores
  I. Use of Selection Procedures for Higher Level Jobs
  J. Interim Use of Selection Procedures
  K. Review of Validity Studies for Currency
60-3.6 Use of Selection Procedures Which Have Not Been Validated
  A. Use of Alternate Selection Procedures To Eliminate Adverse Impact
  B. Where Validity Studies Cannot or Need Not Be Performed
    (1) Where Informal or Unscored Procedures Are Used
    (2) Where Formal and Scored Procedures Are Used
60-3.7 Use of Other Validity Studies
  A. Validity Studies Not Conducted by the User
  B. Use of Criterion-Related Validity Evidence From Other Sources

No. 354 UNIFORM GUIDELINES ON EMPLOYEE SELECTION 401:2277

(1) Validity Evidence
(2) Job Similarity
(3) Fairness Evidence
C. Validity Evidence From Multiunit Study
D. Other Significant Variables
60-3.8 Cooperative Studies
A. Encouragement of Cooperative Studies
B. Standards for Use of Cooperative Studies
60-3.9 No Assumption of Validity
A. Unacceptable Substitutes for Evidence of Validity
B. Encouragement of Professional Supervision
60-3.10 Employment Agencies and Employment Services
A. Where Selection Procedures Are Devised by Agency
B. Where Selection Procedures Are Devised Elsewhere
60-3.11 Disparate Treatment
60-3.12 Retesting of Applicants
60-3.13 Affirmative Action
A. Affirmative Action Obligations
B. Encouragement of Voluntary Affirmative Action Programs

TECHNICAL STANDARDS

60-3.14 Technical Standards for Validity Studies
A. Validity Studies Should be Based on Review of Information About the Job
B. Technical Standards for Criterion-Related Validity Studies
(1) Technical Feasibility
(2) Analysis of the Job
(3) Criterion Measures
(4) Representativeness of the Sample
(5) Statistical Relationships
(6) Operational Use of Selection Procedures
(7) Over-Statement of Validity Findings
(8) Fairness
(a) Unfairness Defined
(b) Investigation of Fairness
(c) General Considerations in Fairness Investigations
(d) When Unfairness Is Shown
(e) Technical Feasibility of Fairness Studies
(f) Continued Use of Selection Procedures When Fairness Studies not Feasible
C. Technical Standards for Content Validity Studies
(1) Appropriateness of Content Validity Studies
(2) Job Analysis for Content Validity
(3) Development of Selection Procedure
(4) Standards for Demonstrating Content Validity
(5) Reliability
(6) Prior-Training or Experience
(7) Training Success
(8) Operational Use
(9) Ranking Based on Content Validity Studies
D. Technical Standards for Construct Validity Studies
(1) Appropriateness of Construct Validity Studies
(2) Job Analysis for Construct Validity Studies
(3) Relationship to the Job
(4) Use of Construct Validity Study Without New Criterion-Related Evidence
(a) Standards for Use
(b) Determination of Common Work Behaviors

DOCUMENTATION OF IMPACT AND VALIDITY EVIDENCE

60-3.15 Documentation of Impact and Validity Evidence
A. Required Information
(1) Simplified Recordkeeping for Users With Less Than 100 Employees
(2) Information on Impact
(a) Collection of Information on Impact
(b) When Adverse Impact Has Been Eliminated in the Total Selection Process
(c) When Data Insufficient to Determine Impact
(3) Documentation of Validity Evidence
(a) Type of Evidence
(b) Form of Report
(c) Completeness
B. Criterion-Related Validity Studies
(1) User(s), Location(s), and Date(s) of Study
(2) Problem and Setting
(3) Job analysis or Review of Job Information
(4) Job Titles and Codes
(5) Criterion Measures
(6) Sample Description
(7) Description of Selection Procedure
(8) Techniques and Results
(9) Alternative Procedures Investigated
(10) Uses and Applications
(11) Source Data
(12) Contact Person
(13) Accuracy and Completeness
C. Content Validity Studies
(1) User(s), Location(s), and Date(s) of Study
(2) Problem and Setting
(3) Job Analysis—Content of the Job
(4) Selection Procedure and Its Content
(5) Relationship Between Selection Procedure and the Job

(6) Alternative Procedures Investigated
(7) Uses and Applications
(8) Contact Person
(9) Accuracy and Completeness
D. Construct Validity Studies
(1) User(s), Location(s), and Date(s) of Study
(2) Problem and Setting
(3) Construct Definition
(4) Job Analysis
(5) Job Titles and Codes
(6) Selection Procedure
(7) Relationship to Job Performance
(8) Alternative Procedures Investigated
(9) Uses and Applications
(10) Accuracy and Completeness
(11) Source Data
(12) Contact Person
E. Evidence of Validity From Other Studies
(1) Evidence from Criterion-Related Validity Studies
(a) Job Information
(b) Relevance of Criteria
(c) Other Variables
(d) Use of the Selection Procedure
(e) Bibliography
(2) Evidence From Content Validity Studies
(3) Evidence From Construct Validity Studies
F. Evidence of Validity From Cooperative Studies
G. Selection for Higher Level Jobs
H. Interim Use of Selection Procedures

DEFINITIONS
60-3.16 Definitions

APPENDIX
60-3.17 Policy Statement on Affirmative Action (see section 13B)
60-3.18 Citations

Title 31—Money and Finance: Treasury
CHAPTER 1—MONETARY OFFICES: DEPARTMENT OF THE TREASURY
PART 51—FISCAL ASSISTANCE TO STATE AND LOCAL GOVERNMENTS

Uniform Guidelines on Employee Selection Procedures (1978); Interim Regulation

1. 31 CFR part 51 is amended by revising § 51.53(b) to read as follows:

§ 51.53 Employment discrimination.

* * * * *

(b) Employee selection procedures.

The Equal Employment Opportunity Commission, the Civil Service Commission, the Department of Justice and the Department of Labor in carrying out their responsibilities in insuring compliance with Federal equal employment opportunity law, have promulgated Uniform Guidelines on Employee Selection Procedures to assist in establishing and maintaining equal employment opportunities; 29 CFR part 1607; 5 CFR 300.103(c); 990-1 (book 3) of the Federal Personnel Manual; 28 CFR 50.14, and 41 CFR 60.3. The Uniform Guidelines on Employee Selection procedures appear as appendix A to this part. Among other things, these guidelines recognize the unlawfulness of the use of any employee selection procedures (including tests and minimum education levels) which disqualify a disproportionate number of persons on grounds of race, color, religion, sex, or national origin and which have not been properly validated or otherwise justified in accordance with Federal law. Recipient governments may not use a selection procedure that is inconsistent with the Uniform Guidelines on Employee Selection Procedures.

* * * * *

2. Part 51 is further amended by adding Appendix A—Uniform Guidelines on Employee Selection Procedures (1978) as adopted at 43 FR 38290, August 25, 1978.

[FR Doc. 78-25592 Filed 9-8-78; 8:45am]

APPENDIX C

Standard Form 171, Personal Qualifications Statement

Standard Form 171
Personal Qualifications Statement

IMPORTANT
READ THE FOLLOWING INSTRUCTIONS CAREFULLY BEFORE FILLING OUT YOUR STATEMENT

- You must furnish all requested information. The information you provide will be used to determine your qualifications for employment. DO NOT SEND A RESUME IN LIEU OF COMPLETING THIS STATEMENT.
- If you fail to answer all questions on your Statement fully and accurately, you may delay consideration of your Statement and may lose employment opportunities. See the Privacy Act Information on the reverse of this sheet.
- So that it is understood that you did not omit an item, please write the letters "N/A" (Not Applicable) beside those items that do not apply to you, unless instructions indicate otherwise.

GENERAL INSTRUCTIONS

- If you are applying for a specific Federal civil service examination:
  - Read the examination announcement or the Qualifications Information Statement for the position to be certain that your experience and education are qualifying.
  - If a written test is required, follow the filing instructions on the admission card.
  - If no written test is required, mail this Statement to the Office of Personnel Management Area Office specified in the announcement or on the Qualifications Information Statement.
  - Be sure to include all other forms required.
  - If you have a change of name or address, notify the Office of Personnel Management Area Office with which you filed this Statement.
  - You may want to make a copy of this Statement for your personal use.
  - Please typewrite or write legibly or print clearly in dark ink.

INSTRUCTIONS RELATING TO SPECIFIC ITEMS

ITEM 13. Lowest Grade or Salary

- Enter the lowest grade or the lowest salary you will accept. You will not be considered for any lower grades or salary. You will be considered for any higher grades or salaries for which you qualify as specified in the examination announcement or the Qualifications Information Statement.

ITEM 16. Other Government and International Agencies

- The Office of Personnel Management is occasionally requested to refer for employment consideration the names of eligibles on competitive registers to State and local government agencies, congressional and other public offices, and public international organizations. Indicate your availability by checking the appropriate boxes. Your response to this question will not affect your consideration for other positions.

ITEM 18. Overnight Travel

- Indicate the number of nights per month you are willing to be away from home in a travel status. Some jobs require nearly constant travel of two or three weeks every month while others require infrequent, short or occasional extended periods of travel. You will be considered for positions requiring travel based on the number of nights per month for which you indicate travel availability.

ITEM 20. Active Military Service and Veteran Preference

- Five-point veteran preference is granted to veterans who receive an honorable or general discharge from the armed forces:
  (a) after active duty during the periods April 6, 1917 to July 2, 1921 and December 7, 1941 to July 1, 1955;
  (b) after more than 180 consecutive days of active duty, any part of which occurred after January 31, 1955 and before October 15, 1976.
  NOTE—Service under an initial period of active duty for training under the "6-month" Reserve or National Guard programs is not creditable for veteran preference; and
  (c) after service in a campaign for which a campaign badge has been authorized.

- Non-disabled veterans who retired at or above the rank of major or its equivalent are not eligible for veteran preference after October 1, 1980.

- You will be required to furnish records to support your claim for five-point preference only at the time of your appointment.

- Ten-point veteran preference is granted to:
  (a) disabled veterans; and
  (b) veterans awarded the Purple Heart.
  Ten-point veteran preference is granted in certain cases to:
  (a) unmarried widows and widowers of veterans;
  (b) spouses of disabled veterans; and
  (c) mothers of deceased or disabled veterans.
  If you claim ten-point veteran preference, submit Standard Form 15, Claim for 10-Point Veteran Preference, and the required proof with this application. Obtain SF 15 and information on provisions of the Veteran Preference laws at any Federal Job Information Center.

- A clemency discharge does not meet the Veteran Preference Act requirement for discharge under honorable conditions. Accordingly, no preference may be granted to applicants with such discharge.

ITEM 21. Experience

- Fill in these experience blocks carefully and completely. A large part of your qualifications rating depends upon a thorough description of your experience and employment history.

- If you fail to give complete details, you may delay consideration of your Statement. Your description of duties may be verified with former employers.

- If you supervise or have supervised other employees, be sure to indicate the number and kind (and grades, if Federal Government) of employees supervised, and describe your duties as a supervisor under Description of Work.

- Volunteer Experience—You may receive credit for pertinent religious, civic, welfare service and organizational work performed with or without compensation. Show the actual amount of time spent in such work (for example, average hours per week or month). Complete all the items just as you would for a compensable position.

- Use separate blocks if your duties, responsibilities, or salary have changed materially while working for the same employer. Treat each such change as a separate position.

PLEASE READ ADDITIONAL INSTRUCTIONS ON BACK OF THIS SHEET

ITEM 21. Experience (Continued)

NOTE—Experience gained more than 15 years ago may be summarized in one block if it is not pertinent to the type of position you applied for.

- Include your military or merchant marine service in separate blocks in order and describe major duty assignments.
- Indicate in each block of Item 21 the name under which you were employed if it was different from the name in Item 6 of this Statement. Show former name in parentheses after "Description of duties and accomplishments in your work."
- Indicate any period of unemployment exceeding three months and your address at that time on the last line of the preceding experience block.
- Block A—Describe your present position in this block. Indicate if you are now unemployed or if you have never been employed.
- Blocks B and C—Describe in Block B the position you held just before your present position and continue to work backwards using Block C.
- Enter the average number of hours per week you work. If you work part time, indicate the average number of hours per week you work.
- Description of Work—Describe each job briefly, including required skills and abilities. Describe any specialties and special assignments, your authority and responsibility, your relationships to others, your accomplishments, and any other factors which help to describe the job.
- If your job contains experience in more than one type of work (for example: carpentry and painting, or personnel and budget) estimate and indicate the approximate percentage of time spent in each type of work. Place the percentages in parentheses at the end of the description of work.
- If you need additional experience blocks:
  —Use Standard Form 171-A, Continuation Sheet; or
  —A plain sheet of paper approximately 8 by 10½ inches in size. Be sure to include all of the information requested in Item 21.
  If you need additional space to describe a position held:
  —Continue in Item 34, Space for Detailed Answers; or
  —Continue on a plain sheet of paper.
- Identify each plain sheet of paper used by showing your name, birth date, examination or position title, and the block under Item 21 from which the description is continued.
- Attach all supplemental sheets to the top of page 3.

ITEM 32. Relatives Employed by the United States Government

- A Federal official (civilian or military) may not appoint any of his or her relatives or recommend them for employment in his or her agency, and a relative who is appointed in violation of this restriction cannot be paid. Therefore it is necessary to have information about your relatives who are working for the Federal Government. In listing relative(s) in answer to question 32 include: father; mother; son; daughter; brother; sister; uncle; aunt; first cousin; nephew; niece; husband; wife; father-in-law; mother-in-law; son-in-law; daughter-in-law; brother-in-law; sister-in-law; stepfather; stepmother; stepson; stepdaughter; stepbrother; stepsister; half brother, and half sister.

CERTIFICATION

- Be careful that you have answered all questions on your Statement correctly and considered all statements fully so that your eligibility can be decided on all the facts. Read the certification carefully before you sign and date your Statement.
- Sign your name in ink.
- Use one given name, initial or initials, and last name.

PRIVACY ACT INFORMATION

The Office of Personnel Management is authorized to rate applicants for Federal jobs under Sections 1302, 3301, and 3304 of Title 5 of the U.S. Code. We need the information you put on this form to see how well your education and work skills qualify you for a Federal job. We also need information on matters such as citizenship and military service to see whether you are affected by laws we must follow in deciding who may be employed by the Federal Government. We cannot give you a rating, which is the first step toward getting a job, if you do not answer these questions.

We must have your Social Security Number (SSN) to keep your records straight because other people may have the same name and birthdate. The SSN has been used to keep records since 1943, when Executive Order 9397 asked agencies to do so. The Office of Personnel Management may also use your SSN to make requests for information about you from employers, schools, banks, and others who know you, but only as allowed by law. The information we collect by using your SSN will be used for employment purposes and also for studies and statistics that will not identify you.

Information we have about you may also be given to Federal, State, and local agencies for checking on law violations or for other lawful purposes. We may also notify your school placement office if you are selected for a Federal job.

PLEASE DETACH THIS INSTRUCTION SHEET BEFORE SUBMITTING YOUR STATEMENT

APPENDIX C

Personal Qualifications Statement
Read instructions before completing form

Form Approved:
OMB No. 3206-0012

1. Kind of position (job) you are filing for (or title and number of announcement)	
2. Options for which you wish to be considered (if listed in the announcement)	
3. Home phone — Area Code / Number	4. Work phone — Area Code / Number / Extension
5. Sex (for statistics only) ☐ Male ☐ Female	6. Other last names ever used
Name (Last, First, Middle)	
Street address or RFD no. (include apartment no., if any)	
City / State / ZIP Code	
8. Birthplace (City & State, or foreign country)	
9. Birth date (Month, day, year)	10. Social Security Number

11. If you have ever been employed by the Federal Government as a civilian, give your highest grade, classification series, and job title

Dates of service in highest grade (Month, day, and year)
From   To

12. If you currently have an application on file with the Office of Personnel Management for appointment to a Federal position, list (a) the name of the area office maintaining your application, (b) the position for which you filed, and (if appropriate) (c) the date of your notice of rating, (d) your identification number, and (e) your rating

DO NOT WRITE IN THIS BLOCK
FOR USE OF EXAMINING OFFICE ONLY

Material ☐ Submitted ☐ Returned
Entered register:
Notations:
Form reviewed:
Form approved:

Option	Grade	Earned Rating	Preference	Aug. Rating

☐ 5 Points (Tent.)
☐ 10 Pts. 30% or More Comp. Dis.
☐ 10 Pts. Less Than 30% Comp. Dis.
☐ Other 10 Points
☐ Disallowed
☐ Being Investigated

Initials and date

THIS SPACE FOR USE OF APPOINTING OFFICER ONLY
Preference has been verified through proof that the separation was under honorable conditions, and other proof as required

☐ 5-Point ☐ 10 Points 30% or More Compensable Disability ☐ 10 Points Less Than 30% Compensable Disability ☐ 10-Point Other

Signature and title

Agency   Date

13. Lowest pay or grade you will accept	14. When will you be available for work? (Month and year)
PAY $ ____ per ____ OR GRADE ____	

15. Are you available for temporary employment lasting YES NO
(Acceptance or refusal of temporary employment will not affect your consideration for other appointments.)
A. Less than 1 month?
B. 1 to 4 months?
C. 5 to 12 months?

16. Are you interested in being considered for employment by YES NO
A. State and local government agencies?
B. Congressional and other public offices?
C. Public international organizations?

17. Where will you accept a job? YES NO
A. In the Washington, D.C. Metropolitan area?
B. Outside the 50 United States?
C. Anyplace in the United States?
D. Only in (specify locality)

18. Indicate your availability for overnight travel.
A. Not available for overnight travel
B. 1 to 5 nights per month
C. 6 to 10 nights per month
D. 11 or more nights per month

19. Are you available for part-time positions (fewer than 40 hours per week) offering YES NO
A. 20 or fewer hours per week?
B. 21 to 31 hours per week?
C. 32 to 39 hours per week?

20. Veteran Preference Answer all parts If a part does not apply to you, answer "NO" YES NO
A. Have you ever served on active duty in the United States military service? (Exclude tours of active duty for training in Reserves or National Guard)
B. Have you ever been discharged from the armed services under other than honorable conditions? You may omit any such discharge changed to honorable or general by a Discharge Review Board or similar authority
If "YES", give details in item 34.
C. Do you claim 5-point preference based on active duty in the armed forces?
If "YES", you will be required to furnish records to support your claim at the time you are appointed
D. Do you claim 10-point preference?
If "YES," check the type of preference claimed and complete and attach Standard Form 15, "Claim for 10-Point Veteran Preference," together with the proof requested in that form.

Type of Preference: ☐ Compensable Disability 30% or More ☐ Compensable Disability Below 30% ☐ Non-compensable Disability ☐ Purple Heart Recipient ☐ Spouse ☐ Widow(er) ☐ Mother

E. List dates, branch, and serial number of all active service (enter "N/A", if not applicable)

From   To   Branch of Service   Serial or Service Number

THE FEDERAL GOVERNMENT IS AN EQUAL OPPORTUNITY EMPLOYER

Standard Form 171 (Rev. 1 79)
Office of Personnel Management
FPM Chapter 295

PREVIOUS EDITION USABLE 7540-00-935-7150 171-107

248 INTERVIEWING

APPENDIX C   249

Attach Supplemental Sheets or Forms Here

22. A. Special qualifications and skills (skills with machines, patents or inventions, your most important publications [do not submit copies unless requested], your public speaking and publications experience, membership in professional or scientific societies, etc.)

B. Kind of license or certificate (pilot, registered nurse, lawyer, radio operator, CPA, etc.)	C. Latest license or certificate		D. Approximate number of words per minute	
	Year	State or other licensing authority	Typing	Shorthand

23. A. Did you graduate from high school or will you graduate within the next nine months, or do you have a GED high school equivalency certificate?

Yes	Month and Year	No	Highest grade completed	**B.** Name and location (city and State) of latest high school attended

C. Name and location (city, State, and ZIP Code, if known) of college or university (If you expect to graduate within nine months, give MONTH and YEAR you expect to receive your degree)	Dates Attended		Years Completed		No. of Credits Completed		Type of Degree (e.g., B.A.)	Year of Degree
	From	To	Day	Night	Semester Hours	Quarter Hours		

D. Chief undergraduate college subjects	No. of Credits Completed		E. Chief graduate college subjects	No. of Credits Completed	
	Semester Hours	Quarter Hours		Semester Hours	Quarter Hours

F. Major field of study at highest level of college work

G. Other schools or training (for example, trade, vocational, Armed Forces or business). Give for each the name and location (city, State and ZIP Code, if known) of school, dates attended, subjects studied, number of classroom hours of instruction per week, certificate, and any other pertinent data

24. Honors, awards, and fellowships received

25. Languages other than English. List the languages (other than English) in which you are proficient and indicate your level of proficiency by putting a check mark (✔) in the appropriate columns. Candidates for positions requiring conversational ability in a language other than English may be given an interview conducted solely in that language. Describe in item 34 how you gained your language skills and the amount of experience you have had (e.g., completed 72 hours of classroom training, spoke language at home for 18 years, self-taught, etc.)

	PROFICIENCY							
Name of Language(s)	Can Prepare and Deliver Lectures		Can Converse		Have Facility to Translate Articles, Technical Materials, etc.		Can Read Articles, Technical Materials, etc., for Own Use	
	Fluently	With Difficulty	Fluently	Passably	Into English	From English	Easily	With Difficulty

26. References. List three persons who are NOT related to you and who have definite knowledge of your qualifications and fitness for the position for which you are applying. Do not repeat names of supervisors listed under Item 21: Experience.

Full Name	Present Business or Home Address (Number, Street, City, State and ZIP Code)	Telephone Number (Include Area Code)	Business or Occupation

Page **3**

INTERVIEWING

		YES	NO
	Answer Items 27 through 33 by placing an "X" in the proper column		
27.	Are you a citizen of the United States? ◄		
	If NO, give country of which you are a citizen		
NOTE:	A conviction or a firing does not necessarily mean you cannot be appointed. The circumstances of the occurrence(s) and how long ago it (they) occurred are important. Give all the facts so that a decision can be made.		
28.	Within the last five years have you been fired from any job for any reason? ◄		
29.	Within the last five years have you quit a job after being notified that you would be fired? ◄		
	If your answer to 28 or 29 above is YES, give details in Item 34. Show the name and address (including ZIP Code) of employer, approximate date, and reasons in each case. This information should agree with your answers in Item 21. Experience.		
30. A	Have you **ever** been convicted, forfeited collateral, or are you now under charges for **any felony** or **any** firearms or explosives offense against the law? (A felony is defined as any offense punishable by imprisonment for a term exceeding one year, but does not include any offense classified under the laws of a State as a misdemeanor which is punishable by a term of imprisonment of two years or less.) ◄		
B.	During the past seven years have you been convicted, imprisoned, on probation or parole or forfeited collateral, or are you now under charges for any offense against the law not included in A above? ◄		
NOTE:	When answering A and B above, you may omit (1) traffic fines for which you paid a fine of $50.00 or less, (2) any offense committed before your 18th birthday which was finally adjudicated in a juvenile court or under a youth offender law, (3) any conviction the record of which has been expunged under Federal or State law, and (4) any conviction set aside under the Federal Youth Corrections Act or similar State authority.		
31.	While in the military service were you ever convicted by a general court-martial? ◄		
	If your answer to 30A, 30B, or 31 is YES, give details in Item 34. Show for each offense (1) date (2) charge (3) place (4) court, and (5) action taken		
32.	Does the United States Government employ in a civilian capacity or as a member of the Armed Forces any relative of yours (by blood or marriage)? (See Item 32 in the attached instruction sheet) ◄		
	If your answer to 32 is YES, give in Item 34 for such relatives (1) name (2) present address (including ZIP Code) (3) relationship (4) department, agency, or branch of the armed forces		
33.	Do you receive, or do you have pending, application for retirement or retainer pay, pension, or other compensation based upon military, Federal civilian, or District of Columbia Government service? ◄		
	If your answer to 33 is YES, give details in Item 34. If military retired pay, include the rank at which you retired		

Your Statement cannot be processed until you have answered all questions, including Items 27 through 33 above
Be sure you have placed an "X" to the left of EVERY marker (◄) above either in the YES or NO column

34. Item No.	Space for detailed answers. Indicate Item numbers to which the answers apply

If more space is required, use full sheets of paper approximately the same size as this page. Write on each sheet your name, birth date, and announcement or position title. Attach all sheets to this Statement at the top of page 3

ATTENTION—THIS STATEMENT MUST BE SIGNED
Read the following paragraphs carefully before signing this Statement

A false answer to any question in this Statement may be grounds for not employing you, or for dismissing you after you begin work, and may be punishable by fine or imprisonment (U.S. Code, Title 18, Section 1001). All the information you give will be considered in reviewing your Statement

AUTHORITY FOR RELEASE OF INFORMATION
I have completed this Statement with the knowledge and understanding that any or all items contained herein may be subject to investigation prescribed by law or Presidential directive and I consent to the release of information concerning my capacity and fitness by employers, educational institutions, law enforcement agencies, and other individuals and agencies, to duly accredited Investigators, Personnel Staffing Specialists, and other authorized employees of the Federal Government for that purpose

CERTIFICATION	SIGNATURE (sign in ink)	DATE
I certify that all of the statements made by me are true, complete and correct to the best of my knowledge and belief, and are made in good faith		

APPENDIX C 251

Standard Form 171-A (Rev. 1-79)
Office of Personnel Management
FPM Chapter 295

CONTINUATION SHEET FOR STANDARD FORM 171
PERSONAL QUALIFICATIONS STATEMENT

Form Approved
OMB No. 3206-0012

INSTRUCTIONS—Fill out this form only when necessary for completion of Item 21, "EXPERIENCE," on Standard Form 171. Enclose with your Statement. Typewrite or print clearly in dark ink.

1. Name (Last) (First) (Middle)	2. Birth date (Month, day, year)	3. Kind of position applied for, or name of examination:

Name and address of employer's organization (include ZIP Code, if known)	Dates employed (give month and year) From To	Average number of hours per week
	Salary or earnings Beginning $ per Ending $ per	Place of employment City State

Exact title of your position	Name of immediate supervisor	Area Code Telephone Number	Number and kind of employees you supervised

Kind of business or organization (manufacturing, accounting, social services, etc.)	If Federal service, civilian or military, series, grade or rank, and date of last promotion	Your reason for leaving

Description of work (Describe your specific duties, responsibilities and accomplishments in this job)

For agency use (skill codes, etc.)

Name and address of employer's organization (include ZIP Code, if known)	Dates employed (give month and year) From To	Average number of hours per week
	Salary or earnings Beginning $ per Ending $ per	Place of employment City State

Exact title of your position	Name of immediate supervisor	Area Code Telephone Number	Number and kind of employees you supervised

Kind of business or organization (manufacturing, accounting, social services, etc.)	If Federal service, civilian or military, series, grade or rank, and date of last promotion	Your reason for leaving

Description of work (Describe your specific duties, responsibilities and accomplishments in this job)

For agency use (skill codes, etc.)

Name and address of employer's organization (include ZIP Code, if known)	Dates employed (give month and year) From To	Average number of hours per week
	Salary or earnings Beginning $ per Ending $ per	Place of employment City State

Exact title of your position	Name of immediate supervisor	Area Code Telephone Number	Number and kind of employees you supervised

Kind of business or organization (manufacturing, accounting, social services, etc.)	If Federal service, civilian or military, series, grade or rank, and date of last promotion	Your reason for leaving

Description of work (Describe your specific duties, responsibilities and accomplishments in this job)

For agency use (skill codes, etc.)

THE FEDERAL GOVERNMENT IS AN EQUAL OPPORTUNITY EMPLOYER
7540-00-935-7157   PREVIOUS EDITION USABLE   171-204

APPENDIX D

The Joe Hatton Situation: An Action Maze[1]

Introduction

This exercise illustrates a way of thinking about how you act as a supervisor and the behavioral options available to you. It begins with the statement of a problem that you, the supervisor, are having with one of your subordinates. The decision path you follow in taking action can and probably will differ from the path taken by others. There is no one "correct" path to follow, just as there is no one correct path in real life. The path you take will depend on your attitudes and your choices at each decision point. First, you will be directed to Step 1. Next, based on the information presented in Step 2, you will decide what action you will take as a result of your decision. Then you will turn to the step indicated next to that choice. Other action choices will refer you to other steps in the exercise, so that you will be skipping back and forth among the steps. The exercise will be over when so indicated in the step to which you have turned or when the information in the step tells you to stop. It will be instructive to be able to retrace your decision path; therefore, record your decisions on the decision path record sheet provided.

Features

1. Joe Hatton will respond in the same emotional tone as indicated by your action:

If You Are:	Joe Will Be:
hostile	hostile
aggressive	aggressive
concerned	concerned
friendly	friendly
understanding	understanding

2. Attempts to deal with Joe by urging him to "do better" or by giving him a pep talk will have no impact on him.

3. Information gathered from Joe's fellow workers will be conflicting. In some

---

[1] Based on "The ABMS Hatton Story." Used by permission of the United States Naval Education and Training Command, NAS Pensacola, Pensacola, Florida.

instances the information will support what you know or what another worker says, but in other instances, the information will contradict what you know or what another worker says.

Ending

Ideally the exercise will end with problem disclosure and Joe's willingness to be referred to a professional counselor or counseling program. Your goal in this interview is, first, to persuade Joe to admit that he has a problem and to be willing to discuss it and, second, to get help for Joe from a professional counselor or a professional counseling program. But the exercise may end when your attitude and behavior are determined to be counterproductive for counseling. At that point, you will be told to stop. In either case, whether you achieve the goal of the interview or are told to stop, review your behavior as recorded on the decision path record sheet.

Note as you retrace your steps that to reach a successful outcome you had to shift your mental outlook and purpose several times: reprimand, information-gathering, counseling, persuasion. What would you do differently? What would stay the same? How could you improve your counseling behavior with Joe Hatton?

Decision Path Record Sheet

Action/Decision (Summarize briefly)	Reason	Step
1.		
2.		
3.		
4.		
5.		
6.		
7.		
8.		
9.		
10.		
11.		
12.		
13.		
14.		
15.		
16.		
17.		
18.		
19.		
20.		
21.		

Action/Decision (Summarize briefly)　　　　　Reason　　　　　Step
22.
23.
24.
25.

Situation

You are the quality assurance officer, and you supervise the quality assurance department of an airline company at a major airport. Your department performs quality assurance checks on all engines, associated power plants, and mechanical repairs. Your people must check every phase of work on an aircraft being serviced or overhauled. They are responsible for the final checking of any item completed by another shop that affects safety of flight in any way and the approval of it as ready for flight. This is an immense responsibility, and theoretically the company's best technical, engineering, and maintenance people work for you. All of them are recognized as highly competent, superior workers. Your company has 20 DC-10 aircraft, 35 managers and supervisors, and 250 workers.

Problem

Your general foreman is Joe Hatton. He has a drinking problem that is starting to affect his work. In the past he has been an excellent employee in all respects. He started with the company nine years ago as a mechanic, progressing upward to his current position. He earned his engineering degree in night school, completing it four years ago. He is well liked by almost everyone who works for the company and by customers as well. But in the last few months Joe has been reporting late for work. He has been sloppy and unreliable in performing critical inspections; in other words, his performance has been deteriorating.

Step 1. This morning Joe checked a control surface on a DC-10. The control surface was improperly rigged, but Joe didn't catch it during the inspection because he was drunk. This afternoon the control surface didn't work properly in flight because its tolerances were incorrect. Although the control surface failed in flight and the situation was quite serious, the aircraft was not lost. After it landed, you personally inspected the control surface and determined that Joe's poor inspection had been responsible for the control failure. You remember that this morning you thought you smelled liquor on Joe's breath, but you were not quite sure. You think that now some action must be taken with Joe.
Go to Step 2.

Step 2. Which of the five actions listed below would you take first? Select the first action you would take from those listed and go only to the step you select. Be sure to record your decision, the reason for it, and the step number on the decision path record sheet.

APPENDIX D 255

   a. Call Joe aside when you find him and have a talk with him about his drinking problem.   **Go to Step 9.**
   b. Have Joe confined to the dispensary until he can be released with his problem cured.   **Go to Step 11.**
   c. Discuss the matter with *your* supervisor.   **Go to Step 7.**
   d. Transfer Joe at the next opportunity.   **Go to Step 34.**
   e. Ignore the situation. It was probably just a coincidence that will never happen again.   **Go to Step 41.**

Step 3. You ask some shop members whom you heard laughing to tell you what they found funny. They are too embarrassed to comment, but one of the more outspoken people says:

"We were just laughing at a joke Fred told at lunch. It didn't have anything to do with you or Joe."

What would you do now?   **Return to Step 24 and select another answer.**

Step 4. You decide to ask the others in the shop if they know whether Joe stayed home because he is drunk again. You wonder if he has a drinking problem, a family problem, or a real illness or if there's something else. You talk to several shop members who work with Joe. They seem a little hesitant to talk, but one finally admits that he saw Joe with some blond woman speeding away from the airport during the lunch hour. He reports that Joe "could have been drunk. Anyway, he drove like it."
What would your approach to Joe be now?   **Return to Step 2.**

Step 5. You decide to keep calling Joe's home at regular intervals during the day. Late that afternoon, someone answers the phone. The same woman, still sounding peculiar, says that Joe is not there. After a few minutes during which you try to determine where Joe is and when he will be back, Joe comes to the phone and asks who it is. When you identify yourself, he says: "I can't talk to you now. Good-bye." He hangs up on you.
In the morning when Joe comes to work, what will your approach to him be?
Go to Step 9.

Step 6. You have asked Joe if he really has been ill or has been absent and having problems on the job because of a drinking problem. Joe says:

"Now look, I know the rules! They say that either your own illness or the illness of someone in your family qualifies as allowable sick leave. And it's been one of the two, I can assure you!"

What would your general approach to Joe be?

1. Explain to Joe that you must have proof of illness before sick leave is allowed, that you are in charge and that he should respect this fact. **Go to Step 13.**
2. Tell Joe that his personal problems are his business but that production in the quality assurance department is your business. Tell him that he must "shape up or he'll be fired."   **Go to Step 24.**
3. Say, "I didn't mean it that way, Joe, and I'm sorry you have been having so much trouble. But I'm concerned about how your absences have been affecting your work."   **Go to Step 28.**
4. Tell Joe he is being transferred immediately.   **Go to Step 25.**
5. Transfer Joe at the first opportunity.   **Go to Step 34.**

Step 7. You have decided to talk to your supervisor about your experience with Joe and his apparent threat to quality assurance within the company. Your boss says:

> "Joe Hatton? I always thought he did a good job and always received good reports about him. I'm sorry to hear that he is having problems. Because of his previous excellent record, I was thinking of recommending him for a promotion. There must be a mistake. Why don't you just settle down a little and see if things don't work themselves out?"

Return to Step 2 and decide on your next step.

Step 8. You have decided to call Joe over to a more private place and ask him what is on his mind. He is reluctant to discuss it at first, but then he blurts out:

> "You know very well what's wrong! Everything seems to be messed up. At first it was just at home, but now you're picking on me too! It's enough to drive a man to drink. The least you could do is get off my back. And keep off!"

What general response would you make to Joe following that rather blunt outburst?

1. Remind Joe that you are responsible for quality assurance and that you are the supervisor. Tell him that you are just doing your job and that he should respect you for doing it.   **Go to Step 13.**
2. Suggest that Joe go back to work and cool off and that you will talk to him later about it.   **Go to Step 19.**
3. Warn Joe that if there are any more comments from him like that one, you will see that he is dealt with severely.   **Go to Step 20.**
4. Tell Joe that you think it might help if you discussed it with him. You don't want to intrude, but you are concerned about his absences. **Go to Step 28.**
5. Tell Joe that he will be transferred or fired for insubordination. **Go to Step 25.**

Step 9. In discussing Joe's drinking problem with him, which one of the following general approaches would you take?

APPENDIX D

1. Explain to Joe the importance of sobriety to the shop's safety and quality assurance record. Point out to him the fact that lives and equipment would be endangered if everyone were under the influence of alcohol while on the job. Urge him to try to do better.   **Go to Step 10.**
2. When Joe comes to work Tuesday morning, tell him that his personal problems and drinking problems are his business but that quality assurance is your business. Tell him that he must "sober up or be fired."
Go to Step 24.
3. Wait until Joe brings up the matter of his drinking so as not to embarrass him.   **Go to Step 16.**
4. Ask Joe what difficulty he is having.   **Go to Step 12.**
5. Be friendly, but tell Joe that you are going to place a warning letter in his personnel file that states that he must improve within thirty days.
Go to Step 17.
6. Tell Joe that he is to report to the dispensary until he can be released or transferred.   **Go to Step 34.**

Step 10. You discuss the problem with Joe, and he says: "I'll never come to work drunk again." But the following Monday he fails to come to work. Someone who says she is his wife phones in to say that he is ill. She sounds odd—as if she has been drinking.
What would you do then?

1. Telephone Joe's home to verify his illness.   **Go to Step 14.**
2. Send some inexpensive flowers to Joe's home with a "get well soon" card.
Go to Step 27.
3. Ask others in the crew if they know whether Joe stayed home because he is drunk again (if you have not already asked this today).   **Go to Step 4.**
4. Wait until Joe returns to deal with him.   **Go to Step 26.**
5. Contact a counselor or other professional to get some help on Joe's drinking problem.   **Go to Step 40.**

Step 11. You have Joe confined to the dispensary. He stays there for three weeks under observation and denies his drinking problem. The dispensary's medical doctors believe him and think that Joe has a case of "bad nerves." Joe is released to return to work. When Joe returns to work that afternoon, you detect alcohol on his breath.   **Return to Step 2 to decide your next step.**

Step 12. You have asked Joe what difficulty he is having. He says:

"Well, it's rather personal, and I would rather not talk about it if you don't mind."

What general approach would you follow now?

1. Tell Joe that he is transferred.   **Go to Step 25.**
2. Ask Joe if he has really been ill or has been absent and having problems on the job because of a drinking problem.   **Go to Step 6.**

3. Tell Joe that his personal problems are his business but that quality assurance is your business. Tell him that he must "shape up or he could get fired." **Go to Step 24.**
4. Be friendly, but explain to Joe that you are going to place a warning letter in his personnel file that states that he must improve within thirty days. **Go to Step 17.**
5. Say something like: "Joe, I don't want to butt in where I'm not wanted, but at the same time, you must see how your Monday absences are affecting your work. I'm concerned about this, and I know you are too." **Go to Step 28.**

Step 13. You have told Joe that you are in charge and that he should have more respect for this fact. Joe says:

"Well, one thing I have respect for is myself! Too much respect to stay on with this chicken organization. I quit!"

Joe leaves.

What do you think about your progress at this point?

1. That you might have handled yourself differently somewhere along the line? Would you like a chance to retrace your steps to see what could be done differently? **If so, go to Step 9.**
2. That you did what any supervisor would do to correct his or her personnel and keep them in line and make sure they know who the boss is. If so, the exercise is over for you. **Go to the discussion questions in Step 22.**

Step 14. You telephone Joe's home to verify his illness. There is no answer. *What would you do now?*

1. Keep calling at regular intervals during the day. **Go to Step 5.**
2. Ask your secretary to keep calling. **Go to Step 21.**
3. Wait until Joe returns to work to deal with the matter. **Go to Step 26.**

Step 15. You have responded to Joe: "Have you talked about it with your wife?" Joe says:

"Yes, but she is so wrapped up in her two kids that she won't listen or give me the consideration that I need. I knew I would have problems when I married a divorcée, but I didn't expect this."

What general approach would you follow now?

1. Say: "I'm glad you realized the seriousness of this, and I hope your wife will be considerate enough to help you overcome the problem. Joe, I hope you will try to do better." **Go to Step 10.**

APPENDIX D

2. Say: "It's pretty tough being married to a divorcée with two little kids, I guess."   **Go to Step 33.**
3. Say nothing but continue to listen.   **Go to Step 18.**

∾∾∾

Step 16. You have decided to wait until Joe brings up the matter of his drinking so as not to embarrass him. But he does not bring it up, and he continues to come to work with liquor on his breath and to make mistakes. He has also been absent quite a bit and is absent today.

When (and if) he comes in tomorrow, what approach will you take with him?   **Return to Step 9.**

∾∾∾

Step 17. You have placed a warning letter in Joe's personnel file stating that his performance and attendance must improve within the next thirty days. Joe is absent on each of the next two Mondays, probably because of hangovers.

At this point, what would you do?

1. Warn Joe what will happen if he is absent again on a Monday. **Go to Step 35.**
2. Wait to see if Joe is absent at all during the remainder of his thirty days of probation.   **Go to Step 37.**
3. Transfer Joe at the first opportunity.   **Go to Step 34.**
4. Tell Joe that you don't want to intrude into his personal problems but that you are concerned about how his absences continue to affect his work. **Go to Step 28.**
5. Express to Joe your hope that he will be able to improve his attendance. Then wait to see if he is absent again during the remainder of his thirty days of probation.   **Go to Step 37.**

∾∾∾

Step 18. You decide to say nothing but continue to listen. Joe explains:

"Martha, my wife, devotes all of her time to her two daughters by a previous marriage. She is overbearing and obnoxious. We have a terrible marriage, and she just doesn't care.

"I know I drink, probably more than I should. It's getting to the point that I can't control it anymore. It's destroying my life and my career."

At this point, Joe breaks down and starts to cry. But in a few minutes he continues:

"When I told Martha I need professional help, she started yelling and said she wasn't going to stay married to an institutionalized alcoholic. Frankly, if I took time off for treatment, she'd leave me. Something must be done soon. I'll do anything."

What would be your general approach?

a. Explain to Joe that you understand what he is going through and suggest that he wait two weeks to see how things look then.   **Go to Step 43.**

    b. Tell Joe that his personal problems are his business but that quality assurance is your business. Tell him that he must "shape up or be fired." **Go to Step 24.**
    c. Suggest that Joe attend a meeting of Alcoholics Anonymous or telephone a professional counselor.   **Go to Step 22.**
    d. Explain to Joe that you are going to place a warning letter in his personnel file that states that he must improve within the next thirty days. **Go to Step 17.**

Step 19. After the situation involving Joe and the other employees, things seem calm for the next several days except for occasional loud laughter in Joe's area when you are not nearby. You must schedule extra work for two thirds of your shop on next Saturday and Sunday. Extra work is considered a penalty because no overtime pay is authorized. Compensatory time off is allowed, however. *Would you:*

1. Include Joe in the extra work but say nothing to him directly? **Go to Step 30.**
2. Assign Joe the extra work, but tell him that if he "shapes up" he will not be assigned extra work in the future.   **Go to Step 32.**
3. Tell Joe that you are scheduling him for extra work but ask him to pitch in and be on your team to get the quality assurance department back to where it should be. Stress the importance of each person's doing his or her part. **Go to Step 10.**
4. Explain to Joe that you have wondered what to do to help him improve his performance, as it is affecting the shop's quality assurance standards. Tell him you don't want to schedule him for extra work if it will complicate the problem he is having.   **Go to Step 28.**

Step 20. You have warned Joe that any more comments will cause him to be dealt with severely. He says:

> "That's what I mean by everybody being on my back. Well, I don't have to take it from you! I demand a transfer!"

What do you think about your progress at this point?

1. That you might have handled yourself differently somewhere along the line? Would you like a chance to retrace your steps to see what could be done differently?   **If so, go to Step 9.**
2. That you did what any supervisor would do to correct his or her personnel and keep them in line and make sure they know who is boss. If so, the exercise is over for you.   **Go to the discussion questions in Step 22.**

Step 21. You have asked your secretary to keep calling Joe's home. At 3:30 P.M. your secretary calls you to say that there has been no answer.

When Joe returns on Tuesday morning, what will be your approach to him? **Go to Step 9 to select another approach.**

ᠺᠲᠺᠲᠺᠲ

Step 22. You have suggested that Joe attend an Alcoholics Anonymous meeting or contact a professional counselor for an appointment. Joe agrees to do this, and you have agreed to make the arrangements.
Joe's problem raises some interesting questions that might be discussed:

1. Now that you know some of Joe's problem(s), is it easier or more difficult to handle his situation? Why?
2. Do you think that the company should be understanding and give Joe time off for treatment? Why?
3. Would just his telling you about the problem help Joe? Why?
4. Are you familiar with Alcoholics Anonymous (or other "helping" organizations)? Would you know how to refer someone for treatment? Could you recommend a professional counselor? If your answer is no to any of these questions, find out the answers to them.

END OF THE ACTION MAZE

ᠺᠲᠺᠲᠺᠲ

Step 23. Your boss says: "Well, Joe's story sounded pretty wild to me. Why don't you talk it over with him and let's see how it comes out. I see no reason for me to be there. **Go to Step 8 for your talk with Joe.**

ᠺᠲᠺᠲᠺᠲ

Step 24. It is now Tuesday and you have just talked to Joe this morning. He didn't say anything to you when you made your comments, and he went directly to work when you finished. This afternoon, one of the shop workers tells you that Joe has been telling everybody how badly you treated him. Later this afternoon as you pass Joe, you catch a glimpse of a gesture he makes behind your back. Other people in the shop laugh. When you turn around, Joe is back at work.
What would you do?

1. Do nothing. Continue on your rounds but keep your eye on Joe. **Go to Step 19.**
2. Ask the others who laughed to tell you what they saw. **Go to Step 3.**
3. Warn Joe that he better stick to his work and that he should forget about making comments about and gestures toward you. **Go to Step 19.**
4. Call Joe over to a more private place and ask him what is on his mind. **Go to Step 8.**
5. Tell Joe that you are going to have him transferred. **Go to Step 25.**

ᠺᠲᠺᠲᠺᠲ

Step 25. You have told Joe that he will be transferred (or fired). Do you think that—without previous warning or preparation—you could make this stick? Our guess is that you couldn't. At any rate, here are some questions for you.

262   INTERVIEWING

1. Would your action cause any problem with others in your work force?
2. Were you responding to Joe's feelings with your feelings?
3. Were you admitting to Joe that you didn't know what else to do with him?
4. Is there anything more to know about Joe?

If you have answered yes to any of these questions, you may be admitting that you have something to learn about the management of people. **If so, return to Step 12 and make another choice.** If you have answered no to all four questions, there is evidently no doubt in your mind that how you behave is the correct way. This exercise can teach you no more. **Turn to the discussion questions in Step 22.**

Step 26. You have decided to wait until Joe returns to deal with him.
Go to Step 9 to select your approach to Joe when he returns.

Step 27. You decide to send some inexpensive flowers to Joe's home with a "get well soon" card. Tuesday, when Joe returns, he does not mention the flowers.
What would be your approach to Joe now?   **Go to Step 9 to select your next step.**

Step 28. You have told Joe that you didn't want to intrude but expressed your concern about how his absences and drinking habits were affecting his work. Joe says:

"I know you are concerned, and I have been, too. I'm sorry it's happening, but I just can't help it. I've told my wife that I might lose my job if it keeps up."

What general approach would you follow then?

1. Say: "I'm glad you realize the seriousness of this and hope you can make your wife see it, too. Joe, I hope you will try to do better."   **Go to Step 10.**
2. Say: "Have you talked about it with your wife?"   **Go to Step 15.**
3. Say nothing but continue to listen.   **Go to Step 18.**
4. Impress Joe with the seriousness of his drinking and warn him that he must improve or take the consequences.   **Go to Step 35.**

Step 29. You have removed the warning letter from Joe's personnel file and told him that you hoped he would keep up the good record he has started once again. Joe may or may not be absent on future Mondays, and he may or may not remain sober. There may be future problems. Did you ever wonder what Joe's problem was? Other decision paths led to his telling you—and perhaps you would like to hear him describe his problem. **If so, go to Step 18. After you have read Joe's statement of the problem, go to Step 22 for some discussion questions.**

Step 30. You decide to include Joe in extra work but say nothing to him directly. You inform the other employees that you want them to work.   **Go to Step 36.**

⌒⌒⌒

Step 31. Because Joe was present each Monday for the remainder of the thirty-day period and sober every day, you have told him to "Keep up the good work." Joe says: "I'm certainly trying." Joe's attendance is perfect for the next three weeks, including the overtime work to which he was assigned. During this time, there is no sign of any problem with alcohol.
At the end of this time, what would you do?

1. You would do nothing.   **Go to Step 39.**
2. You would tell Joe that you were removing the warning letter from his personnel file and express the hope that he will be able to keep up the good record he has started once again.   **Go to Step 29.**

⌒⌒⌒

Step 32. You decide to assign Joe extra work, but you tell him that if he "shapes up" he will not be assigned extra work in the future. Joe says nothing and goes back to work.   **Go to Step 36.**

⌒⌒⌒

Step 33. You remarked to Joe how tough it must be to be married to a divorcée with two children. Joe says: "Boy, I'll say!" Then he clams up.
What general approach would you use then?

1. Say: "I'm glad you realize the seriousness of your drinking, and I hope you can make your wife see it, too. Joe, I hope you will try to do better." **Go to Step 10.**
2. Say nothing but continue to listen.   **Go to Step 18.**

⌒⌒⌒

Step 34. You are having Joe report to the dispensary until he can be released or transferred at the next opportunity. That got rid of *your* problem nicely, didn't it? But what about your department? Did you really fulfill your responsibility? What about Joe's potential, feelings, career growth, and nine-year investment in the company? Do you really know what's happening to him?   **Return to your last step and make another decision.**

⌒⌒⌒

Step 35. You have reminded Joe of what will happen if he is absent or drunk again on Monday. Joe is at work the next Monday. But on the following Monday you notice Joe at lunchtime sitting by himself and looking flushed and sick. When you ask him what the trouble is, he says that he feels sick. You send him to the dispensary, and it sends him home. The dispensary informs you that Joe's fever was 103° and that he has the flu. Joe was reported to have told the nurse that he was afraid that you would have him transferred if he stayed home sick, and that's why he came to work. Joe will be out for the next six days.
When Joe returns, what will your approach to him be?

1. Tell Joe that despite his illness, he is still bound by the warning letter because of his Monday absences and that he still must improve.
   Go to Step 24.
2. Tell Joe that you are "wiping the slate clean" and that you hope he has no more trouble in the future.   **Go to Step 10.**
3. Tell Joe that you are sorry he was sick—that you don't want to intrude but wondered if the difficulty he was having with the Monday absences has been cleared up.   **Go to Step 36.**

Step 36. That afternoon, your boss tells you that Joe has accused you of persecuting him.
Would you:

1. Tell your boss that the charges against you are ridiculous and tell him to put them in writing because you are prepared to take them "all the way up the line" if necessary.   **Go to Step 38.**
2. Describe the situation to your boss and tell him that you want to talk with Joe about it. Tell your boss that he can be present while you and Joe talk.
   Go to Step 23.

Step 37. You have waited to see whether Joe will be absent or under the influence of alcohol during the remainder of the thirty days. He is not.
At this point, what action would you take?

1. You do nothing.   **Go to Step 39.**
2. You tell Joe to keep up the good work.   **Go to Step 29.**

Step 38. You have told your boss to put the charges in writing. The next day he hands you a lengthy written statement containing not only Joe's remarks but also comments from three other people in the quality assurance department. After a few minutes, it is apparent to you that there is nothing to be gained by discussing the matter with your boss. You sign the statement so that it can be forwarded to your boss's boss.

So there it is. You may prove that the accusations against you are false and that in order to cover himself, Joe is out to get you. You have a long fight on your hands. Moreover, your relationship with the people in the quality assurance department is likely to deteriorate. Finally, you have not solved Joe's problem—you still have to deal with him.
What do you think about your progress at this point?

1. That you might have handled yourself differently somewhere along the line? Would you like a chance to retrace your steps to see what could be done differently?   **If so, go to Step 9.**
2. That you did what any supervisor would do to correct his or her personnel and keep them in line and make sure they know who is boss. If so, the exercise is over for you.   **Turn to the discussion questions in Step 22.**

Step 39. Because Joe was not absent or under the influence of alcohol for the remainder of the period, you do nothing. Why not? Joe seems to be trying to do what you want him to do. One principle of teaching desired behavior is to reward it when it occurs.   **Go to Step 37 and reward Joe.**

Step 40. For the next three weeks you cannot schedule an appointment with the person in charge of Alcoholics Anonymous or with a professional counselor. This is not the solution you want.
Now what do you do?

1. Make an appointment for Joe to see the counselor in three weeks. **Go to Step 42.**
2. **Go to Step 9 and make another selection.**

Step 41. You have decided to ignore the situation, thinking that it was just a coincidence that is unlikely to happen again. Another "coincidence" like this might kill someone. Consider the possibility that Joe has a debilitating drinking problem (or even some other problem) and that he needs help.   **Return to Step 2 and make another choice.**

Step 42. You have contacted the counselor to make an appointment. The counselor does not consider Joe's case to be an emergency, and so you will have to wait for three weeks. But you don't want to wait that long.   **Go to Step 9 to select your approach for when Joe returns.**

Step 43. You have decided to wait for two weeks to see how things look. After two weeks, there has been no change.   **Return to Step 18 and make another decision.**

Index

Ability tests, for employment, 72
Acceptance, as answering strategy for unlawful questions, 80
Action maze, supervisor evaluation by, 252–265
Address, questions in employment interview on, 73–74
Adverse impact, equal employment opportunity and, 70
Advertising, potential employers found by, 84
Advice, opening of interview requesting, 11
Age, questions in employment interview on, 74
  see also Equal employment opportunity
Age Discrimination in Employment Act of 1967, 69
Analysis and insight, career planning and, 144–145
Anger, appraisal interview for, 133
Antecedents, in counseling interview, 174
Appearance, 5
Application form for employment, 90–93
  of federal government, 244–251
Appraisal interviewing, 126–142
  in academic environment, 127
  anger dealt with, 133
  appraisal systems objectives, 128
  body, 140
  in business setting, 127
  close, 140
  coequality in, 131–132
  conducting, 139–140
  for correction, 129–130
  for counseling, 131
  for criticism of the supervisor, 130–131
  development plan for, 136–138
  employer aspects considered for capacities and attitudes, 134–135
    interaction with others, 135
    performance, 133–134
    performance potential, 135–136
    personal characteristics, 134
    supervisory skills, 135
  environmental variables in, 139, 141
  for goal setting, 131
  guggles used in, 132
  job variables discussed in, 140–141
  language choice and, 138–139
  long-term, 127–128
  mental set and, 138
  mirroring used in, 132
  objectives of, 128–129
  opening, 139–140
  in political sector, 127
  preparing for, 133–139
  for problem-area identification, 130
  questions in, 132, 141–142
  self-solution and, 132–133
  timing and, 138
  see also Career planning
Appraisal system objectives, 128
Aptitude tests
  for career planning, 86
  for employment, 72
Arrest, questions in employment interview on, 74
Assessment, for career planning, 143–144
  questionnaire for, 148–154
  see also Aptitude tests
Assistance, opening in interview requesting, 11
Associates, questions in employment interview on, 75–76
Attention factors, information forfeiture reduced by, 16
Attitudes
  brought to an interview, 6
  listening ability and, 7

267

268 INDEX

Audiovisual aids, information forfeiture reduced by, 17
Awards, questions in employment interview on, 76

Background of problem, in opening of interview, 11
Bearing, as contradictory, 5
Birth certificate, questions in employment interview on, 74
Blacks. See Equal employment opportunity
Body, 10, 12
   of appraisal interview, 140
   of counseling interview, 173–175
   of employment interview, 113, 114–115
   of exit interview, 163
   of persuasive interview, 58–59, 67
Bona Fide Occupational Qualifications (BFOQ), 72–73

California Test of Mental Maturity, 144
Capacities and attitudes of employer, appraisal interview evaluating, 134–135
Career planning, 142–146
   analysis and insight in, 144–145
   assessment in, 143–144, 148–154
   career testing for, 143–144
   change and, 146
   company information for, 87
   counseling for, 143–144
   decision making in, 145
   environmental characteristics of employment for, 86–87
   questionnaire for, 148–154
   reassessment and, 146
   self-appraisal for, 86, 144
   see also Employment interview; Hiring process; Résumé
Career testing, career planning and, 143–144
Challenge, as answering strategy for unlawful questions, 80
Change, career planning and, 146
Chronological résumé, 97–98
Citizenship, questions in employment interview on, 74–75
Civil Rights Act of 1964, Title VII of the, 68–69, 70–71, 72, 177–194
Climate factors in interview
   of appraisal interview, 139, 141
   physical setting, 8, 9
   psychological climate, 8, 10
   social setting, 8, 9
   time dimensions, 8, 9
Close, 10, 12
   of appraisal interview, 140
   of counseling interview, 175
   of employment interview, 112, 113–114, 115
   of exit interview, 163–164
   of persuasive interview, 59, 67
Closed questions. See Questions
Coding results, for survey interviewing, 29
Coequality, in the appraisal interview, 131–132
Coercion, 51
   see also Persuasive interviewing
Cognitive/affective characteristics, of participants in interview, 6–8
College or university employment office, potential employers found in, 84
Color, questions in employment interview on, 75
   see also Equal employment opportunity
Common-ground approach, for opening interview, 11
Communication, 2–4
Communication audit survey instrument, 41–49
Confrontation, as answering strategy for unlawful questions, 80
Confrontation phrases, in counseling interview, 175
Construct validity, selection criteria validity and, 72
Content validity, selection criteria validity and, 72
Contradictory behaviors, in face-to-face interview, 5
Controlled nondirective approach, for counseling, 169
Conviction record, questions in employment interview on, 74
Correction, appraisal interview for, 129–130
Counseling, 167–175
   antecedents in, 174
   appraisal interview for, 129–130
   body, 173–175
   for career planning, 86, 143–144
   close, 175
   closed questions in, 174
   confrontation phrases in, 175
   controlled nondirective, 169
   defensive climate in, 169–170
   direct mirrors for, 173
   directive, 168
   exit interview for, 164
   guggles for, 173
   helping relationship in, 167
   indirect mirrors for, 173–174
   leading questions in, 174
   listening in, 171
   loaded questions in, 174

INDEX

location of, 172
mirroring in, 170, 173–174
nondirective, 168–169
open questions in, 173
opening, 172
preparation for, 172
silences in, 173
supportive climate in, 169–170
Cover letter, for résumé, 102, 105–107
Criterion approach, to persuasion, 55–56, 63
Criterion-related validity, selection criteria validity and, 72
Criticism of the supervisor, appraisal interview for, 130–131
Cues, in employment interview, 115–116

Decision making, career planning and, 145
Defensive counseling climate, 169–170
Development plans, for appraisal interviewing, 136–138
Dexterity tests, for employment, 72
Dickson, William J., 168–169
Direct mirrors, in counseling interview, 173
Directed résumé, 100
Directive counseling, 168
Disabilities, questions in employment interview on, 76
Discrimination
  fair, 71–72
  unfair, 71
  see also Equal employment opportunity
Disparate treatment, equal employment opportunity and, 70

Education, question on in employment interview, 75, 116–117
Emphasis techniques, information forfeiture reduced by, 16
Employment. See Career planning; Employment interview; Equal employment opportunity; Hiring process; Résumé
Employment agencies, in hiring process, 84, 89–90
Employment application form, 90–93
  of federal government, 244–251
Employment interview, 83, 110–125
  applicant's role in, 113, 114–115
  attire for, 115–116
  body, 113, 114–115
  close, 112, 113–114, 115
  employer's role in, 111–114
  job offer in, 122–123
  opening, 113, 114
  panel interviewing in, 121–122
  physical behaviors and cues in, 115–116
  preliminary screening interview, 88
  purpose of, 111
  questions in
    of applicant, 119–121
    Bona Fide Occupational Qualification Test and, 72–73
    of employer, 116–118
    lawful and unlawful, 73–81
    open-ended, 113
    trade questions, 118
  résumé used in, 112, 114
  see also Equal employment opportunity; Hiring process; Résumé
Employment offer, in employment interview, 122–123
Employment Provisions of the Vietnam Era Veterans' Readjustment Assistance Act of 1974, 70
Employment tests, for employment, 72
Entrée, statement of person given in opening of interview providing, 11–12
Environment. See Climate factors in interview
Equal employment opportunity, 68–73
  adverse impact, 70
  Age Discrimination in Employment Act of 1967, 69
  Bona Fide Occupational Qualifications, 72–73
  disparate treatment, 70
  employment interview and, 71–72
  Employment Provisions of the Vietnam Era Veterans' Readjustment Assistance Act of 1974, 70
  employment tests, 72
  Equal Employment Opportunity Commission, 69, 70–71, 183–184
  Equal Employment Opportunity Coordination Council, 192
  Executive Order 11478, 69
  fair discrimination and, 71–72
  for handicapped, 69–70
  job-related criterion and, 72–73
  lack of reasonable accommodation, 71
  perpetuation of past discrimination, 70–71
  Rehabilitation Act of 1973, 69–70
  selection procedure and, 72–73
  Title VII of the Civil Rights Act of 1964 and, 68–69, 70–71, 72, 177–194
  unfair discrimination and, 71
  Uniform Guidelines on Employee Selection Procedures, 69, 70, 72, 195–243
Equal Employment Opportunity Commission (EEOC), 69, 70–71, 183–184
Equal Employment Opportunity Coordinating Council, 192

Ethics, persuasive interviewing and, 53–54
Executive Order 11478, 69
Executive search firms, potential employers found in, 84, 89
Exit interview, 155–156
  benefits of conducting, 157–160
  body, 163
  close, 163–164
  counseling and, 164
  employee termination notice and, 158
  form for, 161–162
  opening, 160, 163
  outplacement and, 164–165
  pitfalls in, 164
  questions in, 163
  termination of employee completed in, 157, 159
  unplanned turnover needing, 155–157
Expectations, listening ability and, 7
External management training survey questionnaire, 38–41
Extracurricular activities, questions in employment interview on, 75

Face-to-face interview
  barriers to sharing information in, 17–18
  questionnaire for, 25, 39–49
Facts, opening interview with, 11
Fair discrimination, 71–72
Family, questions in employment interview on, 79
Feedback, for message generator, 4
Feedforward, 4
Feelings, brought to an interview, 6
Financial position, questions in employment interview on, 75
Follow-up questions. *See* Questions
Friends and associates, questions in employment interview on, 75–76
Furniture, information sharing considering arrangement of, 18

Goal
  opening of interviewing stating, 10–11
  questions in employment interview on, 47
Goal-orientation, in interview, 7
Goal sentence, in persuasive interview, 54, 55, 62
Goal setting, appraisal interview for, 131
Government employment agencies, potential employers found in, 84
Guggles, in counseling interview, 173
Guilford-Zimmerman Temperament Survey, 144

Handicapped, employment opportunities for the, 69–70
  see also Equal employment opportunity
Handicaps, questions in employment interview on, 76
Hawthorne studies, indirect approach in, 168–169
Health, questions in employment interview on, 76
Helping relationship, counseling interview and, 167
Hiring process, 83
  employment agencies for, 89–90
  induction, 89
  job application form, 90–93, 244–251
  job-posting systems, 93–94
  orientation, 89
  placement, 84, 88–89
  positions specifications form for, 84, 85
  recruiting, 84–87, 89–90
  references requested in, 92, 107–108
  retention, 89
  screening, 84, 87–88
  search firm for, 84, 89
  selection, 84, 88
  sources of potential employers, 84, 86, 89–90
  training and development, 84, 89
  see also Career planning; Employment interview; Résumé
Honors, questions in employment interview on, 76
Housing preference, questions in employment interview on, 76–77

Incentive, opening of interview stating, 10–11
Indirect mirrors, in counseling interview, 173–174
Induction, in hiring process, 89
Information, 15, 24
  organizing, 16, 22
  previewing, 16
  summarizing, 17
  see also Informational interviewing
Information forfeiture, 16–17
Information sharing, barriers to, 17–18
Informational interviewing, 15–23
  barriers to information sharing in, 17–18
  information forfeiture and, 16–17
  journalistic reportorial interview and, 6
  language use in, 8
  see also Questions
Intellectual abilities, in interview, 7
Intelligence tests, for employment, 72
Interactions of employer with others, appraisal interview evaluating, 135
Internal job, job posting systems for, 93–94
Interview
  components of, 3–4

definition, 4
purpose, 15
Interview guide, for survey interviewing, 27, 28

Job application form, 90–93
  of federal government, 244–251
Job offer, in employment interview, 122–123
Job-related criterion, in employment selection, 72–73
Job-related goals, questions on in employment interview, 117
Job variables, in the appraisal interview, 140–141
Journalistic reportorial interview, participant motivation in, 6
  see also Informational interviewing

Lack of reasonable accommodation, equal employment opportunity and, 71
Language codes, 3
Language use, 7
  in appraisal interviewing, 138–139
  in informational interviewing, 8
  as message component, 8
  for questions, 18–19
Lawful questions, in employment interview, 73–80
Leading questions. *See* Questions
Legal aspects of employment, lawful and unlawful questions, 73–81
  see also Equal employment opportunity
Length of the interview, 9
Letter résumé, 101
Listening, 7–8
  counseling and, 171
Loaded language, avoidance of, 19
Loaded questions, in counseling interview, 174

Marital status, questions in employment interview on, 77
Media, potential employers found in, 84
Mental quickness, during the interview, 7
Message components, in interview, 8
Message generator, 4
Military service background, questions in employment interview on, 77
Minority groups. *See* Equal employment opportunity
Mirroring, in counseling, 170
Motivational condition, in interview, 6
Motives, brought to an interview, 6

National origin, questions in employment interview on, 77
Negative criticism, 131

Nelson-Denny Reading Test, 144
Nondirective counseling, 168–169
Nonverbal behaviors, in interview, 4

Objectivity, in survey interviewing, 27–28
Open-ended questions. *See* Questions
Opening, 10–12
  of appraisal interview, 139–140
  of counseling interview, 172
  of employment interview, 113, 114
  of exit interview, 160, 163
  of persuasive interview, 58, 66
Oral reaction, information forfeiture reduced by, 16–17
Organization of information, 16
  questions facilitating, 22
Organization membership, questions in employment interview on, 77–78
Orientation, in hiring process, 89
Outcome, opening of interview stating, 10–11

Panel-interviewing, 121–122
Participant analysis, persuasive interviewing and, 56–57, 65–66
Participant behaviors, 4–5
  cognitive/affective characteristics, 6–8
  physical characteristics, 5–6
Performance evaluation, 133–134, 135
  see also Appraisal interviewing
Perpetuating past discrimination, equal employment opportunity and, 70
Personal characteristics of an employer, appraisal interview evaluating, 134
Personal Qualifications Statement, of the federal government, 244–251
Persuasive interviewing, 51–60
  attitudes of interview partner toward proposal, 57, 65–66
  body, 58–59, 67
  close, 59, 67
  coercion in, 51
  criterion approach to, 55–56, 63
  ethics and, 53–54
  goal sentence in, 54–55, 62
  interpersonal relationships of interview partner for, 57, 65
  opening, 58, 66
  participant analysis for, 56–57, 65–66
  personal characteristics of interview partner for, 56–57, 65
  persuasion in, 52–53
  problem analysis for, 54–56, 62–65
  questioning techniques for, 58–59
  respondent perception and, 52–53
Photograph, employment interview requesting, 78
Physical appearance, 5

Physical behaviors, in employment interview, 115–116
Physical characteristics
 of participants in interview, 5–6
 questions in employment interview on, 78
Physical setting, 8, 9
 information sharing prevented by, 18
Placement, in hiring process, 84, 88–89
Position specifications form, 84, 85
Positive criticism, 130
Preliminary screening interview, 88
Preparation, for interview, 7
Prestige, statement of company given in interview opening adding, 12
Preview statement, information forfeiture reduced by, 16
Previewing information, information forfeiture reduced by, 16
Proactive emphasis, information forfeiture reduced by, 16
Probing questions, 21, 22
Problem analysis, persuasive interviewing and, 54–56, 62–65
Problem-area identification, appraisal interview for, 130
Processing results, for survey interviewing, 29
Professional memberships, questions in employment interview on, 77–78
Promotion from within, job-posting systems for, 93–94
Proof of age, questions in employment interview on, 74
Proxemics
 information sharing considering, 17–18
 physical setting of the interview and, 9
Psychological climate, of interview, 8, 10
Publications, questions in employment interview on, 78
Purposeful sharing, in communication, 2–3

Questionnaires. *See* Survey interviewing
Questions
 in appraisal interview, 132, 141–142
 closed, 20–21
  in counseling interview, 174
  in survey interview, 27
 in exit interview, 163
 follow-up, 21, 22
  in questionnaire, 26
 language choice for, 18–19
 lawful and unlawful in employment interview, 73–81
 leading, 21, 22
  in counseling interview, 174
 loaded, 174
 open-ended, 20–21
  in appraisal interview, 132
  biases in, 27
  in counseling, 173
 oral reaction from, 16–17
 pattern of, 22
 in persuasive interview, 58–59
 probing, 21, 22
 trade, 118
 yes-response, 21
  for responsive interview, 58–59
 see also Employment interview

Race, questions in employment interview on, 75
 see also Equal employment opportunity
Rationalization, as answering strategy for unlawful questions, 80
Reassessment, career planning and, 146
Reciprocity, in interview, 7
Recruiting, in hiring process, 84–87
Redirection, as answering strategy for unlawful questions, 80
References
 in hiring process, 92, 107–108
 questions in employment interview on, 78–79
Refusal, as answering strategy for unlawful questions, 80
Rehabilitation Act of 1973, 69
Reinforcing (yes-response) questions. *See* Questions
Relatives, questions in employment interview on, 79
Religion, questions in employment interview on, 79
 see also Equal employment opportunity
Respondent perception, persuasion and, 52–53
Results-oriented résumé, 99
Résumé, 95–107
 chronological, 97–98
 cover letter for, 102, 105–107
 directed, 100
 in employment interview, 112, 114
 functional (results-oriented), 99
 letter, 101
 of new college graduate, 96, 103–104
Retention, in employment, 89
Roethlisberger, Fritz, J., 168–169
Rogers, Carl, 169
Role differences, information sharing prevented by, 18

Salary questions, in employment interview, 120–121
Sample selection, for survey interview, 29

Screening, in hiring process, 84, 87–88
Search firms, in hiring process, 84, 89
Selection, in hiring process, 84, 88
Self-assessment, for career planning, 144
   questionnaire for, 148–154
Self-help exercises, for career planning, 86
Self-reporting techniques, 24
   see also Survey interviewing
Self-solution, in appraisal interview, 132–133
Sensory channels, as message component, 8
Sex, questions in employment interview on, 79
   see also Equal employment opportunity
Sharing, in communication, 2–3
Silences, in counseling interview, 173
Social setting, of interview, 8, 9
Statement of problem, in opening of interview, 10
Strong–Campbell Interest Inventory, 144
Structured questionnaire, 29–37
Summary-preview transitional statements, information forfeiture reduced by, 16
Supervisors
   action maze evaluating, 252–265
   appraisal interview for criticizing, 130–131
Supervisory skills of employer, appraisal interview evaluating, 135
Supportive counseling climate, 169–170
Survey interviewing
   coding and processing results, 29
   costs of, 26–27
   interview guide for, 27, 28
   interviewers trained for, 28–29
   objectivity in, 27–28
   questionnaires, 25
      external management training survey questionnaire, 38–41
      face-to-face, 25, 39–49
      follow-up questions in, 26
      highly structured, 29–37, 48
      highly unstructured, 39–49
      interviewer administering, 26
      objective of, 27
      self-administered, 25–26
      telephone interview, 25, 26, 29–37, 48
   sample selection for, 29
   time frame for, 25

Telephone interviews, 26
   questionnaire for, 25, 26, 29–37, 48
Termination. *See* Exit interview
Time, opening of interview requesting a period of, 12
Time dimensions, of interview, 8, 9
Timing, of appraisal interview, 138
Title VII of the Civil Rights Act of 1964, 68–69, 70–71, 72, 177–194
Trade journals, potential employers found with, 84
Trade questions, in employment interview, 118
Training and development, in hiring process, 84, 89
Transitions, information forfeiture reduced by, 16
Turnover, exit interview for unplanned, 155–157

Unfair discrimination, 71–72
Uniform Guidelines on Employee Selection Procedures (1978), 69, 70, 72, 195–243
Unlawful questions
   in employment interview, 73–81
   responding to, 80–81
Unstructured questionnaire, 39–49

Verbal language codes, 3
Vicarious experience, communication via, 3
Vietnam era, equality of employment for veterans of the, 70
Vocational interest tests, for career planning, 86

Withdrawal, as answering strategy for unlawful questions, 80
Women. *See* Equal employment opportunity
Work experience, questions in employment interview on, 79, 116

Yes-response question. *See* Questions